Studies in Hermeneutics, Christology, and Discipleship

New Testament Monographs, 3

Series Editor
Stanley E. Porter

Studies in Hermeneutics, Christology, and Discipleship

Richard N. Longenecker

SHEFFIELD PHOENIX PRESS

2006

Copyright © 2004, 2006 Sheffield Phoenix Press

First published in hardback, 2004
Reprinted in paperback, 2006

Published by Sheffield Phoenix Press
Department of Biblical Studies, University of Sheffield
Sheffield S10 2TN

www.sheffieldphoenix.com

All rights reserved.
No part of this publication may be reproduced or transmitted
in any form or by any means, electronic or mechanical, including
photocopying, recording or any information storage or retrieval system,
without the publishers' permission in writing.

A CIP catalogue record for this book
is available from the British Library

Typeset by Fairlie Productions, Fairlie, Ayrshire
Printed on acid-free paper by Lightning Source

ISBN 1-905048-68-8

CONTENTS

Preface vi
Original Location of Articles x
Acknowledgments xii
Abbreviations xiii

HERMENEUTICS

1. Three Ways of Understanding Relations between the Testaments—Historically and Today   2
2. A Developmental Hermeneutic: New Treasures as Well as Old   19
3. Can We Reproduce the Exegesis of the New Testament?   34
4. Major Tasks of an Evangelical Hermeneutic: Some Observations on Commonalities, Interrelations, and Differences   72

CHRISTOLOGY

5. Christological Materials within the Early Christian Communities   90
6. The Foundational Conviction of New Testament Christology: The Obedience / Faithfulness / Sonship of Christ   122
7. Some Distinctive Early Christological Motifs   146
8. Whose Child is This?   176
9. The Melchizedek Argument of Hebrews: A Unique Christological Presentation for a Particular Situation   188

DISCIPLESHIP

10. "Son of Man" Imagery: Some Implications for Theology and Discipleship   224
11. Taking up the Cross Daily: Discipleship in Luke–Acts   246

Index of Authors 275
Index of Biblical References 278

PREFACE

The articles in this little volume have been taken over, in the main, as they originally appeared over the span of approximately three decades in various symposium volumes, learned journals, and a couple more popular publications. Based on a conviction that hermeneutics, Christology and discipleship must always be considered together, the articles have been selected to represent the confluence of these three important streams of understanding and commitment. At times an article has been slightly altered, either to bring its content somewhat up-to-date or to conform its style to what is now current. Likewise, there has been some effort to regularize the form of the articles—as, for example, the use of Greek throughout (rather than Greek script in some articles and English transliterations in others, as originally required), an appended "Select Bibliography" for all of the articles, and the standardization of abbreviations. But apart from these rather slight alterations, all of what follows has appeared earlier in various venues with much the same content and much the same form as it appears here.

Pictures at an Exhibition
One of the interesting stories from the world of music is that of the composition of *Pictures at an Exhibition*, which was written in 1874 as a piano suite by the Russian pianist and composer Modest Mussorgsky and orchestrated in 1922 by Maurice Ravel.

The story begins with Mussorgsky's close friend, Victor Hartmann, an architect and occasional painter, dying in 1873 at the age of 39, and with Mussorgsky being absolutely devastated. The following year, in 1874, an exhibition was organized in honor of Hartmann. Mussorgsky, of course, attended the exhibition of his friend's paintings, and his visit to that show became one of the most famous gallery strolls of all time. For in viewing Hartmann's pictures, Mussorgsky was motivated to write a piano suite that would incorporate his musical impressions of ten of Hartmann's artistic works.

Rumor has it that only three of the works that Mussorgsky immortalized actually appeared in the exhibition he attended (*The Ballet of the Unhatched Chicks, Baba Yaga's Hut,* and *The Great Gate of Kiev*), that five were based on pencil drawings he knew Hartmann had drawn (*The Gnome, Tuileries, Bydlo, Samuel Goldenberg and Schmuyle,* and *Catacombs*), and that two were invented "out of whole cloth" by the composer himself (*The Old Castle* and *The Market Place at Limoges*). Be that as it may, at least Mussorgsky was inspired to compose a masterful piano suite that purports to be a musical representation of ten of Hartmann's paintings—with, of course, its famous recurring "Promenade" theme, which suggests a viewer's progress from painting to painting.

Mussorgsky's piano suite is commanding and picturesque, expressing moods of mystery, frenzy, humor, and grandeur. It was, however, a composition that cried out for orchestral color, and a number of composers during the latter part of the nineteenth century and early twentieth century attempted to orchestrate it. It was finally orchestrated in masterful fashion by Maurice Ravel, and that is the version of *Pictures at an Exhibition* that most people know today.

Articles in this Collection
While compiling this little collection of articles, I could not help but think of some analogies that could be drawn between *Pictures at an Exhibition* and the articles in this collection. Certainly, the analogies that might be drawn are not those of my writings vis-à-vis the magnificent compositions of Modest Mussorgsky and Maurice Ravel. Nor have they anything to do with my talents, expertise, or lifestyle vis-à-vis those of Mussorgsky or Ravel. Rather, the analogy I found myself constantly drawing in compiling this collection of articles was with the paintings of Victor Hartmann, that nineteenth-century artist whose work would have been entirely forgotten were it not for transpositions into another medium by Mussorgsky and Ravel. In particular, I found myself resonating with (1) the somewhat disparate character of the eleven articles here presented vis-à-vis the ten artistic works (whether paintings, pencil sketches, or possibly even imaginary images) that Mussorgsky claimed to be interpreting, and (2) the need for others to interpret more adequately, in whatever medium, the collection of paintings or articles for future posterity.

Studies in Hermeneutics, Christology, and Discipleship

The articles included in this volume of collected studies are not all equal in size, identical in treatment, or originally written with the same intent. Some may be more like paintings and others more like pencil sketches—though, of course, I would vigorously deny that any of them were composed "out of whole cloth." Rather, they have all been written with a desire to be true to the apostolic message and to the intent of the New Testament writers, and with a hope that they will be stimulating, challenging and helpful to whomever might read them—including whoever will read them in their present form.

The articles have been arranged in what has seemed to their author a logical order, though, admittedly, logical placement is more evident for some of them than for others. Some readers may prefer another arrangement. It is our conviction, however, that hermeneutics, Christology and discipleship must always be considered together. So while tempted to deal with each of these topics in separate volumes, and thereby be able to incorporate other materials that have been previously published, I have decided to limit the present selection of articles for the sake of drawing together these three subjects.

The theses expressed in the first four articles on hermeneutics undergird and motivate much of what I have written elsewhere in monographs and commentaries. The present collection of articles does not, of course, represent a full development of the subject, but simply highlights a number of the hermeneutical issues that I believe to be important for biblical exegesis and biblical theology. For more developed treatments of some of these issues, I would ask the reader to turn to my *Biblical Exegesis in the Apostolic Period* (Grand Rapids: Eerdmans, 1975, 2nd ed., 1999) and my *New Wine into Fresh Wineskins: Contextualizing the Early Christian Confessions* (Peabody: Hendrickson, 1999).

The five articles on Christology, likewise, do not make up a complete study of the material on the subject in the New Testament. Rather, I have attempted to deal with matters that I felt have been neglected or need a measure of clarification. Should time, strength, wit, and God's grace allow, I would like to do more. For a more developed treatment of one strand of early christological conviction, I would ask the reader to turn to my *The Christology of Early Jewish Christianity* (London: SCM, 1970; repr. Baker, 1981; repr. Regent, 2001).

Preface

The final section of two articles on discipleship is where, indeed, "the rubber meets the road." The topic is one that lends itself to all sorts of permutations. Most often it is dealt with only devotionally (as I have done also in other venues). What I wanted to do here was to treat the subject in a paradigmatic fashion both exegetically and theologically, trusting that God by his Spirit will direct the reader into much greener pastures with far more expansive horizons.

Only some of the articles included in this volume originally included a bibliography. All of them now, however, have an appended "Select Bibliography." The primary purpose for these selected bibliographies is not to support everything that is said or quoted in the particular article, but to aid the reader's further study of the subject.

ORIGINAL LOCATION OF ARTICLES

1. "Three Ways of Understanding Relations between the Testaments— Historically and Today"—Original Article: "Three Ways of Understanding Relations between the Testaments—Historically and Today," in *Tradition and Interpretation in the New Testament: Essays in Honor of E. Earle Ellis for his 60th Birthday*, ed. G. F. Hawthorne with O. Betz. Tübingen: Mohr; Grand Rapids: Eerdmans, 1987, 22-32.

2. "A Developmental Hermeneutic: New Treasures as Well as Old"—Original Article: "A Developmental Hermeneutic: New Treasures as Well as Old," in *New Testament Social Ethics for Today*. Grand Rapids: Eerdmans, 1984; Vancouver: Regent Publishing, 1993, 16-28.

3. "Can We Reproduce the Exegesis of the New Testament?"—Original Article: "Can We Reproduce the Exegesis of the New Testament?" *Tyndale Bulletin* 21 (1970) 3-38.

4. "Major Tasks of an Evangelical Hermeneutic: Some Observations on Commonalities, Interrelations and Differences"—Original Article: "Major Tasks of an Evangelical Hermeneutic: Some Observations on Commonalities, Interrelations and Differences," *Bulletin for Biblical Research*, 14 (2004) 45-58.

5. "Christological Materials within the Early Christian Communities" —Original Article: "Christological Materials within the Early Christian Communities," in *Contours of Christology in the New Testament*, ed. R. N. Longenecker. MNTS. Grand Rapids: Eerdmans, 2005.

6. "The Foundational Conviction of New Testament Christology: The Obedience/ Faithfulness / Sonship of Christ"—Original Article: "The Foundational Conviction of New Testament Christology: The Obedience / Faithfulness / Sonship of Christ," in *Jesus of Nazareth: Lord and Christ. Essays on the Historical Jesus and New Testament Christology* [*Festschrift* I. Howard Marshall], ed. J. B. Green and M. Turner. Carlisle: Paternoster; Grand Rapids: Eerdmans, 1994, 473-88.

7. "Some Distinctive Early Christological Motifs"—Original Article: "Some Distinctive Early Christological Motifs," *New Testament Studies* 14 (1968) 526-45.

8. "Whose Child Is This?"—Original Article: "Whose Child Is This?" *Christianity Today*, vol. 34, no. 18 (December 17, 1990), 25-28.

9. "The Melchizedek Argument of Hebrews: A Unique Christological Understanding for a Particular Situation."—Original Article: "The Melchizedek Argument of Hebrews: A Study in the Development and Circumstantial Expression of

Original Location of Articles

New Testament Thought," in *Unity and Diversity in New Testament Theology: Essays in Honor of George E. Ladd*, ed. R. A. Guelich. Grand Rapids: Eerdmans, 1978, 161-85.

10. "'Son of Man' Imagery: Some Implications for Theology and Discipleship"—Original Article: "'Son of Man' Imagery: Some Implications for Theology and —Discipleship," *Journal of the Evangelical Theological Society* 18 (1975) 3-16.

11. "Taking Up the Cross Daily: Discipleship in Luke–Acts"—Original Article: "Taking Up the Cross Daily: Discipleship in Luke–Acts," in *Patterns of Discipleship in the New Testament*, ed. R. N. Longenecker. MNTS. Grand Rapids: Eerdmans, 1996, 50-76.

ACKNOWLEDGMENTS

The author and publisher are grateful to the following for permission to reproduce essays first published by them:

Eerdmans Publishing Company for (1) "Three Ways of Understanding Relations between the Testaments—Historically and Today," in *Tradition and Interpretation in the New Testament: Essays in Honor of E. Earle Ellis for his 60th Birthday*, ed. G. F. Hawthorne with O. Betz (Tübingen: Mohr; Grand Rapids: Eerdmans, 1987), 22-32; (2) "A Developmental Hermeneutics: New Treasures as Well as Old," in R. N. Longenecker, *New Testament Social Ethics for Today* (Grand Rapids: Eerdmans, 1984; repr. Vancouver: Regent Publishing, 1993), 16-28; (3) "Christological Materials within the Early Christian Communities," in *Contours of Christology in the New Testament*, ed. R. N. Longenecker (MNTS; Grand Rapids: Eerdmans, 2005); (4) "The Foundational Conviction of New Testament Christology: The Obedience / Faithfulness / Sonship of Christ," in *Jesus of Nazareth: Lord and Christ. Essays on the Historical Jesus and New Testament Christology* [*Festschrift* I. Howard Marshall], ed. J. B. Green and M. Turner (Carlisle: Paternoster; Grand Rapids: Eerdmans, 1994), 473-88; (5) "The Melchizedek Argument of Hebrews. A Unique Christological Understanding for a Particular Situation," in *Unity and Diversity in New Testament Theology: Essays in Honor of George E. Ladd*, ed. R. A. Guelich (Grand Rapids: Eerdmans, 1978), 161-85; and (6) "Taking Up the Cross Daily: Discipleship in Luke-Acts," in *Patterns of Discipleship in the New Testament*, ed. R. N. Longenecker (MNTS; Grand Rapids: Eerdmans, 1996), 50-76.

Tyndale Press for "Can We Reproduce the Exegesis of the New Testament," *TB* 21 (1970) 3-38.

Editor of the *Bulletin for Biblical Research* for "Major Tasks of an Evangelical Hermeneutic: Some Observations on Commonalities, Interrelations and Differences," in *BBR* 14 (2004) 45-58.

Cambridge University Press for "Some Distinctive Early Christological Motifs," *NTS* 14 (1968) 526-45.

Editor of *Christianity Today* for "Whose Child Is This?," in *Christianity Today*, vol. 34, no. 18 (December 17, 1990) 25-28.

Editor of the *Journal of the Evangelical Theological Society* for "'Son of Man' Imagery: Some Implications for Theology and Discipleship," *JETS* 18 (1975) 3-16.

ABBREVIATIONS

Reference Works

APOT *Apocrypha and Pseudepigrapha of the Old Testament*, 2 vols., ed. R. H. Charles (1913, repr. 1963).
BAG *A Greek-English Lexicon of the New Testament and Other Early Christian Literature*, W. F. Arndt and F. W. Gingrich (1957).
JE *Jewish Encyclopedia*, 12 vols., ed. I. Singer (1901–1906).
M-M *The Vocabulary of the Greek Testament, Illustrated from the Papyri and Other Non-Literary Sources*, J. H. Moulton and G. Milligan (1930, 1963).
OTP *The Old Testament Pseudepigrapha*, 2 vols., ed. J. H. Charlesworth (1983, 1985).
Str-Bil *Kommentar zum Neuen Testament aus Talmud und Midrasch*, 6 vols., H. L. Strack and P. Billerbeck (1922–61).
TDNT *Theological Dictionary of the New Testament*, 9 vols., ed. G. Kittel and G. Friedrich, trans. G. W. Bromiley. Grand Rapids: Eerdmans, 1964–74 (from *TWNT*).
TWNT *Theologisches Wörterbuch zum Neuen Testament*, 10 vols., ed. G. Kittel and G. Friedrich. Stuttgart: Kohlhammer, 1933–78.

Series (Commentaries, Texts and Studies)
AB Anchor Bible
BNTC Black's New Testament Commentary
CGT Cambridge Greek Testament
EBC Expositor's Bible Commentary
HNT Handbuch zum Neuen Testament
HNTC Harper's New Testament Commentary
HTKNT Herders Theologischer Kommentar zum Neuen Testament
HEARTS Harvard Theological Studies
MNTS McMaster New Testament Studies
MNTC Moffatt New Testament Commentary
NIGTC New International Greek Testament Commentary
NovTSup Novum Testamentum Supplements
UNTIL New Testament Library
SBLMS Society of Biblical Literature Monograph Series
SBT Studies in Biblical Theology

Studies in Hermeneutics, Christology, and Discipleship

SH	Scripta Hierosolymitana
SNTSMS	Society for New Testament Studies Monograph Series
WBC	Word Biblical Commentary

Journals

ALUOS	Annual of Leeds University Oriental Society
ASTI	Annual of the Swedish Theological Institute
BA	Biblical Archeologist
BASOR	Bulletin of the American Schools of Oriental Research
BBR	Bulletin for Biblical Research
Bib	Biblica
BJRL	Bulletin of the John Rylands University Library
BSac	Bibliotheca sacra
BZ	Biblische Zeitschrift
CBQ	Catholic Biblical Quarterly
CJT	Canadian Journal of Theology
CTJ	Calvin Theological Journal
CTM	Concordia Theological Monthly
ExpT	The Expository Times
EvT	Evangelische Theologie
HeyJ	Heythrop Journal
HTR	Harvard Theological Review
HUCA	Hebrew Union College Annual
Int	Interpretation
IEJ	Israel Exploration Journal
JAAR	Journal of the American Academy of Religion
JBL	Journal of Biblical Literature
JETS	Journal of the Evangelical Theological Society
JJS	Journal of Jewish Studies
JQR	Jewish Quarterly Review
JSJ	Journal for the Study of Judaism
JSNT	Journal for the Study of the New Testament
JTS	Journal of Theological Studies
JTSA	Journal of Theology for South Africa
Jud	Judaism
MGWJ	Monatsschrift für Geschichte und Wissenschaft des Judentums
MTZ	Münchener theologische Zeitschrift
NovT	Novum Testamentum
NRT	Nouvelle revue théologique
NTS	New Testament Studies
Numen	Numen: International Review for the History of Religions
OTS	Oudtestamentische Studiën
RB	Revue biblique

Abbreviations

RHPR	*Revue d'histoire et de philosophie religieuses*
RSR	*Recherches de science religieuse*
RQ	*Revue de Qumran*
SBU	*Symbolae biblicae uppsalienses*
SJT	*Scottish Journal of Theology*
SR/S	*Studies in Religion / Sciences religieuses*
Them	*Themelios*
Theol	*Theology*
TLZ	*Theologische Literaturzeitung*
TRu	*Theologische Rundschau*
TS	*Theological Studies*
TSK	*Theologische Studien und Kritiken*
TTZ	*Trierer theologische Zeitschrift*
VT	*Vetus Testamentum*
ZKG	*Zeitschrift für Kirchengeschichte*
ZNW	*Zeitschrift für die neutestamentliche Wissenschaft*
ZTK	*Zeitschrift für Theologie und Kirche*

Part I

HERMENEUTICS

1

THREE WAYS OF UNDERSTANDING RELATIONS BETWEEN THE TESTAMENTS—HISTORICALLY AND TODAY

Understanding relations between the Old Testament (the Jewish Scriptures, which have been accepted by Christians as their Scriptures as well) and the New Testament (the distinctly Christian Scriptures) has always been of great importance in Christian hermeneutics. Any discussion of the Christian gospel vis-à-vis the Mosaic law, for example, rests heavily on how one views the relation of the testaments, as does also every analysis of how the New Testament writers use the Old Testament. In fact, one's understanding of how the two testaments are related—whether consciously explicated or simply assumed—determines in large measure what kind of Christian theology one espouses, what kind of Christian gospel one proclaims, and what kind of Christian lifestyle one practices.

Often we hear of the differences between early "mainstream" Christianity and Marcionism; in certain quarters, of the polarities between Reformed and Dispensational theologies. In actuality, however, discussions regarding the relation of the testaments have historically been tripartite (i.e., related to or executed by three parties), not simply bipartite—with similar tripartite discussions continuing in full vigor today. In what follows, I would like to sketch out in rather broad strokes the major lines or contours of these discussions, dealing first historically with the three main streams of thought in the early church—that is, Marcionite, Alexandrian, Antiochian—and then indicating how and where similar features corresponding to those three basic approaches continue today.

1. *Marcion*

Marcion of Sinope (a village of Pontus in northeastern Asia Minor, along the southern shore of the Black Sea) was in second- and third-century Christendom "like a figure standing just off-stage but casting his shadow over every player on it."[1] While we know of him mainly through Irenaeus's *Adversus haereses* (against both Gnostics and Marcion) and the third edition of Tertullian's *Adversus Marcionem* (the third edition of 208 CE being the only extant edition; the first edition probably appeared in 198 CE without Book 5)—together, of course, with passing references to him by such diverse writers as Origen, Cyril of Jerusalem, and Pelagius—Marcion's influence on the Christianity of second-century Asia Minor seems to have been immense, and his impact on the theology of almost all Christian writers living elsewhere in the Roman empire is evident at almost every point in their writings.

Claiming fidelity to Paul, Marcion laid stress on Paul's critique of the Mosaic law and concluded (1) that the revelation that came in Jesus Christ is opposed to the teaching of the Jewish Scriptures, (2) that the God of the New Testament is entirely other than the God of Judaism, and, therefore, (3) that Christians must repudiate everything associated with the Jewish law and everyone "too close kindred with Judaism,"[2] including even the Jerusalem apostles. Sometime around 140 CE Marcion compiled a truncated version of the New Testament that contained only ten letters of Paul (minus the Pastorals, and, of course, Hebrews) and the Gospel according to Luke—all with omissions and alterations to suit his understanding of Christianity. At the head of his *Apostolikon* ("Apostolic Writings") stood Galatians, which Marcion saw as the interpretive key to the Christian religion vis-à-vis Judaism and the Mosaic law.

As Marcion understood it, Galatians was directed against Judaism and everything Jewish. It declares the abolition of the Jewish law and repudiates the Creator God of the Jewish Scriptures. Thus as Marcion read Galatians, he saw, for example, 1:6-9 as setting up a sharp contrast between Paul's preaching and the tenets of Judaism, with the angel from heaven of 1:8 who preached another gospel being a messenger of this Jewish Creator God, whom Paul opposed. He interpreted the Hagar–Sarah allegory of 4:21-31 as representing two distinctly different "revelations" (not "testaments"), the former being the Jewish religion that Paul directs his converts to cast out. And he

---

[1] M. F. Wiles, *The Divine Apostle: The Interpretation of St Paul's Epistles in the Early Church* (Cambridge: Cambridge University Press, 1967), 49.

[2] Cf. Tertullian, *Adversus Marcionem* 5.3.1.

insisted that Paul's words of 6:14, that "through the cross of our Lord Jesus Christ ... the world has been crucified to me and I to the world," have reference to the renunciation of the Jewish God and the Jewish law.[3] Nor did the Jerusalem apostles fare any better with Marcion, for they proclaimed, as he understood it, an entirely different gospel, which is why Paul says in 2:11-21 that he censured Peter at Antioch for not walking uprightly according to the truth of the Christian gospel.[4]

Marcion's radical separation of the Christian gospel from the Jewish Scriptures and the Mosaic law, which Tertullian labels "his special and principal work,"[5] struck at the very roots of the fundamental Christian conviction regarding the continuity of God's revelation and redemptive activity in Jesus of Nazareth with God's earlier revelations and actions as recorded in the Jewish Scriptures. It was, therefore, of vital concern to the church at large, and Christian writers of Marcion's day and following often took great pains to deny any such separation and to affirm the positive features of Paul's attitude toward the Mosaic law.

2. *Early Responses to Marcion*

Irenaeus (130–200 CE) and Tertullian (160–after 220 CE) wrote refutations of Marcion's position. Neither of them, of course, was from Alexandria, but they laid the foundations for an approach to the Old Testament that would be carried further by the Alexandrian Fathers, particularly Origen. Irenaeus was from the Roman province of Asia (in the area of Asia Minor) and had been instructed as a youth by Polycarp of Smyrna. Most of his adult ministry, however, was carried on in Gaul, where in 178 CE he became Bishop of Lyons. Tertullian was born in Carthage, the city-state port on the north coast of Africa (nine miles northeast of modern Tunis). He was trained in Roman legal rhetoric and only became a Christian as an adult. After his conversion he wrote apologetic works defending Christianity, polemical works attacking various heresies, and a variety of works on moral and ethical subjects. Jerome speaks of him as a presbyter,[6] but

---

[3] *Ibid.* 5.2-4. Marcion's dualism, while not developed, is implicit throughout his treatment of Galatians, if Tertullian's account represents him aright.
[4] *Ibid.* 5.3.6-7.
[5] *Ibid.* 1.19.4.
[6] Jerome, *De viris illustribus* 3.53.

1. *Understanding Relations between the Testaments*

most modern scholars doubt that he belonged to the clergy. Ultimately he became a Montanist and used the same vigor in attacking orthodox Christianity as he had previously exhibited in defending it.

Tertullian's *Adversus Marcionem*, as the title suggests, is given over entirely to a refutation of Marcion—his general position in Books 1–3; his treatment of Luke's Gospel in Book 4; and his interpretation of the ten letters of Paul in Book 5. While it represents the "mainstream" Christendom of the Ante-Nicene Church Fathers, it is certainly the most devastating polemic against Marcion of the day. Tertullian agreed with Marcion on the importance of Galatians vis-à-vis Judaism: "We too claim that the primary epistle against Judaism is that addressed to the Galatians."[7] But Tertullian went on to insist that Marcion was terribly wrong to renounce the Creator God and set aside the Jewish Scriptures, for both the abolition of the law and the establishment of the gospel derive from the Creator's own ordinance and are rooted in the prophecies of the Jewish Scriptures.[8] So Tertullian argued that it is the same God as preached in the gospel who had been known in the law, though "the rule of conduct" is not the same.

Specifically, Tertullian insisted that Galatians must be understood as teaching that the Christian renunciation of the law stems from the Creator's own will and came about through the work of the Creator's Christ. As for the Jerusalem apostles, he saw them as basically one with Paul in soteriology and christology, though he says that their

---

[7] Tertullian, *Adversus Marcionem* 5.2.1.

[8] Tertullian even argued that Paul is prefigured in the Old Testament: "Among those figures and prophetical blessings over his sons, when Jacob had got to Benjamin he said, 'Benjamin is a ravening wolf; until morning he will still devour, and in the evening will distribute food' [Gen 49:27]. He foresaw that Paul would arise from the tribe of Benjamin, a ravening wolf devouring until the morning, that is, one who in his early life would harass the Lord's flock as a persecutor of the churches, and then at evening would distribute food, that is, in declining age would feed Christ's sheep as the doctor of the Gentiles. Also the harshness at first of Saul's pursuit of David, and afterwards his repentance and contentment on receiving good for evil [cf. 1 Sam 18] had nothing else in view except Paul in Saul according to tribal descent, and Jesus in David by the Virgin's descent from him" (*ibid.* 5.1.5-6). And again: "For he [Isaiah] says, 'I will take away from Judaea,' among other things, 'even the wise master-builder' [Isa 3:3]. And was not that a presage of Paul himself, who was destined to be taken away from Judaea, which means Judaism, for the building up of Christendom? For he was to lay that one and only foundation which is Christ" (*ibid.* 5.6.10).

faith in those early days was "unripe and still in doubt regarding the observance of the law"—just as Paul's practice was inconsistent at times (e.g., in circumcising Timothy, Acts 16:3), though only "for circumstances' sake." As for the "false brothers brought in unawares," they were Jewish Christians who perverted the gospel by their retention of the old rule of conduct. Their endeavors, however, Tertullian held. came to an end when Peter, James and John officially sanctioned the legitimacy of Paul's mission by giving to him and Barnabas "the right hand of fellowship" (cf. *ibid.* 5.3 *passim*).

So Tertullian, on the basis of his reading of Galatians, taught that the law was meant by God for the early instruction of his people; but that with the fulfillment of his redemptive purposes in the coming of Christ, God abolished the law that he himself had appointed ("Better he than someone else!")—though God also confirms the law (i.e., the moral law) in society to the extent that he must.[9] As for Marcion's deletions in Galatians (deleting 1:18-24; 2:6-9a; 3:6-9; and parts of 3:10-12, 14a, 15-25; 4:27-30, with extensive alterations in 4:21-26), Tertullian exclaimed: "Let Marcion's eraser be ashamed of itself."[10] And as for Marcion's theology generally, Tertullian's attitude is epitomized at the very beginning of his work: "The most barbarous and melancholy thing about Pontus [dismal as the region is of itself] is that Marcion was born there."[11]

---

[9] *Ibid.* 5.2.1-4. On Tertullian's views on God as having both abolished and confirmed the law, caution is needed. Only here does he speak in an unqualified manner of God having abolished the law. Usually he distinguishes between (1) the ceremonial aspect of the law, which was abolished, and (2) the moral aspect, which was confirmed and heightened by Christ (cf. *De pudicitia* 6.3-5; *De monogamia* 7.1; *De oratione* 1.1).

[10] *Ibid.* 5.4.2.

[11] *Ibid.* 1.1.4. Immediately following that statement, Tertullian goes on to describe Marcion as: "Fouler than any Scythian [a hated people of southern Europe who lived in what is now the southern Russian provinces and Rumania], more roving than the waggon life [i.e., gypsy kind of life] of the Sarmatian [a nomadic Indo-Iranian people who were related to the Scythians], more inhuman than the Massagete [a large tribe of despised people who lived beyond the Caspian and Aral Seas and were thought by some to be a branch of the Scythians], more audacious than an Amazon [in Greek legend a race of warrior women who were supposed to have lived on the Coast of the Black Sea and in the Causasus Mountains], darker than the cloud (of Pontus) [the sky of Pontus being considered always overcast], colder than its [Pontus's] winter, more brittle than its [Pontus's] ice, more deceitful than the Ister [an ancient name for the Danube River], more

3. The Alexandrian Fathers

Building on the deep desire of Christians to keep the Jewish Scriptures for the Christian church (*à la* Irenaeus and Tertullian)—which meant, in turn, minimizing the negative and maximizing the positive features of Paul's attitude toward the Mosaic law—the Alexandrian Fathers developed a distinctive approach to matters having to do with the relation of the testaments, particularly Clement of Alexandria and Origen. We often think of the Alexandrians as simply allegorist. But allegorical exegesis was only a tool they picked up from certain Jewish teachers of their city to enhance their own approach to the Scriptures[12]—a tool that was eventually discarded by their successors, though their basic approach found rootage extensively within catholic Christendom.

Clement of Alexandria was a convert to Christianity in adult life, and, after a long spiritual pilgrimage, settled in Alexandria as a pupil of Pantaenus, whom he succeeded as head of the catechetical school there during 190–202 CE. He left Alexandria when severe persecution of Christians broke out under Septimus Severus, and died in Asia Minor about 214 CE. While Clement's extant works are far fewer than

---

craggy than Causasus [the region in southeast Europe between the Black Sea and the Caspian Sea, which is divided by the Caucasus Mountains]. Nay more, the true Prometheus [a major god of Greek mythology], Almighty God, is mangled by Marcion's blasphemies. Marcion is more savage than even the beasts of that barbarous region. For what beaver was ever a greater emasculator than he who has abolished the nuptial bond? What Pontic mouse ever had such gnawing powers as he who has gnawed the Gospels to pieces? Verily, O Euxine [the Latin name for the Black Sea], thou hast produced a monster more credible to philosophers than to Christians. For the cynic Diogenes [c. 400–325 BCE] used to go about, lantern in hand, at midday to find a man, whereas Marcion has quenched the light of his faith and so lost the God whom he had found." Though eloquently expressed, it would be difficult in all of the writings of antiquity to find a more devastating invective or pejorative characterization.

[12] C. Siegfried, *Philo von Alexandria* (Jena: Dufft, 1875), 16-37, and H. A. A. Kennedy, *Philo's Contribution to Religion* (London: Hodder & Stoughton, 1919), 32-34, have shown that "there can be little question that Philo stood in a long succession of allegorical interpreters of the Old Testament. The practice had been reduced to a kind of science" (Kennedy, *ibid.*, 32). Clement reveals his awareness of this line of interpreters when he refers to a second-century BCE Alexandrian Jew named Aristobulus who used allegorical exegesis in writing a series of works on the Mosaic law (cf. *Stromata* 5.14.97).

those of his extremely prolific successor, Origen, there can be no doubt as to how he viewed the Mosaic law and the relation of the Old and New Testaments. Most succinct is the following quotation from "The Rich Man's Salvation":

> Now the works of the law are good—who will deny it? For "the commandment is holy" [Rom 7:12], but only to the extent of being a kind of training, accompanied by fear and preparatory instruction, leading on to the supreme lawgiving and grace of Jesus [cf. Gal 3:24]. On the other hand, "Christ is the fulfillment [πλήρωμα, not τέλος] of the law unto righteousness to every one who believes" [Rom 10:4], and those who perfectly observe the Father's will he makes not slaves, in the manner of a slave, but sons and brothers and joint-heirs [cf. Gal 3:26–4:7].[13]

Thus, contra Marcion, Clement of Alexandria affimred that (1) as to the nature of the law, it is "good" and "holy"; (2) as to the purpose of the law, it was given to be "a kind of training, accompanied by fear and preparatory instruction"; (3) as to the focus of the law, that is to be found in its "leading on to the supreme law-giving and grace of Jesus"; (4) as to Christ's work in relation to the law, "Christ is the fulfillment of the law"; (5) as to the Christian's status before God, it is one of being righteous apart from the law—no longer slaves under the law but "sons and brothers and joint-heirs"; and (6) as to the Christian's responsibility to God, it is to believe and perfectly observe the Father's will. All of this, in general, sounds eminently Christian. In the hands of Origen, however, such affirmations received an explication that sets them apart as being distinctive.

Origen (185–254 CE), the precocious and pious son of the Greek grammarian and Christian martyr Leonides, became head of the Christian catechetical school in Alexandria at the youthful age of eighteen in 203 CE, at a time of great persecution and when the church in Egypt lacked leadership. During his lifetime he published a prodigious number of critical, exegetical, theological, apologetic and practical writings. There is extant among all these materials, however, no complete Greek commentary on Galatians—only a few translated fragments in Latin. So we are left without direct knowledge of how Origen specifically interacted with Marcion. Yet we are not left to

---

[13] Clement, *Quis dives salvetur?* 9.2; see *Stromata* 4.130.3 for the other occasion where Clement uses πλήρωμα in speaking of Christ as the fulfillment of the Mosaic law (commenting on Rom 10:4).

wonder how Origen understood the issues dealt with in Galatians, for there are several direct statements and numerous hints on these matters in the many Greek portions we have of his commentaries on Matthew, John and Romans, in the Latin fragments (admittedly few) of his Galatians commentary that have been preserved by Pamphilus and Jerome, and in the two hundred or so extant homilies we have from Origen on various biblical passages. In addition, in *De principiis* Origen spells out quite explicitly his principles of biblical interpretation.

In *Contra Celsum*, which was written near the end of his life, Origen uses Gal 5:17 in support of his sharp distinction between the flesh and the spirit—with primacy, of course, given to the spirit.[14] Earlier in *De principiis* he made this same distinction, using Gal 5:17 there in support as well.[15] So it seems safe to say, though without access to his Greek commentary on Galatians itself, that Galatians with its flesh–spirit dichotomy was foundational for Origen's thought. Likewise, the Hagar–Sarah allegory of Gal 4:21-31 seems to have been foundational for his exegetical method, for in *Contra Celsum* it is that passage which he uses to justify his allegorical or spiritual exegesis.[16] And in that same work, Gal 2:15 is used to buttress his

---

[14] Origen, *Contra Celsum* 8.23.

[15] Origen, *De principiis* 1.3.4; 3.2.3; 3.4.1-5.

[16] *Contra Celsum* 4.44: "Scripture frequently makes use of the histories of real events in order to present to view more important truths, which are but obscurely intimated; and of this kind are the narratives relating to the 'wells' and to the 'marriages' and to the various acts of 'sexual intercourse' recorded of righteous persons, which, however, it will be more seasonable to offer an explanation in the exegetical writings referring to those very passages. But that wells were constructed by righteous men in the land of the Philistines, as related in the book of Genesis, is manifest from the wonderful wells which are shown at Ascalon, and which are deserving of mention on account of their structure, so foreign and peculiar compared to that of other wells. Moreover, that both young men and female servants are to be understood metaphorically, is not our doctrine merely, but one which we have received from the beginning from wise men, among whom a certain one [i.e., Paul] said, when exhorting his hearers to investigate the figurative meaning: 'Tell me, you that read the law, do you not hear the law? For it is written that Abraham had two sons: the one by a bond maid; the other by a free woman. But he who was of the bond woman was born after the flesh; he of the free woman was by promise. Which things are an allegory, for these are the two covenants: the one from Mount Sinai, which genders to bondage, which is Agar' [Gal 4:21-24]. And a little after, 'But Jerusalem which is above is free,

evaluation of Paul vis-à-vis the Jerusalem apostles (he was "mightier than they")[17] and Gal 2:12 to support his understanding of their character (they had "not yet learned from Jesus to ascend from the law that is regulated according to the letter to that which is interpreted according to the spirit").[18]

It is in his extant Romans commentary, however, where we find Origen dealing extensively with Paul's teaching on the law. There he notes that not every reference to law in Paul's writings has the Mosaic law in view, and so insists that distinctions must be made in Paul's usage if we are to understand his meaning.[19] He lists six ways in which the word "law" is used and illustrates them from Romans and other of Paul's letters: (1) the Mosaic law according to the letter (Gal 3:10, 19, 24; 5:4); (2) Mosaic law according to its spiritual sense (Rom 7:12, 14); (3) natural law (Rom 2:14); (4) Mosaic history (Gal 4:2); (5) the prophetic books (1 Cor 14:21); and, though this sense is suggested only somewhat tentatively, (6) the teachings of Christ (1 Cor 9:21).[20] With regard to his distinction between the Mosaic law and natural law, Origen posits that the presence or absence of the article with νόμος is of help, though he never claims this to be an invariable rule.[21]

More particularly, when commenting on Paul's teaching regarding the Christian's relation to the Mosaic law, Origen—in concert with Irenaeus, Tertullian, and the Alexandrian Fathers generally—separated the law into two parts: (1) the ceremonial laws of Leviticus, which, interpreted according to the flesh, have come to an end with Christ; and (2) the moral requirements of the law, which have been

---

which is the mother of us all' [Gal 4:26]. And anyone who will take up the Epistle to the Galatians may learn how the passages relating to the 'marriage' and the 'intercourse with the maid-servants' have been allegorized—the Scripture desiring us to imitate not the literal acts of those who did these things, but (as the apostles of Jesus are accustomed to call them) the spiritual."

[17] *Ibid.* 7.21.

[18] *Ibid.* 2.1; though Origen goes on to offer a partial justification for Peter and his associates, arguing that "certainly it was quite consistent that those should not abstain from the observance of Jewish usages who were sent to minister to the circumcision."

[19] Origen, *Commentarii ad Romanos* on Rom 3:19 (*PG* 14.958).

[20] Origen, "Fragments on Romans," ed. H. Ramsbotham, *JTS* 13 (1912) 216-18 (on Rom 2:21-25) and 14 (1913) 13 (on Rom 7:7).

[21] *Commentarii ad Romanos* on Rom 3:21 (*PG* 14.959).

retained and amplified by Christ.²² And when relating gospel and law, while not without an understanding of the gospel as the historical fulfillment of the law, "his main emphasis," as Maurice Wiles has pointed out, "was placed on the more static and less dynamic conception of the already present but hidden spiritual meaning of the law."²³ For example, in commenting on Rom 6:14, Origen interprets "you are not under law but under grace" as a contrast between the letter of the law and the spirit of the law, without any attention to historical developments either within or between the testaments.²⁴

It is, in fact, this separation of the Mosaic law into its ceremonial and moral parts that characterizes Origen's thinking. And it is no exaggeration to say that this same general approach to relations between the testaments and many of these same features of interpretation have become ingrained in much of Christian theology throughout the centuries and today.

4. *The Antiochian Fathers*

At Antioch of Syria, however, another brand of Christian interpretation arose—one which owed much to Origen for its critical spirit and grammatical precision, but also stood in opposition to many of the Alexandrian exegetical tenets and to their general hermeneutical approach. John Chrysostom (345–407 CE), who became famous in his native Antioch as a great Christian leader and outstanding preacher ("John the Golden Mouth") and who then served as Archbishop of Constantinople from 398 CE to his death in 407 CE, is certainly one of the most important of the Antiochian Fathers. Theodore of Mopsuestia (died 429 CE), who was born in Tarsus but lived in Antioch, was a colleague of Chrysostom, and became Bishop of the ecclesiastical see of Mopsuestia, is likewise important. Also Theodoret (393–460 CE), a native of Antioch and a disciple of Theodore, who later became Bishop of Cyrrhus in Syria.

Chrysostom and his Antiochian colleagues, of course, shared a common Christian faith with Origen and the Alexandrian Fathers. But they differed widely in their general hermeneutical approach to the

---

[22] *Ibid.* on Rom 8:3 and 11:6; cf. Irenaeus, *Adversus haereses* 4.16.4; Tertullian, *De pudicitia* 6.3-5; *De monogamia* 7.1; *De oratione* 1.1; *Apostolic Constitutions* 6.20.

[23] Wiles, *Divine Apostle*, 65.

[24] Origen, *Commentarii ad Romanos* on Rom 6:1 (*PG* 14.1035).

Scriptures and on many exegetical matters. For while the Alexandrians, in concert with Irenaeus and Tertullian, did everything they could to assure that Paul's opposition to the law was kept to a minimum—and so tended to view relations between the testaments in somewhat static fashion—the Antiochian Fathers emphasized historical developments and redemptive fulfillment, and so understood differently Paul's teaching on such matters as the Christian gospel and the Mosaic law and the Christian's relation to the Mosaic law.

Likewise, the Antiochian Fathers stood diametrically opposed to allegorical exegesis and denied the legitimacy of separating the Mosaic law into two unequal parts—that is, the ceremonial law, which came to an end with Christ, and the moral law, which was reaffirmed by Christ. And while they acknowledged that Paul used the word law differently in his writings to refer at times to natural law or to the whole Old Testament, as well as to the Mosaic law, they tended not to appeal to these distinctions in explicating difficult passages, but preferred to interpret such passages along the lines of only one sense per passage for the word law. So, for example, whereas Origen held that Paul's use of law changed frequently and without notice in Romans 7, Chrysostom insisted that the interpretation of Romans 7 must be in terms of the Mosaic law throughout, with other ideas about natural law and/or a paradisal command to be ruled out altogether.[25]

Themes of development and fulfillment come to the fore at many places in the Antiochian Fathers' treatment of the New Testament. For example, though he refused to separate gospel and law into opposing forces, Chrysostom was not prepared to see the Mosaic law as an ethical guide for Christians. Thus on Paul's statement, "Now that faith has come, we are no longer under the supervision of the law; for you are all sons of God through faith in Christ Jesus" (Gal 3:25-26), Chrysostom writes:

> The Law, then, as it was our tutor, and we were kept shut up under it, is not the adversary but the fellow-worker of grace. But if when grace is come it continues to hold us down, it becomes an adversary; for if it confines those who ought to go forward to grace, then it is the destruction of our salvation. If a candle which gave light by night kept us, when it became day, from the sun, it would not only not benefit, it

---

[25] Chrysostom, *Homiliae in Romanos* 12.6, on Rom 7:12; though in treating Rom 2:14-15 he distinguished between written law, natural law, and law as revealed in action.

would injure us. And so does the Law, if it stands between us and greater benefits. Those then are the greatest traducers of the Law who still keep it, just as the tutor makes a youth ridiculous by retaining him with himself when time calls for his departure.[26]

And though he failed to apply the verse either to the anti-semitism prevalent in his day or to male chauvinism, in a remarkable sermon delivered at Constantinople toward the end of his life Chrysostom interpreted Gal 3:28 as having relevance for the question of slavery. Thus while agreeing generally with Christians of his day that slavery is "the penalty of sin and the punishment of disobedience," Chrysostom went on to assert:

> But when Christ came he annuled even this, for in Christ Jesus "there is no slave nor free." Therefore, it is not necessary to have a slave; but if it should be necessary, then only one or at most a second ... Buy them and after you have taught them some skill by which they may maintain themselves, set them free.[27]

In so speaking, Chrysostom was knowingly breaking away from a common Christian view that since slavery arose because of sin it could only be eradicated in the eschaton when God deals finally with sin.[28] Based on a more dynamic understanding of redemption, Chrysostom argued for an application of the gospel to the question of slavery even here and now—not just reserving such matters for the future.[29]

It is fair to say, then, that the Antiochian Fathers, while not denying continuity with the redemptive activities of God throughout history, had a livelier sense of historical development and redemptive fulfillment than did their Alexandrian counterparts. For while the concept of continuity between the testaments was important for both the Alexandrian and Antiochian Fathers (contra Marcion), the Alexandrians tended to understand continuity in terms of identity and sameness whereas the Antiochians saw it in terms of development—a development that retained the essence of the gospel throughout, but

---

[26] Chrysostom, *Commentary on Galatians* on Gal 3:25-26.

[27] Chrysostom, *Homily 40* on 1 Corinthians 10, in *The Homilies of S. John Chrysostom, Archbishop of Constantinople, on the First Epistle of St Paul the Apostle to the Corinthians*, Part II (Oxford: Parker, 1839), 580.

[28] *Ibid.*: "I know I am annoying my hearers, but what can I do? For this purpose I am appointed and I will not cease speaking so."

[29] Cf. R. N. Longenecker, *New Testament Social Ethics for Today* (Grand Rapids: Eerdmans, 1984), 60-65.

with genuine growth of understanding and varieties of expression both within and between the testaments. So because of their more dynamic approach to the Scriptures, the Antiochian Fathers treated questions concerning gospel and law, relations between the two testaments, and the place of the Mosaic law in the Christian life differently from the Alexandrians.

5. *The Situation Today*

It would be presumptuous to attempt to draw straight lines between the three approaches sketched out above and the situation today. Much has transpired in the intervening centuries to break down the lines of distinction and even to muddle the issues. Yet similar tendencies exist in various contemporary theologies. And while it may seem to some more meddling than illuminating to do so, I would like here to indicate how and where features similar to the ancient Marcionite, Alexandrian and Antiochian approaches to the Scriptures exist today—though, of course, in different dress and called by other names.

Taking as the central feature of Marcion's approach the dichotomy between the testaments, at least two systems of interpretation today may be said to exhibit Marcionite tendencies. On the left of the theological spectrum, Rudolf Bultmann and many of his followers, with their understanding of revelation as momentary in nature and historically unconnected, have expressed little interest in the Jewish Scriptures as prolegomena for the Christianity of the New Testament. Further, they have considered the use of the Jewish Scriptures to demonstrate a promise–fulfillment theme and the attempt to link the two testaments together in terms of some overarching salvation-history scenario to be innovations on the part of the New Testament evangelists and other writers, and not intrinsic to the consciousness of Jesus or his earliest followers. Rather, they have preferred to focus on the theological anthropology of Paul and John, interpreting their writings in ways that incorporate certain gnostic and dualistic features.

On the theological right, Dispensationalism, too, exhibits a number of Marcionite tendencies—particularly in its sharp distinctions between Israel and the Christian church, the dispensations of "law" and "grace," "kingdom ethics" and "gospel ethics," and even between Jesus and Paul. Building on a distinctive ecclesiology, it tends to make Paul's letters the essential Christian canon within the New Testament

Scriptures, viewing these writings in ways that are (like those of Bultmannianism) often reminiscent of gnostic and dualistic thought. In effect, interpreters on both the left and the right of today's theological spectrum tend to share certain Marcionite tendencies in their approaches to the question of the relation of the testaments—even though they are hardly on speaking terms theologically, and often seem not even to be cognizant of one another's existence.

An Alexandrian approach to the Scriptures (apart from its use of allegorical exegesis, which came to be used less and less) became dominant in catholic Christendom, and can be seen rather clearly in the more traditional forms of Roman Catholicism, Reformed Theology, and Puritan Theology—diverse as these groups are from one another in their specific doctrinal formulations. For in Alexandrian thought and in these three more contemporary forms of Christian theology the relationship between the testaments is taken to be essentially one of identity or sameness, with what appear to be innovations in later formulations only seen as more precise explications and applications of what was already implicit in the earlier statements. The analogy to be drawn is that of a syllogism, where what appears to be an innovation in the conclusion is really only a logical deduction already contained in the major and minor premises, and so new only in the sense that it had not been explicitly seen to have been the case before. Thus all doctrinal and ethical issues are argued first on the basis of the Old Testament and then from the more explicit data of the New Testament—attempting, thereby, to demonstrate the oneness of biblical teaching. Likewise, balance between the testaments is sought in both the church's "liturgy" and its "canon law" (whether or not these explicit terms are used). Extremes of an Alexandrian approach are to be found in the "Free" Presbyterians of Scotland and the "Theonomy" advocates of the Bible Belt in the States, though these groups are only rather extreme examples of an approach to the Scriptures that has deep rootage in the Christian church today.

With the surging tide of Alexandrian thought flooding Christendom, an Antiochian approach to the relation of the testaments has often been relegated to the backwaters of the church's consciousness. Martin Luther, however, at least in his Galatians commentary of

1535-38 (though seemingly without being aware of it himself),[30] stood firmly in the Antiochian tradition, with this approach to the relation of the testaments being carried on by many Lutherans today particularly where the "younger" Luther is looked to more than Melanchthon and the supposedly "older" Luther. Its revival is also to be seen in the modern Biblical Theology movement, though some of its extremes have come to expression in that movement as well.

In effect, this approach stresses both continuity and genuine innovations in redemptive history. It appeals by way of illustration to the growth of a plant, where stalk, leaves and flower are not just reproductions of an original seed, yet where growth is always controlled by—and to be judged by—what is inherent in the seed itself. Yet it calls on us to appreciate the fulness of growth by looking first of all at the flowering plant itself, and only then to go back to an analysis of the seed. Thus, on such an approach, doctrinal and ethical issues are dealt with first of all on the basis of the data of the New Testament and then related to that of the Old Testament—recognizing genuine growth of understanding and variations of expression both within each of the testaments and between the testaments. Likewise, liturgy and canon law are constructed to reflect the supremacy of God's revelation in Christ and the present working of the Spirit, without denying the importance of God's past revelations and activities as contained in the Jewish Scriptures.

Lines of demarcation cannot always be clearly drawn, either between ecclesiastical groups or within them. For example, Anglicans

---

[30] In 1519 Luther published a commentary on Galatians that was largely dependent on Jerome and Erasmus, who, in turn, were largely dependent on Origen and the Alexandrian tradition. Then in 1523 he produced an abbreviated and revised form of his 1519 work, which in its omissions and changes began to depart from both (see *Luthers Werke* [Weimar, 1884], 2.436-758; *Luther's Works*, ed. J. Pelikan [St Louis: Concordia, 1964], 27.151-410). During the fall semester of 1531, however, Luther gave another series of lectures on Galatians at the University of Wittenburg. That series was taken down in full by three of his students and published in 1535. It was then republished with revisions in 1538 as his definitive exposition of Galatians (*Luthers Werke*, 40 and 40; *Luther's Works*, 26 and 27a; see Luther's Preface in the Weimar edition [40^1] where he acknowledges all that his students have taken down from his lectures as his own [pp. 33-37]). In his 1535-38 Galatians commentary Luther frequently opposes Jerome on matters of exegesis and interpretation, occasionally taking issue with Erasmus' *Paraphrase on Galatians* [1518 or 1519] as well.

with their broad ecclesiastical structures and Baptists with their aversion to many such structures seem to be able to countenance an alliance of all three approaches. Yet while lines cannot always be clearly drawn, tendencies can be recognized and ingrained presuppositions (even my own Antiochian proclivities) must be tested.

Without a doubt, presupposed approaches always influence our hermeneutics and exegesis. Hermeneutical theory and exegesis, however, must not be allowed to be simply controlled by our presuppositions. Rather, analyses of the biblical data must be allowed to constantly test, challenge and correct (where necessary) our ingrained approaches. So it is necessary to recognize how relations between the testaments have been understood historically and what mental baggage we each have inherited in order that we may be properly critical in carrying out the work of biblical interpretation today.

SELECT BIBLIOGRAPHY

Aleith, Eva Hoffman. *Das Paulusverständnis in der alten Kirche*. Berlin: Töpelmann, 1937.
_____. "Das Paulusverständnis des Johannes Chrysostomus," *ZNW* 38 (1939) 181-88.
Attwater, Donald. *St John Chrysostom: Pastor and Preacher*. London: Harvill, 1959.
Bigg, Charles. *The Christian Platonists of Alexandria*. Oxford: Clarendon, 1886, repr. 1913.
Blackman, E. Cyril. *Marcion and his Influence*. London: SPCK, 1948.
Buri, Fritz. *Clemens Alexandrinus und der paulinische Freiheitsbegriff*. Zurich: Niehmans, 1939.
Butterworth, George W. *Origen on First Principles*. London: SPCK, 1936.
Chase, Frederic H. *Chrysostom: A Study in the History of Biblical Interpretation*. Cambridge: Deighton, Bell, 1887.
Daniélou, Jean. *Origen*, trans. W. Mitchell. London, New York: Sheed & Ward, 1955.
Gordan, Peter. *Principles of Patristic Exegesis: Romans 9–11 in Origen, John Chrysostom, and Augustine*. New York, Toronto: Mellen, 1983.
Grant, Robert M. *The Letter and the Spirit*. London: SPCK, 1957.
Hanson, Richard P. C. *Allegory and Event: A Study of the Sources and Significance of Origen's Interpretation of Scripture*. London: SCM; Richmond: John Knox, 1959.

1. Understanding Relations between the Testaments 18

Harnack, Adolf. *Marcion: The Gospel of the Alien God*, trans. J. E. Steely and L. D. Bierma. Durham: Labyrinth, 1990 (translation of *Marcion: Das Evangelium vom fremden Gott*. Leipzig: Hinrichs, 1921).

Lawson, John. *The Biblical Theology of Saint Irenaeus*. London: Epworth, 1948.

Lightfoot, Joseph B. "The Patristic Commentaries on This Epistle," in *Saint Paul's Epistle to the Galatians*. London: Macmillan, 1890 (10th ed.), 227-36 (on Galatians specifically, though also with reference to various ways that the early Church Fathers interpreted Paul generally).

Schelkle, Karl H. *Paulus Lehrer der Väter: Die altkirchliche Auslegung von Röm 1–11*. Düsseldorf: Patmos, 1936, 1958.

Schneemelcher, Wilhelm. "Paulus in der griechischen Kirche des zweiten Jahrhunderts," *ZKG* 75 (1964) 1-20.

Schweizer, Eduard. "Diodore von Tarsus als Exeget," *ZNW* 40 (1941) 33-75.

Seeseman, H. "Das Paulusverständnis des Clemens Alexandrinus," *TSK* 107 (1936) 312-46.

Souter, Alexander. *A Study of Ambrosiaster*. Cambridge: Cambridge University Press, 1905.

_____. *The Character and History of Pelagius' Commentary on the Epistles of St Paul*. London: Oxford University Press, 1916.

_____. *The Earliest Latin Commentaries on the Epistles of St Paul*. Oxford: Clarendon, 1927.

Turner, C. H. "Greek Patristic Commentaries on the Pauline Epistles," in *A Dictionary of the Bible*, ed. J. Hastings. New York: Scribner's; Edinburgh: T. & T. Clark, 1904. Extra Volume, 484-531.

Werner, Jakob. *Der Paulinismus des Irenaeus*. Leipzig: Hinrichs, 1889.

Wickert, Ulrich. *Studien zu den Pauluskommentaren Theodors von Mopsuestia als Beitrag zum Verständnis der antiochenischen Theologie*. Berlin: Töpelmann, 1962.

Wiles, Maurice F. *The Divine Apostle. The Interpretation of St Paul's Epistles in the Early Church*. Cambridge: Cambridge University Press, 1967.

2

A Developmental Hermeneutic
New Treasures as Well as Old

At the conclusion of his parables of the kingdom, Matthew's Gospel portrays Jesus as asking his disciples, "Have you understood all these things?" (13:51). When they answered "Yes," he gave them another parable or parabolic saying: "Every teacher of the law who has been instructed about the kingdom of heaven is like the owner of a house who brings out of his storeroom new treasures as well as old" (13:52).

1. *Analysis of the Parabolic Saying*

Many features of this brief, concluding parable or parabolic saying are fairly easy to understand. The "kingdom of heaven" is certainly the reign of God as proclaimed by Jesus and then focused in Jesus, for the use of "kingdom" in Matthew is christocentrically oriented throughout. Likewise, "the teacher of the law who has been instructed about the kingdom" is one who is committed to and instructed by Jesus—that is, a Christian teacher,[1] not some Jewish scribe trained in Pharisaic traditions. It is also obvious that the parable has something to do with how Christians are to interpret divine revelation and apply its message to their day, for it comes at the end of a group of seven

---

[1] The use of μαθητειθείς ("who has been discipled/trained/instructed") in 13:52 has often been seen as a pun on the name Matthew (μαθθαῖος), and so a veiled reference to the evangelist himself or a "school" that honored his name. Benno Przybylski, however, has shown that the use of "disciple" in Matthew's Gospel refers to "people in general who have accepted (13:52; 27:57) or will accept (28:19) the teaching of Jesus"—that is, Christians generally, not just a circle of learned men within the evangelist's community (*Righteousness in Matthew and his World of Thought* [Cambridge: Cambridge University Press, 1980], 109-10). Cf. also J. D. Kingsbury, *The Parables of Jesus in Matthew 13: A Study in Redaction-Criticism* (London: SPCK, 1969), 126-29.

parables that do just that for the disciples. Further, the parable suggests that in interpretation it is Jesus' pattern that is to be in some way the paradigm for Christian teachers—that is, just as Jesus' pattern of ministry is to be the paradigm for Christian discipleship (cf. Matt 10:25: "It is enough for the student to be like his teacher, and the servant like his master"), so Jesus' manner of interpretation is to have some bearing on how Christians interpret and apply Scripture. Thus just as Jesus is portrayed in Matthew's Gospel as a new and better Moses (esp. in chapters 5–7), so here his disciples are exhorted to be new and better scribes of the kingdom.

The most difficult feature in this parabolic saying, however, is Jesus' comparison of Christian teachers to a householder "who brings out of his storeroom new treasures as well as old." What did Jesus mean by "new" and what by "old"? As Christians today who seek to interpret and proclaim the Christian message, what are we to understand by the phrase "new treasures as well as old" and how are we to relate the new and the old?

Most commentators have concluded that what is meant here by "old" and "new" is what we would refer to as "the religion of Israel" and "the proclamation of the New Testament"—that is, "the old dispensation of Judaism," "the Mosaic law," and/or "the preparatory events and promises of the Old Testament" vis-à-vis "the new dispensation that has come with Christ," "the fulfillment of the Mosaic law in Jesus' ministry," and/or "Jesus' work and teaching."[3] Some understand "old" and "new" to refer more broadly to some such concept as "the Holy Scriptures" and "the disciples' own inward experience of what true religion is"—or even "the Old Evangel of the Bible" and "the new insights of recent scholarship." And a few have

---

[3] E.g., A. W. Argyle: "The ideal disciple is a rabbi with understanding of the Kingdom, who can therefore bring forth from a well-stored mind the old, i.e., the riches of Old Testament truth, and the new, i.e., the riches of the new teaching of Jesus" (*The Gospel according to Matthew* [Cambridge: Cambridge University Press, 1963], 108); D. Hill: "*What is new and what is old*: these phrases probably connote either traditional Jewish teaching on the Kingdom of God which had now been renewed completely by the presence of Jesus, or the ancient OT promises which had found fulfilment in Jesus' person and teaching" (*The Gospel of Matthew* [London: Marshall, Morgan & Scott, 1972], 240). Cf. also the commentaries by T. H. Robinson, R. V. G. Tasker, F. V. Filson, W. F. Albright, et al.

2. A Developmental Hermeneutic

despaired of ever being able to determine what these words might have meant, either to Jesus or to the evangelist Matthew.[4]

Recently, however, there has been a tendency to view the old and new of Matt 13:52 in terms of (1) the gospel proclamation, which has as its focus the ministry and teaching of Jesus, and (2) fuller understandings and new applications of that proclamation for various new circumstances faced by Christian prophets and teachers—including, of course, Matthew's own shaping of the Jesus tradition in his Gospel for his own community and audience.[5] And with this interpretation I am in general agreement. So I propose that here Jesus speaks of the Christian teacher as one who is (1) rooted in the gospel proclamation (i.e., its foundation in the salvation history of the Old Testament and its focus in the work and person of Jesus Christ, together with its derived principles and described practices) *and* (2) relevant to current contexts and circumstances by understanding more fully and applying more adequately that proclamation to his or her own situation.

2. The Conjunction of Old and New in the Bible

Throughout the Bible there is the conjunction of the old and the new. God's revelation of his will in the Old Testament was given progressively in Israel's history, being related to his personal relations with his people (e.g., through the covenants) and his redemptive

---

[4] E.g., B. T. D. Smith: "It is impossible to determine the original meaning of the words" (*S. Matthew* [Cambridge Greek Testament], ed. A. Nairne [Cambridge: Cambridge University Press, 1950], 141). F. C. Grant wrote, "This precious saying described the Christian teacher," but preferred to say nothing as to what it might mean (*Nelson's Bible Commentary*, VI [New York: Thomas Nelson, 1962], 78).

[5] E.g., E. Schweizer: "The true teacher of the Law has learned from Jesus to see both the old and the new together (cf. Wisd. 8:8)—God's Law, and its new interpretation proclaimed by Jesus and realized in all that he does. Or is Matthew thinking of Jesus' own teaching, and its new interpretation in the 'learned' decisions of the community of disciples (16:19; 18:18)?" (*The Good News according to Matthew*, trans. D. E. Green [Atlanta: John Knox, 1975], 315); F. W. Beare: "The 'old' and the 'new' could mean the ancient Law of Israel, written and oral, on the one hand; and the interpretation and application given to it by Jesus, on the other. But we are tempted to feel that for the evangelist it means the tradition of the teaching given by Jesus and the interpretation and application which is now supplied by the evangelist" (*The Gospel according to Matthew* [San Francisco: Harper & Row, 1981], 317).

activity on their behalf (e.g., in the Exodus). And this progressive revelation, while important and applicable for that day, also pointed forward toward future, fuller revelations of God that would culminate in the coming of God's Anointed One, the Messiah (cf., e.g., Gen 3:15; Deut 18:15, 18; Jer 31:31-34; Mal 3:1).

In the Old Testament the "latter prophets" reinterpreted the "former prophets" and the "writings" in order to make new applications of the words of the Mosaic law—not opposing the former, but expressing their significance more fully and applying their message to new situations. Perhaps the most obvious example of this conjunction of old and new in the Old Testament is in Daniel 9, where Jeremiah's prophecy of seventy years (cf. Jer 25:12-14) is reinterpreted to mean "seventy heptads" and to have eschatological significance beyond what was initially thought (cf. esp. vv 1-3, 20-27). Another is in Psalm 110, where the Canaanite chieftain Melchizedek of Genesis 14 is brought into the lineage of Israel as one of the nation's ancient worthies (cf. v 4).

In the New Testament there is a similar conjunction of old and new. The earliest preaching of the apostles was cast almost entirely in functional categories, as, for example, in Acts 2:22-24:

> Jesus of Nazareth was a man accredited by God to you by miracles, wonders and signs, which God did among you through him, as you yourselves know. This man was handed over to you by God's set purpose and foreknowledge; and you, with the help of wicked men, put him to death by nailing him to the cross. But God raised him from the dead, freeing him from the agony of death, because it was impossible for death to keep its hold on him.

It was a message that stressed God's intervention in human affairs in Jesus of Nazareth and focused on God's redemption of humanity through what Jesus as Israel's Messiah did. Presupposed in that message, of course, were many theological nuances. But full-blown theological formulations and developed ethical stances were, at first, largely held in the substratum of the apostles' earliest preaching and appear only in the overtones of their message.

As Jews, the earliest believers in Jesus possessed a basic theology regarding God's person and divine redemption, as well as basic instructions about how they were to live in response to God's actions on their behalf. As Christians, however, their distinctive theological affirmations were derived from God's self-revelation and redemptive

2. A Developmental Hermeneutic   23

activity in Jesus of Nazareth, and their ethical exhortations were focused on the example and teaching of Jesus as illuminated, applied and energized by the Holy Spirit. They seem to have worked in their thinking from functional categories—that is, what God did in and through the ministry of Jesus—to theological, ontological, and speculative categories—that is, how all of this should be understood, who Jesus was (and is), why it all came about, and what it means for everyday living. So in the New Testament we have a record of how these early believers began to work out the nuances of their basically functional "new covenant" stance—under, as we Christians believe, the guidance of God's Spirit—into a rudimentary system of Christian doctrine and a rudimentary style of Christian living. Thus the New Testament, paralleling the Old Testament in this regard, contains both (1) a record of God's progressive revelation of himself and his unfolding redemption on behalf of humanity, and (2) accounts of his people's developing endeavors to work out the theological ramifications and ethical implications of that revelation and redemption.

Jesus' promise of the Spirit as recorded in John 14–16 includes the expectation that there would be fuller understandings of his teachings and ministry on the part of his disciples in the future—fuller understandings not divorced from Jesus but rooted in all that Jesus said and did:

> I have much more to say to you, more than you can now bear. But when he, the Spirit of truth, comes, he will guide you into all truth. He will not speak on his own; he will speak only what he hears, and he will tell you what is yet to come. (16:12-13)

In at least two places in John's Gospel there are references to biblical interpretation as being more perceptive after Jesus' ascension, and suggestions that the ministry of the Spirit was understood by the earliest Christians to include advances in the understanding of Scripture. In John 2 we are told that it was only after Jesus' resurrection that his disciples understood Ps 69:9 in the context of Jesus' ministry:

> His disciples remembered that it is written: 'Zeal for your house will consume me.' ... After he was raised from the dead, his disciples recalled what he had said. Then they believed the Scripture and the words that Jesus had spoken (2:17, 22).

And in John 12, of Jesus' entry into Jerusalem and the use of Psa 118:25-26 and Zech 9:9 in that connection, we are told:

> At first his disciples did not understand all this. Only after Jesus was glorified did they realize that these things had been written about him and that they had done these things to him (12:16).

In these two accounts, one at the beginning of the evangelist's "Book of Signs" (i.e., chs 2–12) and the other at its close, the disciples are portrayed as coming to understand certain actions and sayings of Jesus in light of the Old Testament only at a later time—along, of course, the general lines of interpretation laid out by Jesus, but without any direct word from him.

In fact, each of the four Gospels in its own way evidences how the canonical evangelists attempted to be both true to the proclamation they had received and relevant to the particular situations that they faced. Each of their Gospels is a recasting of the original gospel tradition to meet specific issues and concerns within their respective communities addressed, as redaction criticism so abundantly illustrates.

Likewise, Paul's letters evidence this wedding of old and new in their pastoral applications of the Christian gospel to various theological and ethical problems in the churches. One particularly obvious conjunction of what Jesus was known to have taught and Paul's application of the thrust of that teaching for a somewhat different situation can be found in 1 Corinthians 7. For while in 7:10-11 he quotes a saying of Jesus as settling one matter ("To the married I give this command; not I, but the Lord"), in 7:12-16 (and probably throughout 7:17-40 as well), with regard to a further matter (or matters) on which the church possessed no explicit word of Jesus, Paul speaks as one authoritatively expressing the gospel's intent: "To the rest I say this; I, not the Lord" (v 12; cf. also v 2: "I have no command from the Lord, but I give a judgment as one who by the Lord's mercy is trustworthy," and v 40: "In my judgment, ... and I think that I have the Spirit of God.").

But these are only rather obvious examples. I have said much more by way of attempting to demonstrate this point theologically and ethically in my commentary on Galatians (Dallas: Word, 1990) and my book *New Testament Social Ethics for Today* (Grand Rapids: Eerdmans, 1984; repr. Vancouver: Regent College Publishing, 1997).

3. *Christian Theology as a Story of Development*

The history of Christian theology is a story of development. In the Bible we have the record of God's progressive revelation and unfolding redemption: first in Israel's history, then (pre-eminently) in Jesus' ministry, and finally in the apostolic church's witness. But this record is coupled with accounts of the developing endeavors of God's people to work out the theological ramifications and ethical implications of that revelation and redemption.

Neither the Bible as a whole nor the New Testament in particular gives us the final word on the formulation of Christian theology or Christian ethics—at least, not final in the sense that nothing more can or need be said. Rather, the New Testament (building on the Jewish Scriptures) is the touchstone for Christian theology and the benchmark for Christian living. It presents the proclamation of God's definitive word to humankind in the person and ministry of Jesus of Nazareth, and it gives us the paradigm of how the implications involved in God's revelatory and redemptive activity were begun to be spelled out in the apostolic period. To learn the full story of Christian theology and Christian ethics to date, one must also be a student of church history and open to the guidance of God's Spirit. For under the guidance of the same Spirit who inspired the biblical writings (1) there has been a progressive illumination throughout the centuries of the church's existence of the meaning and significance of God's definitive activity in Jesus Christ, and (2) there are continuing challenges and opportunities to think both creatively and in a Christian manner today. To be a Christian theologian and Christian ethicist in this day, therefore, requires (1) extensive familiarity with the Scriptures, (2) extensive familiarity with church history, (3) discernment in appreciating the essence and direction of the biblical statements, (4) discernment in distinguishing between advances and pitfalls in the history of Christian thought, being able to identify the lines of continuity that exist between every true advance and the New Testament, the touchstone for Christian faith and benchmark for Christian practice, and (5) creative ability to say what all this means for Christian faith and life today amid the complexities of varying ideologies and competing lifestyles.

The New Testament, therefore, is not a textbook on systematic theology or a treatise on Christian ethics. It is a record of God's revelation and redemption in Jesus Christ and a record of the church's initial attempts to understand and state what all that means. To be biblical is not to say only what the New Testament says, "nothing more and nothing less," as some would claim. Rather, biblical Christians realize that the Bible, history, and reason all come into play in constructing a Christian theology: the first, as the touchstone for truth and benchmark for living, pointing out the path to be followed both theologically and ethically; the second, as a record of how the church has tread that path throughout the centuries, with attention to both the advances and the pitfalls; the third, in determining where the history of Christian theology and ethics has been in continuity with its revelational base and how Christian theology and ethics should be expressed today.

Admittedly, the concept of development in theology is a relatively modern one. Jewish interpreters saw their work in terms of conservation, distillation, and application, but not as a creative enterprise or an objective advance of content. Jesus ben Sirach, for example, the author of the early second-century "wisdom" writing we call *Sirach* (or *Ecclesiasticus*, "The Church's Book," as Jerome called it), thought of himself as "one that gleans after the grape-gatherers" (i.e., the Sages) and whose work was to distill for posterity the essence of the Sages' wisdom (cf. *Sirach* 33:16-18). So, too, the Pharisees, the apocalyptic writers, the Dead Sea Covenanters, the tannaitic and amoraitic rabbis of the Talmud, the Gaonim, and the Rishonim (e.g., Rashi and Maimonides)—to name only a few prominent schools of Jewish interpretation—saw their tasks mainly (if not exclusively) in terms of conservation, distillation, and application.

Likewise, the Church Fathers, the medieval exegetes, and even the Reformers (Luther, Calvin, *et al.*) viewed their treatments of Scripture not as developments but as summaries (*compendia*) and distillations. They might have looked on their writings as being creative in the sense of an increasing subjective understanding and contemporary applications. But they would not have considered them developments in the content of Christian theology. Nor did they have any awareness of developments within Scripture.

Yet virtually all modern historians of theology agree that, despite their claims to the contrary, almost all of the Jewish and Christian interpreters mentioned above have, in fact, produced writings that go beyond being merely "*compendia* with contemporary applications." In a real sense, each in his own way has been creative and has treated

Scripture in a manner that has affected theology objectively, whether Jewish or Christian.

4. Nineteenth-Century Expressions of Developmental Thinking

It was in the latter half of the nineteenth century that the concept of development assumed prominence in theology. People were conscious of significant achievements in science, technology, exploration, trade, and the arts, and so began to view all human endeavor, both quantitatively and qualitatively, in terms of progress.

More significantly for our purposes, a number of works were written during the latter decades of the nineteenth century by eminent theologians representing all shades of the theological spectrum and advocating a developmental understanding of the progress of Christian doctrine since the close of the New Testament canon—with some also arguing for a development of doctrine within the canon. John Henry Newman's *An Essay on the Development of Christian Doctrine* (1845), which he wrote in large part to justify and explain his own religious pilgrimage from an earlier evangelical stance to his later espousal of Roman Catholicism, was seminal. But just as important were Robert Rainy's *The Delivery and Development of Christian Doctrine* (1874), Adolf Harnack's *Outlines of the History of Dogma* (1886; first English translation in 1905), and James Orr's *The Progress of Dogma* (1901).

With respect to the theology of the apostle Paul, which is always a major interest of mine, it was Auguste Sabatier (1839–1901) who, as a young scholar in his early thirties, first proposed a developmental hypothesis for an understanding his thought and attempted to trace out what he called the "progressive character of Paulinism" (*The Apostle Paul: A Sketch of the Development of His Doctrine* [French original, 1870; English translation, 1896]). A number of German scholars followed Sabatier's lead and attempted to work out a developmental understanding of Paul's thought generally. Among them were Hermann Karl Lüdemann (*Die Anthropologie des Apostels Paulus und ihre Stellung innerhalb seiner Heilslehre. Nach den vier Hauptbriefen*, 1872), Otto Pfleiderer (*Der Paulinismus: Ein Beitrag zur Geschichte der urchistlichen Theologie*, 1873), and Bernhard Weiss (*Lehrbuch der biblischen Theologie des Neuen Testaments*, first published in 1868, but revised extensively through 1893). More particularly, Ernst G. G. Teichmann (*Die paulinischen Vorstellungen von Auferstehung und Gericht,* 1896) and Heinrich Julius Holtzmann (*Lehrbuch der neutestamentliche Theologie,* 1897) focused on the development of Paul's eschatological thought.

Likewise, a number of British scholars during the last half of the nineteenth century added their voices in support of a developmental understanding of Paul. Among them were Joseph B. Lightfoot (see particularly his "The Chronology of St Paul's Life and Epistles," which were his lecture notes of 1863 and published posthumously in *Biblical Essays* in 1893) and George Matheson (*The Spiritual Development of St Paul,* 1897). Special attention was given to Paul's eschatological development by Henry StJohn Thackeray (*The Relation of St Paul to Contemporary Jewish Thought,* 1900) and Robert Henry Charles (*A Critical History of the Doctrine of the Future Life in Israel, in Judaism, and in Christianity,* 2nd rev ed., 1913).

Not everyone, of course, has accepted the concept of development in either Scripture or the history of doctrine—and even when espoused, it has been variously explained. Further, the twentieth century has witnessed less concern about developmental theories than was evident during the latter half of the nineteenth century. Nonetheless, there still continues in many quarters a lively interest in such an understanding of Christian theology generally and Scripture in particular, both in Protestant and Catholic circles and among both evangelical and liberal scholars—whether it is called "the development of doctrine" (as among most Protestant theologians), "the evolution of thought" (as among more radical theologians), or "the unfolding of revelation" (as among Roman Catholic theologians).

5. Three Models of Development

Yet while many today are prepared to speak of the development of Christian doctrine over the past two millennia, and while some would also speak of development within the Scriptures themselves (whether under the rubric of "progressive revelation" or the more mundane "evolution of religion"), three quite different models of development have been proposed.[6] First, there are those who take the relationship of later formulations to earlier foundations to be essentially one of identity or sameness, with what appear to be later innovations only

---

[6] On these three models, see M. F. Wiles, *The Remaking of Christian Doctrine* (London: SCM, 1974), 4-9.

2. A Developmental Hermeneutic

more precise explications and applications of what was already implicit earlier. The analogy to be drawn is that of a syllogism, where what appears to be an innovation in the conclusion is only a logical deduction drawn from the major and minor premises and is new only in the sense that it had not been seen to be the case before. This was the attitude of the Alexandrian Fathers (e.g., Clement of Alexandria, Origen),[7] and it continues to be the view of development taken in many Roman Catholic, Reformed, and Puritan circles that are more traditionally oriented.

A second model proposed for understanding development is one that speaks of both continuity with a foundational core and genuine growth in conceptualization and expression. It is a model that appeals by way of analogy to the relationship between a growing plant and its original seed; and it argues that real growth always involves genuine innovations of structure (e.g., the stalk, leaves, and flower of a plant are not just reproductions of the original seed), yet that growth is always controlled and judged by what is inherent in the seed itself. It is a model that speaks of "organic growth" (as did the Roman Catholic Cardinal John Henry Newman; also the evangelical Scottish Presbyterians Robert Rainy and James Orr), which encourages us to look for germinal expressions that incorporate within themselves indications of a proper course of development and by which we may test all succeeding developments, and which calls on us to attempt to trace out the various and often varying stages of growth as they appear at different times and under diverse circumstances thereafter. This was the approach of the Antiochian Fathers (e.g., John Chrysostom and his colleague Theodore of Mopsuestia),[8] and it has come to characterize, I believe, the methodology of the more constructive theologians of our day, whatever their particular confessional stance.

A third way of understanding development is one that emphasizes innovations in the growth of doctrine and minimizes any necessary prepositional connection with the foundational core. It stresses environmental and ideological changes in history that have brought about innovative, even contradictory, reformulations of Christian thought. And it justifies its use of the adjective "Christian" in these

---

[7] On an "Alexandrian" approach to Paul among the Ante-Nicene Fathers, see M. F. Wiles, *The Divine Apostle: The Interpretation of St Paul's Epistles in the Early Church* (Cambridge: Cambridge University Press, 1967), *passim*.

[8] On an "Antiochian" approach, see Wiles, *Divine Apostle, passim*.

reformulations not on the basis of any prepositional correspondence to earlier doctrines but on the similarity of a particular writer's religious aim and faith. This is the model of an existentialist writing of Christian theology with its insistence on the historically unconnected and momentary nature of God's encounter with humanity. It has come to expression most vocally in New Testament circles in the writings of Rudolf Bultmann and his disciples.[9]

While, admittedly, scholars differ on what is meant by "the development of Christian doctrine," almost all speak of the history of Christian thought as a story of development. Our own view is in line with an "organic" understanding (the second model above), using the analogy of an original seed to the stalk, leaves, and flower of a plant. Better yet, the analogy could be of a young man fervently in love with a young woman, whose early expressions of love may incorporate many psychological and physiological presuppositions unrecognized by him and whose early love letters may fail to express all that his heart and mind feel, but who, as he grows in understanding and draws on the stock of ideas available to him in his culture, comes over a period of time to be able to understand more adequately and to express more fully his love, together with its ramifications and implications.

This is not to imply that theological development is always a continuous and culminative growth in only one direction. Seed sometimes grows in spurts and in aberrant ways—and, sadly, so does love. In theology, therefore, as in all of life, there is the need to develop healthy growth patterns, to be able to identify factors of continuity as well as features of development, and to be conservative in our reaching back to our revelational base as well as creative in our moving forward to a fuller understanding, a more faithful explication, and a better application. Thus, as there is the conjunction of old and new in the Bible, so there has been the conjunction of old and new throughout the history of Christian thought. And it is this realization that we must keep in mind in seeking to understand New Testament theology and New Testament ethics in our day.

---

[9] It is also found in Wiles's "non-incarnational" approach to theology in his *Remaking of Christian Doctrine*.

2. A Developmental Hermeneutic

6. *A Proposed Understanding of New Testament Theology and Ethics*

The New Testament is no textbook on theology. Nor is it a compendium of ethical theory. Rather, what we have in the New Testament is the proclamation of the Christian gospel and an enunciation of its theological and ethical principles—coupled with descriptions of how that proclamation and its principles were put into practice in various situations during the apostolic period. Its proclamation and principles, I argue, are to be taken as normative. The way that its proclamation and principles were put into practice in the first century, however, should be understood as signposts at the beginning of a journey that point out the path to be followed if we are to reapply that same gospel in our day.

It will not do simply to ask, "What does the New Testament proclaim or teach about this or that theological matter?, or, "Does the New Testament say anything explicit concerning this or that ethical issue?"—with the intent being merely to repeat in those same words and same applications what it proclaims or teaches, but to remain silent where no express statement is given or no particular application is made. Such an approach assumes the record to be a static codification of theological affirmations and ethical maxims.

Rather, what we need to do is ask, What principles derived from the gospel proclamation and New Testament teaching are important for our own theological and ethical understanding today?, and What practices in application of these principles does the New Testament describe as setting a paradigm for our reapplication of those principles? In answering such questions, we need to be both as expert as possible in historical-cultural-grammatical exegesis and as open as possible to the Spirit's guidance so as to be able to distinguish between declared principles and described practices.

The church of the first century and the writers of the New Testament did not settle every theological issue and every ethical concern in advance, simply because they were not omniscient and could not know in advance all of the theological issues or ethical concerns that have arisen during the past two thousand years. Nor did God by his Spirit so illuminate them that they could. What they did do, however, was highly significant, both for Christian faith and doctrine and for Christian living: they proclaimed the message of new life in Christ and they began to work out the implications of that gospel for the situations they encountered—not always, admittedly, as fully or as adequately as we might wish from our later perspectives, but appropriately for their day and pointing the way to a fuller understanding and more adequate application in later times.

We should not try to make out the New Testament writers to be all-knowing and all-wise in every area of theological or ethical concern—or, conversely, disparage them because they were not. Instead, I suggest, we ought as Christians to (1) attempt to recapture the essence of their proclamation and the principles of the Christian gospel that have ramifications for our own reconstruction of theology and our own ethical living, both personal and societal, and (2) endeavor to follow the path that they marked out in the application of that gospel and its principles in their day, seeking to carry on their work in fuller and more significant ways today. In so doing, I believe, we will be expressing the mandate given by Jesus to his disciples and all his followers throughout the ages, as recorded in Matt 13:51: "Every teacher of the law who has been instructed about the kingdom of heaven is like the owner of a house who brings out of his storeroom new treasures as well as old."

SELECT BIBLIOGRAPHY

Bruce, Frederick F. *Tradition: Old and New*. Exeter: Paternoster, 1970.
Burkill, T. A. *The Evolution of Christian Thought*. Ithaca, London: Cornell University Press, 1971.
Chadwick, Owen. *From Bossuet to Newman: The Idea of Doctrinal Development*. Cambridge: Cambridge University Press, 1957, 2nd ed., 1987.
Daniélou, Jean. *The Development of Christian Doctrine Before the Council of Nicaea*, trans. and ed. J. A. Baker. London: Darton, Longman & Todd, 1964.
Hanson, Richard P. C. *Tradition in the Early Church*. London: SCM, 1962.
_____. *The Continuity of Christian Doctrine*. New York: Seabury, 1981.
Harnack, Adolf. *Outlines of the History of Dogma*, trans. E. K. Mitchell. New York: Funk & Wagnalls, 1893 (from 3rd German edition of 1886); repr. Boston: Beacon, 1957.
Kelly, J. N. D. *Early Christian Doctrines*. New York: Harper, 1958.
McGrath, Alister E. *The Genesis of Doctrine: A Study in the Foundations of Doctrinal Criticism*. Oxford: Blackwell, 1990.
Newman, John Henry. *An Essay on the Development of Christian Doctrine*. London: James Toovey, 1845.
Orr, James. *The Progress of Dogma*. London: Hodder & Stoughton, 1901.

Pelikan, Jaroslav *Development of Christian Doctrine: Some Historical Prolegomena*. New Haven, London: Yale University Press, 1969.
_____. *Historical Theology. Continuity and Change in Christian Doctrine*. London: Hutchinson; New York: Corpus, 1971.
Rainy, Robert. *The Delivery and Development of Christian Doctrine*. Cunningham Lectures of 1873. Edinburgh: T. & T. Clark, 1874.
Sabatier, Auguste. *The Apostle Paul: A Sketch of the Development of his Doctrine* (French original, 1870; first English translation, 1896). London: Hodder & Stoughton, 1906.
Thiselton, Anthony C. *The Two Horizons: New Testament Hermeneutics and Philosophical Description*. Exeter: Paternoster; Grand Rapids: Eerdmans, 1980.
Toon, Peter. *The Development of Doctrine in the Church*. Grand Rapids: Eerdmans, 1979.
Walgrave, Jan Hendrik. *Unfolding Revelation: The Nature of Doctrinal Development*. Philadelphia: Westminster, 1972.
Wiles, Maurice F. *The Making of Christian Doctrine*. Cambridge: Cambridge University Press, 1967.
_____. *The Remaking of Christian Doctrine*. London: SCM, 1974.

3

CAN WE REPRODUCE THE EXEGESIS OF THE NEW TESTAMENT?

The New Testament's use of the Old Testament is a topic of perennial concern to the Christian church. And this is especially true today, what with (1) rising interest in the field of hermeneutics generally, and (2) new data from somewhat analogous materials as supplied by recent discoveries, particularly from the Dead Sea Scrolls. Such terms as "midrash," "pesher," "*sensus plenior*," "theological exegesis," "corporate personality," "typology," "fulfillment motif," "*Gemeindetheologie*," and the like, have become rather fixed entities in current theological discussion, witnessing to the currency of the topic at hand.

Involved in any treatment of biblical exegesis in the New Testament are the dual issues of the descriptive (i.e., What exactly took place?) and the normative (i.e., How obligatory or relevant are such exegetical practices today? On what basis? How can they be employed?). It is with these two matters that this article concerns itself, proposing first to elucidate the exegetical patterns within the New Testament in light of contemporary Jewish practices and then to deal with the question of the normative character of these practices in view of various suggestions offered today.

It is a recurring thesis of this essay that a great part of our problem in answering such a question as "Can we reproduce the exegesis of the New Testament?" lies in (1) our failure to understand correctly the nature of *pesher* exegesis at Qumran and in the New Testament, (2) our inability to appreciate the circumstantial character of some of the exegesis in the New Testament, and (3) our uncertainties regarding the relation of the descriptive and the normative in the New Testament. I have therefore taken it upon myself to attempt some explanation of Jewish practices before dealing directly with the New Testament itself, believing that only with such a background are we able to answer with any degree of precision such questions as "Ought we

3. Can We Reproduce the Exegesis of the NT? 35

attempt to reproduce the exegetical practices of the New Testament?" and "Are we able so to do?" Admittedly, space and time allow matters to be presented in only broad outline. Yet perhaps even a cursory overview will be of aid in establishing some guidelines.

1. *Exegetical Practices of First Century Judaism*

Three methods of interpreting the sacred text have come to characterize the three most significant hermeneutical divisions within Judaism in the period roughly contemporary with the first Christian century.

Midrash Exegesis
For rabbinic interpreters, and presumably for the earlier Pharisees as well, the central concept in interpretation was that of "midrash." The word comes from the verb דרש ("to resort to," "to seek"; fig. "to read repeatedly," "to study," "to interpret"), and strictly denotes an interpretive exposition—however derived and irrespective of the type of material treated. The expositions of the Gemaras and the Midrashim, therefore, while using various exegetical methods, are referred to as either "Midrash Halakah" or "Midrash Haggadah"—the term "midrash" covering the range of hermeneutical devices involved, with the qualification "halakah" or "haggadah" having reference to the type of material.

Midrash must be defined according to its stages of development. It is in the Babylonian Talmud that midrash exegesis is distinguished from *peshat* or literal interpretation.[1] In such a context,

> the term 'midrash' designates an exegesis which, going more deeply than the mere literal sense, attempts to penetrate into the spirit of the Scriptures, to examine the text from all sides, and thereby to derive interpretations which are not immediately obvious.[2]

But for the tannaitic period (i.e., from Rabban Hillel through Judah the Prince), the distinction between *peshat* as the literal sense of Scripture and *derash* as a derivative exposition of hidden meanings seems not to have been consciously invoked. In the Palestinian Gemaras and the earlier Midrashim, the verbs פשט and דרש are used synonymously—which is the basis for Jacob Lauterbach's contention that

---

[1] *B. Hullin* 6a; *b. Erubin* 23b; *b. Yebamoth* 24a. Also, of course, in the later cabbalist writings.

[2] S. Horovitz, "Midrash," *JE*, 8.548.

before the period of the Amoraim, distinctions between *peshat* exegesis and midrash exegesis were not made: "the Tannaim believe that their Midrash was the true interpretation and that their 'derash' was the actual sense of Scripture, and therefore 'peshat'."[3]

That there was a development in both the methodology and the terminology of Pharisaic exegesis is most easily illustrated by the progress from (1) Hillel's seven "middoth" or exegetical rules, to (2) Ishmael's thirteen exegetical rules, to (3) Eliezer ben Jose ha-Gelili's thirty-two rules during only the space of a century and a half.[4] Yet it remains possible to postulate a basic continuity of practice between the earlier Tannaim and the later Amoraim. The fact of the necessity for Hillel's seven rules, for example, presupposes a use of midrash exegesis in its more technical sense in the early first century CE[5]—though only a few examples in this more technical sense are able to be credited to Hillel himself, and, significantly, all of them are relatively simple in character.[6]

We may, therefore, take it that Pharisaic teachers within first century Judaism not only (1) understood the Old Testament historically and literally, for which the talmudic writings provide abundant evidence, (2) exposed the text to a mild allegorical treatment at times, of which there are a few extant examples,[7] and (3) worked the language of Scripture allusively into the very fabric of their formulations, which is also evident throughout, but that they also (4) employed a midrashic interpretation that sought to draw out the hidden meanings within the text over and above what could be considered the obvious or plain meaning. In so doing, as George Foot Moore long ago expressed matters, they developed:

> an atomistic exegesis, which interprets sentences, clauses, phrases, and even single words, independently of the context or the historical occasion, as divine oracles; combines them with other similarly

---

[3] J. Z. Lauterbach, "Peshat," *JE*, 9.653.

[4] For listings of these three sets of Middoth or exegetical rules, see H. L. Strack, *Introduction to the Talmud and Midrash* (New York: Meridian Press, 1959), 93-98.

[5] On the antiquity of the middoth ascribed to Hillel, see *ibid.*, 93-94.

[6] Cf. *Leviticus Rabbah* 1.5; 34.3; *j. Pesahim* 33a; *tos. Erubin* 4.7; *b. Shabbath* 19a; *b. Kiddushin* 43a.

[7] See *infra*, "Allegorical Exegesis."

detached utterances; and makes large use of analogy of expressions, often by purely verbal association.[8]

In days when Sadducees (until their demise) rejected the validity of the Oral Law, Gentiles scorned not only the written laws but also the oral traditions of the Jews, and the faithful within Israel required guidance for living in an alien milieu, it was considered necessary both to establish the Oral Law on a solid footing in Scripture and to explicate Holy Writ to cover every situation of life. And this halakic concern extended over into haggadic matters, so that the same methods were followed there as well.

Midrash exegesis, then, ostensibly takes its point of departure from the biblical text itself (though psychologically it may be motivated by other factors) and seeks to explicate the hidden meanings contained therein by means of agreed upon hermeneutical principles in order to contemporize the revelation of God for the people of God. It may be briefly characterized by the maxim: "That has relevance to This"—that is, what is written in Scripture has relevance to our present situation. Or, as Renée Bloch described it:

> 1. Its point of departure is Scripture; it is a reflection or meditation on the Bible.
> 2. It is homiletical, and largely originates from the liturgical reading of the Torah.
> 3. It makes a punctilious analysis of the text, with the object of illuminating obscurities found there. Every effort is made to explain the Bible by the Bible, as a rule not arbitrarily but by exploiting a theme.
> 4. The biblical message is adapted to suit contemporary needs.
> 5. According to the nature of the biblical text, the midrash either tries to discover the basic principles inherent in the legal sections, with the aim of solving problems not dealt with in Scripture (*halakhah*); or it sets out to find the true significance of events mentioned in the narrative sections of the Pentateuch (*haggadah*).[9]

Or, again, as Birger Gerhardsson defined it:

> Midrash is normally composed out of already-existing material, accepted as authoritative because it comes from the Scripture or the tradition. Using this raw material, the new is evolved. Naturally new terms, new phrases, new symbols and new ideas are introduced, but

---

[8] G. F. Moore, *Judaism in the First Centuries of the Christian Era* (Cambridge, MA: Harvard University Press, 1927), 1.248.

[9] Quoted in G. Vermes, *Scripture and Tradition in Judaism*. Leiden: Brill, 1961 (second edition 1973), 7.

the greater part is taken from that which already exists in the authoritative tradition. Midrash starts from a [sacred] text, a phrase or often a single word; but the text is not simply explained—its meaning is extended and its implications drawn out with the help of every possible association of ideas.[10]

Pesher Exegesis

The exposition in the materials from Qumran is often introduced by the term "pesher," a word meaning "solution" or "interpretation" and coming from the Aramaic *pishar*. There are also instances where "midrash" is so used, most significantly for our purposes in the first lines of the comments on Pss 1:1 and 2:1-2,[11] though in these cases the word seems to have the non-technical meaning found in earlier rabbinism.[12]

The Dead Sea sectarians considered themselves to be the divinely elected community of the final generation of the present age, living in the days of "messianic travail" before the eschatological consummation. Theirs was the task of preparing for the coming of the Messianic Age and/or the Age to Come. And to them applied certain prophecies of the Old Testament that were considered to speak of their situation and circumstances. While it is true in general that "the members of the community conceive[d] of themselves as repeating in a later age the experience of their remote forefathers in the days of Moses,"[13] it must also be recognized, as F. F. Bruce has pointed out, that they did not think of the prophecies in question as the message of God that was significant in an earlier situation but now, *mutatis mutandis*, also relevant to them. Rather, they looked upon those selected passages as being exclusively concerned with them.[14] And therefore, following

---

[10] B. Gerhardsson, *The Testing of God's Son*, trans. J. Toy (Lund: Gleerup, 1966), 14.

[11] *4QFlor* 1 and 14. For a discussion of the five occurrences of "midrash" in the texts published to date [i.e., 1970] from Qumran, and in four reported instances, see A. G. Wright, "The Literary Genre Midrash: Part One" and "The Literary Genre Midrash: Part Two," *CBQ* 28 (1966) 105-38, 417-57 (116-17).

[12] Cf. *ibid.*, 117-18.

[13] T. H. Gaster, *The Dead Sea Scriptures* (Garden City: Doubleday, 1964), 4; cf. W. D. Davies, *The Setting of the Sermon on the Mount* (Cambridge: Cambridge University Press, 1964), 26n, 33.

[14] F. F. Bruce, *Biblical Exegesis in the Qumran Texts* (London: Tyndale; Grand Rapids: Eerdmans, 1960), 16-17. On the selected nature of the passages

almost every prophetic statement cited, there is the recurrence of the word פשר, which may be variously translated as "the interpretation of this is," "this refers to," or "this means."

In an early study of Qumran's exegetical practices, W. H. Brownlee distilled the essence of the exegesis in the Habakkuk Commentary (*1QHab*) to thirteen propositions,[15] which thirteen points have been found to be generally representative of all of the other commentaries as well. Brownlee's first point, that "everything the ancient prophet wrote has a *veiled, eschatological meaning*," has reference to the community's understanding of itself as God's righteous remnant in the period of eschatological consummation. Here Qumran distinguishes itself from rabbinic interpretation, for while in the talmudic literature there is a contemporizing treatment of Holy Writ that seeks to make God's Word relevant to the present circumstances and on-going situations, among the Dead Sea covenanters the biblical texts were considered from the perspective of imminent apocalyptic fulfillment.

Brownlee's second point regarding "*forced, or abnormal construction of the Biblical text*" concerns *1QHab*'s more than fifty deviations from the MT (apart from the purely orthographic), of which several vary from all known versions of the LXX and Targums as well,[16] and the four cases where the Old Testament text is read as though it were multiform—that is, not only as though each word has several meanings but also that the text itself has more than one wording, one appearing in the quotation and the other in the comment following.[17]

The problem of textual variations and dual readings at Qumran is a difficult one. In the present state of uncertainty regarding the history of the MT and early recensions of the LXX, a final solution seems out

---

treated at Qumran, see C. Roth, "The Subject Matter of Qumran Exegesis," *VT* 10 (1960) 51-68 (esp. 52, 56), though without accepting the implications that Roth draws for a first-century CE Zealot identification.

[15] W. H. Brownlee, "Biblical Interpretation among the Sectaries of the Dead Sea Scrolls," *BA* 14 (1951) 54-76 (60-62).

[16] For a tabulation of the "Principal Variants," see W. H. Brownlee, *The Text of Habakkuk in the Ancient Commentary from Qumran* (Philadelphia: Society of Biblical Literature, 1959), 108-13.

[17] On the dual readings of Hab 1:8; 1:11; 1:15-16, and 2:16, see *ibid.*, 118-23; also K. Stendahl, *The School of St Matthew and its Use of the Old Testament* (Lund: Gleerup, 1954; Philadelphia: Fortress, 1958, second edition 1967), 186-89.

of the question. Stendahl tends to favor *ad hoc* creations in many of these cases.[18] Brownlee, however, is more cautious in saying:

> Though deliberate alteration may have played a part in the formation of the Hab. text utilized in DSH, it is probably resorted to but rarely. Many divergent texts were current from which one might well select the reading most advantageous to the purpose at hand.[19]

Until further evidence is forthcoming on the state of the Hebrew, Greek, and Aramaic texts in this early period, we do well to withhold judgment on the matter. It may well be that in some cases *1QHab* reflects *ad hoc* textual creations or deliberate corrections of existing versions by an expositor or group of expositors within the community. Or the phenomenon may be entirely one of selection among variants.

In the remaining eleven characteristics of his listing, Brownlee has clearly demonstrated that the mode of exegesis used by the Qumran covenanters is strikingly similar to that of rabbinic midrash. Thus many have followed him in labeling the exegesis of the Qumran commentaries a "midrash pesher," considering it comparable to rabbinic "midrash halakah" and "midrash haggadah" and to be distinguished from them only in regard to literary form and content.[20]

But, though it is often done, it is not sufficient to define *pesher* simply as midrashic exegesis that (1) displays a greater audacity in its handling of the text and (2) is coupled to an apocalyptic orientation.[21] Such a characterization is true as far as it goes, but it does not touch

---

[18] Stendahl's reaction, while favoring *ad hoc* creations, is rather mixed: "The relation between DSH, the MT and the Versions is of great interest. In many cases DSH appears to be created *ad hoc*. What is more remarkable is that some of these readings are supported by one or more of the Versions" (*School of St Matthew*, 189). Stendahl later builds on this *ad hoc* understanding in his treatment of Matthew's formula quotations, though concludes his section on the textual variations in *1QHab* by stating: "We must rather presume that DSH was conscious of various possibilities, tried them out, and allowed them to enrich its interpretation of the prophet's message, which in all its form was fulfilled in and through the Teacher of Righteousness" (*ibid.*, 190).

[19] Brownlee, *Text of Habakkuk*, 117-18.

[20] Cf. Brownlee, "Biblical Interpretation," 76. Note Stendahl's agreement in priorities and nomenclature (*School of St Matthew*, 184), and M. Burrows's objection based on the priority of literary form (*The Dead Sea Scrolls* [London: Secker & Warburg, 1955], 211-12).

[21] E.g., Stendahl, *School of St Matthew*, 193; Brownlee, "Biblical Interpretation," 54-76.

3. Can We Reproduce the Exegesis of the NT? 41

upon the vital factor in Qumran hermeneutics. For central in the consciousness of the covenanters of Qumran was what might be called the "*raz* (mystery)–*pesher* (interpretation) revelational motif," which is found explicitly stated in the comments on Hab 2:1-2:

> God told Habakkuk to write the things that were to come upon the last generation, but he did not inform him when that period would come to consummation. And as for the phrase, "that he may run who reads," the interpretation [*pesher*] concerns the Teacher of Righteousness to whom God made known all the mysteries [*razim*] of the words of his servants the prophets.[22]

And this is echoed in the treatment of Hab 2:3:

> The last period extends beyond anything that the prophets have foretold, for "the mysteries of God are destined to be performed wondrously."[23]

Further, to read the Dead Sea Hymns of Thanksgiving (*1QH*) not only as an expression of the Teacher of Righteousness himself, whether written directly by him or derived from his oral teaching,[24] but also with the *raz–pesher* motif in mind, is illuminating. Repeatedly there occurs the idea of having been given the interpretation of divine mysteries, which are then to be shared with the people. Representative of this theme is *1QH* 4.26-29:

> Through me hast Thou illumined the faces of full many, and countless be the times Thou hast shown Thy power through me. For Thou has made known unto me Thy deep, mysterious things, hast shared Thy secret with me and so shown forth Thy power; and before the eyes of full many this token stands revealed, that Thy glory may be shown forth, and all living know of Thy power.[25]

The men of Qumran seem not so much conscious of following a rabbinic mode of exegesis as of recreating the Danielic pattern of interpretation. For in Dan 9:24-27, Jeremiah's prophecy of seventy years is reinterpreted by the angel Gabriel to mean seventy heptads of years,[26] and in Dan 11:30 Balaam's prophecy regarding "the ships of

---

[22] *1QHab* 7.1-5.

[23] *1QHab* 7.7-8, accepting Gaster's literal rendering of the maxim (*Dead Sea Scriptures*, 280, n. 25).

[24] Cf. J. T. Milik, *Ten Years of Discovery in the Wilderness of Judaea*, trans. J. Strugnell (London: SCM, 1959), 40.

[25] Cf. also *1QH* 1.21, 2.13.

[26] See Jer 25:11-12; 29:10.

Kittim" is employed to denote a Roman fleet.[27] In the Aramaic portion of Daniel, that is in 2:4–7:28, there are thirty occurrences of the word *peshar*, with the greater part of the material contained therein appropriately able to be classed as "Theme and Variations on the *Raz–Pesher* Motif": Nebuchadnezzar's dream of the metallic human image, and Daniel's interpretation (ch 2); Nebuchadnezzar's dream of the gigantic tree and its fall, and Daniel's interpretation (ch 4); the writing on the wall at Belshazzar's banquet, and Daniel's interpretation (ch 5), and Belshazzar's dream of the composite animal, and Daniel's interpretation (ch 7). "In the Book of Daniel," as F. F. Bruce aptly notes, "it is clear that the *raz*, the mystery, is divinely communicated to one party, and the *pesher*, the interpretation, to another. Not until the mystery and the interpretation are brought together can the divine communication be understood."[28] And, as Bruce comments further:

> This principle, that the divine purpose cannot be properly understood until the *pesher* has been revealed as well as the *raz*, underlies the biblical exegesis in the Qumran commentaries. The *raz* was communicated by God to the prophet, but the meaning of that communication remained sealed until its *pesher* was made known by God to His chosen interpreter. The chosen interpreter was the Teacher of Righteousness, the founder of the Qumran community.[29]

Extensive consideration has been given to whether *pesher* exegesis as found in the Scrolls is to be classed as "commentary" or as "midrash." But the discussions have usually been carried on solely in categories pertinent to either a commentary form or a mode of exegesis, and largely ignore the factor wherein the Dead Sea community felt itself to be distinctive. In fact, Qumran's *pesher* treatment of the Old Testament is neither "commentary" nor "midrash." "It does not," as Cecil Roth has pointed out, "attempt to elucidate the Biblical text, but to determine the application of Biblical prophecy or, rather, of certain Biblical prophecies: and the application of these Biblical prophecies in precise terms to current and even contemporary events."[30]

---

[27] See Num 24:24.
[28] Bruce, *Biblical Exegesis in the Qumran Texts*, 8.
[29] Ibid., 9.
[30] Roth, "Subject Matter of Qumran Exegesis," 51-52.

3. Can We Reproduce the Exegesis of the NT? 43

The crucial question in defining *pesher* in the Dead Sea texts has to do with the point of departure. In contradistinction to rabbinic interpretation, which spoke of "That has relevance to This," the Dead Sea covenanters treated Scripture in a "This is That" fashion. Or as Karl Elliger put it as early as 1953: "Seine Auslegung gründet sich also nicht auf den Text allein, sondern in noch stärkerem Masse und im entscheidenden Punkte auf eine besondere Offerbarung."[31]

Biblical exegesis at Qumran, then, was considered to be first of all revelatory and/or charismatic in nature. Certain of the prophecies had been given in cryptic and enigmatic terms, and no one could understand their true meaning until the Teacher of Righteousness was given the interpretive key. In a real sense, they understood the passages in question as possessing a *sensus plenior* (i.e., a "fuller sense") that could be ascertained only from a revelational standpoint[32]—believing, in effect, that the true message of Scripture was only heard when prophecy and interpretation were brought together. The understanding of the Teacher with regard to certain crucial passages and the guidelines he laid down for future study were to be the touchstones for all further exegesis,[33] and members were strictly forbidden to incorporate extraneous opinion "in any matter of doctrine or law."[34]

We need not suppose that interpretation ceased with the Teacher of Righteousness himself, or that the Dead Sea texts preserve only interpretations explicitly given by him. Rather, he sounded the keynote and set the paradigm in his treatment of certain prophecies, and the

---

[31] K. Elliger, *Studien zum Habakuk-Kommentar vom Toten Meer* (Tübingen: Mohr–Siebeck, 1953), 155; see also 154-64. Elliger's main point is paralleled in the treatment of Bruce, *Biblical Exegesis in the Qumran Texts*, 7-19, and J. A. Fitzmyer, "The Use of Explicit Old Testament Quotations in Qumran Literature and in the New Testament," *NTS* 7 (1961) 297-333 (310), though the sharp dichotomy that Elliger draws between a revelational perspective and a midrashic mode of exegesis may be legitimately questioned.

[32] Cf. Fitzmyer, "Use of Explicit Old Testament Quotations," 332. On the *sensus plenior* in Roman Catholic theology, see R. E. Brown, *"Sensus Plenior" of Sacred Scripture* (Baltimore: St Mary's University, 1955); idem, "The *Senus Plenior* in the Last Ten Years," *CBQ* 25 (1963) 262-85.

[33] *1QH* 2.11-13: "Thou hast set me as a banner in the vanguard of Righteousness, as one who interprets with knowledge deep, mysterious things; as a touchstone for them that seek the truth, as standard for them that love correction."

[34] *1QS* 5.15-16.

membership met in study cells and communal sessions to carry on investigations along the lines set out for them by their teacher. In such meditations on the text, of course, exegetical methods at hand were employed.

We cannot deny midrashic modes of treatment at Qumran, but we must not allow them to take ascendancy in our definition of *pesher* interpretation. If we must use the term "midrash" of Qumran exegesis, perhaps such a term as "charismatic midrash" should be employed to distinguish it from the "scholastic midrash" of the rabbis.[35] As in Daniel 5, where the interpretation is understood to be a divine revelation given through Daniel to the king and yet explicated in terms of a midrash on the cryptic מנא מנא תקל ופרסין, so with the community on the shores of the Dead Sea. Exegesis at Qumran stands between Daniel and the rabbis, and is a matter of both revelatory stance and midrashic mode—though, it must be insisted, in this order.

Allegorical Exegesis

The most prominent Jewish allegorist known is Philo of Alexandria (c. 20 BCE–50 CE). In an endeavor to (1) safeguard the transcendence of God against every form of anthropathism,[36] (2) vindicate Hebrew theology before the court of Grecian philosophy,[37] and (3) contemporize the sacred accounts so as to make them relevant to then current situations and experiences,[38] Philo treated the Old Testament as a corpus of symbols given by God for humanity's spiritual and moral benefit that must be understood in other than a literal or historical manner. For him, the historical and *prima facie* meaning must be pushed aside, even counted as offensive, to make room for the

---

[35] Brownlee refers to H. L. Ginsberg calling the Teacher of Righteousness a "charismatic exegete" ("Biblical Interpretation," 60n).

[36] Cf. *De posteritate Caini* 4; *Quod Deus immutabilis sit* 59; *De sacrificio Abelis et Caini* 95; see S. Sowers, *The Hermeneutics of Philo and Hebrews: A Comparison of the Interpretation of the Old Testament in Philo Judaeus and the Epistle to the Hebrews* (Richmond: John Knox, 1965), 22-23.

[37] Cf. *Quis rerum divinarum heres sit* 214; *Quod omnis probus liber* 57; *De mutatione nominum* 167-68; *De migratione Abrahami* 128; *De specialibus legibus* 4.61; *Quaestiones et solutiones in Genesin* 2.6, 3.5, 4.152.

[38] S. Sowers, citing S. Sandmel and G. Kuhlmann, speaks of Philo's work as "a religious existentialism somewhat like the kind of interpretation fashionable because of Kierkegaard" (*Hermeneutics of Philo and Hebrews*, 32, n.9).

intended spiritual meaning that underlies them.[39] Exegesis of Holy Writ was for him an esoteric and mystic enterprise that, while not without its governing principles,[40] was to be dissociated from any literal interpretation however defined.

Philo, it is true, was not universally admired, and he may not represent the entirety of hellenistic Judaism at this point. But his exegetical methods were not unique to himself. C. Siegfried and H. A. A. Kennedy have shown that "there can be little question that Philo stood in a long succession of allegorical interpreters of the Old Testament. The practice had been reduced to a kind of science."[41] Clement of Alexandria mentions a second-century BCE Alexandrian Jew by the name of Aristobulus who used allegorical exegesis in a series of works on the Mosaic law.[42] The *Letter of Aristeas* includes one instance of a mild allegorical treatment in its portrayal of the High Priest Eleazer's defense of the Jewish dietary laws[43]—which, judging from Josephus's extensive paraphrase of the *Letter of Aristeas* and his specific references to it,[44] suggests that it was probably widely known.

Jacob Lauterbach has identified two groups of Palestinian Pharisees active prior to the time of Rabbi Judah the Prince, the *Dorshe Reshumot* and the *Dorshe Hamurot*, who employed a mild allegorical exegesis in their treatment of Scripture—whose work was gradually repudiated, though not entirely purged, in the tightening up of Judaism at the end of the second century CE.[45] And Joseph Bonsirven and

---

[39] For Philo, "der buchstäbliche Sinn ist lediglich der Körper, der den allegorischen also die Seele umschliesst" (O. Michel, *Paulus und seine Bibel* [Gütersloh: Bertelsmann, 1929; second edition, 1972], 106). Cf. also C. Siegfried, "Philo Judaeus," *JE* 10.7.

[40] Philo speaks of "canons of allegory" (*De somniis* 1.73; *De specialibus legibus* 1.287) and "laws of allegory" (*De Abrahamo* 68); cf. also C. Siegfried, *Philo von Alexandria als Ausleger des Alten Testament, an sich selbst und nach seinem geschichtlichen Einfluss betrachtet* (Jena: Dufft, 1875), 165-68.

[41] Kennedy, *Philo's Contribution to Religion*, 32; see also 32-34. Cf. also Siegfried, *Philo von Alexandria*, 16-37.

[42] *Stromata* 5.14-97.

[43] *Letter of Aristeas* 150-70. See esp. 150: "For the division of the hoof and the separation of the claws are intended to teach us that we must discriminate between our individual actions with a view to the practice of virtue."

[44] *Antiq.* 12.2.1-15 (11-118).

[45] J. Z. Lauterbach, "The Ancient Jewish Allegorists in Talmud and Midrash," *JQR* 1 (1911) 291-333, 503-31.

David Daube have presented significant papers in support of the existence of an early Pharisaic allegorical exegesis within Palestine itself.[46] In addition, the Dead Sea Scrolls include a number of examples of allegorical interpretation, representative of which is the treatment of Hab 2:17 in *1QHab* 12.3-4: "'Lebanon' stands here for the Communal Council, and 'wild beasts' for the simple-minded Jews who carry out the Law."[47] But though allegorical exegesis was widespread within first century Judaism, it was not dominant in Palestine.

Some Concluding Observations
What then can be concluded regarding the exegetical practices of first-century Judaism? Or, so as not unduly to complicate matters and to speak only to our immediate concern, perhaps we ought to ask: What then can be concluded regarding the exegetical practices of first-century *Palestinian* Judaism?

In common, all Palestinian Jews seem to have held the convictions (1) that the biblical text, being divinely inspired, is extremely rich in content, (2) that the task of the interpreter is to deal with both the obvious and the hidden meanings contained therein, and (3) that the methods used in this task, whether literal, midrashic, or mildly allegorical, are not to be too sharply distinguished, since all may be legitimately employed in the explication of Holy Writ. Where they differed was on (1) the stance or point of departure in the exegetical enterprise, and (2) the purpose. In a Pharisaic tradition, one started with the Scriptures and sought by means of a detailed exegesis to make its principles relevant to the contemporary situation. For the men of Qumran, however, the days of eschatological consummation were upon them and their teacher had been given the revelatory key

---

[46] Bonsirven cites several cases of allegorical treatment of biblical legislation in the talmudic materials that fly in the face of prohibitions against allegorical interpretation of halakic passages ("Exégèse allégorique chez les rabbins tannaites," *RSR* 23 [1933] 522-24); Daube develops a thesis that the whole system of rabbinic exegesis initiated by Hillel about 30 BCE was based on hellenistic models ("Rabbinic Methods of Interpretation and Hellenistic Rhetoric," *HUCA* 22 (1949) 239-64), and argues that "in the eyes of the Rabbis, the Bible, since it enshrined the wisdom of God, contained various layers of meaning ... A word might have an ordinary sense and one or two allegorical senses at the same time ("Alexandrian Methods of Interpretation and the Rabbis," in *Festschrift Hans Lewald* [Basel: Helbing & Lichtenhahn, 1953], 27-44 [38]).

[47] Cf. also *1QMic* 8-10; *CDC* 6.2-11 (8:2-10); 7.9-20 (9:2-9).

for a proper understanding of the mysteries of God—and so their biblical interpretations were charismatic in nature, stressing the note of fulfillment. In the process, feeling that they alone correctly understood the Old Testament prophecies, greater liberties were taken with the biblical text. In effect, they engaged in textual criticism on a theological basis.

2. Exegetical Patterns in the New Testament

The Jewish roots of the New Testament make it *a priori* likely that its basic presuppositions and exegetical practices would resemble those of contemporary Judaism to some extent. This has long been established with regard to rabbinic writings (especially in relation to Paul), and it is becoming increasingly evident from the Qumran materials as well.

In view of these data, we must abandon the mistaken idea that the New Testament writers' treatment of the Old Testament was either (1) an essentially mechanical process, whereby explicit "proof texts" and exact "fulfillments" were brought together, or (2) an illegitimate twisting and distortion of the ancient texts. It is true that literal fulfillment of a direct sort evidences itself as one factor in the New Testament. The Christian claim to continuity with the prophets could hardly have been supported were there no such cases. And it is also true that from a modern perspective the exegesis of the early Christians often appears forced, particularly when judged only by modern criteria. But neither approach does justice to the essential nature of New Testament hermeneutics, for both ignore basic patterns of thought and common exegetical methods used in the Jewish milieu in which the Christian faith came to birth.

There is little indication in the New Testament that the authors themselves were conscious of using a variety of exegetical genres or of following particular modes of interpretation. At least they seem to make no sharp distinctions between what we would call historical-grammatical exegesis, illustration by way of analogy, midrash exegesis, *pesher* interpretation, allegorical treatment, or interpretation based on a "corporate solidarity" understanding. All of these appear in their writings in something of a blended and interwoven fashion. What they were conscious of, however, is interpreting the Old Testament (1) from a christocentric perspective, (2) in conformity with a Christian tradition, and (3) along christological lines. And in their exegesis there is the interplay of Jewish presuppositions and practices, on the one hand, with Christian commitments and perspectives, on the other, which were joined to produce a distinctive interpretation of the Old Testament.

Pesher Motifs in Early Jewish Christianity
It is in the material attributed to the earliest disciples and associates of Jesus that the New Testament's use of the Old Testament most closely approximates Qumran exegesis—that is, in the Gospel of Matthew, the Gospel of John, the preaching of Peter and other early Jewish-Christian leaders reported in Acts, the First Epistle of Peter,[48] and the Epistle of James. There is, indeed, a literal use of the Old Testament (particularly in the quotation of explicit prophecies) and an allusive use, but the dominant manner in which the Old Testament is employed within these materials is that of a *pesher* treatment.

In seeking to understand Matthew's use of the Old Testament, it is well to remind ourselves of a phenomenon in the First Gospel that has been often noticed and variously explained—that is, that many parallels between the life of Jesus and the experience of the nation Israel in its early days seem to be drawn, especially in the earlier chapters of the Gospel. As even a cursory glance at a "synopsis" of the Gospels reveals, Matthew's presentation in the first half of his work varies noticeably from the arrangements of both Mark and Luke. The First Evangelist seems to be following a thematic order in the structuring of his Gospel wherein, by means of Hebraic concepts of "corporate solidarity" and "typological correspondences" in history, Jesus is portrayed as the embodiment of ancient Israel and the antitype of God's earlier redemptive activity.

And to this should be coupled the idea of a *pesher* handling of the biblical text and application of its meaning. For as has been frequently pointed out, particularly since Krister Stendahl's 1954 monograph on the composition of the First Gospel, there is a striking similarity between Matthew's formula quotations and the exegesis of *1QHab*.[49]

---

[48] Introductory issues for 2 Peter are similar to those for Jude, but cannot be treated here. I personally accept both as authentic, though neither yields evidence of pertinence for the question at hand.

[49] See Stendahl, *School of St Matthew*. Whether or not the mixed text-form of the Matthean formula quotations is unique to Matthew or shared by the other synoptic evangelists is a question that need not detain us here (cf. R. H. Gundry,

There are differences, of course. In addition to the obvious fact that the introductory formulae vary, there is a difference of degree in the liberty taken with the text itself. Matthew's readings can be supported more adequately, though not entirely, by known variants than can those of *1QHab*. And there is a decided difference in the application of the biblical texts. For whereas both employ a "this is that" theme in their treatments, Matthew does not necessarily pre-empt the narrative so as to make it meaningless in its earlier context while Qumran treated the texts as pertinent only to the present situation.[50] But in that Matthew's formula–fulfillment quotations (1) have their point of departure in the "this" (the Christ-events) and move on to the "that" (the Old Testament passages), (2) are employed to demonstrate the fulfillment of certain prophetic words and actions in the present rather than to elucidate principles in the text that have relevance to the present, and (3) are affected in their textual form by the application made, it is correct to speak of them as *pesher* treatments.

To summarize in a paragraph or two the evidence in support of Stendahl's thesis is impossible. Nor is it necessary in such an essay as this, especially in view of the prominence of his monograph. I would only express my basic agreement with Stendahl on the point in question (though without committing myself to his "School" hypothesis). And I would suggest that we must understand Matthew's use of the Old Testament along the lines of the Jewish concepts of "corporate solidarity" and "typological correspondences" in history coupled to the Christian convictions of present "eschatological fulfillment" and "Messianic presence"—with these basic presuppositions coming to expression through a *pesher* treatment of certain Old Testament passages, resulting in a christocentric interpretation.

The remaining question as to whether Matthew's textual deviations are to be explained on the basis of a selection of variants or in certain cases as *ad hoc* creations (or, independent corrections of existing texts) must remain for the present unresolved. Until more is known about the state of the biblical text prior to Jamnia, it is necessary to

---

The Use of the Old Testament in St Matthew's Gospel [Brill: Leiden, 1967]). It is the distinctive application of the Old Testament and the type of mixed biblical text employed that sets Matthew apart from the rest, not just the fact of a mixed text.

[50] Cf. Bruce, *Biblical Exegesis in the Qumran Texts*, 16-17.

reserve judgment⁵¹—though whether the phenomenon is one of selection or creation, a *pesher* treatment is involved.

It is in John's Gospel that we find the closest parallel to Matthew's fulfillment quotations and treatment of the Old Testament. In the Fourth Gospel the fulfillment theme appears in the quotations approximately a dozen times: (1) in the Baptist's application of Isa 40:3 to his own person and ministry (1:23); (2) in the people's attribution of Ps 118:25 to Jesus (12:13); (3) in three of the five quotations credited to Jesus (6:45; 13:18; 15:25), two of which are introduced by ἵνα πληρωθῇ; (4) in Jesus' justification for employing a christocentric approach to Scripture ("Moses ... wrote of me," 5:39-47); and (5) in the seven quotations attributed to the evangelist himself, six of which are formula quotations and five of which are introduced by ἵνα πληρωθῇ (2:17; 12:15, 38, 40; 19:24, 36, 37).

Whereas Matthew's portrayal of Jesus seems to have been developed generally along the lines of the Messiah as the embodiment of Israel and its history (at least in the first half or so of the Gospel), John appears to have thought of Jesus in terms of the center of the nation's life. He constantly relates his presentation to the Jewish festivals,⁵² emphasizes communal celebrations and social gatherings,⁵³ and presents Jesus as central in every relationship.⁵⁴ But though the imagery varies slightly, the presuppositions are the same as those inherent in the First Gospel. And the treatment of Scripture is comparable—especially so in the case of the seven quotations credited to the evangelist himself, which in application and purpose are closely parallel, if not identical, to Matthew's formula citations.

The texts of John's quotations, of course, evidence less deviation from known versions than those of Matthew, reflecting stronger LXX influence. But as with the similar phenomena in Matthew and at Qumran, our evidence is insufficient to make a final determination

---

⁵¹ Cf. F. M. Cross, Jr, "The History of the Biblical Text in the Light of Discoveries in the Judean Desert," *HTR* 57 (1964) 281-99; *idem*, "The Contribution of the Qumran Discoveries to the Study of the Biblical Text," *IEJ* 16 (1966) 81-95; P. W. Skehan, "The Biblical Scrolls from Qumran and the Text of the Old Testament," *BA* 28 (1965) 87-100.

⁵² John 2:13; 5:1; 6:4; 7:2; 10:22; 11:55; 12:1; 13:1; 19:14.

⁵³ E.g., John 2:1ff.; 12:2ff.; 13:1–18:1.

⁵⁴ Esp. John 7:37ff.; 8:12ff.

3. Can We Reproduce the Exegesis of the NT? 51

regarding whether the deviants are the products of selection or *ad hoc* creations.

Assuming the speeches of Acts to be abstracts of early Christian proclamation and the epistles of James and 1 Peter to contain early sermonic material, we may presume to employ these portions in determining the use of Scripture in the preaching of the earliest Jewish Christians.

It is usually held that the source of Old Testament quotations and allusions in the Acts and the epistles of James and 1 Peter is the LXX.[55] And on the basis of this observation, it is often concluded either (1) that the phenomenon of Greek citations credited to Aramaic speaking preachers lies heavily against the authenticity of the records, or (2) that the LXX was the Bible of the earliest Christians. Both the observation and the positions that spring from it, however, neglect to take into consideration the degree of assimilation to the LXX that has been affected by the author himself or the amanuensis of the work in question.[56]

As is inevitable in any historical account, the quotations in Acts are at least one step removed from their original source. And it may reasonably be supposed that their textual form, if originally deviant on the basis of a Semitic variant, would be brought into greater conformity to the LXX—if for no other reason, for the sake of the Greek-speaking audience. Such could likewise be the case with James and 1 Peter, directed as they are to Diaspora Jews and, at least for 1 Peter, evidencing the presence of an amanuensis (cf. 1 Pet 5:12). Max Wilcox has shown that while the citations of the Old Testament in Acts are fairly representative of the LXX in general, the allusions, because they are less capable of exact definition, seem to have escaped a process of assimilation.[57] In addition, J. de Waard argues that the LXX alone is not sufficient to explain the textual phenomena of the quotations in Acts, asserting that four biblical citations in Acts (3:22-23; 7:43; 13:41; 15:16) are prime examples of where "certain New

---

[55] Note the seminal article of W. K. L. Clarke, "The Use of the Septuagint in Acts," in *The Beginnings of Christianity*, 5 vols., ed. F. J. Foakes Jackson and K. Lake (London: Macmillan, 1920–33), 2.66-105.

[56] Cf. M. Wilcox, *The Semitisms of Acts* (Oxford: Clarendon, 1965), 20.

[57] *Ibid.*, 20-55.

Testament writings show affinities to the DSS as regarding the Old Testament text."[58]

It seems, therefore, that we are here confronted with two issues: (1) the problem of pre-Jamnia variants, and (2) the phenomenon of possible assimilation. Until further evidence is available, we are well advised to leave open the question of textual deviation in early Christian preaching. We may suspect a similar *pesher* treatment of the text as seen in Matthew and to an extent in John, but we are without data of sufficient strength either to affirm or deny it.

In the use of the Scriptures, however, we need have little reticence in asserting a *pesher* approach as having been prominent in early Jewish-Christian preaching. Peter, writing about 63 CE, explicitly records his attitude toward the Old Testament prophecies in saying:

> The prophets who prophesied of the grace that is yours searched and inquired concerning this salvation, inquiring regarding what person or time was indicated by the Spirit of Christ within them when predicting the sufferings of Christ and the subsequent glory. It was revealed to them that they were serving not themselves but you, in the things which have now been announced to you by those who preached the gospel to you through the Holy Spirit sent from heaven—things into which angels desire to look.[59]

While he did not use the terms "mystery" and "interpretation," the thought of the apostle is strikingly parallel to that of the *raz–pesher* motif at Qumran.

And the exegetical practice of Peter, as seen in the quotations credited to him in Acts and those of his First Epistle, evidences the importance he placed on a *pesher* understanding of Scripture. There are instances where he treats the Old Testament in a midrashic fashion alone—that is, where he begins with the passage in question, actualizes its content and applies its principles, but does not enter into a demonstration of fulfillment.[60] In the majority of cases, however, Peter uses a "this is that" *pesher* theme, as can be seen in:

---

[58] J. de Waard, *A Comparative Study of the Old Testament Text in the Dead Sea Scrolls and in the New Testament* (Leiden: Brill, 1965; Grand Rapids: Eerdmans, 1966), 78.

[59] 1 Pet 1:10-12.

[60] E.g., 1 Pet 1:16 (quoting Lev 11:44; 19:2; 20:7); 3:10-12 (quoting Ps 34:12-16); 5:5 (quoting Prov 3:34). In 1 Pet 1:24-25 (quoting Isa 40:6, 8) there seems to appear a merging of midrash and *pesher* treatments.

1. The "stone" citations of 1 Pet 2:6-8 and Acts 4:11, quoting Isa 28:16, Ps 118:22, and Isa 8:14, the point being that this stone is Christ.

2. The statements regarding Judas in Acts 1:20, quoting Pss 69:25 and 109:8. While the first of Hillel's exegetical rules is employed, arguing that that which is said regarding the unrighteous in general applies specifically to the betrayer of the Messiah, the aspect of fulfillment gives the treatment a *pesher* flavor as well.

3. The application of Joel 2:28-32 (MT 3:1-5) to the Pentecost outpouring of the Spirit in Acts 2:17-21, stating explicitly that "this is that which was spoken by the prophet Joel."

4. The argument in Acts 2:25-28 that David's words recorded in Ps 16:8-11 were really prophetic, and that in the resurrection of Jesus their true character has been recognized and their prediction fulfilled.

5. The application in Acts 2:34-35 of Ps 110:1 to the ascension of Jesus, insisting that this is that of which the Psalm really spoke.

6. The "prophet citation" of Acts 3:22-23, quoting Deut 18:15, 18,[61] and possibly alluding to Lev 23:29. Christ is "that prophet," the prophet "like unto me [Moses]," concerning whom Moses exhorted and warned the people to hear.

The "this is that" *pesher* motif also appears in the church's ascription of Ps 2:1-2 to the contemporary situation of Sadducean opposition to the preaching of Jesus (Acts 4:25-26), in Philip's proclamation of Jesus on the basis of Isa 53:7-8 (Acts 8:32-33), and in James's application of Amos 9:11 to the issue at the Jerusalem Council (Acts 15:16-17). Perhaps it is also implicit in Stephen's address of Acts 7 and in James's seemingly strange use of the fulfillment formula in Jas 2:23.

Jesus as Source and Paradigm

The "this is that" *pesher* motif, as contrasted with the "that has relevance to this" theme of the rabbis, well characterizes the distinctive treatment of Scripture by the early Jewish Christians. But it also signals a difference of perspective, and, on the analogy with Qumran, points to an originating source. Karl G. Kuhn's maxim that "in Palestinian Christianity, Jesus of Nazareth and the redemptive significance

---

[61] On the correlation of the textually aberrant τοῦ προφήτου ἐκείνου of Acts 3:23 with the reading הנבי of Deut 18:18 in *4QTestimonia*, see J. A. Fitzmyer, "4QTestimonia and the New Testament," *TS* 18 (1957) 513-37 (537); de Waard, *Comparative Study of the Old Testament Text*, 24.

of his person is the creative element"⁶² is true of early Christian hermeneutics as well. For convinced of his Messiahship and Lordship—by means of the convergence of his historical presence among them, the witness of the Spirit, and the validation of the resurrection—the early Christians began with Jesus as the "certain and known quality."⁶³ In him they witnessed a creative handling of the Scriptures that became for them both the source of their own understanding and the pattern for their treatment of the Old Testament.

The selection of Old Testament passages quoted in the New indicates a highly original and creative approach to Scripture. C. H. Dodd has pertinently observed that "creative thinking is rarely done by committees, useful as they may be for systematizing the fresh ideas of individual thinkers, and for stimulating them to further thought. It is individual minds that originate."⁶⁴ And he concludes in words that cannot be improved upon: "To account for the beginning of this most original and fruitful process of rethinking the Old Testament we found need to postulate a creative mind. The Gospels offer us one. Are we compelled to reject the offer?"⁶⁵

Not only can it be reasonably argued that the selection of messianically relevant Old Testament portions is to be credited to Jesus himself, but also it should be noted that all of the Gospels record that he treated selected biblical verses in a genuinely creative fashion employing a *pesher* interpretation of the verses in question.

According to Luke's Gospel, Jesus began to expound Scripture in terms of a fulfillment theme very early in his ministry. In Luke 4:16-21, he enters the synagogue at Nazareth and is called upon to read the lesson from the prophet Isaiah. He reads Isa 61:1-2, rolls up the scroll, hands it to the attendant, sits down to speak, and proclaims: "Today this scripture is fulfilled in your ears." In John's Gospel the theme of fulfillment is just as explicitly stated in the denunciation of the

---

⁶² K. G. Kuhn, "The Lord's Supper and the Communal Meal at Qumran," *The Scrolls and the New Testament*, ed. K. Stendahl (New York: Harper & Row, 1957), 86.

⁶³ Using the phrase of J. Barr, *Old and New in Interpretation* (London: SCM, 1966), 139, though in opposition to his point.

⁶⁴ C. H. Dodd, *According to the Scriptures: The Sub-Structure of New Testament Theology* (London: Nisbet, 1952), 109-10.

⁶⁵ *Ibid.*, 110.

Pharisees by Jesus in John 5:39-47. The passage begins with a rebuke of his antagonists' false confidence, proceeds to give an unfavorable verdict on their attitudes and interpretations, and climaxes in the assertion: "If you believed Moses, you would have believed me; for he wrote of me." If we had only these two passages, it would be possible to claim that Jesus himself gave the impetus to the use of the fulfillment theme and *pesher* exegesis in early Christianity.

But the demonstration of Jesus' employment of the fulfillment theme and his own *pesher* treatment of the text does not depend on these two portions alone. In addition, the following instances should be noted:

1. His application of Isa 6:9-10 in Matt 13:14-15 in explanation of his use of parables.

2. His paraphrase of Isa 29:13 (possibly collating it with Ps 78:36-37) in rebuke of the scribes and Pharisees from Jerusalem, introducing the quotation with the words "Isaiah prophesied concerning you, saying."

3. His quotation of Zech 13:7 in Matt 26:31 and Mark 14:27 with regard to his own approaching death, directly invoking the "this is that" *pesher* motif and altering the tenses, number and vocabulary of the LXX in the process.

4. His application of the conflated texts of Mal 3:1 and Isa 40:3 to John the Baptist in Matt 11:10 and Mark 1:2-3, saying by way of introduction (in Matthew's Gospel): "This is he of whom it is written," and altering the pronouns and verbs of the LXX reading.

5. His citation of Ps 118:22-23, "The stone that the builders rejected has become the head of the corner," in Mark 12:10-11, implying fulfillment in his own person.

6. His application of Isa 53:12 directly to himself in Luke 22:37, saying first that "it is necessary that that which is written be fulfilled in me" and then that "that concerning me [in the prophecy of Isaiah] has fulfillment."

7. His allusion to the message of Isa 54:13 and Jer 31:33 in John 6:45, making the point that the words "and they shall all be taught of God" (as the prophet's message may be freely rendered) apply to his teaching and his ministry generally.

8. His application of the lament of Ps 41:9 to his betrayal by Judas in John 13:18, introducing the citation by ἵνα πληρωθῇ and using synonyms for the LXX rendering.

9. His application of the lament of Pss 35:19 and 69:4, "hated without a cause," to himself in John 15:25, using the ἵνα πληρωθῇ introductory formula and changing the participle of the LXX to a finite verb (though probably only to conform to sentence structure in its new context).

10. His interpretation of Ps 110:1 as reported by all three synoptic evangelists (Matt 22:41-46; Mark 12:35-37; Luke 20:41-44, arguing on the basis of David's acclamation that the Messiah must be considered as more than just a junior David, a "second David," or even "the son of David," with all of the nationalistic connotations that that title evoked, and implying that David's true intent found fulfillment in his person.

Assuming the canonical Gospels to be giving at least a substantially accurate account of Jesus' use of the Scriptures, it must be asserted that Jesus' own treatment of the Old Testament was remarkably similar, if not essentially identical, to that of the earliest Jewish Christians. It can, of course, be argued that this similarity only indicates that the accounts of Jesus' usage were fabricated by the authors of the Gospels themselves and that the whole is a product of *Gemeindetheologie*. But it can also be postulated, more plausibly I believe, that Jesus himself was both the source and the pattern for early Christian interpretation—that is, (1) that certain biblical passages that he interpreted continued to be interpreted in the same way by the earliest Christians (e.g., Isa 53:12 in Mark 15:28 and Isa 53:7-8 in Acts 8:32-33, and less directly elsewhere; the "stone" citations in Acts 4:11 and 1 Pet 2:6-8; and Ps 110:1 in Acts 2:34-36 and a number of times in Hebrews) and (2) that his treatment of these passages furnished the paradigm for further exegetical endeavors within the early apostolic community.[66]

---

[66] Cf. C. F. D. Moule's excellent treatment of Jesus' use of the Old Testament in his *The Birth of the New Testament* (London: Black; New York: Harper & Row, 1962, second edition 1966), 62-70, 84-85. See also Fitzmyer, "Use of Explicit Old Testament Quotations," 315-16; A. von Rohr Sauer, "Problems of Mesianic Interpretation," *CTM* 35 (1964) 566-74; B. Gerhardsson, *Memory and Manuscript*, trans. E. J. Sharpe (Lund: Gleerup, 1961), 225-34, though with Gerhardsson's thesis tempered by the comments of Davies in *Setting of the Sermon on the Mount*, 465-66.

Midrash and Pesher Motifs in Paul

It may be considered axiomatic that Paul shared, at least generally, the current Jewish exegetical presuppositions and Jewish-Christian attitudes toward Scripture. His own personal history would lead us to expect this[67] and his writings evidence it.[68] Further, Dodd has shown that a common body of Old Testament material underlies the Pauline exegesis and that of other New Testament writers.[69]

But while there are broad areas of agreement between the Jerusalem apostles and Paul, there also appear differences of hermeneutical approach and practice. We must not magnify the variations into any dichotomous cleavage. On the other hand, however, we cannot merely equate Paul's exegetical habits with those mentioned earlier.

Together with the earliest Jewish Christians, Paul understood the Old Testament christologically. And he worked from the same two fixed points: (1) the Messiahship and Lordship of Jesus, as validated by the resurrection and as witnessed to by the Spirit, and (2) the revelation of God in the Scriptures of the Old Testament. But though in his own experience a true understanding of Christ preceded a proper understanding of Scripture, in his exegetical endeavors he habitually began with Scripture and moved on to Christ. As C. H. Dodd has observed (even while constructing his important thesis regarding the common area of agreement underlying all New Testament interpretation), "Paul in the main tries to start from an understanding of the biblical text just as it stands in its context."[70] While the Jerusalem apostles placed the revelation of God in Jesus the Messiah "neben dem Text," so that both stood starkly side-by-side, Paul's treatment evidences not quite this rather wooden juxtaposition but a placing of Scripture as central within a larger context of christological awareness. And while the early Jewish-Christian leaders characteristically began with Jesus the Christ and moved on to an understanding of the

---

[67] Cf. R. N. Longenecker, *Paul, Apostle of Liberty* (New York: Harper & Row, 1964), 21-64.

[68] Cf., e.g., H. StJ. Thackeray, *The Relation of St Paul to Contemporary Jewish Thought* (London: Macmillan, 1900); Michel, *Paulus und seine Bibel* (1929); W. D. Davies, *Paul and Rabbinic Judaism: Some Rabbinic Elements in Pauline Theology* (London: SPCK, 1948^1, 1955^2, 1970^3; Philadelphia: Fortress, 1980^4); E. E. Ellis, *Paul's Use of the Old Testament* (London: Oliver & Boyd, 1957).

[69] Dodd, *According to the Scriptures*, esp. 23.

[70] *Ibid.*, 23.

Old Testament from this christocentric perspective, Paul usually starts with the text itself and seeks via a midrashic explication to show christological significance. There is an area of overlapping. But whereas the exegesis of early Jewish Christianity has its closest contemporary parallel known to date with the *pesher* exegesis of Qumran, Paul's treatment of the biblical texts is more closely related to that of Pharisaism.[71]

This is not to value one approach or method more highly than the other. Both Paul and the Jerusalem apostles viewed the relations of the revelation in Jesus and the revelation in the Old Testament as complementary, as well as supplementary. And, undoubtedly, both would have acknowledged the legitimacy of the other's practice, as each seems to do unconsciously at those points where they overlap. It is only to point out that the Pauline approach to the Old Testament and Paul's own biblical apologetic varies to an extent from that practiced by the earliest Jewish Christians, and to suggest that this difference is due in large measure to differences of training, individual spiritual experience, and ideological environments confronted in their respective missionary enterprises.

A common feature in the Pauline quotations is the Pharisaic practice of "pearl stringing"—that is, of bringing to bear on one point of an argument passages from various parts of the Old Testament, both to support the argument and to demonstrate the unity of Scripture. This is most obviously done in the citations of Rom 3:10-18 (joining five passages from the Psalms and one from Isaiah), Rom 10:18-21 (joining verses from Psalm 18, Deuteronomy 32, and Isaiah 65), Rom 15:10-12 (joining verses from Deuteronomy 32, Psalm 116, and Isaiah 11), and Gal 3:10-13 (joining verses from Deuteronomy 21 and 27, Habakkuk 2, and Leviticus 18)—and it appears also in Rom 9:25-29, Rom 11:8-10, and 2 Cor 6:16-18. In addition, a midrashic treatment of the Old Testament is evident in at least such passages as Rom 10:6-10

---

[71] W. F. Albright, although here a bit extreme, nonetheless is generally correct and stresses a point too often overlooked in insisting that "St. Paul's interpretation of the Old Testament follows the Greek hermeneutics of the Mishnah rather than the quite different type of interpretation found in the Essene commentaries on the books of the Bible" (*New Horizons in Biblical Research* [Oxford: Oxford University Press, 1966], 51).

(the word is nigh, even in the mouth and in the heart),[72] 1 Cor 10:1-6 (the rock that followed in the wilderness),[73] 2 Cor 3:12-18 (Moses' veil that still blinds),[74] Gal 3:16 (seed and seeds),[75] and Eph 4:8-10 (Christ's ascent implies descent as well).[76] And even the two cases of a somewhat mild allegorical interpretation in 1 Cor 9:9-10 (not muzzling the ox) and Gal 4:21-31 (Hagar and Sarah) find as close parallels in rabbinic practice as anywhere else.[77]

But is there any evidence of a *pesher* treatment of the Old Testament by Paul? Three matters warrant comment here: (1) textual deviations, (2) a "this is that" fulfillment motif, and (3) a *raz–pesher* understanding of the prophetic message.

Earle Ellis has shown that of the ninety-three Old Testament portions cited by Paul, either singly or in combination, thirty-eight diverge from all known versions of the LXX and MT. He further argues

---

[72] On Deut 30:11-14. For references to Jewish parallels, see Thackeray, *Relation of St Paul to Contemporary Jewish Thought*, 187. Note also what appears to be a rabbinic rebuttal to Paul in *Deut. Rabbah* 8.6, with, interestingly, the same exegetical method employed.

[73] Probably on Num 21:17. Regarding the rabbinic treatment of this passage and the legend that developed, see Ellis, *Paul's Use of the Old Testament*, 66-70.

[74] On Exod 34:33-35. Regarding the rabbinic principle followed here of parallelling two passages that have one term in common and interpreting them in light of one another, see J. Jeremias, "Zur Gedankeführung in den paulinischen Briefen," in *Studia Paulina*, ed. G. Sevenster and W. C. van Unnik (Haarlem: Bohn, 1953), 149-51.

[75] On Gen 13:15; 17:7; 24:7. Cf. D. Daube, *The New Testament and Rabbinic Judaism* (London: Athlone, 1956), 438-44.

[76] On Ps 68:18. G. B. Caird speaks of Paul "Christianizing the Rabbinic exegesis of the Pentecostal psalm" ("The Descent of Christ in Ephesians 4, 7-11," in *Papers Presented to the Second International Congress on New Testament Studies Held at Christ Church, Oxford, 1961* (Studia Evangelica, II), ed. F. L. Cross [Bonn: Akademie Verlag, 1964], 543). A form of the rabbinic argument of inference is used in Eph 4:9. On a targumic basis for the text of Eph 4:8, see *ibid.*, 540-41; Thackeray, *Relation of St Paul to Contemporary Jewish Thought*, 182; and Wilcox, *Semitisms of Acts*, 25. Conversely, crediting the form of the text to an early Christian "midrash pesher," see Ellis, *Paul's Use of the Old Testament*, 144, and B. Lindars, *New Testament Apologetic: The Doctrinal Significance of the Old Testament Quotations* (London: SCM, 1961), 52-56.

[77] Paul's treatment of 1 Cor 9:9-10 should be compared to the rabbinic treatments in *Gen. Rabbah* 44.1 and *Lev. Rabbah* 13.3, as well as to the often cited Philonic parallel of *De sacrificio Abelis et Caini* 260. On rabbinic allegorical exegesis, see *supra*, "Allegorical Exegesis."

that about twenty of these give evidence of a *pesher* type molding of the text.[78] In almost all of these latter instances, he points out, "the variation seems to be a deliberate adaptation to the NT context; in some cases the alteration has a definite bearing on the interpretation of the passage."[79]

The problem, of course, is to what extent these deviations are (1) explainable on the basis of contemporary variants now extinct and not *ad hoc* creations, and (2) distinctive to *pesher* exegesis and not also true of rabbinic midrashic treatments? In the present state of our knowledge regarding extant versions of the biblical text during the first Christian century, definiteness about the first issue is manifestly impossible and opinions about the second are a matter of judgment.

Earle Ellis, following Stendahl's handling of similar phenomena in Matthew's Gospel, tends to view many of these as *ad hoc* creations of Paul in working out his *pesher* approach to Scripture. Yet, significantly I believe, Ellis also notes that what he calls "the *pesher* method" is "not used extensively in Paul's quotations" and that where it does occur "it often appears to go behind the Greek to reflect an interpretation of the Hebrew *ur*-text" and that "some of the most significant instances appear to point back to a pre-Pauline usage in the early Church."[80]

Whether it be judged a process of selection among variants or the creation of interpretive readings—and after deducting the maximum of renderings that could stem from a tradition within the early church—the conclusion is inevitable that Paul felt somewhat free in his handling of the Old Testament text as we know it. T. W. Manson has rightly characterized Paul at this point, as well as the Jerusalem apostles, in saying:

> The meaning of the text was of primary importance; and they seem to have had greater confidence than we moderns in their ability to find it. Once found it became a clear duty to express it; and accurate reproduction of the traditional wording of the Divine oracles took second place to publication of what was held to be their essential meaning and immediate application.[81]

---

[78] Ellis, *Paul's Use of the Old Testament*, 11-16, 139-47.
[79] *Ibid.*, 144.
[80] *Ibid.*, 146. Probable pre-Pauline text forms include Rom 12:19; 1 Cor 14:21; 15:45; 2 Cor 6:16ff.; Eph 4:8.
[81] T. W. Manson, "The Argument from Prophecy," *JTS* 66 (1945) 135-36.

But the question must be asked: Is this true only of *pesher* exegesis, or does it also find parallels in rabbinic midrash as well? I would suggest that *pesher* interpretation is somewhat wrongly understood if it is defined only on the basis of deviations in the form of the biblical text, for rabbinic midrash differs more quantitatively than qualitatively at this point.

In regard to the "this is that" fulfillment motif, Paul's letters indicate that he used it very sparingly. 1 Cor 15:3-5 twice employs the phrase "according to the scriptures." But the context and manner of citation suggest that Paul is here using a confessional formula of earlier Christians who themselves made use of the fulfillment theme. His inclusion of their words indicates his agreement, but the verbal expression itself probably did not originate with him. In 2 Cor 6:2 the apostle asserts that the "acceptable time" and "the day of salvation" spoken of in Isa 49:8 are upon us "now," and in Gal 4:4 he speaks of "the fullness of time" as having taken place in God's sending of his Son—both passages reflecting his consciousness of living in the days of eschatological consummation. But only in his sermon in the synagogue at Antioch of Pisidia, as recorded in Acts 13:16-41, is Paul represented as making explicit use of the fulfillment theme. And that, of course, is directed to a Jewish audience. It seems, therefore, that Paul's habit in his Gentile mission was not to attempt a demonstration of eschatological fulfillment in any explicit manner. Evidently such a procedure would carry little weight with those unaccustomed to think in terms of historical continuity and unschooled in the Old Testament.

With regard to Paul and a *raz–pesher* understanding of the prophetic message, the following observation and comment by F. F. Bruce provide significant starting points for the discussion:

> In the Greek versions of the Septuagint and Theodotion, this term *raz*, wherever it occurs in Daniel, is represented by μυστήριον, ... [and] it is helpful to bear this in mind when we meet the word μυστήριον in the Greek New Testament.[82]

Now Paul employs μυστήριον some twenty times, and in a number of ways. But in three instances in his use of the term he seems to be definitely involving himself in a *raz–pesher* understanding of the unfolding of redemptive history:

---

[82] Bruce, *Biblical Exegesis in the Qumran Texts*, 8.

1. In the doxology of Rom 16:25-27, where he identifies "my gospel" as being "the preaching of Jesus Christ according to the revelation of the *mystery* that was kept secret for long ages ["times eternal"], but is now disclosed and through the prophetic writings is made known to all nations."[83]

2. In Eph 3:1-11, where he speaks of "the *mystery* made known to me by revelation, which was not made known to the sons of men in other generations as it has now been revealed to his holy apostles and prophets by the Spirit—the *mystery* hidden for ages in God who created all things."

3. In Col 1:26-27, where he mentions "the *mystery* hidden for ages and generations but now made manifest to his saints."

What is this "mystery"? From his reference to "my gospel" in Rom 16:25 (cf. also Rom 2:16), coupled with his insistence in Gal 1:11-12 that his gospel came to him by means of "a revelation of Jesus Christ," we may take it that this mystery was something that he considered to be uniquely his. And this consciousness of distinction comes to expression again in Eph 3:6-8, where he explicitly associates the "mystery" to which he had been given the interpretive key with his Gentile ministry and the equality of Jews and Gentiles before God. Evidently, then, Paul's gospel, which had been given by revelation, was not a gospel that differed in kerygmatic content from the proclamation of the early church, but a gospel that included a new understanding of the pattern of redemptive history in these finals days—a gospel that involved the legitimacy of a direct approach to Gentiles and the recognition of the equality of Jews and Gentiles before God.

Paul could not claim the usual apostolic qualifications, as expressed in John 15:27 and Acts 1:21-22. His understanding of the Old Testament could not be directly related to the teaching and example of the historic Jesus. And he was dependent on the early church for much in the Christian tradition, as his letters frankly evidence. But he had been confronted by the exalted Lord, had been directly commissioned an apostle by Jesus himself, and considered that he had been given the key to the pattern of redemptive history in the present period. The Jerusalem apostle had the key to many of the prophetic mysteries, but he had been entrusted with a *pesher* that was uniquely his. Together, they combined to enhance the fullness of the gospel.

---

[83] Understanding the καί of verse 25 to be explicative.

Some Concluding Observations

I have not even touched upon exegetical patterns in the Epistle to the Hebrews. That is a large issue, which space and time forbid us to deal with here. What I have sought to demonstrate is that in the literature attributed to the earliest disciples and associates of Jesus there is the interplay of Jewish presuppositions and exegetical practices with a Christian commitment and perspective that, by means of a *pesher* treatment of the Old Testament, produced a distinctive interpretation. The early Jewish Christians were not so much interested in commentaries on the biblical texts or the application of principles to specific developments in the present as they were in demonstrating redemptive fulfillment in Jesus of Nazareth. Thus they took a prophetic stance on a revelatory basis and treated the Old Testament more charismatically than scholastically. Having had their eyes opened by Jesus so that they might understand the Old Testament correctly, they were able to see previously ignored meaning in the nation's history and to apprehend the enigmatic in the prophetic word. Their major task was thus to demonstrate that "this" that is manifest in the person and work of Jesus "is that" recorded in the Old Testament. And in that they felt they possessed a more adequate knowledge of the real meaning of Scripture than elsewhere available, they were not afraid to select among variants the text they believed would best convey Scripture's true meaning—possibly, at times, even to create a wording to express that meaning—and to treat the passage in a creative fashion.

Paul's use of the Old Testament, however, is not just the same as that found in the materials representative of early Jewish Christianity. While he shared common presuppositions, a common body of *testimonia* biblical material, and a common attitude toward the relationship of meaning and traditional wording in the Old Testament texts, he differed in his closer affinity to rabbinic exegetical norms, his infrequent use of a fulfillment apologetic, and his consciousness of a difference in revelational insight into the redemptive purposes of God. Training, spiritual experience, and audience varied, and these factors evidence themselves in a difference of exegesis.

3. *The Reproduction of New Testament Exegesis Today*

Having surveyed the hermeneutics of first century Judaism and delineated representative exegetical patterns in the New Testament, the question with which we began this article directly confronts us: "Can we reproduce the exegesis of the New Testament?"

Various Answers Currently Given

The question is of renewed and vital interest today, and various answers are currently being given to it. Answering negatively are those represented by what might be called "classical liberalism" and "unreconstructed Bultmannianism," who assert the impossibility of any such endeavor since (1) much of the exegesis of the New Testament is an arbitrary distortion and ingenious twisting of the biblical texts, which go beyond the limits of any proper hermeneutic,[84] and (2) the self-understanding of contemporary people and the critical-historical thought of modern theology separates us from the methodology of the New Testament.[85]

Those responding negatively do not deny that the Old Testament is important for the study of the New Testament. They insist, however, that the Old Testament represents a religion that stands outside of and apart from the religion of the New, and that it must therefore be treated not as prolegomena to the gospel but as a witness to the gospel on the part of a religion that is essentially distinct from the gospel. The New Testament writers, not realizing this, engaged in demonstrating continuity and fulfillment. But from our more advanced perspective, we now see how impossible such an endeavor was—and, of course, is today.

Where a positive answer to our question is given, it is usually expressed in one or the other of the following ways:

1. Most conservative interpreters (whether orthodox or quasi-orthodox in theology) hold—or, at least "feel"—that on so vital a

---

[84] Cf., e.g., S. V. McCasland, "Matthew Twists the Scriptures," *JBL* 80 (1961) 143-48, who went so far as to assert that Matthew's treatment illustrates the words of 2 Pet 3:16 regarding "ignorant and unstable" men who twist Scripture to their own destruction.

[85] Cf., e.g., F. Baumgärtel, "The Hermeneutical Problem of the Old Testament," in *Essays on Old Testament Interpretation*, ed. C. Westermann, trans. J. L. Mays (London: SCM, 1963), 134-59; see also R. Bultmann, "Prophecy and Fulfilment," in *ibid.*, 50-75.

matter as the New Testament's use of the Old, the descriptive is also the normative, and so believe themselves committed to explain the principles underlying the exegesis of the New Testament in order that these same procedures might be followed today. Few would accept the rather flexible axiom of Coccejus (the eighteenth century Dutch Reformed theologian who opposed what he viewed as a scholastic method of studying theology of his day in favor of a more scriptural method) that "the words of Scripture signify all that they can be made to signify." But many, taking their cue from such earlier influential writers as F. W. Farrar,[86] insist that the exegetical methods of Christ and the apostles must control Christian exegetical practices today.[87]

2. Many existential exegetes (particularly the so-called "post-Bultmannians") insist, to quote Walther Eichrodt, that it is "open to us to go beyond the New Testament types and to mention other similar correspondences,"[88] since the faith that ties together the Old and New Testaments into an essential unity is ours as well. These interpreters agree with the classical liberals and Bultmannians in their disavowal of any real continuity of detail between the testaments and in their insistence that "modern scientific exegesis cannot be simply derived from its use within the New Testament."[89] But they assert that because of the continuity of faith that exists between prophets, apostles, reformers, and ourselves, each—though in his own way and using materials of relevance to his own times—must engage in a similar exegetical task. Thus, to quote Hans Walter Wolff, "the witnessing word waits on its encounter with each new hearer."[90]

---

[86] F. W. Farrar, *History of the Interpretation of the Bible* (London: Macmillan, 1886), esp. 434-36.

[87] Cf., e.g., L. Berkhof, *Principles of Bible Interpretation* (Grand Rapids: Baker, 1950), 140ff., who, in discussing the interpreter's handling of the "mystical sense of Scripture," begins by saying: "The necessity of recognizing the mystical sense is quite evident from the way in which the New Testament often interprets the Old."

[88] W. Eichrodt, "Is Typological Exegesis an Appropriate Method?," in *Essays on Old Testament Interpretation*, 244.

[89] *Ibid.*, 231.

[90] H. W. Wolff, "The Hermeneutics of the Old Testament," in *Essays on Old Testament Interpretation*, 164. In addition to the articles cited above by Eichrodt

3. A number of Roman Catholic scholars have recognized that the New Testament frequently explicates the Old Testament along the lines of what they have called a *sensus plenior* (or, "fuller sense"), and have credited the origin of this fuller sense in one way or another to the historical Jesus. Following out their doctrine of a dual basis of revelational authority, they then go on to insist that in like manner theology today can carry on the New Testament exegetical procedures only as it is guided by the "Magisterium of the Church," which is the expression of the "Mystical Body of Christ."[91]

Evangelicals generally have found themselves unhappy with the presuppositions underlying (1) the "No" answers of classical liberals and Bultmannians, and (2) the "Yes" responses of post-Bultmannian and Roman Catholic interpreters, and so have held themselves—in their sympathies, if not always in their formal practice—to some form of the thesis that the descriptive is also in some manner normative for exegesis today. In light of the nature of New Testament exegesis, however, especially as illumined to a great extent by first-century Jewish practice, the question must be raised: Is there not a better way to solve the problem of relationships?

A Proposed Solution
It is the thesis of this essay that at least three matters must be taken into account when asking about the relation of New Testament exegesis and a proper hermeneutic today. In the first place, it is essential that we understand the nature of *pesher* interpretation in the New Testament. Second, there is the necessity of recognizing that in certain instances midrashic and allegorical exegesis seem to be used in the New Testament somewhat circumstantially. And third, some determination must be made as to the relation of the descriptive and the normative in biblical interpretation. Involved in all three of these matters is the question of the extent to which Christianity

---

and Wolff, note the seminal article in the same volume by Gerhard von Rad, "Typological Interpretation of the Old Testament."

[91] Cf., e.g., R. Bierberg, "Does Sacred Scripture Have a *Sensus Plenior*?," *CBQ* 10 (1948) 182-95; E. F. Sutcliffe, "The Plenary Sense as a Principle of Interpretation," *Bib* 34 (1953) 333-43; Brown, *"Sensus Plenior" of Sacred Scripture* (1955); idem, "Sensus Plenior in the Last Ten Years," *CBQ* 25 (1963) 262-85.

3. Can We Reproduce the Exegesis of the NT?

today—particularly orthodox Christianity, which is the perspective from which I speak—is committed not only to the apostolic faith and doctrine but also to the apostolic practice.

As Christians, our commitment is not to the Teacher of Righteousness and his associates at Qumran, even though they claimed to have spoken in a revelatory manner. Rather, as Christians, to quote Fenton J. A. Hort:

> Our faith rests first on the Gospel itself, the revelation of God and his redemption in His Only begotten Son, and secondly on the interpretation of that primary Gospel by the Apostles and Apostolic men to whom was Divinely committed the task of applying the revelation of Christ to the thoughts and deeds of their own time. That standard interpretation of theirs was ordained to be for the guidance of the Church in all after ages, in combination with the living guidance of the Spirit.[92]

As students of history we can appreciate something of what was involved in their exegetical methods, and as Christians we commit ourselves to their conclusions. But apart from a revelatory stance on our part, I suggest that we cannot reproduce their *pesher* exegesis. While we may sometimes sound as if we are speaking direct from the courts of heaven (hopefully, only inadvertently), and while we legitimately seek continuity with our Lord and his apostles in matters of faith and doctrine, we must also recognize the uniqueness of Jesus as the true interpreter of the Old Testament and the distinctive place he gave to the apostles in the explication of the prophetic word.[93]

That New Testament authors used the Old Testament somewhat circumstantially is seen first of all in the distribution of the biblical quotations in their writings, particularly in Paul's letters. Accepting for the moment Earle Ellis's count of ninety-three Old Testament passages cited by Paul (and some count must be accepted as a working standard, though the distinction between a quotation and an allusion is admittedly often quite elusive), the frequency of occurrence in the various Pauline letters is both interesting and instructive: in Romans, 52 Old Testament portions are quoted; in 1 Corinthians, 16; in 2 Corinthians, 9; in Galatians, 10; in Ephesians, 4; in 1 Timothy, 1; and in 2 Timothy, 1—while in 1 Thessalonians, 2 Thessalonians, Colos-

---

[92] F. J. A. Hort, *The Epistle of St James* (London: Macmillan, 1909), ix.
[93] Note the consciousness of the centrality of the apostles in early Christian tradition as expressed in such passages as John 15:27, Eph 2:20 and Rev 21:14.

sians, Philemon, Philippians, and Titus, Old Testament quotations, as such, do not appear.[94] Probably we will never be able to explain this phenomenon fully. It cannot be attributed just to the size of a letter in question, for Galatians, while relatively brief, is proportionately full of Old Testament quotations. More likely it has to do with the character of the audience addressed, the problems faced, and the immediate purpose of the author—factors that involve something of a circumstantial rationale. And while this phenomenon is most easily illustrated in the letters of Paul, simply because of the number of letters with which we have to work in the Pauline corpus, it is probably true of the other New Testament writers as well.

Not only in distribution, however, but also in the manner in which the biblical portions are employed in certain instances may we postulate a circumstantial character in the citations. David Daube, for example, has proposed that in Paul's treatment of "seed" and "seeds" in Gal 3:16, not only is the apostle using a midrashic mode of interpretation but also responding to a judaizing conception of what it means to be Abraham's "seed"—and that, in addressing his converts who were troubled by the exegesis of the Judaizers, "he deliberately furnishes them with a deeper application."[95]

Such a proposal is pregnant with possibilities, immediately suggesting that Paul is here meeting and outclassing his antagonists on their own grounds—and so, that the specific form of his argument should be understood somewhat circumstantially. And what is true here may also be true elsewhere, particularly in the midrashic exegesis of Rom 10:6-10 (the word being nigh, even in the mouth and the heart), 1 Cor 10:1-6 (the rock that followed in the wilderness), and 2 Cor 3:12-18 (the Mosaic veil that still blinds)—as well as in the allegorical treatment of Hagar and Sarah in Gal 4:21-31.

Admittedly, this whole subject of a circumstantial use of the Old Testament by Paul and others in the New Testament deserves a much fuller explication and discussion than this article is able to provide.[96] I

---

[94] Ellis, *Paul's Use of the Old Testament*, esp. Appendix I (A). See also Appendix I (B), where allusions and parallels in the Pauline letters to the Old Testament are listed.

[95] Daube, *New Testament and Rabbinic Judaism*, 441.

[96] For a number of other examples, see my commentaries on *Galatians* (WBC; Dallas: Word, 1990) and *Acts* (EBC; Grand Rapids: Zondervan, 1981; 2nd ed.

would only here propose that the instances cited above are examples of portions that need to be treated in such a fashion, and that this matter of circumstantial exegesis must be taken into account in any discussion of the normative character of New Testament exegetical methods and procedures.

What, then, can be said to our question "Can we reproduce the exegesis of the New Testament?" I suggest that we must answer both "No" and "Yes." Where that exegesis takes on a revelatory character, where it is atomistic or allegorical, or where it is avowedly circumstantial, "No."[97] Where, however, it treats the Old Testament in a more literal fashion, following the course of what we would speak of today as critical-historical-grammatical exegesis, "Yes." Our commitment as Christians is to the reproduction of the apostolic faith and doctrine, and only secondarily, if at all, to the apostolic exegetical conventions and practices.

Orthodoxy has always distinguished between the descriptive and the normative in other areas—as, for example, in such matters as ecclesiastical government, the apostolic office, and charismatic gifts, to name only a few. I propose that in the area of exegesis, as well, we may appreciate the manner in which the interpretations of the various New Testament writers were derived and need to reproduce their conclusions by means of a critical-historical-grammatical exegesis, but we cannot assume that their exegetical methods are necessarily the norm for our exegesis today.

SELECT BIBLIOGRAPHY

This bibliography contains materials published before 1970. A more extensive listing of materials up to 1999 can be found in the second edition of my *Biblical Exegesis in the Apostolic Period* (Grand Rapids: Eerdmans, 1999).

2005), as well as my forthcoming commentary on *Romans* (NIGTC; Grand Rapids: Eerdmans).

[97] While given facetiously, C. F. D. Moule's comment is illustratively appropriate: "I wish I had lived in the age of פשר. I would have shown how II Kings vi.5f. is an account of St. Paul's conversion in code: the lost axe-head was שאול; what rescued it was עץ!" ("Fulfilment Words in the New Testament: Use and Abuse," *NTS* 14 (1968) 293-320 [297, n. 2]).

Bonsirven, Joseph. *Exégèse rabbinique et exégèse paulinienne*. Paris: Beauchesne, 1939.
Brown, Raymond E. *The "Sensus Plenior" of Sacred Scripture*. Baltimore: St Mary's University, 1955.
Bruce, Frederick F. *Biblical Exegesis in the Qumran Texts*. London: Tyndale; Grand Rapids: Eerdmans, 1960.
Brownlee, William H. "Biblical Interpretation among the Sectaries of the Dead Sea Scrolls," *BA* 14 (1951) 54-76.
_____. *The Text of Habakkuk in the Ancient Commentary from Qumran*. Philadelphia: Society of Biblical Literature, 1959.
Cross, Frank M., Jr, "The History of the Biblical Text in the Light of Discoveries in the Judean Desert," *HTR* 57 (1964) 281-99.
_____. "The Contribution of the Qumran Discoveries to the Study of the Biblical Text," *IEJ* 16 (1966) 81-95.
_____ and S. Talmon, eds. *Qumran and the History of the Biblical Text*. Cambridge, MA: Harvard University Press, 1975.
Daube, David. "Rabbinic Methods of Interpretation and Hellenistic Rhetoric," *HUCA* 22 (1949) 239-64.
_____. "Alexandrian Methods of Interpretation and the Rabbis," in *Festschrift Hans Lewald*. Basel: Helbing & Lichtenbahn, 1953, 27-44.
Davies, William D. *Paul and Rabbinic Judaism. Some Rabbinic Elements in Pauline Theology*. London: SPCK, 1948^1, 1955^2, 1970^3; Philadelphia: Fortress, 1980^4.
Dodd, Charles H. *According to the Scriptures: The Sub-Structure of New Testament Theology*. London: Nisbet, 1952.
Fitzmyer, Joseph A. "4QTestimonia and the New Testament," *TS* 18 (1957) 513-37; repr. in his *Essays on the Semitic Background of the New Testament*. Missoula: Scholars, 1971, 59-89.
_____. "The Use of Explicit Old Testament Quotations in Qumran Literature and in the New Testament," *NTS* 7 (1961) 297-333; repr. in his *Essays on the Semitic Background of the New Testament*. Missoula: Scholars, 1971, 3-58.
Jeremias, Joachim. "Paulus als Hillelit," in *Neotestamentica et Semitica*, ed. E. E. Ellis and M. Wilcox. Edinburgh: T. & T. Clark, 1969, 88-94.
Lauterbach, Jacob Z. "The Ancient Jewish Allegorists in Talmud and Midrash," *JQR* 1 (1911) 291-333 and 503-31.
Le Déaut, Roger. "Apropos d'une définition du Midrash," *Bib* 50 (1969) 395-413; ET = "Apropos a Definition of Midrash," trans. M. C. Howard, *Int* 25 [1971] 259-83.
Lindars, Barnabas. *New Testament Apologetic: The Doctrinal Significance of the Old Testament Quotations*. London: SCM, 1961.
Michel, Otto. *Paulus und seine Bibel*. Gütersloh: Bertelsmann, 1929; 2nd ed., 1972.

Moule, Charles F. D. "The Church Explains Itself: The Use of the Jewish Scriptures," in his *The Birth of the New Testament*. London: Black; New York: Harper & Row, 1962; second edition, 1966, 53-85.

———. "Fulfilment Words in the New Testament: Use and Abuse," *NTS* 14 (1968) 293-320; repr. in his *Essays in New Testament Interpretation*. Cambridge: Cambridge University Press, 1982, 3-36.

Roberts, Bleddyn J. "The Dead Sea Scrolls and the Old Testament Scriptures," *BJRL* 36 (1953) 75-96.

———. "Bible Exegesis and Fulfillment in Qumran," in *Words and Meanings: Essays Presented to D. W. Thomas*, ed. P. R. Ackroyd and B. Lindars. Cambridge: Cambridge University Press, 1968.

Stendahl, Krister. *The School of St Matthew and its Use of the Old Testament*. Lund: Gleerup, 1954; Philadelphia: Fortress, 1958, 2nd ed., 1967.

Thackeray, Henry StJohn. *The Relation of St Paul to Contemporary Jewish Thought*. London: Macmillan, 1900.

Vermes, Geza. *Scripture and Tradition in Judaism*. Leiden: Brill, 1961; 2nd ed., 1973.

———. "The Qumran Interpretation of Scripture in its Historical Setting," *ALUOS* 6 (1966-68) 85-97.

Waard, Jan de. *A Comparative Study of the Old Testament Text in the Dead Sea Scrolls and in the New Testament*. Leiden: Brill, 1965; Grand Rapids: Eerdmans, 1966.

Wolfson, Harry A. *Philo: Foundations of Religious Philosophy in Judaism, Christianity and Islam*, 2 vols. Cambridge, MA: Harvard University Press, 1947.

Wright, Addison G. "The Literary Genre Midrash: Part One" and "The Literary Genre Midrash: Part Two," *CBQ* 28 (1966) 105-38, 417-57 (also published as *The Literary Genre Midrash*. Staten Island: Alba House, 1967).

4

MAJOR TASKS OF AN EVANGELICAL HERMENEUTIC
Some Observations on Commonalities, Interrelations, and Differences

Hermeneutics—the theory, method and practice of how to read, understand, and use biblical texts—is at the heart of Christian identity, has profound effects on the formulation of Christian theology, informs every aspect of Christian living, and gives guidance to the church's proclamation and mission. It is, in fact, foundational for every reading of Scripture, every expression of Christian conviction, and all Christian living, whether personal or corporate.

Hermeneutics is a vast and extensive subject. It can hardly be treated adequately in such a short presentation as this. Nonetheless, the major tasks of an evangelical hermeneutic may here be profitably highlighted, with some observations made with respect to their commonalities, interrelations and differences. Elsewhere I have written in some detail about the New Testament's use of the Old Testament and its normativeness for us today in our reception and contextualization of the Christian gospel.[1] All I want to do here is offer something of a position paper that sets out an overview of my own understanding of a proper evangelical hermeneutic—suggesting in the process what I believe to be a viable set of answers to the question posed long ago in my 1969 Tyndale lecture, which appeared as the lead article in the

---

[1] See esp. my *Biblical Exegesis in the Apostolic Period* (Grand Rapids: Eerdmans, 1975, 2nd ed. 1999) and my *New Wine into Fresh Wineskins: Contextualizing the Early Christian Confessions* (Peabody: Hendrickson), 1999; also such articles as *idem*, "Can We Reproduce the Exegesis of the New Testament?" *TB* 21 (1970) 3-38; *idem*, "'Who Is the Prophet Talking About?' Some Reflections on the New Testament's Use of the Old," *Them* 24 (1987) 3-16; and *idem*, "Prolegomena to Paul's Use of Scripture in Romans," *BBR* 7 (1997) 145-68.

4. Major Tasks of an Evangelical Hermeneutic

Tyndale Bulletin of 1970: "Can we reproduce the exegesis of the New Testament?"[2]

1. *The Interpretive / Descriptive Task*

The first task in the hermeneutical enterprise is to understand the words, thoughts and intentions of the biblical writers in their particular contexts. This is the vitally important *interpretive* or *descriptive* task, which must be undertaken by all interpreters, whatever their theological commitments.

Evangelicals, however, go beyond many other interpreters in asserting that all truly Christian thought and all truly Christian living must begin with and be based on the revelation of God as (1) given in the experience of the nation Israel in the Old Testament, (2) uniquely expressed in the person and work of Jesus of Nazareth, (3) interpreted and proclaimed by the apostolic witness of the early church, and (4) illuminated and applied by the Holy Spirit. The Christian faith, evangelicals insist, is a religion of revelation, with that revelation being primarily concerned with the "Good News" (εὐαγγέλιον, 'the gospel') regarding Jesus of Nazareth, who is Israel's promised Messiah, humanity's accredited Lord, and the Word of God incarnate—and, just as importantly, who by his obedient life and sacrificial death made possible for all people redemption from sin and death and reconciliation to God. It is a message (1) witnessed to by "the law and the prophets" in the Old Testament and (2) proclaimed and explicated by the apostolic writers in the New Testament (which together with the Old Testament "law and prophets" constitute the "word of God" inscripturated), and that is (3) illuminated and applied by God's Spirit, who has always been active by way of revelation, interpretation, application, and enabling.

But while the Christian faith is a religion of revelation, it is also a historical religion. For it is based on what God has done redemptively in history, how the early church was led by God to understand his redemptive working in Jesus the Christ, and how that gospel message was proclaimed during the apostolic period—laying emphasis on the essential content of that proclamation, but also noting the various forms and methods that were used to convey and spell out the nuances of that proclamation to diverse audiences of that day. So in seeking to

---

[2] *TB* 21 (1970) 3-38 (as cited above in footnote 1).

understand the words, thoughts and intentions of the biblical writers, attention must not only be directed to the revelatory and transcultural features of their message, but also to the cultural contexts, specific situations, particular concerns, and distinctive exegetical conventions of their day that influenced and were used by them in declaring, explicating, and nuancing that message when addressing their various audiences.

Further, in seeking to explicate the revelation of God as given and interpreted in the New Testament, we must consider not only "innerbiblical" exegesis—that is, so-called "intertextuality" or "interpreted intertextuality" (which, however, all too often means "intratextuality"; that is, focusing exclusively on the parallels and echoes that exist between the Old Testament and the New Testament)—but also "extrabiblical" exegesis, which involves comparative analyses of the themes and practices of the New Testament writers vis-à-vis the conventions, themes, and practices found in the Greco-Roman world generally and the writings and traditions of Second Temple Judaism in particular. Despite protests from some scholars, I believe it is impossible to give a fair hearing to the interpretations of the New Testament writers without also interacting with the exegetical presuppositions, procedures and practices found in the writings of Second Temple Judaism or Early Judaism—that is, in the Jewish apocryphal, pseudepigraphical, and apocalyptic writings, the Dead Sea Scrolls, and the later rabbinic codifications of earlier Pharisaic teaching. For, as Geza Vermes has aptly pointed out:

> In inter-testamental Judaism there existed a fundamental unity of exegetical tradition. This tradition, the basis of religious faith and life, was adopted and modified by its constituent groups, the Pharisees, the Qumran sectaries, and the Judeo-Christians. We have, as a result, three cognate schools of exegesis of the message recorded in the Bible, and it is the duty of the historian to emphasize that none of them can properly be understood independently of the others.[3]

All this means that, in undertaking this first interpretive or descriptive task of the hermeneutical enterprise, I want always to try to understand better (1) the content and thrust of the New Testament writers' interpretations of Scripture *and* (2) the exegetical methods they used in arriving at those interpretations and conveying them to their

---

[3] G. Vermes, "The Qumran Interpretation of Scripture in Its Historical Setting," *ALUOS* 6 (1966–68) 85-97 (95).

4. Major Tasks of an Evangelical Hermeneutic 75

respective audiences by reference to both an "inner-biblical" exegesis and an "extra-biblical" exegesis. Further, in direct response to the question "Can we reproduce the exegesis of the New Testament?," I find it necessary to make a distinction between (1) that which was divinely (also often humanly) intended to be the essential, transcultural message of the various New Testament writers, and (2) the cultural, circumstantial, time-bound methods they used to convey and support that message in their day. Together with all evangelical and most constructive scholars, I consider the content and thrust of the New Testament proclamation to be normative for Christian faith and doctrine. Departing from some of my evangelical colleagues, however, I view the exegetical conventions, procedures and methods used by the writers of the New Testament to convey and support that message to be culturally and circumstantially conditioned—particularly when they worked from certain exegetical conventions of their day and engaged in what I define as "midrash," "pesher," "allegorical," or *ad hominem* exegesis—and so not formative for my own exegetical practice.

In effect, by means of today's literary-critical-historical tools—which, admittedly, are themselves always culturally conditioned, since exegesis is always a human endeavor—I seek to understand the content and thrust of a biblical writer's proclamation, recognizing always that such matters are presented in the garb of the cultural, temporal, societal and circumstantial forms of the day. It is the Good News of God's redemptive activity in human history on behalf of all people—which is set out in preliminary and promissory fashion in the Old Testament, uniquely expressed in the person and work of Jesus of Nazareth, proclaimed and interpreted by the apostolic witness of the New Testament, and illuminated and applied by the Holy Spirit—that I want to highlight and set forth as clearly as possible in my descriptive treatment of the Scriptures. For it is "the truth of the gospel" (to use the expression that Paul used in Gal 1:5, 14 for what he saw to be central and most important in Christian proclamation) that is the essential matter, and thus the normative feature of Scripture. At the same time, however, I also want to understand, as best I am able, the exegetical principles and procedures, together with the then-current rhetorical and epistolary conventions, that the New Testament writers used, in various contexts and as they developed certain themes, to convey and support that central proclamation. For an understanding of their exegetical methods, together with an appreciation of their rhetorical modes of persuasion and epistolary practices, enables me better to grasp, appropriate, and contextualize for my own situation and society what is being presented.

2. The Transformational Task

The second major task of an evangelical hermeneutic has to do with appropriating the biblical message for personal and corporate living. This is the *transformational* task, which involves commitment to the message of the biblical writers and openness to God's Spirit to make operative in one's life what was meant to be normative in the gospel proclamation. For all evangelicals and most constructive biblical scholars—though there may be differences among them as to exactly what should be seen as normative and how the essentials of that gospel are to be expressed—the transformational task in the hermeneutical enterprise is no less important than the descriptive.

The major commonality between the first, the interpretive or descriptive task, and this second, the transformational task, is that both are concerned with what is perceived to be the heart and core of the biblical message—that is, amidst all the various presentations of the biblical writers and all their differing styles, conventions, procedures, and methods in presenting their materials, both tasks are concerned primarily with the central content and thrust of the biblical proclamation. A major difference between the two tasks, however, is that, whereas the first is based on one's own research and reflection, the second involves a personal response of faith and commitment and comes about principally, if not entirely, through the mediation of the Christian church. We may think of ourselves solely in individualistic terms, and so flaunt our supposed individualism. But as Miroslav Volf has rightly pointed out: "It is from the church that one receives the content of faith, and it is in the church that one learns how faith is to be understood and lived."[4]

As we mature in our Christian faith, we tend to forget how *communal* was the context for our original awareness of the message of the gospel, how *elemental* were many of our earliest reasons for believing that gospel, and how *functional* was our turning to Christ for

---

[4] M. Volf, *After Our Likeness: The Church as the Image of the Trinity* (Grand Rapids: Eerdmans, 1998), 163.

salvation. As we think back to those earlier days, we cannot help but recall that for all practical purposes the mediation of faith in our own lives proceeded less (if at all) by way of personal research and reflection and more (if not entirely) by way of the mediation of the community of faith, the Christian church as broadly defined, and our response of faith and commitment to what was given us. Usually that mediation came by way of various Christian "significant others," such as family members or friends. And often our response became "saving faith" not only in a very elemental, functional fashion, but also on the basis of a minimum of knowledge content—sometimes, in fact, a body of knowledge that was exceedingly superficial or even erroneous, though with even that being used by God in unexpected ways to bring us to himself.[5]

Down through the centuries the Christian church has used various external aids to bring about transformation in the lives of its parishioners. Liturgy, music, hymnody and architecture have often been used effectively for such a purpose—though, admittedly, without always being able to accomplish fully that purpose. Less worthy attempts to engender faith and devotion have been by means of supposed relics of the saints, embellished stories about Christian martyrs, and objects associated with the historical Jesus (e.g., the Shroud of Turin, or, of late, the James Ossuary)—sometimes, in cer-

---

[5] Calvin's comment on Isa 7:10-12 (where God spoke through the prophet Isaiah to Ahaz, king of Judah: "Ask the Lord your God for a sign, whether in the deepest depths or in the highest heights") provides an apt insight into one of the ways in which God works: "As the Lord knew that King Ahaz was so wicked as not to believe the promise, so he enjoins Isaiah to confirm him by adding a sign. For when God sees that his promises do not satisfy us, he makes additions to them suitable to our weakness, so that we not only hear him speak, but likewise behold his hand displayed, and thus are confirmed by an evident proof of the faith" (*Commentary on the Book of the Prophet Isaiah*, trans. W. Pringle [Edinburgh: Calvin Translation Society, 1850], 239). Ahaz, of course, did not want a sign, for he had no desire to respond positively to any message from God. So in pseudo-piety he replied: "I will not ask; I will not put the Lord to the test." But the amazing thing is that God offered to give Ahaz any sign that would convince him of God's working and God's ways.

The main point of Calvin's comment is that miraculous signs are only given in support of God's promises, and so should not be viewed as superior to God's word. But Calvin also makes the point that God speaks to us in ways "suitable to our weakness." And as people of faith, looking back in hindsight, we all must confess that God has often done just that in our own religious experiences.

tain circles, by means of various contemporary forms of atomistic exegesis (as in ancient midrashic treatments), revelatory identifications (as in ancient pesher treatments), and/or allegorical parallels (as in ancient allegorical treatments), which all too often depend more on the ingenuity of the preacher or commentator than on the text being expounded.

The focus of the transformational task in Christian theology, however, is (1) the work and teaching of Christ, as portrayed and contextualized in the New Testament, and (2) the ministry of the Holy Spirit, who makes operative in the lives of individual believers and society today Christ's work and teaching. Thus the principal exhortations in the New Testament regarding transformation are to be found in such passages as:

> Phil 2:5: "Let the same mind be in you that was in Christ Jesus" (which introduces the early church's Christ-hymn of 2:6-11); and,
>
> 1 Pet 2:21: "Christ suffered for you, leaving you an example, so that you should follow in his steps" (which introduces the early Christian confessional material of 2:22-23, with phraseology and allusions drawn from Isaiah 53).

And so, when speaking about how believers in Christ are to live their new lives "in Christ," the New Testament writers refer to (1) *the example of Jesus* and (2) *the teaching of Jesus* as the material content for such living (cf., e.g., the parallels to Jesus' teaching in such passages as Rom 12:1–15:13; 1 Thess 4:1-12; James; and 1 Peter), as well as to (3) *the work of the Holy Spirit* in recalling, illuminating, and bringing to effect Jesus' teaching in the lives of his followers (cf., e.g., John 14:26; Gal 5:16-26).

The common feature in both the descriptive and the transformational tasks of an evangelical hermeneutic is, therefore, the centrality of the gospel, which is rooted in a preparatory and promissory fashion in the Old Testament and proclaimed and interpreted in the New Testament. Likewise, interrelations between the descriptive and the transformational are viewed as important in an evangelical hermeneutic, for what is understood to be normative must also be appropriated for Christian thought to be truly formed and Christian living to truly take place. There is, however, usually no endeavor on the part of evangelicals to reproduce the exact forms by which that gospel proclamation was originally presented or supported, whether as expressed in the Old Testament or reflected in the New Testament—particularly, as is our present concern, to attempt to reproduce the exact exegetical conventions, procedures, practices, or methods of the New Testament writers so as to enhance the transformational process.

As Christians we need to remember that our original positive response to the gospel did not include any correlative acceptance of such cultural forms or exegetical conventions. We may have come later to understand something about how that gospel was clothed in its New Testament portrayals in somewhat diverse cultural garb for differing first-century audiences—and, hopefully, to appreciate something of the appropriateness of the New Testament writers' contextualizations of that message in their day. Our original perception, however, while probably more intuitive than reasoned, was entirely proper: that there is an essential distinction between the normative, transcultural nature of the gospel message and the cultural, circumstantial, time-bound methods that the New Testament writers used to convey and support that proclamation. It was the Holy Spirit who taught us this truth at the time of our conversion. And like Paul's converts in the province of Galatia who became confused regarding a somewhat similar matter, we need always—even as we grow older in the Christian faith and become more knowledgeable about the Scriptures—"keep in step with the Spirit" (cf. Gal 5:25).

3. *The Contextualization Task*

The third major task of an evangelical hermeneutic has to do with the expression of the Christian gospel in the various cultural contexts and specific situations of today. This is the contemporary *contextualization* task, which is a vitally important concern for all missiologists, whatever their theological persuasion—and should be, as well, for all evangelicals. For the central mandate of the Christian church is that given by Jesus himself as recorded in the final verses of Matthew's Gospel:

> All authority in heaven and on earth has been given to me. Therefore go and make disciples of all nations, baptizing them in the name of the Father and of the Son and of the Holy Spirit, and teaching them to obey everything I have commanded you. And surely I will be with you always, to the very end of the age.[6]

---

[6] Matt 28:18-20.

4. Major Tasks of an Evangelical Hermeneutic

In my *New Wine into Fresh Wineskins*, which is subtitled *Contextualizing the Early Christian Confessions*, I have set out and attempted to explicate three theses: (1) that the "new wine" of the gospel has been encapsulated in the early Christian confessional materials that are incorporated by the writers of the New Testament into their writings—broadly speaking, in "hymns" (poetic portions), *homologiai* (formulaic prose passages), and single-statement affirmations—and that many of these confessional materials can be identified by means of form-critical analyses developed during the past century (Part 1); (2) that the New Testament writers often used these confessional materials as a basis for and to structure and support their presentations in addressing their respective audiences and speaking to particular issues, thereby contextualizing that "new wine" of the gospel into the "fresh wineskins" of differing cultures and circumstances (Part 2); and (3) that in their contextualizations of those early Christian confessions the New Testament writers not only highlighted for their addressees the central features of the Christian gospel—that is, the "new wine" of the early proclamation—but also give guidance as to how we should contextualize that gospel in the differing cultural contexts and circumstances of our day—that is, the "fresh wineskins" of today (Part 3). I will not attempt here to spell out, justify, or deal with the implications of those three theses. This is what my 1999 monograph is all about. All I want to do in this presentation is to point out that the contextualization of the gospel in the various cultural contexts, situations and circumstances of today is also of great importance for an evangelical hermeneutic, and to speak to the issue of how this third task, that of contemporary contextualization, relates to the previous two mentioned above, which we have called the descriptive and the transformational tasks.

For the sake of brevity, perhaps the issues can most easily be brought to the fore by asking three rather elemental, yet profound, questions—questions that have perennially perplexed Christians down through the centuries and to which various answers have been given: (1) Why in the New Testament do we have four canonical Gospels and not just one written Gospel, since, after all, there is only one gospel? (2) Why in the New Testament do we have seven, ten, or thirteen (as I believe) letters of Paul to various Gentile churches and leaders in the Gentile churches, when he was the "apostle to the Gentiles" and had only one message? And, (3) why in the New Testament

4. Major Tasks of an Evangelical Hermeneutic   81

do we have such other writings as not only the so-called "Acts of the Apostles" (the second part of Luke's composition), but also the homily or sermon to the Hebrews, the epistles or tractates of James, Peter, John, and Jude, and the Johannine apocalypse, when we already have the four Gospels and Paul's letters—which twofold collection of writings seems to have sufficiently nourished most believers in Christ during the first three or four Christian centuries, and has been taken by many today to be sufficient for their own spiritual health?

There are those who have treated (and continue to treat) the Bible generally, and the New Testament in particular, as a textbook on Christian theology and a compendium of Christian ethics—if not always in theory, at least in practice. So they have all too often tried to harmonize the four Gospels into one literary presentation; to view Paul's letters as all saying the same thing, only on different occasions; and to interpret Acts and the "hinder parts" of the New Testament (i.e., Hebrews through Revelation) almost exclusively in terms of the statements and norms found in the canonical Gospels and Paul. Such an approach seeks to highlight the features of unity and revelational authority that can legitimately be claimed for the Bible generally and the New Testament in particular. But it fails to take into account the factors of contextualization, development, and diversity also present in those writings.

My thesis is that what we have in the New Testament are (1) *declarations* of the gospel and the ethical principles that derive from the gospel, as principally contained in the early Christian confessions, and (2) *descriptions* (whether in the form of Gospels, letters, accounts of representative exploits, sermons, tractates, or an apocalypse) of how that gospel proclamation and its inherent principles were contextualized in diverse cultural contexts, circumstances, and situations during the apostolic period. The proclamation and principles, because expressive of God's salvific work in Christ Jesus and highlighted in the early Christian confessions, are to be viewed as normative for Christian thought and life. The ways in which that proclamation and those principles were put into practice in the first century, however, should be understood as contextualizations for a particular time, culture and circumstance.

In effect, the four Gospels, Paul's letters, the Acts of the Apostles, and the other writings of the New Testament—all of which we as evangelicals believe were written under the Spirit's direction, and so will not lead us into error when rightly understood—function (1) to highlight the central and essential features of the Christian gospel, *and* (2) to reflect the contextualizations and usages appropriate for the conveyance of that gospel in various circumstances and situations of the first century. What is *declared* in the early Christian confessions, based on the apostolic proclamation of the Good News in Christ Jesus and its implied principles, is normative for Christian thought and living. What is *described* with regard to the various contextualizations of that gospel for diverse situations and cultures can, indeed, be appreciated on their own merits, but need not be viewed as normative for Christian faith and doctrine today. Nonetheless, though not normative, those descriptions of how the gospel was contextualized in the apostolic period of the Christian church give us guidance today by way of examples as to how we should contextualize that same gospel for our own particular times, cultures, and circumstances.

If all of this be true—or, at least, only approximately true—then questions about relationships between this third task of an evangelical hermeneutic, that of contextualizing the gospel today, and those of the first two, the descriptive and the transformational, seem rather obvious. Common to all three is an emphasis on the centrality and normativity of the gospel as presented by the writers of the New Testament, with the Good News that was discovered in the first task (the "interpretive" or "descriptive") and appropriated for personal and corporate living in the second task (the "transformational") being always the starting point for and content of what is to be contextualized in this third task of the hermeneutical enterprise. But as with the transformational, the task of contextualizing the gospel today does not call on Christians to reproduce the specific exegetical conventions, procedures or practices of the New Testament writers—whether viewed as something intrinsic to the gospel proclamation, as something traditional that one hesitates to set aside, or as something that in some way would enhance a contemporary contextualization. In fact, the question "Should we not (or, 'Ought not we attempt to') reproduce the exegesis of the New Testament?," while often pious in motivation and wanting to be holistic in theology, only serves to add something extraneous to the normativity of the gospel proclamation, and so by its addition may very well divert attention from what is truly central and essential. And the question "Can we reproduce the exegesis of the New Testament?" actually sets up an impossibility.

For while many of the exegetical practices and conventions of the New Testament may be viewed as having been significant in their day—particularly when addressed to a certain distinctive situation or a certain audience with a particular mind-set—they lack the power to convince in the different cultures, circumstances, and situations of today.

The New Testament portrays how the "new wine" of the gospel of Christ was poured into the "fresh wineskins" of first-century Jewish and Gentile circumstances. In so doing, it not only highlights the gospel and its principles but also gives guidance by way of example as to how to contextualize that self-same gospel in different contexts, situations and circumstances—even in different cultures and at later times. Our contextualization task today is how to "pour" that "new wine" of the Christian gospel into the "fresh wineskins" of the cultures and circumstances of our day. For when either the "newness" of Jesus' work and teaching *or* the "freshness" of new situations or different cultures (whether those of the first century or today) is ignored, the result is, as Matthew's Gospel puts it, the perversion of the gospel *or* the spoiling of the situations in which the gospel is proclaimed, or both. But when both the "new wine" and the "fresh wineskins" are honored—allowing them to interact with one another in a proper fermentation process (in what I have called in my 1999 monograph a "Synergistic-Developmental Model" of contextualization)—"both are preserved" (Matt 9:17).

4. *Some Concluding Remarks*

I find it absolutely necessary to make a distinction between (1) the central, transcultural message of the New Testament writers, and (2) the circumstantial, cultural, and time-bound methods they used to convey and support that message. Together with most evangelical and constructive scholars, I consider the content and thrust of the gospel proclamation in the New Testament to be normative. Departing from some of my evangelical colleagues, however, I view the conventions, procedures, and methods used by the writers of the New Testament in conveying and supporting that proclamation of Good News in their day to be often culturally and circumstantially conditioned— particularly when they work from certain exegetical conventions of their day and engage in what I define as "midrash," "pesher," "allegorical," or *ad hominem* exegesis—and therefore not formative for my own Christian life, thought, or exegetical practice.

In effect, by means of today's literary-critical-historical tools—which, admittedly, because exegesis is always a human endeavor, are themselves culturally conditioned—I seek to understand the content and thrust of the biblical writers' proclamation, recognizing always that such matters are presented in the garb of the cultural, circumstantial, and temporal expressions of their day. It is the Good News of God's redemptive activity in human history on behalf of all people, as expressed preeminently in the work and person of Jesus the Christ, that I want to highlight and set forth as clearly as possible in my descriptive treatment of Scripture, for therein lies "the truth of the gospel" (to use Paul's phrase for what is at the heart of matters in Gal 2:5 and 14; cf. "the truth of Christ" in 2 Cor 11:10 and "the word of the truth of the gospel" in Col 1:5) that is the essential matter and normative feature of Scripture. At the same time, however, I also want to understand, as best I am able, the exegetical principles, proedures, and practices that the writers used to convey and support that central proclamation—in various contexts and as they developed various themes—for such an understanding (1) enables me to better grasp, appropriate and proclaim the content and thrust of what is presented, and (2) aids me by way of example to recontextualize that message in conventions and forms more suited to the cultural contexts and circumstances of today.

Scripture itself evidences a number of places where theological statements and ethical exhortations are supported by cultural means and methods that were considered at the time both legitimate and meaningful, but which could be thought suspect at a later time. In the Old Testament, for example, among the various ways for discerning God's will and conveying God's message were such things as dreams, visions, ecstatic utterances, the fleece of sheep, necromancy, the Urim and Thummim in the breastplate of the high priest, the braying of a donkey, and some rather crude and even rude symbolic actions of various prophets. All of these were meaningful and significant in their day and served to explicate God's message. But though acknowledged in Heb 1:1 as having been appropriate vehicles for the divine message ("In the past God spoke to our ancestors through the prophets in many and various ways"), they are nowhere in Scripture set out as normative procedures to be necessarily followed.

Likewise in the New Testament, after considering who might be qualified—and after praying to God for direction—the early apostles cast lots in order to determine a successor for Judas (Acts 1:15-26). Some earnest Christians, such as the Amish, Old Order Mennonites, and early Moravians, have continued this practice in determining God's will for leadership in their respective communities, God's direction for their communal order and service, and many matters having to do with Christian living. But most Christians view this method as culturally conditioned and not normative for believers today.

And this same distinction between (1) the transcultural, essential message of the New Testament, together with its inherent theological and ethical principles, and (2) the culturally conditioned methods used in the support and expression of that message, which are described in the New Testament but not set out as being normative, has been accepted by most Christians today with respect to a number of other features in the New Testament as well—unless, of course, some form of "restorationism" or "primitivism" is espoused. For example, Christians desire to be in continuity with the theologies of Christian baptism and the Lord's Supper as set out in the New Testament, but they differ widely as to how those sacraments should be practiced—with most feeling no need to reproduce exactly the specific forms or practices of the earliest believers as described in the New Testament. Likewise, Christians today commonly make a distinction in their ecclesiology between the New Testament principles of church government ("church order" or "community formation") and the explicit New Testament practices, and so build their denominational policies and ecclesial structures on what they consider to be biblical principles *and* effective organization patterns of the day, without attempting to reproduce the exact structures of church organization as reflected in the New Testament.[7]

Further, this distinction between the normative and the described can be found in abundance in the area of ethics, whether personal or social. In personal ethics, for example, Christians are challenged and feel themselves bound by their Lord's teaching on humility and mutual acceptance (though, sadly, not always sufficiently so), but usually feel no similar compulsion to continue his practice of foot

---

[7] For an explication of such matters, see *Community Formation in the Early Church and in the Church Today*, ed. R. N. Longenecker (Peabody: Hendrickson, 2002).

washing; while in social ethics they look to the principles of Jesus' teaching and the gospel proclamation for guidance, but usually feel no need to reproduce the precise social circumstances or specific communal relations of the earliest believers in Jesus.

It is often assumed, and sometimes argued, that "apostolic faith and doctrine" *and* "apostolic exegesis" are, in some way, both normative for the faith, proclamation, and practice of Christians today—and so both, in some manner, should be expressed in any contemporary contextualization of the gospel. It is a stance often motivated by reverence and piety. It is an assertion that claims to be biblical and holistic, and it calls on biblical exegetes to be both traditional and creative. All of this may be considered, at least to an extent, highly laudable. But a truer evangelical hermeneutic, I make bold to suggest, is one that (1) distinguishes between the central, transcultural, normative proclamation of the gospel in the New Testament and the circumstantial, cultural, time-bound methods used by the New Testament writers to convey and support that message, (2) views its major tasks as having to do not only with an interpretation or description of apostolic history, theology and exegesis, but also with personal transformation and contemporary contextualization, and (3) understands the commonalities, interrelations, and differences between these three tasks along the lines we have sketched out above.

SELECT BIBLIOGRAPHY

Allison, Dale C., Jr. *The New Moses: A Matthean Typology*. Minneapolis: Fortress, 1993.

Bandstra, Andrew J. "Interpretation in 1 Corinthians 10:1-11," *CTJ* 6 (1971) 5-21.

Barrett, C. Kingsley. "The Interpretation of the Old Testament in the New," in *The Cambridge History of the Bible*, ed. P. R. Ackroyd and C. F. Evans. Cambridge: Cambridge University Press, 1970, 1.377-411.

Bateman, Herbert W. *Early Jewish Hermeneutics and Hebrews 1:5-13: The Impact of Early Jewish Exegesis on the Interpretation of a Significant New Testament Passage*. New York: Lang, 1997.

Black, Matthew. "The Christological Use of the Old Testament in the New Testament," *NTS* 18 (1971) 1-14.

_____. "The Theological Appropriation of the Old Testament by the New Testament," *SJT* 39 (1986) 1-17.

Bock, Darrell L. "Evangelicals and the Use of the Old Testament in the New," *BSac* 142 (1985) 209-23, 306-19.

4. Major Tasks of an Evangelical Hermeneutic

Brown, Raymond E. "The *Sensus Plenior* in the Last Ten Years," *CBQ* 25 (1963) 262-85.

_____. "Matthew's Formula Citations of Scripture," in his *The Birth of the Messiah: A Commentary on the Infancy Narratives in Matthew and Luke*. Garden City: Doubleday, 1977, 96-104 (plus 596-98 in the 1993 updated edition).

Bruce, Frederick F. *This Is That: The New Testament Development of Some Old Testament Themes*. Exeter: Paternoster, 1968.

Caird, George B. "The Exegetical Method of the Epistle to the Hebrews," *CJT* 5 (1959) 44-51.

Deichgräber, Reinhard. *Gotteshymnus und Christushymnus in der frühen Christenheit: Untersuchungen zur Form, Spache, und Stil der frühchristlichen Hymnen*. Göttingen: Vandenhoeck & Ruprecht, 1967.

Dodd, Charles H. *The Apostolic Preaching and its Developments*. London: Hodder & Stoughton, 1936.

_____. *According to the Scriptures: The Sub-Structure of New Testament Theology*. London: Nisbet, 1952; New York: Scribner's, 1953.

Ellis, E. Earle. *Paul's Use of the Old Testament*. Edinburgh: Oliver & Boyd; Grand Rapids: Eerdmans, 1957; repr. Grand Rapids: Baker, 1981.

France, Richard T. *Jesus and the Old Testament: His Application of Old Testament Passages to Himself and his Mission*. London: Tyndale; Downers Grove: InterVarsity, 1971; repr. Grand Rapids: Baker, 1982.

Goppelt, Leonhard. *TYPOS: The Typological Interpretation of the Old Testament in the New*, trans. D. V. Madvig (from 1939 German edition). Grand Rapids: Eerdmans, 1982.

Harnack, Adolf. "Das alte Testament in den paulinischen Briefen und in der paulinischen Gemeinden," *Sitzungsberichte der preussischen Akademie der Wissenschaften zu Berlin* (1928), 124-41.

Hays, Richard B. *Echoes of Scripture in the Letters of Paul*. New Haven, London: Yale University Press, 1989.

Juel, Donald. *Messianic Exegesis: Christological Interpretation of the Old Testament in Early Christianity*. Philadelphia: Fortress, 1988.

Karris, Robert J. *A Symphony of New Testament Hymns: Commentary on Philippians 2:5-11, Colossians 1:15-20, Ephesians 2:14-16, 1 Timothy 3:16, Titus 3:4-7, 1 Peter 3:18-22, and 2 Timothy 2:11-13*. Collegeville: Liturgical Press, 1966.

Longenecker, Richard N. *The Christology of Early Jewish Christianity*. London: SCM, 1970; repr. Grand Rapids: Baker, 1981; repr. Vancouver: Regent College Publishing, 2001.

_____. *Biblical Exegesis in the Apostolic Period*. Grand Rapids: Eerdmans, 1975, 2nd ed., 1999.

_____. *New Wine into Fresh Wineskins: Contextualizing the Early Christian Confessions*. Peabody: Hendrickson, 1999.

Michel, Otto. *Paulus und seine Bibel*. Gütersloh: Bertelsmann, 1929, 1972^2.

Moule, C. F. D. "Fulfilment-Words in the New Testament: Use and Abuse," *NTS* 14 (1968) 293-320.

Vermes, Geza. *Scripture and Tradition in Judaism*. Leiden: Brill, 1961, 1973².

_____. "The Qumran Interpretation of Scripture in Its Historical Setting," *ALUOS* 6 (1966–68) 85-97.

_____. "Jewish Studies and New Testament Interpretation," *JJS* 31 (1980) 1-17.

_____. "Jewish Literature and New Testament Exegesis: Reflections on Methodology," *JJS* 33 (1982) 362-76.

Part II

CHRISTOLOGY

5

CHRISTOLOGICAL MATERIALS WITHIN THE EARLY CHRISTIAN COMMUNITIES

Christology, or what may be defined as theological interpretation of the person and work of Jesus of Nazareth, did not arise in a vacuum. It was, Christians believe, rooted in the Jewish Scriptures, developed by prophets and seers in the Religion of Israel and Second Temple Judaism, expressed in the ministry of a rather obscure Jewish prophet, teacher, and miracle worker of Galilee, and held in the memory of that prophet's earliest followers, who proclaimed him to be Israel's promised and long-expected Messiah. But its central features seem also to have been incorporated into certain materials that circulated—whether orally or in written form, or both—within the early Christian communities. And it was from these materials that Paul in his letters, the evangelists in their Gospels, and the other writers of the New Testament drew in formulating their respective portrayals and presentations of Jesus.

The identity and reconstruction of these early christological materials is, of course, highly conjectural. We do not have any independent access to them. Their existence, nature and contents—in fact, everything about them—must be inferred by means of form-critical and tradition-critical analyses of the New Testament into which it is believed they have been incorporated. Nevertheless, most scholars are convinced (1) that there existed among early believers in Jesus various oral and written christological materials, (2) that these materials were first formed and used in the contexts of worship, preaching and teaching, (3) that these materials gave guidance to the authors of the New Testament in their presentations and arguments, and (4) that it is possible to identify some of these early materials and to describe some of their essential features.

5. Christological Materials

This is not to deny the impact of Jesus' teaching and ministry on his earliest disciples, nor to minimize the significance of eye-witness reports and the church's memory of such reports. Nor is it to devalue the importance of either oral tradition or the work of God's Spirit in the nascent church. But these are matters not easily accessible to literary analysis or historical investigation, and so must be left to the domains of informed speculation and personal faith.

Our thesis in this article is that—in addition to personal remembrances, eye-witness reports, the communal memory of the early church, and the work of God's Spirit in the retention and interpretation of all these recollections about Jesus of Nazareth—it needs also to be recognized that there circulated within the early Christian communities various christological materials, both written and oral, which brought much of that earlier testimony together and were used by the writers of the New Testament in their portrayals and presentations. Four such bodies of material we want to highlight here: (1) passion narratives and reports, (2) an eschatological tractate and traditions, (3) a Logia or Sayings collection, and (4) confessional portions—with, undoubtedly, other related materials also existing within the early Christian communities.

1. Passion Narratives and Reports

An emphasis on the death of Jesus on a cross is prominent throughout the New Testament and a major feature in all of its various strands and strata. A number of early Christian hymns and confessions quoted in the New Testament attest to the centrality of Jesus' death on a cross in early Christian thought—as, for example, the reference to Christ being "obedient unto death, even death on a cross" in Phil 2:8, which serves as the focal point of the hymn of 2:6-11; and the statement "Christ died for our sins" in 1 Cor 15:3b, which stands at the head of the material quoted in 15:3b-5 and is buttressed by the affirmation that this was "according to the Scriptures" (cf. also such portions as quoted in Gal 3:13; Rom 3:25; and Col 1:20). And Paul repeatedly declares that the focus of his preaching in his mission to Gentiles was "the cross" and "Christ crucified" (e.g., 1 Cor 1:17-18, 23; 2:2; Gal 3:1).

Further, while the canonical Gospels must certainly be seen as more than just "passion narratives with extended introductions," as Martin Kähler once called them (cf. his *The So-Called Historical Jesus and the Historic, Biblical Christ*, trans. C. E. Braaten [Philadelphia:

Fortress, 1964; 1st German ed., 1892], 80 n. 11), there can be no doubt that Jesus' death on a cross is a major emphasis of all four of the canonical evangelists. Its depiction, in fact, constitutes the climax of each of their Gospels. About fifteen percent of the total amount of material in the four New Testament Gospels is made up of passion narratives. So prominent was Jesus' death on a cross in the consciousness of the early Christians that at many places in the New Testament the terms "death" and "cross" appear as metonymies for all that Christ did in accomplishing human redemption.

Such a focus of concern and frequency of emphasis have raised a number of critical questions. Three, in particular, call for consideration here: (1) What was the rationale for emphasizing Jesus' death on a cross?, (2) Was there a connected passion narrative (or narratives) within the early church?, and (3) In what context (or contexts) were these early passion materials formed and used?

What was the Rationale for Emphasizing Jesus' Death on the Cross?
Ultimately, of course, the rationale for the death of Jesus on a cross is rooted in the sovereign will and purposes of God—which are matters that I must leave to the realm of mystery and the greater expertise of theologians. Historically, however, the rationale for Jesus' death on a cross among the earliest Jewish believers in Jesus seems to have been, largely, apologetically and biblically based.

The greatest problem that faced Jews who believed in Jesus as God's Messiah was the declaration of Deut 21:23: "Anyone who is hung on a tree is under God's curse." The statement originally had reference to the exposure of a criminal executed for a capital offense, whose lifeless body was to be hung on a tree for public ridicule. But it came to be understood among Jews as referring also to the impalement or crucifixion of a living person on a pole or cross (with, of course, the pole or cross viewed as parts of a tree). Paul reflects the general Jewish repugnance of the idea of a crucified Messiah when he speaks in Gal 5:11 and 1 Cor 1:23 of the "scandal" of Christ having been put to death by crucifixion on a cross.

The earliest believers in Jesus, however, seem to have resolved this problem of a crucified Messiah by viewing God's curse of Christ on the cross as his sharing humanity's curse—that is, as an "interchange" wherein Christ participated in our life and bore God's judgment on sin in order that we might participate in his life and death (i.e., his "active" and "passive" obedience) and thereby receive righteousness before God. Morna Hooker has aptly and amply explicated this New Testament understanding (see her "Interchange in Christ," *JTS* 22 [1971] 349-61; *idem*, "Interchange and Atonement," *BJRL* 60 [1976] 462-81; *idem*, "Interchange and Suffering," in *Suffering and Martyrdom in the New Testament*, ed. W. Horbury and B. McNeil [Cambridge: Cambridge University Press, 1981], 70-83; *idem*, "Interchange in Christ and Ethics," *JSNT* 25 [1985] 3-17; cf. also K. Berger's use of the expression *ein Tauschgeschäft* in "Abraham in der paulinischen Hauptbriefen," *MTZ* 17 [1966] 52). In what is probably an early Christian confessional portion, Gal 4:4-5, for example, speaks of God's Son as having been "born under the law" so that he could redeem those who are under the law and make them God's sons and daughters. Thus Christ's death on a cross was interpreted as being not punitive but redemptive (cf. Gal 3:13; see also 2 Cor 5:21).

In addition, early Jewish believers in Jesus looked to their sacred Scriptures, that is, to what Christians later called the Old Testament, for biblical justification for the death of Jesus on a cross. C. H. Dodd has shown how certain *testimonia* passages drawn from the Old Testament—particularly Isa 52:13–53:12, Psalm 22, and Zechariah 9–14—served as an apology for Jesus' passion and provided the substructure for all of early Christian theology (*According to the Scriptures*, esp. 72, 92-93, 127).

Joachim Jeremias and Christian Maurer have also noted the many allusions to Isa 52:13–53:12 in the passion narratives of the Gospels and argued that the figure of the suffering Servant depicted in Isaiah was applied by the early Christians to Jesus (cf. J. Jeremias, "παῖς θεοῦ," *TDNT*, 5.700-12; C. Maurer, "Knecht Gottes und Sohn Gottes," "Knecht Gottes und Sohn Gottes in Passionsbericht des Markusevangeliums," *ZTK* 50 [1953] 1-38). And Barnabas Lindars, while recognizing that the focus of early Christian proclamation was on the resurrection (as he does in his second chapter), has insisted that it was impossible to speak of the resurrection of Jesus without attaching, as well, some positive significance to his death (*New Testament Apologetic: The Doctrinal Significance of the Old Testament Quotations* [London: SCM; Philadelphia: Westminster, 1961], 75). So he set out what he called the "passion apologetic" of the early church (as he does in his third chapter), laying particular emphasis on allusions to Isaiah 53, quotations from the "Passion Psalms" (i.e.,

Psalms 22, 31, 34, 41, 69 and 109), and references to Zechariah 9–14 that can be found in the passion narratives of the canonical Gospels (*ibid.* 75-137).

The exact nature of the passion apologetic found in the four Gospels of the New Testament can be legitimately debated. Morna Hooker is quite right to point out the precariousness of building too much on allusions to the Isaian Servant passages in the canonical passion narratives and to object to differentiating too sharply between the Servant of the Lord and known figures of messianic expectation in Second Temple Judaism (cf. *Jesus and the Servant* [London: SPCK, 1959]; see also her *The Son of Man in Mark* [London: SPCK; Montreal: McGill University Press, 1967]). And Douglas Moo has done scholarship a service in clarifying many matters regarding the use of Scripture in Judaism and early Christianity, highlighting the "remarkably unified interpretation" of the Old Testament passages used by the evangelists in their passion narratives, and directing us back to the teaching of Jesus himself for an ultimate explanation of the interpretations found in those passion narratives (cf. *The Old Testament in the Gospel Passion Narratives* [Sheffield: Almond, 1983]). But that passion materials of some type existed before the writing of our New Testament—and, further, that their formulations were motivated in large part by apologetic and biblical concerns—seems to be an axiom that deserves credence.

Was There a Connected Passion Narrative (or Narratives) within the Early Church?
Accepting the presence of passion materials within the early church, the further question arises: Was there a connected passion narrative (or narratives) within the early church?

Resemblances between the Synoptic Gospels and the Fourth Gospel in their portrayals of Jesus' final week in Jerusalem are impressive. One might have expected a certain similarity among the three synoptic evangelists, for their portrayals of Jesus' ministry before that final week are similar. But the fourth evangelist's passion narrative is also remarkably similar to those of the other three—even though his earlier portrayal of Jesus' pre-passion ministry is in many ways quite different from theirs. In fact, of the approximately six percent of material in John's Gospel that can be paralleled with the Synoptic Gospels, almost all of it occurs in the fourth evangelist's account of

5. Christological Materials 95

Jesus' sufferings and death in Jerusalem. And it is this coming together of the four Gospels in their respective passion narratives that has often suggested to interpreters that all four of the evangelists were drawing on either an earlier stereotyped oral tradition or an earlier connected written account in their portrayals of Jesus' passion—or, perhaps, on earlier connected accounts, whether oral or written, that overlapped extensively.

Likewise it needs to be noted that, while there are somewhat differing traditions regarding Jesus' pre-passion ministry reflected in the Synoptic Gospels and John's Gospel, there are a number of rather surprising verbal agreements and parallels of content between the synoptic evangelists and the fourth evangelist in their passion narratives—all of which suggest something of a common tradition or similar source materials being used by all four evangelists. For example, both Mark and John (though not Matthew or Luke) agree on such relatively minor linguistic matters as (1) Jesus being anointed with "pure nard" (Mark 14:3; John 12:3), (2) the "300 denarii" (Mark 14:5; John 12:5), (3) Peter going "into" the courtyard of the high priest (Mark 14:54; John 18:15), (4) Peter "warming" himself at the fire in the high priest's courtyard (Mark 14:54, 67; John 18:18, 25), (5) the cry "crucify him" in the imperative (Mark 15:14; John 19:15), and (6) the mention of the "Day of Preparation" (Mark 15:42; John 19:31). And both Luke and John (though not Matthew or Mark) include material regarding (1) Joseph of Arimathea taking Jesus' body down from the cross, wrapping it in linen cloth, and burying it in a new tomb (Luke 23:53; John 19:41), and (2) the risen Jesus appearing to his disciples in Jerusalem, where he taught and commissioned them (Luke 24:36-49; John 20:19-29)—the latter passage in Luke's Gospel being frequently referred to as "a bolt out of the Johannine sky."

Agreements and disagreements between the passion narratives of the four Gospels have been set out rather generally by Joachim Jeremias in his *Eucharistic Words of Jesus* (see pages 89-96). On the basis of his observations, Jeremias has posited a four-stage development of the Passion Narrative: (1) an early kerygmatic confession, as now appears in 1 Cor 15:3b-5; (2) a "short account," which began with the arrest of Jesus, (3) a "long account," which included "the triumphal entry, the cleansing of the temple, the question about Jesus' authority, the Last Supper with the announcement of betrayal, Gethsemane, arrest of Jesus, trial before the Sanhedrin, denial of Peter, the condemnation by Pilate, the crucifixion, the empty grave"; and (4) expansions of the then existing narrative "by the addition of particular incidents and blocks of traditional material into the forms which we now have in the four gospels" (*ibid.*, 96). In a sentence that concludes the scenario as set out above, Jeremias added the following caveat: "It goes without saying that these four stages are only milestones in a much more colourful and complicated development" (*ibid.*).

There has been a rather general consensus among scholars (1) that some sort of connected passion narrative existed within the early church, and (2) that this connected passion narrative became one of the chief sources for the writing of our Synoptic Gospels and Fourth Gospel. In 1970, for example, Raymond Brown, expressing what he believed to be a "centrist" view of the matter, stated:

> Critical scholars of diverse tendencies (Bultmann, Jeremias, and Taylor, to name a few) agree that the Marcan Passion Narrative is composite and that one of Mark's chief sources was an earlier consecutive account of the passion" (*The Gospel according to John* [Garden City, NY: Doubleday, 1970], 787 and 789).

And Brown went on to say that this "earlier consecutive account of the passion" was not only the basic source for the passion accounts of the three synoptic evangelists but also the primary source for the passion account of the fourth evangelist (*ibid.*).

Several studies since the early 1970s, however, have tended to cast doubt on the hypothesis of a connected passion narrative that all of the canonical evangelists used in writing their Gospels. Eta Linnemann, for example, argued that we must distinguish between "independent reports" (*Berichte*) and a "connected account" (*Erzählung*), and concluded from her analysis of the passion narratives that the four evangelists worked from a collection of "independent reports" rather than a "connected account" (*Studien zur Passionsgeschichte* [Göttingen: Vandenhoeck & Ruprecht, 1970). Ludgar Schenke highlighted the need for scholars to distinguish more carefully between tradition and redaction in the evangelists' passion portrayals (*Der Passionsbericht nach Markus* [Gütersloh: Mohn, 1974]; see also his *Der gekreuzigte Christus* [Stuttgart: Katholisches Bibelwerk, 1974], which builds on his earlier, more extensive *Auferstehungsverkündigung und leeres Grab* [Stuttgart: Katholisches Bibelwerk, 1969]). Detlev Dormeyer developed a "redactional vocabulary" for the passion narratives of the Gospels by studying statistical relationships between the terms used in them and terms used elsewhere in early tradition and the evangelists' pre-passion portrayals, and so proposed a more exact linguistic method for distinguishing between tradition and redaction (cf. his *Die Passion Jesu als Verhaltensmodell* [Münster: Aschendorff, 1974]). And many recent studies of the passion narratives have followed the lead of these scholars.

The problem, of course, is how to evaluate relations between tradition and redaction in the canonical passion narratives. Distinctive redactional features in the four individual portrayals seem to negate the view that they are to be understood as simply the product of a stereotyped oral tradition—or, as "the Papias tradition" has often been understood, simply the preaching of Peter, which was recorded verbatim by Mark and then followed by Matthew and Luke (perhaps also John). Yet agreements (or, at least, resemblances) between the passion accounts of the four evangelists, which are extensive and often quite precise, provide a solid foundation for postulating that some form (or forms) of a connected passion narrative (or narratives) existed within the early Christian communities and that it was used by the evangelists in their accounts of Jesus' final ministry in Jerusalem and death on a cross.

It may be (1) that there existed more than one form or version of the passion narrative, as well as various other passion reports, among the early Christians—with each of those narratives possessing a certain "sense of center," but also being somewhat different (as seems to be the case for the portrayals of Jesus' pre-passion ministry given by Mark, Matthew and Luke vis-à-vis that presented by John)—and (2) that the synoptic evangelists depended heavily on one of these forms and the fourth evangelist on another, though with all four knowing of other materials as well. It is some such thesis that I myself believe the evidence suggests.

We may never, however, be able to spell out the exact nature of the passion materials that were extant among the earliest believers in Jesus. Nonetheless, we can still feel confident in assuming that the New Testament authors had various source materials at their disposal, which circulated within the Christian communities of their day, and that one important set of such materials was made up of (1) a connected passion narrative or narratives, and, perhaps, (2) various other individual passion reports.

In What Context (or Contexts) were These Passion Materials Formed and First Used?

The earliest Christians viewed themselves as (1) witnesses to the resurrection of Jesus (cf. Acts 1:22b) and (2) proclaimers of all that that most startling event in human history involved (cf. Acts 2:24-36; 3:13-15; 4:2, 10-11, 33; 5:30-32, 40-41; 13:30-37; 17:18, 31b-32; 23:6; 24:21; see also 1 Corinthians 15). But "one of the first tasks which the Church had to undertake in defence of its claims," as Barnabas Lindars has pointed out, "was to explain the suffering and death of Jesus the Messiah" (*New Testament Apologetic*, 75).

Where did the early believers look for such a passion apologetic? Obviously, they turned to their ancient Scriptures. But their understanding of their sacred Scriptures had been revolutionized by the ministry and teaching of Jesus. So, as Lindars went on to argue, (1) while actual quotations from Isaiah 53 are not numerous in the New Testament, "allusions to it are embedded so deeply in the work of all the principal [New Testament] writers that it is certain that it belongs to the earliest thought of the primitive Church" (*ibid.* 77; though for better nuancing, see Hooker, *Jesus and the Servant*), and (2) while Jesus is not recorded as having used the Isaian title Servant of the Lord with reference to himself, "the enigmatic Son of Man seems to include this idea in certain contexts (*ibid.*, 78; though for a better explication of Son of Man imagery, see Hooker, *Son of Man in Mark*). And thus as Lindars concludes:

> [Jesus'] instruction to the disciples about his coming Passion is likely to have made use of this prophecy [i.e., generally Isaiah 53, but more particularly "the enigmatic Son of Man" imagery] at least sufficiently to give it a secure place in their thought. When a Passion apologetic was required, it was there ready-made in the teaching which they had received (*New Testament Apologetic*, 78).

Such a passion apologetic would have been necessary for both (1) those within the early Christian communities, in affirmation of their new self-identity, and (2) those outside the Christian communities, in proclamation to them of the "good news" of the gospel—which would necessarily have included a biblically based apologetic that was calculated to overcome their obstacles to belief. We may, therefore, rather confidently assume that the early passion narrative(s) and reports—which were developed within the early Christian communities and used by the canonical evangelists in their respective passion

5. *Christological Materials* 99

narratives—were formed in the contexts of (1) the affirmation of believers, who needed support for their new self-identity and understanding, and (2) the proclamation of Jesus' resurrection, ministry and person to non-believers, who required a biblical apologetic for the death of Jesus on a cross.

2. *An Eschatological Tractate and Traditions*

Another set of materials that evidently circulated among the earliest believers in Jesus—which materials, it seems, were used by the writers of the New Testament in their christological presentations—has to do with futuristic eschatology. These materials come to focus particularly in the Olivet Discourse of Mark 13, Matthew 24–25 and Luke 21.

Critical questions regarding the Olivet Discourse and its auxiliary eschatological traditions are legion, with hardly any passage in the New Testament more controversial than this one. Only three matters of a source-critical and tradition-critical nature, however, are directly relevant to our purposes here—with these three questions being somewhat parallel to those three asked earlier regarding the passion narrative(s) and passion reports: (1) What was the rationale for these eschatological materials?, (2) Was there a connected Olivet Discourse circulating within the early church?, and (3) In what context (or contexts) were these early eschatological materials formed and first used?

What was the Rationale for These Eschatological Materials?
There is no doubt that the New Testament lays heavy emphasis on "realized eschatology"—that is, on the eschatological age of redemption as having dawned or been "inaugurated" in the ministry and person of Jesus of Nazareth. This is declared quite straightforwardly in an early Christian confession incorporated by Paul in Gal 4:4-5, which begins with the declaration: "When the time had fully come, God sent his Son," and ends with the affirmation: "in order that we might receive the full rights of sons" (or, "adoption as God's children"). But realized eschatology is not the whole story. "Futuristic eschatology" also has an important place in all of the portrayals and presentations of the New Testament.

C. H. Dodd, even while emphasizing realized eschatology, has shown how the catechetical tradition of the early church (as reflected in the New Testament) included not only "theological dogmas" and "ethical precepts" but also a number of futurist statements given as "eschatological motives," with these eschatological motivational materials tending "to gravitate to the close of the *catechesis*" (cf. "The 'Primitive Catechism' and the Sayings of Jesus" [1968, which is a "partly re-written, with additional matter" version of his 1959 article], esp. 11-14 and 18-24). Included in these eschatological hortatory materials are such matters as (1) warnings about future false christs and false prophets (cf. Matt 7:22ff.; 1 Thess 5:3; 2 Thess 2:2ff.; 1 Tim 4:1ff.; 2 Tim 4:1ff.; 2 Pet 3:3ff.; Rev 13; 16:12ff.; 17:1ff.); (2) references to future persecutions and sufferings of God's people (1 Thess 1:6; 3:1-4; 2 Thess 1:4-7; 1 Pet 4:12-19; Rev 11:3-13; 13:11-13); (3) statements about future judgments on Jerusalem and its people (Matt 23:34-36; Luke 11:49-51; 13:1-5; 19:41-44; 23:27-31; 1 Thess 2:16; 2 Thess 2:4ff.); and (4) calls to watchfulness in the light of Christ's near but incalculable parousia (1 Thess 5:1-11; 2 Thess 1:5; 1 Pet 1:13; 4:7; 5:8; Rev 3:2ff.; 16:15). And it is just such futuristic and hortatory statements that appear in the Olivet Discourse.

The basic rationale for these eschatological materials in the early church was not to spell out some sort of eschatological timetable, as can be found in the writings of various apocalyptic authors of Second Temple Judaism. Rather, it was to call believers in Jesus to discernment and watchfulness in the midst of adverse situations (cf. Hooker's emphasis on Mark 13 as being both prophetic in content and apocalyptic in form, or as "prophetic-apocalyptic," in *Son of Man in Mark*; idem, "Trial and Tribulation in Mark XIII," *BJRL* 65 [1982] 78-99; see also G. E. Ladd's earlier article, "Why Not Prophetic-Apocalyptic?" *JBL* 76 [1957] 192-200). Futuristic eschatology in these passages functions much as it does in the Old Testament—that is, as a prophetic summons to a seriousness of purpose, a life lived in holiness and justice, and a watchful expectation that awaits God's future actions. The only real difference in the New Testament eschatological passages is that the prophetic call is christologically oriented, with a focus on the parousia or "coming" of Christ.

Was There a Connected Olivet Discourse Within the Early Church?
Scholarly study of the Olivet Discourse over the past couple centuries has been both extensive and intensive. During the last half century, however, there have been a number of important source-critical and

tradition-critical treatments of this eschatological unit of material. Notable among the more recent treatments has been that of George Beasley-Murray, who in 1954 (and continuing on through 1993) has done scholarship a service in charting the course of the debate and critiquing various arguments used to deny the discourse to Jesus (cf. his *Jesus and the Last Days: The Interpretation of the Olivet Discourse* [Peabody: Hendrickson, 1993], which incorporates in revised form his earlier *Jesus and the Future* [London: Macmillan, 1954] and his *A Commentary on Mark Thirteen* [London: Macmillan, 1957]).

Significant critical studies of the Olivet Discourse have also been produced by Lars Hartman, who in 1966 noted that the Olivet Discourse may appropriately be identified as a midrash on the book of Daniel (cf. his *Prophecy Interpreted: The Formation of Some Jewish Apocalyptic Texts and of the Eschatological Discourse Mark 13 par.* [Uppsala: Gleerup, 1966]), though he did not pay much attention to its parabolic and hortatory materials, and Jacques Dupont, who from 1968 through 1978 explicated a number of the source-critical and tradition-critical issues of pertinence to the discourse's parables and exhortations (cf. his "La parabole du figuier qui bourgeonne [Mc, XIII, 28-29]," *RB* 75 [1968] 526-48; "La parabole du maître qui rentre dans la nuit [Mc 13, 34-36]," in *Mélanges Béda Rigaux* [Gembloux: Duculot, 1970], 89-116; "La ruine du temple et la fin des temps dans de discours de Marc 13," in *Apocalypses et théologie de l'espérance*, ed. L. Monloubou [Paris: Cerf, 1977], 207-69; and "La persécution comme situation missionnaire [Marc 13, 9-11]," in *Die Kirche des Anfangs: Festschrift für H. Schürmann* [Freiburg: Herder, 1978], 97-114). Likewise of significance are the treatments of Desmond Ford, who in 1979 investigated the origin and significance of the expression "the abomination of desolation" in Mark 13:14 and Matt 24:15 and spelled out its relation to similar references in 1 and 2 Thessalonians and the Johannine Apocalypse (*The Abomination of Desolation in Biblical Eschatology* [Washington: University Press of America, 1979]), and David Wenham, who in 1984 argued that the Olivet Discourse reflects "an elaborate and substantial pre-synoptic tradition," which, as the title of his book suggests (*The Rediscovery of Jesus' Eschatological Discourse* [Sheffield: JSOT, 1984]), must be seen to have been ultimately rooted in the circumstances and teaching of Jesus himself.

There have also been a number of important exegetical and redaction-critical studies of the Olivet Discourse in various commentaries on the Synoptic Gospels, as well as significant comments in various interpretive treatments of the Thessalonian letters and the Johannine Apocalypse. On the source-critical and tradition-critical issues that are involved, however, the works by Beasley-Murray, Hartman, Dupont, Ford, and Wenham have, each in its own way, been high points in the contemporary discussion. And what has seemed most significant to the majority of source-critical and tradition-critical scholars in answering the question "Was there a connected Olivet Discourse within the early church?" is the fact that the contents of the discourse are attested widely and at various places in the New Testament—not only in the Synoptic Gospels, but also in 1 and 2 Thessalonians and the Johannine Apocalypse.

Assuming Markan priority, Matthew 24 follows Mark 13 more closely than does Luke 21. The differences in the accounts may only be redactional in nature. It may be, however, that one tradition of the discourse lies behind Mark and Matthew and another tradition lies behind Luke—or, perhaps, separate traditions are to be seen as lying behind all three Gospels. Nonetheless, the three presentations of the three synoptic evangelists are in substantial agreement, and that agreement suggests that there existed within the early church an eschatological body of teaching.

Likewise, similarities between Paul's words in 1 and 2 Thessalonians about what is to precede the End and the evangelists' statements regarding the same in the Olivet Discourse are considerable, and suggest that their traditions must in some way be related. Admittedly, verbal similarities—such as the use of θροεῖσθαι, "to be disturbed" or "frightened" (2 Thess 2:2; cf. Mark 13:7; Matt 24:6) and σημεῖα καὶ τέρατα, "signs and wonders" (2 Thess 2:9; cf. Mark 13:22; Matt 24:24); also the expressions ὁ ἄνθρωπος τῆς ἀνομίας, "the man of lawlessness," and ὁ υἱὸς τῆς ἀπωλείας, "the son of destruction" (2 Thess 2:3), which have frequently been seen as synonymous with τὸ βδέλυγμα τῆς ἐρημώσεως, "the abomination of desolation" (Mark 13:14; Matt 24:15)—are, of themselves, rather slight and may be variously ascribed. But the parallels of ideas and structure are strong, with such parallelism being especially evident when comparing 2 Thess 2:1-12 with the first part of the Olivet Discourse in Mark 13:5-22. Further, the portraits of the varied manifestations of the Antichrist in Revelation 11, 13, 14, 16, 17 and 20 embody many of the characteristic features found in Daniel, the Olivet Discourse of the Synoptic Gospels (esp. Mark 13), and Paul's Thessalonian letters (esp. 2 Thessalonians 2).

This phenomenon of multiple attestation certainly points to a source or sources within the early Christian community on which the three synoptic evangelists, Paul (and/or his followers), and John the Seer drew. In its earliest form that source (or sources) was undoubtedly oral, with Jesus' teaching about the End having made a deep impression on his disciples, and so retained in their memory and often repeated. A written account (or accounts), however, probably also came about at an early time in the church's existence. For not only would the early believers in Jesus, when facing persecution, have wanted a more tangible record on which they could rely, but also would have desired to preserve in rather fixed form Jesus' teaching that was foundational for their new eschatological existence and orientation. So it may be assumed that they cherished not only accounts about Jesus' passion and resurrection, but also records about what he taught with regard to his coming parousia.

In What Context (or Contexts) were These Eschatological Materials Formed and First Used?
It is impossible to read the Olivet Discourse in the Synoptic Gospels without being impressed by both (1) the remarkable similarities between the three accounts and (2) the different inclusions, recastings, and emphases of each of the evangelists. Nor is it possible to read the related eschatological materials of the Thessalonians letters and the Johannine Apocalypse without being impressed by both commonalities and differences.

The basic interpretive features of the Olivet Discourse suggest a highly creative mind as its originator. The church's witness is that it was Jesus who first interpreted Daniel and the other Old Testament prophets in such a way as to produce the distinctive elements of early Christian eschatology. C. H. Dodd once pertinently observed:

> Creative thinking is rarely done by committees, useful as they may be for systematizing the fresh ideas of individual thinkers, and for stimulating them to further thought. It is individual minds that originate (*According to the Scriptures*, 109-10).

And he concluded his observation in words that cannot be improved on:

> To account for the beginning of this most original and fruitful process of rethinking the Old Testament we found need to postulate a creative mind. The Gospels offer us one. Are we compelled to reject the offer? (*ibid.*, 110).

On the one hand, therefore, we are compelled to affirm in the words of Bruce Vawter:

> That Jesus actually made such a prophecy, in view of his consistent eschatological teaching on the soonness of a divine visitation on Jerusalem and Judea, his conviction of the decisiveness of his own role in the workings of salvation history, and his reading of the temper of the times, there is absolutely no reason to question. His words are in the tradition of Israel's prophecy (cf. Jer. 7:1-15; Ezek. 24:15-23) and have not been simply made up by Christian writers in the light of later events (*The Four Gospels*. Dublin: 1967, 322).

On the other hand, however, it needs also to be recognized that the early church went beyond merely remembering Jesus' words and creatively applied his teaching in the Olivet Discourse to its own circumstances in various ways.

One particularly illuminating observation, which has often been made, is that the Olivet Discourse in all three of its versions in the Synoptic Gospels forms both a conclusion to the teaching ministry of Jesus and an introduction to the evangelists' passion narratives. So it seems proper to believe that the Olivet Discourse, together with various other auxiliary traditions, were used by the early church in contexts having to do with both catechetical instruction and evangelistic proclamation.

3. A Logia or Sayings Collection

A third set of materials that seems to have circulated within the early Christian communities, and which appears to have been used by the authors of the New Testament in their various christological presentations, is a collection of Logia (i.e., "words") or Sayings of Jesus—material that has been designated "Q" (from the German word "Quelle," which means simply "source"). This is a collection of sayings of Jesus that has been compiled by scholars in one of three ways: (1) from the verbatim or near-verbatim sayings that appear in about one-sixth of Matthew's Gospel and one-sixth of Luke's Gospel, but not in Mark—that is, the so-called "double tradition" (which is a "minimalist" definition of "Q"), or (2) from such verbal agreements in the double tradition *plus* other sayings in Matthew and Luke that display a general agreement of sense to those with explicit verbal agreements (which is the "generally accepted" definition of "Q"), or (3) from both the verbal and the general agreements in the double tradition *plus* a few sayings that appear in "the triple tradition," which would include some that appear in Mark, or that are included only by Matthew or only by Luke—assuming that for some reason the other Gospel omitted them (which is a "maximalist" definition of "Q").

The contents of such a postulated "Q" or Sayings source are usually estimated to have been about 220-235 verses, depending on whether it is reconstructed according to a "minimalist," "generally accepted," or "maximalist" definition. Most scholars, however, acknowledge that such a source may have been larger than any of our contemporary reconstructions of it. For the evangelists Matthew and Luke, who seem to have independently omitted a few passages found in their principal narrative source, that is in Mark's Gospel, may also have independently omitted some of the material that appeared in their Sayings source, that is in the Logia or "Q".

There are, of course, all sorts of critical issues that could be raised regarding such a hypothetical Sayings source. Four questions, however, are directly relevant to our purposes here: (1) Were teachings of Jesus preserved by his early followers?, (2) Was there a Logia or Sayings collection that circulated among Christians prior to the writing of our canonical New Testament?, (3) What was the nature of this postulated Sayings collection?, and (4) In what context (or contexts) was this Sayings collection formed and first used?

Were Teachings of Jesus Preserved by His Early Followers?
It can hardly be doubted that the teachings of Jesus were preserved in some form by his early followers. Jews during the periods of Second Temple Judaism (c. 200 BCE–120 CE) and early Rabbinic Judaism (c. 120–500 CE) commonly preserved teachings of their rabbis. This is what the Mishnah and Babylonian Gemaras (i.e., the Talmud) are all about, as well as tangent materials found in the Tosephta ("the Additions"), the Palestinian Gemaras, and many of the Midrashim. It may also be the basis for many of the central writings of the Dead Sea Scrolls—in particular, the *Thanksgiving Psalms* or *Hodayot*, which are

preserved in two copies from cave 1 (i.e., *1QH*ᵃ and *1QH*ᵇ) and six copies from cave 4 (i.e., 4Q427–432), and the *pesher* commentaries on such biblical books as Genesis (*4QpGen*), Isaiah (*4QpIsa*), Hosea (*4QpHos*), Nahum (*4QpNah*), and the Psalms (*4QPs*), most of which appear in multiple copies. Many scholars, in fact, posit that the *Hodayot* and *pesher* commentaries at Qumran stemmed, at least ultimately, from the "Teacher of Righteousness" himself (whoever he was).

Paul's letters evidence a lively retention of the teachings of Jesus among the early Christians. In 1 Thess 4:1-12, for example, when giving ethical instruction to his Gentile converts at Thessalonica, Paul speaks in words that sound very much like the ethical teaching of Jesus as later recorded in the Synoptic Gospels. In 1 Thess 4:13–5:11 he speaks about the future coming of Jesus using expressions that are reminiscent of many of Jesus' eschatological statements, as also later recorded in the Synoptic Gospels—once even, in 1 Thess 4:15-17, including a further "word of the Lord," which evidently here means a teaching of Jesus that was known to Paul (and, presumably, to many in the early church) but was not incorporated by the canonical evangelists into their writings (i.e., an *agraphon* or "unwritten saying"). And in 2 Thess 2:1-12, as we noted above, there are significant parallels of ideas and structure with the first part of the Olivet Discourse as later recorded in Mark 13:5-22.

Further, in 1 Cor 7:10, when speaking about marriage to his Gentile converts at Corinth, Paul gives the general Christian maxim that "a wife should not separate from her husband"—which, he insists, is not just his opinion (cf. v 12), but a command that stems from the Lord Jesus: "I give this command, not I but the Lord" (παραγγέλλω, οὐκ ἐγὼ ἀλλὰ ὁ κύριος). In 1 Cor 9:14, when speaking about the right of Christian apostles to receive remuneration, he cites a teaching of Jesus: "In the same way, the Lord commanded (οὕτως καὶ ὁ κύριος διέταξεν) that those who preach the gospel should receive their living from the gospel." And throughout the ethical exhortations of Rom 12:1–15:13 there appear numerous reminiscences of Jesus' teaching.

Matthew and Luke also testify to a lively interest in the preservation of Jesus' teachings within the early church, for one-sixth of each of their Gospels is given over to sayings of Jesus that go beyond what appears in Mark—in addition, of course, to the Olivet Discourse, which appears in all three Gospels, and a few other sayings that

Matthew and Luke share with Mark. Likewise, the *Gospel of Thomas* and the *Gospel of Philip*, which are collections of Jesus' sayings found at the site of Nag Hammadi (or, at Chenoboskin, as the village was called earlier) in Egypt, evidence a continuing interest in Jesus' teachings among certain sectarian Christians of the second century. There has, of course, been extensive debate regarding the dating of these Nag Hammadi "Gospels" and their relation to the canonical Gospels. But however these matters are finally resolved, it should at least be noted that both sets of Gospels—whether canonical or sectarian—highlight the fact of an interest among early Christians in the preservation of Jesus' teachings.

The statement of Eusebius (c. 260–339), who was bishop of Caesarea and an eminent church historian, regarding Papias of Hierapolis (who flourished about 130 CE), whom Eusebius identified as "John's hearer" (whether John the disciple or John the Elder, if, indeed, they are to be distinguished) and "an associate of Polycarp," offer further testimony to a continuing interest in Jesus' teaching within the early church. For Eusebius says that Papias was the author of "five books" entitled *Expositions of the Logia* (i.e., 'Sayings', 'Declarations', or 'Oracles') *of the Lord*, which volumes, Eusebius says, existed in his day (*Ecclesiastical History* 3.39.1)—though, sadly, they evidently became extinct sometime after Eusebius wrote in the first part of the fourth century.

Was There a Sayings Collection that Circulated Among Early Christians?
Given that early believers in Jesus preserved in some fashion the teachings of their Lord, the question, however, still persists: Was there a Logia or Sayings collection that circulated among early Christians prior to the writing of our canonical New Testament? All that can really be said to such a query is that the New Testament writers themselves seem to suggest such a collection as then existing within the early Christian communities—whether written or transmitted orally—and that such an hypothesis makes sense historically.

The major evidence in favor of an early Sayings collection stems from the study of literary relations between the three Synoptic Gospels. Most Christians up through the nineteenth century generally assumed some sort of primitive oral gospel, which circulated among the early Christians and was used by the four evangelists in the writing of their respective Gospels. In the nineteenth century, however, attention was focused on the remarkable parallels of language and structure between the Synoptic Gospels, as well as on their distinctive differences, and explanations for the composition of these Gospels were proposed in terms of literary interdependence and the sources that they used. Thus there developed a twofold explanation of, first, the common *narrative* of the Synoptic Gospels (i.e., "the triple tradition") and then of the extensive number of verbatim and near-verbatim *sayings* of Jesus that appear in Matthew and Luke, but not in Mark (i.e., "the double tradition"): (1) that for the common narrative material, Mark's Gospel was not only "medial" (so Karl Lachmann in 1835) but also "prior" (so C. H. Weisse in 1838), and (2) that for the many sayings found in Matthew and Luke but not in Mark, we must postulate a Sayings source (so H. J. Holtzmann in 1863), which can be designated "Q" (so Johannes Weiss in 1890).

These literary analyses and conclusions were first undertaken and drawn up by liberal scholars, and so many conservative Christians have viewed them with suspicion. But the hypothesis of an early Sayings collection, whether written or orally stereotyped, has become accepted by most conservative New Testament scholars as well. For as Raymond Brown concisely puts it (assuming, of course, the basic validity of the "Two Source Theory"), "the existence of Q ... remains the best way of explaining the agreements between Matt and Luke in material they did not borrow from Mark" (*An Introduction to the New Testament* [New York: Doubleday, 1997], 122).

The hypothesis of an early Sayings collection is further supported by Paul's repeated distinctions in 1 Corinthians between what Jesus commanded and his own statements as an apostle. These distinctions are most evident in 7:10 ("I give this command, not I but the Lord") and 9:14 ("in the same way, the Lord commanded"), where Paul quotes in an *ad sensum* manner the teachings of Jesus on particular problems within the Corinthian church, and in 7:12 ("I say, not the Lord") and 7:25 ("I have no command of the Lord, but I give my opinion as one who by the Lord's mercy is trustworthy"), where he acknowledges that he has no express teaching of Jesus on a particular matter but tells his converts that what he is writing them is his own opinion—which, of course, he believes to be trustworthy. Such distinctions, however explained, suggest not only that Paul knew of a collection of Jesus' sayings but also that his Gentile converts at Corinth knew of such a collection as well. More to the point, they suggest that both he and they knew what that Sayings collection contained (i.e., where he quotes Jesus' teaching) and what it did not contain (i.e., where he goes beyond the recorded teaching of Jesus and attempts to contextualize the Christian gospel with respect to the problems faced by his converts).

Mention should also be made of the numerous parallels in the ethical teaching that appear particularly in Romans, 1 and 2 Thessalonians, Ephesians, 1 Peter, and James. These parallels suggest the existence of a common body of catechetical material within the early church from which their respective writers drew. To spell out these parallels and to argue for a common source would take far more time and space than the constraints of the present article allow. E. G. Selwyn has done that with respect to the parallels between 1 Peter and 1 and 2 Thessalonians, which he believed can also be found in Romans, Ephesians and James, and on the basis of his investigation has argued that they evidence "a high degree of interdependence ... on a common stock of teaching" (*The First Epistle of St Peter* [London: Macmillan, 1947], 19). His argument, in fact, is that the ethical teaching of 1 Peter—as well as that of 1 and 2 Thessalonians, Romans, Ephesians and James—builds on the *verba Christi* (i.e., "the words of Christ"), "which were collected at an early date explicitly as words of the Lord, and therefore inspired," and which "lie below the surface of the Epistle [of 1 Peter], and usually not far below it" (*ibid.*, 23; see the extensive treatments in his "Introduction," Section 3: "Sources Underlying the Epistles," 17-24, and his Essay II: "On the Inter-Relation of 1 Peter and other N.T. Epistles," 365-466).

What was the Nature of This Postulated Sayings Collection?
This postulated Sayings collection, as reconstructed from materials in the Synoptic Gospels, seems to have consisted almost entirely of sayings of Jesus and a few short parables. It probably had very little narrative material. Only three narrative portions can be claimed to have been included: one on the temptation of Jesus; another on the centurion's sick servant; a third on the disciples of John the Baptist coming to see Jesus. Its content may have been essentially what was referred to by Eusebius, quoting Papias with reference to Matthew: "Matthew compiled the Logia [i.e., the 'Sayings' or 'Oracles', which, however, the early church usually assumed to be Matthew's Gospel]

in the Hebrew language [i.e., Aramaic], and everyone interpreted [or, 'translated'] them as he was able" (*Ecclesiastical History* III.39.16). Nevertheless, most reconstructions of "Q" today follow Luke's order and use the traditional chapter and verse designations of Luke's Gospel—since Luke's version of any particular saying of Jesus is usually shorter and more terse, whereas Matthew's, while at times more Palestinian in its imagery, is often more expansive and interpretive, with most of the sayings of Jesus in Matthew's Gospel worked into larger sermonic sections of the evangelist's presentation.

There is a strong sapiential (i.e., "wisdom") tone to Q. For as reconstructed from the Synoptic Gospels, the Jesus of "the non-Markan sayings found in Matthew and Luke" is primarily a Jewish sage who taught wisdom and gave ethical instruction. This need not imply that the earliest Christian message was only ethical—without any eschatological or christological features—as those who speak of Q as a "Q Gospel" or "The First Gospel" usually assume. The Old Testament has a wide variety of content and literary genre (e.g., historical narrative, prophecy, psalms, wisdom literature), and cannot be judged on the basis of only one type of writing. Likewise, the Dead Sea Scrolls exhibit diverse materials (e.g., organizational codes, *pesher* commentaries, *testimonia* collections, Psalms of Thanksgiving, a Temple Scroll, a War Scroll, and even a Copper Scroll), as does also the later rabbinic literature (e.g., *halakah*, or "ethical rules for living," being dominant in the Mishnah, Tosephta and Gemaras, with *haggadah*, or "expositions, sermons and everything else," prominent in the Midrashim). So the early believers in Jesus seem to have possessed not only a Logia or Sayings collection, but also, as we have argued above, (1) passion narrative(s) and reports and (2) eschatological tractate(s) and traditions. And each of these bodies of material, it may be postulated, served to enhance the fullness of the gospel within the early Christian congregations.

But even if, for the sake of argument, one accepts Q as something of a "Gospel," it needs to be recognized that such a reconstructed group of sayings is not entirely devoid of either eschatology or christology. "There is," as Raymond Brown points out with respect to postulated Q, "a strongly eschatological thrust in the warnings, woes, and some of the parables" (*An Introduction to the New Testament*, 120). More pertinent for our purposes, however, are Brown's observations regarding Q's christology:

5. Christological Materials

Many would attribute to Q a low christology since in it Jesus emerges simply as a Sophist or Cynic wisdom teacher. Yet the Q Jesus is to come and baptize with the Holy Spirit, as proclaimed by JBap (3:16-17; 7:18-23). He is greater than Solomon and greater than Jonah the prophet (11:31-32). He is portrayed as the Son of Man who will come in judgment (17:23-27, 30, 37) and as the Son of Man who is rejected and suffers in his lifetime (7:31-35; 9:57-60). He is the Son to whom all has been given; he is known only by the Father, and only he knows the Father (Luke 10:22). It is insufficient simply to call Jesus Lord; one must hear his words and do them if one is to survive (6:46-49). Jerusalem must bless him (13:34-35), and one must prefer him over family (14:26-27). He can proclaim with assurance that in the kingdom those who follow him will sit on thrones, judging the twelve tribes of Israel [evidently alluding to 22:29-30]. Such a Jesus is far more than a wisdom teacher (*ibid.*, 120).

In What Context (or Contexts) was This Sayings Collection Formed and First Used?

We need not here get involved with trying to trace out stages of growth in Q. Nor need we try our hand at attempting to discern diversity among the various Christian groups where such a Sayings collection was used—nor to posit some original locality for its formation, whether at Jerusalem, Antioch, or elsewhere. These are matters reflecting a high degree of speculation and that probably depend more on a particular scholar's propensities than the data itself. They may, in fact, be no better than Papias's statement (as cited above) that "Matthew compiled the Logia [assuming 'Logia' here means 'Sayings' or 'Oracles,' and not 'Gospel'] in the Hebrew language [i.e., Aramaic], and everyone interpreted [or, 'translated'] them as he was able" (*Ecclesiastical History* III.39.16).

It is possible that some of the differences of wording between the Q sayings in Matthew and the Q sayings in Luke are attributable to variant copies of an original Sayings source. Or it may be that there were somewhat different Greek translations of an original Aramaic version—as would, of course, be inevitable among translations. This latter understanding is what seems to be suggested by Papias's statement that "everyone interpreted [or, 'translated'] them as he was able."

But however matters of provenance may eventually (if ever) be resolved, it seems necessary to postulate (1) that there existed within the early church a collection of the sayings of Jesus, (2) that this

Sayings collection was principally ethical in nature, (3) that it was first formed in catechetical and/or teaching contexts, and (4) that it was known and used widely in various Christian communities. Such a Sayings collection seems to have been known and used even in Gentile churches, such as those at Thessalonica, Corinth and Rome. In fact, to judge by statements in 1 Cor 7:10, 12, 25 and 9:14, both Paul and his Gentile converts seem to have known not only what was included in that sayings collection but also what was not included.

4. Confessional Portions

A further body of material to be highlighted here consists of what may generally be called "confessional portions," which appear to have been widely known within the early Christian communities and were incorporated by the authors of the New Testament into their writings. The verb "confess" and the noun "confession" are commonly used today in a legal sense to refer to the admission of guilt. In the New Testament, however, as well as in the church's language drawn from the New Testament, "confess" and "confession" most often signal statements of belief that express basic theological and christological convictions—with those statements taking various forms (e.g., hymns, formulaic prose, single-statement affirmations), depending on the circumstances in which they came about (e.g., worship, prayer, preaching, liturgy, teaching, catechism, apologetic discourse).

Eduard Norden's analyses of "artistic prose" in the ancient world (*Die antike Kunstprosa vom VI. Jahrhunderts vor Christus in die Zeit der Renaissance*, 2 vols. [Leipzig: Teubner, 1898; repr., 1983]) inaugurated the modern form-critical study of ancient writings. Building on his analyses, Johannes Weiss began the study of hymnodic materials in Paul's letters ("Beiträge zum paulinischer Rhetorik," in *Theologische Studien* [Festschrift B. Weiss], ed. C. R. Gregory, *et al.* [Göttingen: Vandenhoeck & Ruprecht, 1897], 165-247), Eduard von der Goltz took up the study of prayer among the earliest Christians (*Das Gebet in der ältesten Christenheit* [Leipzig: Hinrichs, 1901), Alfred Seeberg attempted to reconstruct the earliest Christian catechism (*Der Katechismus der Urchristenheit* [Leipzig: Deichert, 1903; repr. Munich: Kaiser, 1966]), and Norden himself went further to apply his own form-critical principles to further analyses of New Testament prayers and hymns (*Agnostos Theos: Untersuchungen zur Formengeschichte religöser Rede* [Leipzig:

Teubner, 1913; repr., 1956]). And throughout the twentieth century the study of early Christian confessional materials has been widely and vigorously pursued (for details, see my *New Wine into Fresh Wineskins*, ch. 1).

Discussion of these early Christian confessional materials has frequently been carried on under such rubrics as "hymns," "prayers," "formulas of faith," "catechetical teachings," "liturgical formulations," "ecclesial traditions," and/or "narrative stories"—with the transliterated Greek terms *kerygma* ("proclamation"), *paradosis* ("tradition"), *didache* ("teaching"), and *homologia* ("confession") often used as descriptive titles. But as Ethelbert Stauffer long ago observed: "Many confessions were hymn-like and many hymns were creed-like" (*New Testament Theology*, trans. J. Marsh [London: SCM, 1955], 237). Contemporary scholars tend to speak of all these materials as simply "confessions."

A number of matters having to do with these confessional materials call for both scholarly and pastoral treatment, and I have attempted to do that, at least to an extent, in my *New Wine into Fresh Wineskins* [1999]. Three questions, however, are directly relevant to our purposes here: (1) Were confessional portions circulating among the early Christian communities prior to the writing of our canonical New Testament?, (2) What was the nature of these early Christian confessions?, (3) In what context or contexts were these confessional materials formed and first used?

Were Confessional Portions Circulating Among the Early Christian Communities?
The writers of the New Testament did not use quotation marks or indentations to mark off confessional material quoted or used in their compositions. The identification of early Christian hymns (i.e., poetic portions of worship and praise) and *homologiai* (i.e., formulaic prose statements and affirmations), which have been incorporated into the New Testament, depends almost entirely on form-critical and tradition-critical analyses of the writings of the New Testament authors.

Scholars over the past century have had their own variations and refinements with respect to method. Nonetheless, despite some differences, there is widespread critical agreement with regard to the legitimacy of the following criteria for the identification of early Christian hymns:

1. The presence of parallel structures (*parallelismus membrorum*) that reflect either Jewish or Hellenistic poetic conventions, or both;

2. The presence of words and phrases not characteristic of a particular New Testament author (i.e., *hapax legomena*)—or, if appearing elsewhere in that author's writings, not with the meaning or in the manner found elsewhere in his other writings—suggesting that the material in question was probably composed by someone else;

3. A preference for participles over finite verbs, suggesting an original oral provenance for the material rather than the literary setting in which it now appears;

4. The frequent use of the relative pronoun ὅς ("who") to begin passages;

5. Contextual dislocations, which may be either poetic material breaking into a prose section or doctrinal material breaking into an ethical section, or both;

6. The continuance of a portion after its content has ceased to be relevant to its immediate context; and,

7. The affirmation of a basic Christian conviction, which usually has to do with the work or person of Jesus Christ.

Many of the form-critical criteria used to identify early Christian hymns in the New Testament are, of course, also used to identify early Christian *homologiai*. In particular, the following criteria are usually considered to be also relevant for the identification of formulaic, but non-poetic, confessional materials:

1. The presence of parallel structures (i.e., *parallelismus membrorum*) even though the material is not poetry;

2. The presence of expressions used only once in a particular author's writings (i.e., *hapax legomena*), or words or phrases not used in that manner elsewhere in that author's writings;

3. A preference for participles over finite verbs; and,

4. An affirmation regarding the work or person of Jesus Christ.

Added to this list have been such other linguistic indicators as:

5. Christological Materials

5. The appearance of the noun "confession" (ὁμολογία) to signal the content of such early Christian material, either expressed or implied;

6. The use of the verb "confess" (ὁμολογέω) with a double accusative or an infinitive to introduce a direct or an indirect quotation;

7. The use of ὅτι (the so-called *hoti recitativum*) to introduce a direct or an indirect quotation;

8. The use of verbs having to do with preaching (εὐαγγελίζω, κηρύσσω, or καταγγέλλω), teaching (διδάσκω), or witnessing (μαρτυρέω or μαρτύρομαι) to introduce confessional material; and,

9. The use of a participial construction or a relative clause to introduce the material in question.

The most obvious early Christian hymns in praise of God are those found in Rom 11:33-36 and Rev 15:3b-4. The most commonly accepted early Christian hymns extolling Christ are Phil 2:6-11, 1 Tim 3:16b, and 1 Pet 2:22-23. The most widely acknowledged *homologiai*, or formulaic prose confessional statements, are 1 Cor 15:3b-5, Rom 1:3b-4, Rom 3:24-26, Gal 3:26-28, Gal 4:4-5, and Heb 1:3. The material in Col 1:15-20 is also considered by most New Testament scholars to be an early christological hymn. It could, however, just as well be seen as a *homologia*, or formulaic prose confessional portion, for its lyrical quality and strophic structure are not readily identifiable.

We modern readers seem to have difficulty in identifying the confessional materials that have been incorporated by the New Testament authors into their writings. That is possibly because we have lost the thread of the narrative structure of early Christian proclamation. More likely, however, it is because we have never heard the hymns sung, the confessions repeated, or the affirmations made in the context of corporate worship, and so cannot recognize them when we come across them on the pages of the New Testament. Nonetheless, even though it may be possible to identify only some of these early Christian hymns, *homologiai*, and single-statement affirmations—perhaps, one might venture to say, as many as forty or fifty, with others still remaining to be identified—scholars are reasonably convinced that such materials were incorporated by the writers of the New Testament into their compositions.

What was the Nature of These Early Christian Confessions?
The hymns and formulaic prose statements that are incorporated within the New Testament appear to have been originally devotional in nature, expressing the early believers' praise to God and adoration of Christ in the context of corporate worship. This may seem hardly surprising. For confessions in the biblical sense are faith expressions, and memorable faith expressions take form most commonly in the context of corporate worship—whether that worship is planned or spontaneous.

Further, the christological confessional materials of the New Testament, as differentiated from the purely theocentric confessional materials, reflect a narrative substructure or story line in which Jesus Christ is the main character. Each confession, whether in the form of poetry or prose, narrates a portion of the story about Jesus as God's redemptive agent. We cannot, of course, say whether or not all of the addressees of the New Testament writings already knew each of the confessional portions quoted. What can be affirmed, however, is that these confessions, whether cited in whole or in part, were meant to remind readers of the basic story about Jesus—a story that they already knew and that was foundational for their new lives "in Christ."

It needs also to be noted that the early Christian hymns and formulaic prose confessional statements of the New Testament are dominantly functional—that is, that they affirm what "God in Christ" has done and is doing redemptively, rather than speculate about ontology. This functional emphasis is particularly prominent in the confessions found in Paul's earlier letters (e.g., Gal 1:4; 3:13; 4:4-5; 1 Cor 15:3b-5; Rom 3:24-26), which, as the earliest writings of the New Testament, presumably incorporate some of the earliest Christian confessional materials. Very soon, however, ontological categories that were inchoate in the earlier confessional affirmations seem also to have come to the fore (e.g., Heb 1:3; John 1:1-14).

Finally, and perhaps more obviously, it needs to be constantly kept in mind that the confessional portions that appear in the New Testament use the language and metaphors of their day in speaking about the work of Christ and its significance (e.g., to cite only the most obvious, Rom 3:24-26; Col 1:15-20; Heb 1:3; John 1:1-14). Some of this language and some of these expressions may seem a bit out of place in the context of the respective writings in which they appear. And they often require considerable translation into modern parlance

5. Christological Materials

to be understood today. Nonetheless, they were important as foundation stones, building blocks, and points of contact for the writers of the New Testament in their presentations and for their addressees in their understanding (for further on the nature and contents of these early Christian confessional materials, see my *New Wine into Fresh Wineskins*, ch. 2).

In What Context (or Contexts) were These Confessional Materials Formed and First Used?
Observations regarding the nature of early Christian confessional materials in the New Testament—that is, their devotional nuances, their reflections of a narrative story line that focused on Jesus, their functional affirmations, and their use of the language and metaphors of the day—all seem to locate their original formation and first use in the corporate worship of the early believers in Jesus, whenever and wherever that took place.

Paul's letters indicate that some of this confessional material was cast into poetic form and sung as hymns in corporate worship. In 1 Cor 14:26 he alludes to the singing of hymns in corporate worship ("When you come together, everyone has a hymn ...."); in Col 3:16-17 and Eph 5:19-20 there are explicit exhortations to include in the church's worship "psalms, hymns, and spiritual songs," which are to be directed in christocentric fashion ("in the name of the Lord Jesus" and "through him") to God the Father. Outside the Pauline corpus, the existence of such confessional materials is suggested by references in Hebrews to confessing Jesus (3:1), confessing the faith (4:14), and confessing one's Christian hope (10:23)—perhaps also in Jude to "the faith" (v 3) and "the most holy faith" (v 20).

More important, however, are the early hymns and prayers within the New Testament that both reflect various Jewish nuances and express distinctively Christian ideas. The most obvious of these hymnic prayers or prayerful hymns are the canticles of Mary, Zechariah, and Simeon in the infancy narrative of Luke 1–2 and the songs of praise to God and the victorious Lamb in Revelation 4, 5, 7 and 15. These New Testament hymns are comparable to the hymns of praise directed to God in the Jewish Scriptures (cf. the "Song of Moses" in Exod 15:1-18, which is echoed in the "Song of Miriam" in Exod 18:21; the "Song of Deborah" in Judg 5:1-31; and the "hymns" of Psalms 8–9, 29, 33, 65, 67–68, 96, 98, 100, 103–105, 111, 113–14,

117, 135–36, 145–50), as well as in some of the writings of Second Temple Judaism (cf. *Judith* 16:1-17; *Sirach* 51:01-12) and many of the hymns contained in the Qumran texts (esp. in *1QH*, the *Hodayot* or *Thanksgiving Psalms/Hymns*).

It may be postulated with some confidence, therefore, that the early Christian confessional materials incorporated within the New Testament were first formed and used within the context (or contexts) of corporate worship within the early church. Their use by the various writers of the New Testament may have varied (cf. my *New Wine into Fresh Wineskins*, chs 3–5). And their use certainly needs to be revived today (cf. *ibid.*, chs 6–7). But originally, it seems, these confessions were formed and used as formulaic statements, whether as hymns or *homologiai*, in the corporate worship of the early church.

5. Conclusion

Luke tells us that in writing his Gospel he (1) had the precedents of "many others" (πολλοί) who had written accounts of God's redemptive work in the ministry of Jesus, (2) took the opportunity to investigate the various traditions that had been "handed on to us" (παρέδοσαν ἡμῖν), and (3) used sources that depended ultimately on eyewitness reports (Luke 1:1-4). John tells us that his Gospel should not be taken as a complete account, but that "Jesus did many other signs in the presence of his disciples, which are not written in this book" (John 20:30).

Paul indicates that both he and his Gentile converts at Corinth knew not only what Jesus taught, but also what was not included in the collection of sayings from which they both seemed to have worked (cf. 1 Cor 7:10 and 9:14 vis-à-vis 7:12 and 7:25)—though, in all likelihood, that collection contained more teachings of Jesus than were later recorded in the Synoptic Gospels (as witness the *agraphon* that Paul quotes in 1 Thess 4:15-17). The various parallels of ethical teaching that exist between Romans, 1 and 2 Thessalonians, Ephesians, 1 Peter, and James, together with resemblances of this material with what we know from the canonical Gospels of the teaching of Jesus, suggest the existence of a common body of catechetical material within the early church from which the respective New Testament writers drew. And there are many places in the New Testament where we are alerted to the fact that the early Christians in their corporate worship sang hymns (e.g., 1 Cor 14:26; Col 3:16-17; Eph 5:19-20; cf. also the

Canticles of Luke 1–2 and the hymns to God and the Lamb of the Johannine Apocalypse) and confessed their faith (e.g., Heb 3:1; 4:14; 10:23; perhaps Jude 3 and 20).

We may not be able to identify or spell out the nature of all of the sources alluded to by the evangelists and the other writers of the New Testament. But we can still feel confident in assuming (1) that there circulated within the early Christian communities various christological materials, (2) that these materials brought together much of the church's early testimony, as based on eye-witness reports, personal remembrances, and oral tradition, and (3) that these materials were used by the writers of the New Testament in their portrayals of and arguments about Jesus of Nazareth, who was acclaimed to be the Messiah or "the Christ." We need to focus our attention redactionally, exegetically, and theologically on the christological presentations of the New Testament (as will take place in the articles that follow). But we also, by means of form-critical and tradition-critical analyses, need to be cognizant of the facts (1) that there existed prior to the writing of our New Testament various christological source materials, such as have been set out in rather elemental fashion above, and (2) that the writers of the New Testament used these materials as building blocks in their portrayals and presentations.

SELECT BIBLIOGRAPHY

Allison, Dale C., Jr. *The Jesus Tradition in Q*. Harrisburg: Trinity Press International, 1997.

Beasley-Murray, George R. *Jesus and the Future: An Examination of the Criticism of The Eschatological Discourse, Mark 13, with Special Reference to the Little Apocalypse Theory*. London: Macmillan, 1954.

_____. *Jesus and the Last Days: The Interpretation of the Olivet Discourse*. Peabody: Hendrickson, 1993 (which incorporates in revised form his *Jesus and the Future*. London: Macmillan, 1954, and his *A Commentary on Mark Thirteen*. London: Macmillan, 1957).

Deichgräber, Reinhard. *Gotteshymnus und Christushymnus in der frühen Christenheit: Untersuchungen zu Form, Sprache und Stil der frühchristlichen Hymnen*. Göttingen: Vandenhoeck & Ruprecht, 1967.

Donahue, John R. "From Passion Tradition to Passion Narrative," in *The Passion in Mark. Studies on Mark 14–16*, ed. W. H. Kelber. Philadelphia: Fortress, 1976, 1-20.

Dodd, Charles H. *The Apostolic Preaching and its Developments.* London: Hodder & Stoughton, 1936.

_____. *According to the Scriptures: The Sub-Structure of New Testament Theology.* London: Nisbet, 1952; New York: Scribner's, 1953.

_____. "The 'Primitive Catechism' and the Sayings of Jesus," in his *More New Testament Studies.* Manchester: Manchester University Press, 1968, 11-29 (an article "partly re-written, with additional matter," originally published in *New Testament Essays: Studies in Memory of T. W. Manson.* Manchester: Manchester University Press, 1959).

Dupont, Jacques. "La parabole du figuier qui bourgeonne (Mc, XIII, 28-29)," *RB* 75 (1968) 526-48.

_____. "La parabole du maître qui rentre dans la nuit [Mc 13, 34-36]," in *Mélanges Béda Rigaux.* Gembloux: Duculot, 1970, 89-116.

_____. "La ruine du temple et la fin des temps dans de discours de Marc 13," in *Apocalypses et théologie de l'espérance,* ed. L. Monloubou. Paris: Cerf, 1977, 207-69.

_____. "La persécution comme situation missionnaire (Marc 13, 9-11)," in *Die Kirche des Anfangs: Festschrift für H. Schürmann.* Freiburg: Herder, 1978, 97-114.

Ford, Desmond. *The Abomination of Desolation in Biblical Eschatology.* Washington: University Press of America, 1979.

Hartman, Lars. *Prophecy Interpreted: The Formation of Some Jewish Apocalyptic Texts and of the Eschatological Discourse Mark 13 par.* Uppsala: Gleerup, 1966.

Hooker, Morna D. *Jesus and the Servant.* London: SPCK, 1959.

_____. *The Son of Man in Mark.* London: SPCK; Montreal: McGill University Press, 1967.

Jeremias, Joachim, and Walther Zimmerli, "παῖς θεοῦ," *TDNT,* 5.654-717 (first part, pp. 654-77, by Zimmerli; second part, pp. 677-717, by Jeremias); earlier English trans. (from German *TWNT,* 5.653-713): idem, *The Servant of God,* trans. H. Knight, et al. London: SCM, 1957.

_____. *The Eucharistic Words of Jesus,* trans. N. Perrin, 3rd ed. rev New York: Scribner's, 1966.

Karris, Robert J. *A Symphony of New Testament Hymns: Commentary on Philippians 2:5-11, Colossians 1:15-20, Ephesians 2:14-16, 1 Timothy 3:16, Titus 3:4-7, 1 Peter 3:18-22, and 2 Timothy 2:11-13.* Collegeville: Liturgical Press, 1966.

Kloppenborg, John S. *Q Parallels: Synopsis, Critical Notes, and Concordance.* Sonoma: Polebridge, 1988.

_____. *The Formation of Q.* Philadelphia: Fortress, 1987; Harrisburg: Trinity Press International, 2nd ed., 1999 (with new Preface).

Lindars, Barnabas. *New Testament Apologetic: The Doctrinal Significance of the Old Testament Quotations.* London: SCM; Philadelphia: Westminster, 1961.

5. Christological Materials

Longenecker, Richard N. *The Christology of Early Jewish Christianity*. London: SCM, 1970; repr. Grand Rapids: Baker, 1981; repr. Vancouver: Regent Publishing, 2001.

———. *New Wine into Fresh Wineskins: Contextualizing the Early Christian Confessions*. Peabody: Hendrickson, 1999.

Maurer, Christian. "Knecht Gottes und Sohn Gottes in Passionsbericht des Markusevangeliums," *ZTK* 50 (1953) 1-38.

Moo, Douglas J. *The Old Testament in the Gospel Passion Narratives*. Sheffield: Almond, 1983.

Wenham, David. *The Rediscovery of Jesus' Eschatological Discourse*. Sheffield: JSOT, 1984.

6

THE FOUNDATIONAL CONVICTION OF NEW TESTAMENT CHRISTOLOGY
The Obedience / Faithfulness / Sonship of Christ

Numerous attempts have been made during the course of the church's history to capture the essence of the gospel by highlighting some central New Testament concept or expression. Much of what has been proposed has frequently been enlightening and helpful. At times, however, particularly when isolated and treated in an exclusivistic fashion, that supposedly central feature has been used to truncate the fullness of the gospel or to deflect Christian thought and action into subsidiary paths, thereby skewing the Christian message.

1. *Some Major Attempts of the Past*

One early attempt to capture the heart of the gospel proclamation was what has been called the "victory motif," as proposed by some of the Church Fathers—that is, that God through the work of Christ on the cross won the final victory over all of the cosmic evil powers, thereby freeing believers from sin, death, the law, and condemnation. Gustaf Aulén in his *Christus Victor* of 1931 and Ragnar Leivestad in his *Christ the Conqueror* of 1954,[1] the two twentieth-century scholars who have done the most to trace out the history of the "victory motif" in the early church, have labeled this motif the "classic idea" of the atonement. Later in the third and fourth centuries, in response to such seemingly logical questions as "Victory over whom?" "Victory where?" and "Victory how?," it became the basis for a "Devil Ransom" theory and "Descensus ad Inferos" doctrine (cf. the Nicene Creed: "He descended into hell").

Another attempt has been to focus on "the body of Christ." This is a metaphor that incorporates important corporate nuances regarding the relationship of believers to Christ and to one another, but it has also been seen in certain circles to have ontological significance as well. In Roman Catholic theology the fact that the church is spoken of in the

Pauline letters as "the body of Christ" has been spelled out to mean that just as Christ walked the hills of Palestine in his physical body so he exists today in his church with its center at Rome—with the result that there now exist (1) two forms of revelation, Scripture *and* ecclesiastical tradition, with the latter being more explicit and the prescribed means for understanding the former, and (2) two forms of redemptive activity, Christ's work *and* the church's work, with the latter being a redoing and application of the former. Most rigidly expressed, the Roman Catholic Church represents itself as God's sole agent of revelation and redemption today, with no salvation available to men and women apart from the ministrations of that church.

The watchword of the Protestant Reformation was "justification by faith." What Luther and his reforming colleagues desired was that people be brought back to a lively consciousness of what Christ had already done on their behalf, thereby putting an end to all thoughts about attaining righteousness by one's own efforts or acceptance before God by one's own actions. So they focused on God's justification of the unrighteous by means of the work of Christ, with concomitant emphases on "Scripture alone" (i.e., apart from ecclesiastical dogma) and "faith alone" (i.e., apart from works). Later as these Reformation principles took root, the idea of "imputation" was viewed, particularly in Reformed theology, as also being a central motif of the gospel—both that of God's imputation of Adam's sin to each individual and God's imputation of Christ's righteousness to the elect. In other circles, however, such concepts as "salvation," "reconciliation," or even "transfer of merit" became important auxiliary ideas to be joined to the central theme of justification.

The twentieth century, too, has witnessed a number of attempts to capture the essence of the gospel in a central motif or expression. One prevalent way has been to focus on the eschatological factor of early Christian proclamation, with various scenarios proposed. Chief among these eschatological proposals are those that go under such names as "Thoroughgoing" or "Consistent Eschatology," "Realized Eschatology," "Inaugurated Eschatology," "Proleptic Eschatology," "Participationistic Eschatology," or "Fulfilled Messianism."

Another method used during the past century to capture the essence of early Christian preaching and teaching has been to highlight the christological titles of the New Testament. Chief among the titles analyzed have been "Christ" (or 'Messiah')," "Son of God," "Lord," and "Son of Man," whether singly or in some combination. Undoubtedly a great deal has been learned about early Christian conviction and Christian understanding has been profited much by means of such an approach. Yet diverse understandings have been proposed as to what each of these titles meant among the earliest believers in Jesus, and so quite diverse implications drawn as to what any one title or complex of titles signified as to the essence of early Christian conviction and proclamation.

The above listing sets out in very rough fashion only some of the more prominent proposals put forward over the course of the past two millennia in an endeavor to capture the essence of the Christian gospel. But even such a rough-hewn sketch raises questions not only as to the possibility of such an enterprise, but also its feasibility and the capability of scholars to carry out such an endeavor. Amid all of the various features within the proclamation of the New Testament, can we, in fact, identify a central affirmation or some foundational conviction that resides at the heart of things? Or to pick up on an expression coined by James Moffatt: Is there an identifiable "sense of center" in all that is variously affirmed in the New Testament? Even more important for our consideration here—particularly since we believe that conviction regarding Jesus of Nazareth lies at the heart of all Christian proclamation—is the question: Is there some basic understanding of the work and person of Jesus of Nazareth that underlies the christology of the New Testament?

2. Our Thesis

The thesis of this article is that the various terms and expressions used in the New Testament with respect to Christ are to be understood as pictorial representations, graphic metaphors, or similes that stem ultimately from a basic conviction having to do with the obedience, faithfulness, and/or sonship of God's Anointed One, the Messiah or Christ—with its corollary being the trustful obedience of every believer in response. In the case of Christ, I suggest that all the titles ascribed to him in the New Testament and all the metaphors used in description of the nature and effects of his work are founded ultimately on the early Christians' conviction regarding the full obedience and entire faithfulness of Jesus of Nazareth, God's Son *par excellence*, with this complete filial obedience being seen as having been exercised throughout his life (i.e., his "active obedience") and coming to ultimate expression in his death on the cross (i.e., his "passive obedience"). In the case of believers, response is in terms of a personal relationship with that Obedient One—or, in Pauline terms, being "in Christ."

In his English lectures on *The Religion of Jesus and the Faith of Paul* of 1923,[1] Adolf Deissmann attempted to mark out the path that he believed Christians, both scholars and lay people, should take in dealing with the various theological terms in Paul's letters. So, for example, when speaking of Paul's teaching on justification, Deissmann argued:

> According to my conception, the doctrine of justification is not the quintessence of Paulinism, but one witness among others to his experience of salvation. Justification is one ancient picture-word, alongside many others. Justification is one note, which, along with many others—redemption, adoption, etc.—is harmonised in the one chord that testifies to salvation.[2]

Similarly, on the variety of terms used by Paul, Deissmann wrote:

> The impression of complexity has only arisen because we have not understood the similes as similes which were synonymous with one another, though to the mind of antiquity they would easily have been so understood. The single so-called Pauline ideas have been isolated by us, and then the attempt has been made to reconstruct a chronological order of salvation, an 'ordo salutis', as our ancestors called it. As a matter of fact, the religion of Paul is something quite simple. It is communion with Christ.[3]

Deissmann's statements, of course, must be seen in the context of his own agenda: that of the primacy of being "in Christ" or "Christ mysticism" in Pauline thought—which is an understanding of Paul that cannot easily be set aside, though it is not the focus of our discussion here. Nonetheless, whatever is thought of Deissmann's overall thesis, his comments regarding the nature of Paul's theological language (as well as that of the New Testament generally) are suggestive and helpful.

More recently, Markus Barth, in his 1971 work on *Justification*, focused his analysis of Paul's understanding of Christ's work on the

---

[1] A. Deissmann, *The Religion of Jesus and the Faith of Paul*, trans. W. E. Wilson (London: Hodder & Stoughton, 1923).
[2] *Ibid.* 271.
[3] *Ibid.* 222-23.

theme "Jesus Christ comes, demonstrating faithfulness to God and man."[4] Barth's emphasis in the central part of his work is stated in the following words:

> The Son is not only sent out by the Father and Judge to be a passive tool, as it were, of God. He also renders *obedience* to his commission by *coming* to fulfil his office. With his advent, "faith came" ... Thus faith in God (or better, faithfulness to God) and love for men are realized in Jesus Christ at the same time in the same deed.[5]

In what follows, I want to spell out the above thesis by way of a rather elementary survey of the major New Testament materials, dealing with them in roughly chronological fashion: first with some of the early Christian confessions that are incorporated within the New Testament writings; then with the letters of Paul; then the canonical Gospels; and finally the Epistle to the Hebrews. The reader needs to be alerted to the fact that, due to the scope of the subject here treated, I have opted to omit citing scholarly support for the various statements made, since any attempt at a proper footnoting would have to be extensive—consuming, in fact, the article's greater amount of space. I can only beg the indulgence of the reader, particularly so since my intent is more suggestive than definitive. Further, the reader needs to be aware that throughout what follows I am using the terms "obedience," "faithfulness," and "son / sonship" with reference to Christ in an equivalent manner. My hope is that such an equivalency of concepts will be seen to be demonstrable from the data cited below.

3. The Early Christian Confessions

That there existed within the early church various Christian confessional formulas is suggested by references in the Pauline corpus to (1) "the traditions" that Paul passed on to his converts (2 Thess 2:15), (2) kerygmatic material that was commonly used within the early church, which Paul received and passed on (1 Cor 15:3; see also v 11), (3) "the form of teaching" to which believers were committed (Rom 6:17), and (4) "the good confession" made by Timothy (1 Tim 6:12). The presence of such confessional formulas is also suggested by

---

[4] M. Barth, *Justification: Pauline Texts Interpreted in Light of the Old and New Testaments*, trans. A. M. Woodruff (Grand Rapids: Eerdmans, 1971), 38-39; cf. also *idem*, "The Faith of the Messiah," *HeyJ* 10 (1969) 363-70.

[5] *Ibid.* 39 (italics his).

statements in Hebrews that speak of "confessing" Jesus (3:1), "confessing the faith" (4:14), and "confessing" one's Christian hope (10:23), as well as statements in Jude that speak of "the faith" and "the most holy faith" (3:20).

Exactly what criteria are to be used for establishing the presence of such early confessional material in any particular New Testament writing has been a matter of continued debate ever since the first proposals made by Eduard Norden in his *Agnostos Theos* of 1912.[6] Likewise, how to distinguish between liturgical formulations, creedal statements, traditional sayings, and hymns—as well, of course, how to identify the provenance of each of these confessional fragments—are matters on which scholars have often been divided. Nonetheless, almost all are agreed that the needs of proclamation, worship, and instruction among the early believers in Jesus brought into existence various Christian confessional materials, and most believe it possible to identify at least some of them within the pages of the New Testament.

The first early Christian confession to be identified in the New Testament, and the one accepted by almost everyone as being most obvious, is the hymnodic portion found in Phil 2:6-11. We need not here rehearse the reasons why this passage is usually seen as a pre-Pauline Christian hymn, nor attempt to analyze its strophic structure or identify its exact provenance. Nor need we enter here into any of the many theological debates that have been based on this passage or use it as the fulcrum for their arguments—as, for example, debates as to whether the nature of the Son is the same as (*homoousios*) or similar to (*homoiousios*) that of the Father; whether preexistence is an attribute of Christ; whether a "kenosis" theory of the incarnation legitimately derives from this passage, and, if so, how it should be understood; whether a "docetic" view of Christ's humanity is expressed in the passage; or what is meant by the exaltation and universal lordship of Christ Jesus—even what is signified by the title "Lord" itself.

All of the above matters are important in any proper analysis of Phil 2:6-11. For if in these verses we possess an early Christian confession

---

[6] E. Norden, *Agnostos Theos: Untersuchungen zur Formengeschichte religiöser Rede* (Leipzig: Teubner, 1913; repr. 1956), which was based on his earlier and more wide-ranging *Die antike Kunstprosa vom VI. Jahrhunderts vor Christus bis in die Zeit der Renaissance*, 2 vols. (Leipzig: Teubner, 1898).

that is set out in the strophic structure of a hymn, then it is of great importance to deal seriously with these issues and concerns when trying to understand the attitudes and commitments of at least one congregation of early Christian believers, whatever may be said about the conceptual orientation or geographical location of those early believers. Constraints of space and time, however, prohibit our dealing with most of these issues in the present article.

Yet one datum of importance that is central in the passage needs to be highlighted here—not only because it is suitable for our present purpose, but also because it has been so often overlooked: that in his actions on behalf of humanity, the one of whom the hymn speaks "became *obedient* unto death" (γεγόμενος ὑπήκοος μέχρι θανάτου). At the very heart of this early Christian hymn, therefore, is an affirmation regarding the complete obedience of Christ. It is an obedience expressed not just "in death," as is so often mistakenly assumed, but an obedience that characterized his entire life and so extended even to the inclusion of death, as the preposition μέχρι ("as far as," "to the extent of," "to the point of") suggests in its emphasis on extent, degree, or measure.

That such an obedience is the focal point of the hymn is signaled by what appears to be Paul's interjectory exclamation at this point: "Even death on a cross!" (θανάτου δὲ σταυροῦ). That the words are to be understood as Paul's own ejaculatory cry of horror is suggested by the fact that they break the strophic structure of the hymn, however that structure is explicitly set out, being inserted between the first half of the hymn on humility (the κατάβασις or "descent" section) and the second half on exaltation (the ἀνάβασις or "ascent" section). And that Paul breaks into the hymn at this point with such an emotive interjection reflects (1) the general Jewish horror regarding the exposure of a dead corpse on a tree, which came during the Second Temple period to include the impalement or crucifixion of a living person on a pole or cross (cf. Deut 21:22-23), and (2) Paul's own early revulsion against any thought of a crucified Messiah, which he knew to be scandalous to Jews (cf. 1 Cor 1:23; Gal 5:11). Likewise, it probably recalls the central problem of early Christians as to how to understand Jesus of Nazareth as Israel's Messiah when he was accursed by God because of having died on a cross—which was a dilemma they resolved by understanding God's curse on Jesus the Messiah as an "exchange curse" (cf. 2 Cor 5:21).

6. Foundational Convictions of NT Christology

But also of importance for our purpose here is to note that Paul's interjected exclamation of Phil 2:8b signals the point of emphasis in his quotation of this early Christian confessional hymn—at least the emphasis in the κατάβασις or "lowering" section, which makes up the first half of the hymn: that the work of Christ is to be understood primarily in terms of his complete obedience, with that obedience expressed throughout his life and extending even to the inclusion of death. It is this kind of obedience that is appealed to throughout the rest of Philippians, first in showing how it was present in the ministries of Paul himself, his colleague Timothy, and the Philippian church's own emissary Epaphroditus, and then in urging that such a paradigm of obedience be worked out in the lives of believers at Philippi as well.

In Gal 4:4-5 there appears another early Christian confessional portion that Paul seems to have drawn, either in whole or in part, from the church's proclamation:

> When the time had fully come, God sent his Son, born of a woman, born under the law, in order to redeem those under the law, so that we might receive adoption as God's children (ἵνα τὴν υἱοθεσίαν ἀπολάβωμεν, lit., "so that we might receive the sonship" or "the full rights of sonship").

It is a confession that seems based, as narrative analysis suggests, on the gospel story as told by the earliest Jewish Christians. And it is a confession used by Paul to support his emphases in Galatians on (1) a believer's true family relationship ("the sonship" or "the adoption" as God's children) when related to God by means of the work of Christ, apart from "the works of the law," and (2) Gentile believers' freedom from the supervision of the Mosaic law.

These verses seem to stem from a Jewish-Christian confessional affirmation, for Paul quotes them to Gentile converts by way of countering judaizing agitators who claimed to be supported by the Jewish-Christian congregation at Jerusalem. But what needs also to be noted here is that central to this confessional portion is a stress on the sonship of Christ, which in a Jewish-Christian context probably carried not so much an ontological nuance as signaled primarily the factor of loving obedience rendered by the Son to the Father.

The statement "God sent his Son" (ἐξαπέστειλεν ὁ θεὸς τὸν υἱὸν αὐτοῦ) may very well have been a formula drawn from Jewish Wisdom writings and used by the early Christians to associate

"Wisdom" with Christ (cf. 1 Cor 1:24, 30), as Eduard Schweizer and others have argued—whether with ontological or functional nuances, or both.[7] But when this formulaic statement was used among Jewish Christians in the context of a confession, Gal 4:4-5 tells us that they spoke of Christ as not only being truly human ("born of a woman") and possessing a representative quality ("the Man") but also as offering a perfect obedience to God the Father ("born under the law," "the Son") on behalf of all those "under the law," that is, all Jews.[8]

Also of importance when dealing with the sonship of Christ in the early Christian confessions is the title "Son of God" in the salutation of Paul's letter to the Romans. The material of Rom 1:3-4 is often seen as an early Christian confession that Paul used to explicate what he means by "his Son"—that is, he is "the one who was a descendant of David, as to his human nature"; but also "the one who was declared to be the Son of God with power, according to his spirit of holiness (or, perhaps, "the Holy Spirit"), by the resurrection of the dead." A two-stage understanding of Christ seems to be here set out. The first identifies him as David's descendant. The second speaks of what God declared him to be on the basis of the character of his life and as evidenced by his resurrection. And for that latter stage the title "Son of God" is used, which in an early Jewish-Christian confession probably referred more to Christ's attitude and actions of obedience than to anything necessarily ontological—though, of course, such an ascription would fit well into later christological developments.

One other early confessional portion could perhaps be cited here in support of our thesis that the obedience or faithfulness of the Son is the underlying conviction of the earliest Christology—though, of course, as one moves on to analyze the various proposed early Christian confessions it becomes more and more difficult both to legitimize their presence and to set out their limits.[9] That particular confessional portion in mind comes after the resumed thesis paragraph of Rom 3:21-23 (or perhaps 3:21-24). It has been argued by Rudolf Bultmann, Ernst Käsemann, *et al.*, to be made up of verses 24-26 (starting with the present participle δικαιούμενοι, "being justified") and by Eduard

---

[7] Cf. my review of E. Schweizer and others in my *Galatians* (WBC; Dallas: Word, 1990), 167-70.

[8] See *ibid.*, 166, 171-72.

[9] Cf. my *New Wine into Fresh Wineskins: Contextualizing the Early Christian Confessions* (Peabody: Hendrickson, 1999), esp. 17, 23-26.

Lohse and others to comprise only verses 25-26 (starting with the relative personal pronoun ὅν, "who"). Based on an analysis of structure, style, *hapax legomena* (i.e., "once used words or expressions"), and distinctive theological content, a compelling case can be made for the presence of an early Christian confessional portion that is here used by Paul in support of his thesis of Rom 3:21-23 (perhaps also v 24) regarding the manifestation of God's righteousness, the witness of Scripture, the work of Christ, and the necessity of faith—though scholars have been almost equally divided as to exactly where that confessional material begins (as well, among some, exactly where it ends).

For my part, I believe Bultmann and company to be right in taking the confession to begin with the participle δικαιούμενοι, "being justified." Accepting such a view, this confessional material may be seen as setting out three graphic metaphors in description of the work of Christ: (1) the legal metaphor of *justification*, "being justified freely by his grace" (v 24a); (2) the civil and social metaphor of *redemption*, "through the redemption that came about by Christ Jesus" (v 24b); and (3) the cultic metaphor of *sacrificial atonement* (whether understood as "propitiation" or "expiation"), "God set him forth as a sacrifice of atonement ("a propitiation" or "an expiation") through faith in his blood" (v 25a). But what needs also to be noted is that all three of these metaphors—as well as everything else said about God's salvific actions in the rest of verse 25b-26—are based on the final statement of the confession, which serves as the climax of the whole passage: "In order that God might be just and the justifier of τὸν ἐκ πίστεως Ἰησοῦ."

That final expression τὸν ἐκ πίστεως Ἰησοῦ is, of course, notoriously difficult to translate. Taking Ἰησοῦ to be an objective genitive, it may mean "the one who has *faith in Jesus*." More likely, however, as we will attempt to demonstrate in the following section when we discuss πίστις Ἰησοῦ Χριστοῦ in Paul's own thought, Ἰησοῦ should here probably be viewed as a subjective genitive and the expression in question understood as "the one who is based on *the faith* [or, *faithfulness*] *of Jesus*." And if this be so, then it needs to be observed that in an early Christian confession that Paul uses in support of his thesis statements in 3:21-23 regarding the present manifestation of God's righteousness, the metaphors "justification," "redemption," and "sacrifice of atonement" ("propitiation" or "expiation") are based on and stem from an underlying conviction regarding the obedient response of Jesus to God his father—that is, conviction regarding the faith or faithfulness of Jesus.

4. *The Letters of Paul*

The above four confessions have been drawn from three of Paul's letters. In a full treatment of early Christian confessional materials it would be necessary to deal not only with what the early believers who originally composed them meant by such statements but also how an author who incorporates them into his writings understood them. For it is possible for writers to quote material for their own purposes without giving full credence to all that is said in the material they quote.

But this is not the case with Paul's use of these four confessions—particularly with respect to their focus on Christ's obedient and faithful sonship. To a degree we have hinted at how Paul used the portrayals of Christ's obedience, as drawn from earlier Christian confessional material, in his exhortations to believers at Philippi, Galatia, and Rome, thereby suggesting (using the literary criterion of multiple attestation) how intrinsic was such a theme to his own theology. And we believe that any more complete contextual study of these confessions and their use by Paul will bear out such an understanding.

More directly relevant here, however, are Paul's own statements—that is, beyond those found in the material he quotes—that focus on the obedience, sonship, and / or faithfulness of Christ. The most obvious reference to the obedience of Christ that can be attributed directly to Paul, and not just to material he quotes, is to be found in Rom 5:19:

> For just as through *the disobedience* (τῆς παρακοῆς) of the one man were "the many" made sinners, so through *the obedience* (τῆς ὑπακοῆς) of the one man will "the many" be made righteous.

In context, this statement must be seen as the second part of a doublet. In the first part, in verse 18:, Paul speaks of the "one trespass" of Adam, which resulted in "condemnation for all humanity," being countered by Christ's "one act of righteousness," which brings about the condition of "righteousness of life for all humanity." Here in the second part of that doublet, in verse 19, he speaks of "the disobedience of the one man [Adam]," which brought about the sinful condition of "the many," being countered by "the obedience of the one man [i.e., the Second Man, Jesus Christ]," which is able to make "the many" righteous. Likewise, when noting the context of Paul's reference to the obedience of Christ, verses 18-19 must be seen as the conclusion of Paul's rather convoluted argument that began back at verse 12, as the joining of the particles ἄρα and οὖ at the beginning of verse 18 suggests.

There are, of course, a number of issues that need to be dealt with in any full consideration of what Paul is saying in verse 19 and its import for the apostle's argument in Romans. Immediately obvious is the question as to whether the parallel statements of verses 18 and 19 should be seen as setting out two distinguishable, though clearly related, phenomena (i.e., Christ's so-called "passive righteousness" in his death and his "active righteousness" throughout his life) or understood in terms of the former being explicated by the latter (i.e., Christ's "one act of righteousness" in his death to be understood in the context of his complete obedience). Further, exactly how 5:12-21: functions in the course of Paul's argument throughout Romans 1–8 is an important issue for any real contextual and exegetical study of Romans. Most commentators believe that there is a break in Paul's argument in these chapters that occurs either between chapters 4 and 5 or between chapters 5 and 6, and so (1) view chapters 1–4 and 5–8 as two phases of the argument (the first on justification; the second on sanctification) or (2) take chapters 1–5 as the argument for justification by faith and chapters 6–8 as depicting the results of justification—with Martin Luther, who favored this latter understanding, even suggesting that 5:12-21 is an excursus appended by Paul to his portrayal of justification in 3:21–5:11. On the other hand, some have proposed that the argument of the first eight chapters of Romans should be seen as set out in two somewhat overlapping or parallel sections, with the break coming between 5:11 and 5:12: the first, that of 1:18–5:11; the second, that of 5:12–8:39 (so, e.g., Philip Melanchthon, Theodore Zahn, Franz Leenhardt, Matthew Black).

I personally favor viewing 5:1-11 as the thesis paragraph for the central section of Paul's argument in Romans, wherein he moves from matters regarding "the righteousness of God" and "justification by faith" (which both he and his addressees accepted) to the proclamation of "peace with God," "reconciliation," being "in Christ," and being "in the Spirit" (which were the major emphases of Paul's preaching). And I understand 5:12-21 as the foundational story of the Christian gospel as Paul proclaimed it to Gentiles in the Greco-Roman world, wherein he set out the spiritual condition of "death" and "condemnation" that all humans experience because of the disobedience of "one man," Adam, and counters that with the spiritual condition of life and righteousness because of the obedience of "one man," Jesus Christ.

On such a view, Paul's reference to the obedience of Christ has a vitally important place in the overall argumentation of Romans. For in his contrast between what Adam brought into human experience (i.e., death and condemnation) and what Christ effected for humanity (i.e., life and righteousness), it is the obedience of Christ that is presented as the basis for all that is proclaimed in 5:1–8:39, which I believe to be the central section of the letter.

But even if the place of 5:12-21 in the overall structure and argument of Romans should be viewed differently, at least it needs to be noted that Paul's reference to the obedience of Christ in verse 19 has an important place at least in the argument of 5:12-21 itself, for it is the basic feature that Paul highlights when he speaks about the work of Christ—whether the two sets of statements in verses 18-19 are to be understood as depicting two related phenomena that come to climax in the second (as may be argued from the paralleling of "death" and "life" only a few verses earlier in 5:10) or as the former being explicated by the latter.

Admittedly, apart from its appearance in the confession of Phil 2:6-11, only here in Rom 5:19 does Paul use the noun "obedience" (ὑπακοή) when speaking about the work of Christ. But theology is more than mathematics; and while the literary-historical criterion of "multiple attestation" is always important, one does not appeal only to frequency counts in support of significance. Further, one needs to couple with this term the cognate expressions and statements that appear in Paul's letters for the idea of obedience. Chief among such cognate ways of expressing Christ's obedience in Paul's writings are (1) the expression "the faith / faithfulness of Jesus Christ [or, of 'Christ Jesus', or simply 'Christ']" and (2) the titles "Son" and "Son of God."

A number of scholars, particularly of late, have come to see that Paul's use of the phrase πίστις ʼΙησοῦ Χριστοῦ has much to do with the subject of Christ's obedience, and, further, that it signals something of vital importance for Paul's christological thought.

Usually, of course, the genitive form of the name "Jesus Christ," "Christ Jesus," or simply "Christ" in the expression is taken as an objective genitive, and so translated "faith *in* Jesus Christ." Some, in fact, insist that that is its only possible translation. Others, however, find in the expression a great deal of christological significance—though, it needs always to be noted, without minimizing the importance of human faith as called for in most of Paul's other uses of the noun "faith" (πίστις).

In addition to its appearance in Rom 3:26b, in what we have proposed above to be part of an early Christian confession, the expression πίστις Ἰησοῦ Χριστοῦ appears elsewhere in Paul's letters at least six times (with the wording of Gal 3:26 in P[46] being a possible, though unlikely, seventh):

> Rom 3:22: "The righteousness of God [is manifested] διὰ πίστεως Ἰησοῦ Χριστοῦ to all who believe."
>
> Gal 2:16 (twice): "Knowing that a person is not justified by the works of the law but διὰ πίστεως Χριστοῦ Ἰησοῦ, even we have believed in Jesus Christ in order to be justified ἐκ πίστεως Χριστοῦ."
>
> Gal 3:22: "The scripture has consigned all things under sin in order that the promise, which is ἐκ πίστεως Ἰησοῦ Χριστοῦ, might be given to those who believe."
>
> Eph 3:12: "... in whom we have boldness and confidence of access διὰ τῆς πίστεως αὐτοῦ."
>
> Phil 3:9: "... not having a righteousness of my own that is based on the law, but that which is διὰ πίστεως Χριστοῦ, the righteousness of God that depends on faith."

Admittedly, the expression is difficult to translate. But when the Greek noun πίστις is understood in terms of the Hebrew noun אמונה, which means both "faith" and "faithfulness," it becomes not too difficult to view Paul as using πίστις Ἰησοῦ Χριστοῦ in much the same way as he uses πίστις τοῦ θεοῦ ("the faithfulness of God") in Rom 3:3 and πίστις Ἀβραάμ ("the faith of Abraham") in Rom 4:16. This may be the case, as well, in that very enigmatic expression ἐκ πίστεως εἰς πίστιν of Rom 1:17, and so we should read "out of faith unto faith" (as the words are literally translated) as meaning "a righteousness that is *based on* [the divine] *faithfulness* and that *results in* [a human response of] *faith*."

In effect, Paul seems to use πίστις Ἰησοῦ Χριστοῦ as something of a set phrase—perhaps drawn from the expression ἐκ πίστεως

Ἰησοῦ in the Christian confessional material that he incorporates in Rom 3:26—to signal the basis for the Christian gospel: that its objective basis is the perfect response of obedience that Jesus rendered to God the Father, both actively in his life and passively in his death. Taking such a view, it needs to be noted that in three of the passages cited above Paul nicely balances the objective basis for Christian faith (i.e., "the faith" or "faithfulness of Jesus Christ") and humanity's necessary subjective response (i.e., "faith"):

> Rom 3:22: "this righteousness of God is 'through the faith / faithfulness of Jesus Christ' (διὰ πίστεως Ἰησοῦ Χριστοῦ) and 'extends to all who believe' (εἰς πάντας τοὺς πιστεύοντας)";
>
> Gal 3:22: "so that the promise, 'which is based on the faith / faithfulness of Jesus Christ' (ἐκ πίστεως Ἰησοῦ Χριστοῦ) 'might be given to those who believe' (δοθῇ τοῖς πιστεύουσιν)"; and,
>
> Phil 3:9: "a righteousness 'that is based on the faith / faithfulness of Christ'" (διὰ πίστεως Χριστοῦ) and 'that depends on faith' (ἐπὶ τῇ πίστει)."

Though it is often claimed that in these three verses we have simply cases of redundancy in Paul's vocabulary, it is probably better to see in the wording of these verses Paul's desire to set out both the objective and the subject bases for the Christian life—that is, both the objective "faith" or "faithfulness" of Christ in obedience to God the Father and the subjective response of "faith" on the part of those whom God reconciles to himself through the work of Christ.

Also of pertinence when attempting to grasp the foundational conviction that underlies Paul's christological thought are the titles "Son" and "Son of God," which among the earliest Jewish believers seem to have been used in a more functional manner to denote Jesus' unique relationship with God and his filial obedience to his Father's will. Admittedly, Paul does not use these titles for Christ as much as do the four evangelists who wrote the canonical Gospels or the writer of the Epistle to the Hebrews (whose usages will be discussed below). Nonetheless, in addition to references to "his Son" and "Son of God" in the confessional materials quoted in Gal 4:4-5 and Rom 1:3-4, Paul uses these titles some thirteen times further in his letters:

> "His Son": Rom 1:3, 9; 5:10; 8:3, 29, 32; 1 Cor 1:9; Gal 1:16; 4:6; 1 Thess 1:10;
> "The Son": 1 Cor 15:28; and
> "Son of God": 2 Cor 1:19; Gal 2:20.

And often these thirteen occurrences, in context, reverberate with the more functional nuance of obedience that is to be found in the materials of early Jewish Christianity—particularly when combined with the motif of Christ's faith or faithfulness or when juxtaposed with statements regarding his death, which function to highlight the extent of Christ's obedience and faithful sonship.

5. The Canonical Gospels

That sonship is a dominant motif in the portrayals of Jesus in the canonical Gospels is beyond dispute. He is presented in them as speaking about God and to God in such a manner as to suggest that God was uniquely his Father, and as referring to himself in both direct and allusive fashion as the "Son" and "Son of God"—not just during or at the end of his ministry but also as a twelve year old boy in the Jerusalem temple, which he called "my Father's house" (Luke 2:49). Even Satan is portrayed as acknowledging this factor as being fundamental in Jesus' self-consciousness, for in two of his three temptations as recorded in Matt 4:1-11 and Luke 4:1-13 it is Jesus' consciousness of having a unique, filial relationship with God that is used as the tempter's point of departure—that is, "If [understood as a first class conditional statement, and so "since"] you are the Son of God"). In fact, as portrayed in the Gospels, it was this filial consciousness that undergirded all of Jesus' ministry and from which he worked in the carrying out his messiahship.

In addition, it needs to be noted that the canonical evangelists evidence a lively consciousness of the unique sonship of Jesus not only by their portrayals and editorial comments, but also by how they arrange their materials and by what they emphasize—particularly the evangelists Mark, Matthew, and John. Indeed, it is not going beyond the evidence to argue that it was this consciousness of Jesus' filial relationship with God that served as the foundational conviction for all that they wrote.

Mark, for example, begins his Gospel with the caption: "The beginning of the gospel about Jesus Christ, the Son of God" (1:1). The first half of his Gospel is concerned with the question of the identity of Jesus, and it concludes with the affirmation of Peter: "You are the Christ!" (8:29). The second half spells out the nature of Jesus' ministry as being that of a suffering Messiah, and it concludes with the acclamation of the Roman centurion: "Surely this man was the

Son of God!" (15:39). Exactly what it was that impressed the centurion and what he meant by "Son of God" may be debated, for he was a Gentile and so probably used the title in something of a polytheistic manner. It is doubtful that he was thinking along the lines of Jesus' full obedience to the Father's will. Nonetheless, even though he may have nuanced his acclamation differently than the early Jewish believers in Jesus would have, Mark evidently considered the centurion to have in this case spoken "better than he knew." So Mark makes the point— whatever the centurion himself might have meant by such an honorific outburst—that in calling Jesus "Son of God" the centurion was using the proper title. In fact, Mark highlights this acclamation by using it as the climax of the second half of his Gospel that deals with the unfolding secret as to the nature of Jesus' messiahship. For in his teaching about the nature of his messiahship (8:31–10:52), during his Jerusalem ministry (11:1–13:37), and throughout his passion (14:1–15:39), Jesus evidenced that he was, indeed, God's obedient Son *par excellence*.

Further, it needs to be noted that all three synoptic evangelists make a point of focusing on the unique sonship of Jesus in their depictions of Jesus' baptism and transfiguration. In the baptism narrative the "voice from heaven," which is a locution for God himself, identifies Jesus as "my beloved Son" (ὁ υἱός μου ὁ ἀγαπητός) and commends his sonship—with Mark 1:11 and Luke 3:22 reading "You are my beloved Son; with you I am well pleased"; Matt 3:17 reading "This is my beloved Son, with whom I am well pleased." In the Transfiguration narrative, the "voice out of the cloud," which again signals God as speaking, refers to Jesus as "my beloved Son" (ὁ υἱός μου ὁ ἀγαπητός) or "my chosen Son" (ὁ υἱός μου ὁ ἐκλελεγμένος) and exhorts the disciples to "listen to him" (with the Matthean version also including a divine commendation)—Mark 9:7, "This is my beloved Son; listen to him"; Matt 17:5, "This is my beloved Son, with whom I am well pleased; listen to him"; Luke 9:35, "This is my chosen Son, listen to him!"

Undoubtedly, all three evangelists felt that they were reproducing the acclamation of the heavenly voice just as they found it in the gospel tradition—if not verbatim (i.e., *ipsissima verba*, "the express words") at least in essence (i.e., *ipsissima vox*, "the express voice" or "meaning"). But the redactional changes that each of the evangelists makes in their respective presentations suggest that they were not just trying to reproduce a tradition about what actually happened, but that they were also attempting, each in his own way, to highlight for their readers the fundamental importance of the sonship of Jesus. They were, in effect, saying: "To understand Jesus, one must see his divine Sonship as basic to all that he did!"

And John's Gospel, while devoid of any baptism or transfiguration narrative, says much the same thing in speaking of Jesus as God's "one and only Son" in 3:16 (ὁ υἱὸς ὁ μονογενής; cf. 1 John 4:9) and 3:18 (ὁ μονογενὴς υἱός), as well as in ascribing that same title to the eternal Logos in 1:14 and 18 of the Fourth Gospel's Prologue—though, admittedly, textual support varies as to whether the adjective "one and only" (μονογενής) in these latter verses modifies "Son" or "God," or with the article alone is to be seen as used substantively. For this is the One who as both God's Son and the eternal Logos not only reveals the Father's purposes, but is in complete compatibility with the Father's will and so expresses true filial obedience.

Among all of the four evangelists, however, Matthew is the one who seems to have been most dominated by a consciousness of Christ's filial obedience. For throughout his Gospel, particularly in the first half, Matthew appears to be often paralleling the life of Jesus and the life of the nation Israel—with that paralleling evidently meant to portray Jesus as "the Jew" who recapitulated in his life and ministry the experiences of the nation, obediently responding to God in a manner that Israel had not. Matthew's Gospel, of course, has a number of themes (some major and some minor), with many of these themes used to organize the presentation—sometimes overtly and extensively; at other times more allusively and in a more limited fashion. It cannot be claimed, therefore, that an emphasis on Jesus' sonship has entirely molded or fashioned all of what Matthew has presented in his Gospel. Yet many commentators believe they can detect echoes and reminiscences of experiences of the nation Israel in Matthew's Gospel, particularly in the first half of his Gospel.

The major parallels that have been often pointed out in Matthew's Gospel between Jesus and the nation of Israel are as follows: (1) a child of promise (1:18-23); (2) deliverance from Herod's slaughter (2:1-18); (3) coming out of Egypt (2:15, 19-21); (4) passing through the waters (3:13-17); (5) entering the wilderness for testing (4:1-17); (6) calling out the "twelve sons of Israel" (4:18-22); (7) giving the law from the mountain (5:1–7:28); (8) performing ten miracles (8:1–9:38); (9) sending out the Twelve to "conquer" the land (10:1-42); (10) feeding the multitudes with "manna" from heaven (14:15-21 and 15:32-39), and (11) being transfigured before his disciples (17:1-8). Not all of these parallels, of course, are equally evident or compelling. But the general parallelism between Jesus and the nation of Israel that is set out in Matthew's Gospel cannot easily be set aside.

Much more could be cited from the Gospels in support of the thesis that the four canonical evangelists possessed a lively consciousness of the unique sonship of Jesus and that they wrote from the perspective of such a foundational conviction. What we have done in this article is simply to highlight some of the most obvious data in support of such a thesis. We must leave it to others to deal with the more allusive and inferential evidence.

One cannot, however, leave the witness of the canonical Gospels in this regard without also referring to what in the Synoptic Gospels is presented as Jesus' last great spiritual struggle before enduring the agony of the cross—that is, his response of complete obedience in his prayer in the Garden of Gethsemane. For in the Gethsemane narratives of the synoptic evangelists Jesus is portrayed as crying out in anguish: "Father, if you are willing, take this cup from me!" But immediately coupled with this cry are his words: "Yet not my will, but yours be done!" (Luke 22:42; cf. Mark 14:36; Matt 26:39). An echo of this event appears in John's Gospel in the words of Jesus: "Now my heart is troubled, and what shall I say? 'Father, save me from this hour'? No, it was for this very reason I came to this hour. Father, glorify your name!" (John 12:27-28). Though the details of the Gethsemane experience differ somewhat in the Synoptic Gospels (e.g., in Matthew, "he fell on his face"; in Mark, "he fell on the ground"; in Luke, "he knelt down"; note also Luke's additions of an angel being present to strengthen him and his sweat being "like great drops of blood"), and though John's Gospel locates this response in a different context, all of the evangelists agree in focusing on Jesus' attitude of complete obedience—which, evidently, they viewed as the only fitting way to express his divine sonship.

6. *The Epistle to the Hebrews*

The argument of the first ten chapters of Hebrews is built along the lines of first a thesis statement in 1:1-2, then what appears to be an early Christian confessional portion in 1:3-4 that is quoted in support of that thesis, and thereafter five biblical portions drawn from the LXX—(1) a catena of passages (Ps 2:7; 2 Sam 7:14; Deut 32:43; Pss 97:7; 45:6-7; 102:25-27) on which the exposition of 1:5–2:4 is based; (2) Ps 8:4-6 on which 2:5-18 is based; (3) Ps 95:7-11 on which 3:1–4:13 is based; (4) Ps 110:4 on which 4:14–7:28 is based, and (5) Jer 31:31-34 on which 8:1–10:39 is based. Chapters 11–13 then exhort the addressees to move forward in their Christian commitments, focusing attention on Jesus "the Pioneer and Perfecter" of their faith (2:9-10; 12:2-3) and being prepared to follow Jesus even to the point of leaving, if need be, their former Jewish allegiances (13:11-14).

The substance of the argument, however, has to do with Christ as "the Son," by whom "in these last days" God has revealed himself and acted redemptively on behalf of his people. And the point of the argument, which comes repeatedly to the fore throughout the epistle's first ten chapters, is that the person and work of the Son—while in continuity with all of God's past words and actions—is to be understood as superior to all of God's previous revelations and redemptive activities. In particular, as the argument of the homiletical epistle unfolds, the Son is presented as superior to angels in his exaltedness (1:5–2:4), to angels in his lowliness and humiliation (2:5-18), to Moses and the law (3:1-6), to Joshua and the possession of the land (3:7–4:13), to the Levitical priesthood (4:14–5:10), to the Melchizedekian priesthood (7:1-28), and to the old covenant and its cultus (8:1–10:39).

One of the most interesting features of the Epistle to the Hebrews is its placement of the theme of the Son's obedience in the context of both (1) ontological affirmations regarding Jesus' divine status and sinlessness, and (2) functional portrayals of his redemptive activities on behalf of humanity. The statement of the writer in 5:8-9 appears, at first glance, somewhat startling in its joining of ontology and function: "Although he was a son, he learned obedience from what he suffered; and once made perfect, he became the source of eternal salvation for all who obey him." That this reference to the Son's obedience as having been perfected during his earthly life is no inadvertence on the part of the author is evidenced by the fact that the same point appears in briefer fashion in 2:10, where it is said that "in bringing many sons and daughters to glory it was fitting that God ... should make the Pioneer of their salvation perfect through suffering," and in 7:28, which speaks of "the Son, who has been made perfect forever." However difficult it may be for scholars today to understand the conjunction of the categories of ontology (i.e., "person") and function (i.e., "work")—or, to reconcile what has been called a "Christology from Above" with a so-called "Christology from Below"—the writer to the Hebrews seems to have had no problem in bringing together both *status* and *process* when speaking about Christ, the Son—that is, with presenting a Christology that has to do with both "being" and "becoming."

But however the categories of ontology and function are to be related in the portrayals of sonship in Hebrews, the important point to note here is that at the heart of the writer's argument about the work of Christ stands the concept of the Son's complete obedience to his heavenly Father. This can be seen throughout the first ten chapters of the epistle. But it appears in a particularly explicit and forceful manner in the final chapter of that sustained argument—that is, in 10:5-7 quoting Ps 40:6-8:

> Therefore, when Christ came into the world, he said: "Sacrifice and offering you did not desire, but a body you prepared for me; with burnt offerings and sin offerings you were not pleased. Then I said, 'Here I am—it is written about me in the scroll—I have come to do your will, O God.'"

For the writer of Hebrews, therefore, the fundamental factor that underlies both the incarnation of the Son and his earthly ministry is that of obedience: "To do your will, O God."

7. Conclusion

Our thesis in this article is that all of the christological titles and all of the metaphors used in the New Testament to describe Christ's work are to be understood as stemming ultimately from the foundational conviction of the early Christians about the full obedience and entire faithfulness of Jesus of Nazareth, God's Son *par excellence*—with that filial obedience seen as having been expressed throughout his life (i.e., his "active obedience") and coming to ultimate expression in his death on the cross (i.e., his "passive obedience"). That does not mean, however, that we should disregard the titles or neglect the metaphors. Much can be learned that is of profit for Christian theology by a contextual and historical study of each of the christological titles and metaphors, for they are given to flesh out the gospel message and highlight areas of significance in different contexts. Further, the impact of the Christian gospel is often greatly enhanced by the proclamation of its message in terms of one or the other of the titles or metaphors used of Christ in the New Testament, especially when suited to the needs of a particular audience or situation. But what needs to be appreciated is that behind all of these pictorial representations, graphic metaphors, and explanatory similes stands the foundational conviction of the early Christians about the obedience, faithfulness, and sonship of Christ—with its corollary being the trustful obedience of the believer in response.

Validation for our thesis is not just to be found in the frequency with which the actual terms "obedience," "faithfulness," and "Son" or "Son of God" appear in the New Testament. It is also to be found in their strategic use by the New Testament letter writers and evangelists, appearing, as we have noted above, in such significant places as an early Christian confessional portion that has been incorporated into a letter (e.g., Phil 2:8; Gal 4:4-5; Rom 1:3-4; 3:26), the thesis of a letter (e.g., Rom 3:21-23; Heb 1:1-2), the propositional statement of a letter (e.g., Gal 2:15-21), a major argument of a letter (e.g., Rom 5:19; Gal 3:22), the caption and conclusion of a Gospel (e.g.. Mark 1:1; 15:39), or woven into the warp and woof of the presentation of a Gospel or epistle (e.g., in Matthew and in Hebrews).

Further validation can be found in the multifaceted way that the concept of Christ's obedient, faithful sonship undergirds many other presentations of the writers of the New Testament. For it not only informs, we believe, christological features, but also matters that are soteriological, ecclesiological, eschatological, ethical, and sacramental in nature—though to demonstrate how this foundational conviction undergirds the presentations of the various New Testament writers in each of these areas would require a full monograph, which is a task that must be left to others.

SELECT BIBLIOGRAPHY

Allison, Dale C., Jr. *The New Moses: A Matthean Typology*. Minneapolis: Fortress, 1993.
Aulén, Gustaf. *Christus Victor: An Historical Study of the Three Main Types of the Idea of Atonement*, trans. A. G. Hebert. London: SPCK, 1950.
Barth, Markus. "The Faith of the Messiah," *HeyJ* 10 (1969) 363-70.

_____. *Justification: Pauline Texts Interpreted in Light of the Old and New Testaments*, trans. A. M. Woodruff. Grand Rapids: Eerdmans, 1971.
Beasley-Murray, George R. *John*. WBC 36. Waco: Word, 1987.
Cullmann, Oscar. *The Christology of the New Testament*, trans. S. C. Guthrie and C. A. M. Hall. London: SCM, 1959.
Deichgräber, Reinhard. *Gotteshymnus und Christushymnus in der frühen Christenheit: Untersuchungen zu Form, Sprache, und Stil der frühchristlichen Hymnen*. Göttingen: Vandenhoeck & Ruprecht, 1967.
Deissmann, Adolf. *Die neutestamentliche Formel "in Christo Jesu."* Marburg: Elwert, 1982.
_____. *The Religion of Jesus and the Faith of Paul*, trans. W. E. Wilson. London: Hodder & Stoughton, 1923.
Hays, Richard B. *The Faith of Jesus Christ: An Investigation of the Narrative Substructure of Galatians 3:1–4:11*. Chico: Scholars: 1983; 2nd ed., Grand Rapids: Eerdmans, 2001.
Hengel, Martin. *The Son of God: The Origin of Christology and the History of Jewish–Hellenistic Religion*. Philadelphia: Fortress, 1976.
Karris, Robert J. *A Symphony of New Testament Hymns: Commentary on Philippians 2:5-11, Colossians 1:15-20, Ephesians 2:14-16, 1 Timothy 3:16, Titus 3:4-7, 1 Peter 3:18-22, and 2 Timothy 2:11-13*. Collegeville: Liturgical Press, 1966.
Leivestad, Ragnar. *Christ the Conqueror*. London: SPCK, 1954.
Longenecker, Bruce W., ed. *Narrative Dynamics in Paul: A Critical Assessment*. Louisville: Westminster / John Knox, 2002.
Longenecker, Richard N. *The Christology of Early Jewish Christianity*. London: SCM, 1970; repr. Grand Rapids: Baker, 1981; repr. Vancouver: Regent Publishing, 2001.
_____. *Biblical Exegesis in the Apostolic Period*. Grand Rapids: Eerdmans, 1975; repr. Vancouver: Regent Publishing, 1993; repr. Exeter: Paternoster, 1995; 2nd ed., Grand Rapids: Eerdmans, 1999.
_____. *Galatians*. WBC 41. Dallas: Word, 1990.
_____. *New Wine into Fresh Wineskins: Contextualizing the Early Christian Confessions*. Peabody: Hendrickson, 1999.
Moule, Charles F. D. "The Intention of the Evangelists," in *New Testament Essays: Studies in Memory of T. W. Manson*, ed. A. J. B. Higgins. Manchester: Manchester University Press, 1959; repr. in *idem*, *The Phenomenon of the New Testament*. London: SCM, 1967.
Norden, Eduard. *Agnostos Theos: Untersuchungen zur Formengeschichte religiöser Rede*. Leipzig: Tübner, 1913; repr. 1956.

7

Some Distinctive Early Christological Motifs

Too often the Christology of early Christianity has been determined by (1) evaluating the hellenistic contribution to the New Testament, subtracting this from the total, and acclaiming the residue to be Semitic and original (oblivious to the intermingling of Hebraic and hellenistic ideologies in first-century Palestine), and (2) working from a predetermined set of convictions as to what was possible in a Hebraic milieu. Now *a prioris* can never be eliminated altogether from any study. Nor should they be condemned *per se*, for without them one would never begin. But they must be checked—both historically and critically.

In large measure this process of "hellenistic subtraction" has been abetted in the past by the nature and paucity of extant materials with which the New Testament could be compared. But with the discoveries of the Dead Sea Scrolls and the Nag Hammadi texts, and the resultant re-evaluation of previously known non-canonical writings, material is now at hand for a new application of the old comparative-religion methodology that gives promise of more adequately based results.

It is the thesis of this article that certain portions of the New Testament stand in direct ideological and conceptual continuity with the Dead Sea Scrolls and related Old Testament apocryphal writings, on the one hand, and the post-apostolic Jewish-Christian materials and related Nag Hammadi texts, on the other; and that by the tracing of parallels of imagery and expression between these three bodies of material—with appropriate allowances for differences of theological outlook and the development of thought—there result some interesting identifications and observations regarding early Christology such as were not possible before. Following out the suggestions and work of others, it is my purpose here to isolate some distinctive Jewish-

Christian themes and conceptual patterns in the New Testament by reference to these earlier Jewish and later Jewish-Christian writings, extrapolating both forward and backward in search of legitimate concurrences.

1. *Critical Assumptions*

Before dealing with specifics of identification and interpretation, some account must be given regarding the critical assumptions on which this study is based. Space permits only the most cursory treatment, with the expectation that some matters will be more fully developed in what follows below.

The distinctive literature of Qumran I take to be reflective of one aspect of the Essene movement in Palestine, and to have been written during the first century BCE and early first century CE. I accept as being generally reliable the conclusions reached in R. H. Charles's two-volume *magnum opus* regarding the dates and provenances of the Old Testament apocryphal material,[1] though with these qualifications: (1) that there is no evidence for the pre-Christian nature of either the "Similitudes" of *1 Enoch* (chapters 37–71 of *Ethiopic Enoch*) or a Greek version of the *Testaments of the Twelve Patriarchs*, and (2) that many of the writings labeled by Charles as "Pharisaic" because of their opposition to Saducean perspectives (I refer especially to *Jubilees*, the Greek and Aramaic portions of *1 Enoch*, and the *Psalms of Solomon*) must now be seen to be within an Essene cycle of influence, whether originally written by Essenes (or "proto-Essenes") or taken over by them.

With regard to the Nag Hammadi texts, I believe they are expressions of heterodox Jewish Christianity within which has blossomed the incipient gnosticism of heterodox Judaism under the stimulus of Greek religious philosophy. The authors themselves were probably not all Jewish Christians. But the conceptual framework within which they work has a definite Jewish background. I would not go so far as to assert their primitive Jewish-Christian character. On the other hand, however, I believe they are not just developments of canonical material. Rather, they should be seen as basically independent of the New Testament Gospels. Following Gilles Quispel, I take the Nag Hammadi "Gospels" to be based on an extra-canonical Jewish-Chris-

---

[1] *APOT*, 2 vols. Cf. now also *OTP*, 2 vols.

7. Distinctive Early Christological Motifs

tian Gospel tradition—perhaps a *Gospel to the Hebrews* and revised materials from a *Logia* collection—and so both independent from and secondary to the four Gospels of the New Testament.[2]

As for the many New Testament apocryphal writings in addition to the thirteen codices at Nag Hammadi—such works as the second-century Gospels, Acts, Preaching, and Apocalypses associated with the names of Peter, James, John, Thomas, the Hebrews, and the Nazarenes—almost all of these are *prima facie* Jewish-Christian in nature and seem to come from a milieu similar to that of the later *Clementine Homilies* (possibly, also, are the bases for the still later *Clementine Recognitions*). Perhaps, as well, there is a Jewish-Christian substratum in the *Didache* and the *Shepherd of Hermas*, though this need not be pressed here.

A number of writings in the New Testament have been seen of late to have closer ideological and conceptual affinities with a sectarian type of Judaism as appears in the texts from Qumran than to any other form of ancient Judaism known to date. I refer particularly to Matthew's Gospel, John's Gospel, the Epistle to the Hebrews, and the so-called "General" or "Catholic" Epistles (especially James and 1 Peter). These I take, along with the Apocalypse, to be "Jewish-Christian" materials in the sense that they both reflect a Jewish-Christian background and are addressed to Jewish Christians and/or potentially interested Jews, whether living in Palestine–Syria or the wider Diaspora.

Paul has indicated in Galatians 2 that the early advance of Christianity took place along the lines of two main missions and within two major spheres of influence: the Jewish-Christian mission, in which James, Peter (or Cephas), and John were most prominent, and the Gentile Christian mission, in which Paul took the lead. These writings just referred to I take to be reflective of this first mission, though with the qualification that they represent varied aspects of that mission at varied stages of its development and not a monolithic entity. For just as the Gentile centers of Paul's evangelization evidence diversity and development, so we should posit the same for the Jewish-Christian mission.

---

[2] Cf. G. C. Quispel, The Jung Codex and Its Significance," in *The Jung Codex. A Newly Recovered Gnostic Papyrus*, trans. F. L. Cross (London: Mowbray, 1955), 37-78 (48-54).

But even more significant than these overtly Jewish-Christian writings for the identification of early Jewish-Christian christological patterns—if for no other reason, because of the early date of the materials in which they are contained—are portions found in the Pauline letters that reflect early Jewish-Christian convictions and early Jewish-Christian stances: (1) snatches of incorporated confessional and hymnodic material (undoubtedly 1 Cor 15:3-5; also Phil 2:6-11; and probably many other portions),[3] and (2) polemic discourse where there is reason to believe that a type of Jewish-Christian argument is being countered (principally in Galatians and Colossians, though of this I must speak later). Also the first part of the Acts of the Apostles may be employed here, for whether its "semitisms" are translation phenomena, the result of a literary use of sources, the conscious or unconscious imitation of the LXX, or a combination of these factors, its author structures his presentation according to these two major cycles of early Christian advance and shows an interest in "archaizing" with respect to the Jewish-Christian mission—whether that treatment by its author be judged to be conscious or derivative.

2. Angelomorphic Christology

Perhaps the methodology here invoked is most readily seen in a consideration of "angelomorphic Christology." Jean Daniélou has demonstrated that terms borrowed from the vocabulary of angelology were used widely up to the fourth century with reference to Christ and the Spirit, and that after that time these expressions tended to disappear because of their ambiguity and the use made of them by the Arians.[4] Of the Ebionites, Tertullian says that they make of Christ a mere man, "though more glorious than the prophets, in that they say that an angel was in him";[5] and Epiphanius reports that "they say that he [Christ] was not begotten of God the Father, but created as one of the archangels ... that he rules over the angels and all the creatures of the Almighty."[6]

---

[3] Cf. now my *New Wine into Fresh Wineskins: Contextualizing the Early Christian Confessions* (Peabody: Hendrickson, 1999), esp. Part I, pp. 5-44.

[4] J. Daniélou, "Trinité et angélologie dans la théologie judéo-chrétienne," *RSR* 45 (1957) 5-41 (ET: "The Trinity and Angelology," in his *The Theology of Jewish Christianity*, trans. J. A. Baker [Chicago: Regnery, 1964] 117-46).

[5] *De carne Christi* 14.5; see also the entire fourteenth chapter.

[6] *Haereses* 20.16.4.

In *Testament of Dan* 6:2 there seems to be a transposition from the Jewish theme of the intercession of the angel Michael for the nation Israel to the Jewish-Christian theme of the mediatorship of Christ along with the defense of Israel, in the exhortation: "Draw near unto God and unto the angel that intercedeth for you, for he is a mediator between God and men, and for the peace of Israel shall he stand up against the kingdom of the enemy."[7] Admittedly, this interpretation is dependent on a Christian provenance for the Greek Testaments. Similarly, and with the same critical problem, *Testament of Levi* 5:6 seems to make this same transposition in Levi's dialogue with the angel and his identification of that angel as "the angel who intercedes for the nation Israel *and* for all the righteous" (italics mine).

In *Clementine Homilies* 18.4 and *Recognitions* 2.42 there is a comparable pattern in the representation of the seventy nations governed by seventy angels, over whom Christ rules as the greatest of the archangels and therefore is called "God of gods." The *Shepherd of Hermas* speaks frequently of the exalted Lord as the "glorious angel," the "most venerable angel," the "holy angel," and the "angel of the Lord," and distinguishes him quite clearly from other angels who are sent by him to guide Hermas.[8]

Even Origen, though not a *Jewish* Christian, comes close to an angelomorphic Christology in his identification of the two seraphim of Isa 6:3 as being Christ and the Holy Spirit.[9] But, interestingly, Origen claims to have received this interpretation from a Hebrew teacher—though whether he means that the germinal idea was received from a non-Christian Jew and he Christianized it or that this was the interpretation of some Jewish-Christian instructor is uncertain, and probably not vitally important here. It is sufficient to note that even in this moderate approach to angelomorphic Christology a Jewish source is cited.

I am not suggesting by citing Ebionite references that I think all Jewish Christians were Ebionites, either in patristic times or in the

---

[7] On the identification of Michael with Christ in early Christian angelomorphic Christology, see, e.g., *Shepherd of Hermas, Similitudes* 8.3.3 and *2 Enoch* 22:4-9. On the correspondence of Melchizedek and Michael at Qumran, see *11QMelchizedek*.

[8] Cf. *Shepherd of Hermas, Visions* 5.2; *Commandments* 5.1.7; *Similitudes* 5.4.4; 7.1-3, 5; 8.1; 2.1; and 9.1.3; 12.7-8.

[9] *De principiis* 1.3.4.

apostolic period, or that only Ebionites used such imagery and expressions. What I am proposing as probable is that various groups within what can be labeled "Jewish Christianity" in the patristic period shared a common body of conceptual imagery and expression, and that angelomorphic Christology was used in both heterodox formulations and more orthodox ones.

That second-century Christian tradition included an angelomorphic representation of Christ is directly attested by Justin in the *Dialogue*:

> But if you knew, Trypho, who He is that is called at one time the Angel of great counsel, and a Man by Ezekiel, and like the Son of man by Daniel, and a Child by Isaiah, and Christ and God to be worshipped by David, and Christ and a Stone by many, and Wisdom by Solomon, and Joseph and Judah and a Star by Moses, and the East by Zechariah, and the Suffering One and Jacob and Israel by Isaiah again, and a Rod, and Flower, and Cornerstone, and Son of God, you would not have blasphemed Him who has now come, and been born, and suffered, and ascended to heaven; who shall also come again, and then your twelve tribes shall mourn.[10]

Here Justin seems to be marshaling titles and giving a précis of the Gospel such as he believes pertinent for a Jewish audience. And it is significant that he begins by identifying Christ as "the Angel of great counsel."

So, too, the *Gospel of Thomas*, while itself opting for a more esoteric evaluation of Jesus, nonetheless acknowledges that angelomorphic Christology was a prominent element in certain Christian circles of the second century—as is indicated in the first part of Logion 13:

> Jesus said to his disciples: Make a comparison to me and tell me whom I am like. Simon Peter said to him: "You are like a righteous angel." Matthew said to him: "You are like a wise philosopher." Thomas said to him: "Master, my mouth is not at all able to bear that I say whom you are like."

It therefore seems well within the evidence to conclude that in the patristic period angelomorphic Christology expressed itself within Jewish-Christian circles, and, to some extent, in the writings of certain Gentile Christians who had been influenced by Jewish or Jewish-Christian patterns of thought.

---

[10] *Dialogue with Trypho* 126.1-2. Cf. also Justin's christological understanding of the "angel of the Lord" in *Dialogue* 55.10; 58.3; 126.4-5.

7. Distinctive Early Christological Motifs

That sources for angelomorphic expression can be found in pre-Christian Judaism is obvious. The Old Testament speaks of the theophanic presence as the "Angel of God," the "Angel of Yahweh," or simply "the Angel,"[11] thereby offering solid biblical support for the Christian attribution of angelomorphic categories to Christ. The LXX indicates an interest in angels in its translations of Deut 32:8, 33:2, and Ps 8:5.

In the Talmud, God is viewed as surrounded by his heavenly courtiers, each with his proper rank and particular function—though it needs also to be noted that in talmudic Judaism "angels, however abundant, have small religious importance."[12] They act in communicating God's message to humans. But the rabbinic attitude toward their conveyance of humans' prayers to God is far less positive, and even ambiguous. A Jerusalem Gemara explicitly forbids prayer via angelic mediation;[13] though the Babylonian Talmud seems to allow it if one prays in Hebrew—the angels being ignorant of Aramaic.[14] But this restriction would seem to limit quite seriously the mediatorial value of angels for the common people (the *'am haaretz*), and, practically speaking, tends to substantiate George Foot Moore's judgment that "in orthodox Judaism they [i.e., angels] were not intermediaries between man and God."[15]

Philo, too, has an angelology. For him, as with Judaism generally, angels serve in the administration of the cosmos and in the communication of revelations. But in his attempt to bridge the gap between the pure Being of God and the world of Becoming, angels were "a considerably vaguer category" than either Logos, who is

---

[11] מלאך אלים: Gen 21:17; 31:11; Exod 14:19; Judg 6:20; 13:6, 9; מלאך יהוה: Gen 16:7-11; 22:11, 15; Exod 3:2; Num 22:22-35; Judg 2:1, 4; 5:23; 6:11-22; 13:3-21; המלאך: Gen 48:16.

[12] C. G. Montefiore and H. Loewe, eds., *A Rabbinic Anthology* (London: Macmillan, 1938), 23.

[13] *J. Berakoth* 13 a: "If a man is in distress, let him not call on Michael or Gabriel, but let him call direct on me, and I will hearken to him straightway." Cf. also *4 Ezra* 7:102-15, where mediation of any kind is explicitly denied.

[14] *B. Shabbath* 12b; *b. Sotah* 33a. The prohibition against prayer in Aramaic is ascribed to R. Judah the Prince. As Roy A. Stewart has pointed out, the prohibition "may be pro-Hebraic rather than anti-angelic" (*Rabbinic Theology: An Introductory Study* [Edinburgh: Oliver & Boyd, 1961], 57).

[15] G. F. Moore, *Judaism in the First Centuries of the Christian Era*, 3 vols. (Cambridge, MA: Harvard University Press, 1927-30), 1.411.

7. Distinctive Early Christological Motifs 152

God's Thought or Reason, or Powers, which are manifestations of divine activity.[16] Angels in the Philonic treatment are subsumed under the broader concept of Powers—though, significantly, they are ruled over by the Logos, the "elder of the angels" (τὸν ἀγγέλων πρεσβύτατον) or the "archangel as it were" (ὡς ἂν ἀρχάγγελον).[17]

Of greatest significance for our purpose here, however, is the angelology of the Dead Sea Scrolls and related apocryphal literature. At the close of a lengthy description of an Essene candidate's initiatory rites, Josephus tells us that the sectarian proselyte was "carefully to preserve the books of the sect and the names of the angels."[18] And the writings found at Qumran—both the distinctively sectarian materials and the works taken over by the group—evidence an elaborate angelology, particularly in the larger portions of *1QS*, *1QH*, *1QM*, and *1 Enoch* 1–36 though also in the fragments. Especially important in this material, however, are features having to do with angelic ministration in the redemption of humanity. For not only are angels considered to superintend the created universe and to act as messengers of God to humans, they also aid people to be acceptable to God,[19] convey people's prayers to the Almighty,[20] and act as intercessors before God on behalf of people as well.[21]

When these matters of redemptive angelic ministration and angelomorphic Christology are extrapolated into the New Testament, interesting correspondences result. We need not dwell on the general angelology of the New Testament, for that is too common to be important here. Nor need we consider the common Jewish theme of

---

[16] Cf. H. A. A. Kennedy, *Philo's Contribution to Religion* (London: Hodder & Stoughton, 1919), 162.

[17] *De confusione linguarum* 146.

[18] *War* 2.8.7 (Loeb); 2.142 (Whiston).

[19] Note, for example, discussions in *1QS* 3.18ff. and *1QM* 13.9-10 regarding the "Angel of Truth" or "Light" as helping people to be acceptable in spite of all that the "Angel of Darkness" or "Hostility" can do to the contrary. Cf. also *11QMelchizedek*.

[20] E.g., *1QH* 6.13; *Tobit* 12:12-15; *3 Baruch* 11–17.

[21] E.g., *1 Enoch* 9:10; 15:2; 99:3, 16; *2 Baruch* 6:7 (also *1 Enoch* 40:9; 47:2; *Testament of Levi* 3:5; 5:6-7, though here methodologically ruled out). On the angelic liturgy and angels as having priestly characteristics at Qumran, see J. Strugnell, "The Angelic Liturgy at Qumran—4Q Serek Sirot 'Olat Hassabbat'," *Congress Volume: Oxford, 1959* (VTSup, 7; Leiden: Brill, 1960), 318-45. Only in Zech 1:12 is there anything similar in the Old Testament.

7. Distinctive Early Christological Motifs 153

the presence of angels in the giving of the Mosaic law in Acts 7:53, Gal 3:19-20, and Heb 2:2, though that is somewhat more to the point. The wide dissemination of this theme via the LXX translation of Deut 33:2 and rabbinic exposition on it, however, makes it difficult to handle with any precision. What does seem significant, however, is (1) the association in certain New Testament passages of angels with Christ and redemption, and (2) that the clearest instances of this association are to be found in polemical portions directed against certain Jewish-Christian views then current.

Assuming a Jewish-Christian identification for the troublers at Galatia (*contra* Johannes Munck, though not going to the other extreme of Hans J. Schoeps and S. G. F. Brandon in equating them with the whole of the Jerusalem Church), Paul's references to angels in that letter are for our purposes here highly significant. For in Gal 1:8 he anathematizes even an angelic revelation if it conflicts with what he has proclaimed, and in Gal 3:19-20 he contrasts the angelic and Mosaic mediated covenant with that which is the better in Christ. Evidently, his converts were beginning to restructure their thinking along angelomorphic lines to the detriment of the primacy and sufficiency of Christ—or, at least, Paul thought that there was this danger inherent in the false teaching that enticed them. And the apostle speaks against it.

Further, in Gal 4:14, in what is probably a play on their reconstituted conceptual imagery, Paul seems to equate the "angel of God" with "Christ Jesus" in his reminder to them that they received him on his former visit "as an angel of God, as Christ Jesus" (ὡς ἄγγελον θεοῦ, ὡς Χριστὸν Ἰησοῦν). In Colossians, assuming some type of syncretistic Jewish-Christian agitation behind the difficulties in the Lycus Valley, Paul speaks in 2:18 of "the worship of angels," by which he probably means, as in the Galatian letter, such prominence given to angelic manifestations and angelomorphic categories as to minimize the uniqueness of Christ.[22]

In the Epistle to the Hebrews, assuming some type of Jewish-Christian audience—whether in Palestine–Syria, Rome, or Corinth—for

---

[22] The assertion in the *Preaching of Peter*, as preserved by Clement of Alexandria and Origen (cf. E. Hennecke, *New Testament Apocrypha*, 2 vols., ed. W. Schneemelcher, trans. and ed. R. McL. Wilson [London: Lutterworth, 1963], 2.100-101), that the Jews worship angels, probably stems from this statement in Col 2:18.

which a return to Judaism was a live option, the opening argument of chapters 1 and 2 on the supremacy of the Son over angelic ministers seems to point to some type of doctrine of redemptive angelology held by the recipients.[23] Perhaps, also, inferences can be drawn from the frequency of angels in the Lucan birth narrative, if this can be related to translation phenomena or to a literary use of sources, as well as in the Matthean infancy account.

But whatever is thought regarding these latter cases in Luke and Matthew, it does seem from the polemic on the part of those in the Gentile mission against certain antagonists and views held within the Jewish mission that angelomorphic Christology, or something approaching it, was an element within Jewish Christianity in apostolic times. Again, this is not to claim that Gentile Christianity and Jewish Christianity stood in essential opposition throughout (though, for the extremes in both groups, this may very well have been the case). It is only to assert that probably just as the Gentile mission operated within a body of conceptual imagery and expression, though with varieties evident within the cycle, so the Jewish mission in its various manifestations shared common patterns of thought and expression. There was undoubtedly a great deal of overlapping. But distinctives also seem evident. And one of these distinctive emphases on the part of Jewish Christians was apparently that of angelomorphic Christology.[24]

---

[23] *11QMelchizedek*, as M. de Jonge and A. S. van der Woude have noted, "illustrates the type of thinking about angels and other heavenly beings which the author of Hebrews is up against" ("11Q Melchizedek and the New Testament," *NTS* 12 [1966] 301-26 [317]).

[24] Wilhelm Michaelis has argued "dass das Urchristentum keine Engelchristologie gekannt hat" (*Zur Engelchristologie im Urchristentum* [Basel: Majer, 1942], 187). But that judgment was leveled against the thesis of Martin Werner that Jewish apocalypticism had an Angel-Messianology (as seen particularly in Dan 7:13, the *Testament of Levi*, and the "Similitudes" of *1 Enoch* 37–71, which was simply carried over into early Christianity—with the result that the church's earliest Christology was essentially an Angel Christology (cf. M. Werner, *Die Entstehung des christlichen Dogmas* [Tübingen: Katzmann, 1941], 302-49). Both methodologically and theologically, however, the material presented above finds little parallel with Werner's treatment, and so is not really affected by Michaelis's negative review.

3. The Name

In the Valentinian *Gospel of Truth*, the theme of the Son as the Name of the Father is explicitly developed at length in 38:6–41:3. The passage begins:

> The Name of the Father is the Son. It is He who, in the principle, gave a name to Him who came forth from Him and who was Himself, and whom He engendered as a Son. He gave Him His Name which belonged to Him—He, the Father to whom belong all things which exist around Him. He possesses the Name; He has the Son. ... One does not pronounce the Name of the Father; but He reveals Himself through a Son. Thus, then, the Name is great.

The *Gospel of Philip*, in Logion 12, also speaks of "the Name that the Father gave to the Son, which is above all things, which is the Name of the Father,"[25] Jean Daniélou has argued that already in *1 Clement* and the *Shepherd of Hermas*, especially in the liturgical sections reflecting traditional material, there are echoes of such an earlier christological attribution, though not anywhere as strong as it appears in the Nag Hammadi Gospels.[26] Gilles Quispel has shown that speculations on the divine Name as a quasi-hypostatic entity active in the mediation of revelation can be observed in pre-Christian esoteric Judaism and Jewish-Christian heterodoxy of the third to sixth centuries.[27] And Gershom Scholem, following out the work of Hugo Odeberg, points out that in later Jewish mystical writings there appear similar speculations on the Angel of the Lord in whom is the Name of the Lord, who is the bearer of all the divine attributes and who is to guide people before the throne of God.[28]

The *locus classicus* for this concept is Exod 23:20-21, where God promises to send an Angel before the people and warns them to take heed to him for "my name is in him." And it finds support in the many Old Testament passages where the divine Name (שם) signals the

---

[25] Cf. also *Gospel of Philip*, Logion 19.

[26] J. Daniélou, *The Theology of Jewish Christianity*, trans. J. A. Baker (Chicago: Regnery, 1964), 151-57.

[27] G. Quispel, "The Jung Codex and Its Significance," in *The Jung Codex. A Newly Recovered Gnostic Papyrus*, trans. F. L. Cross (London: Mowbray, 1955), 68-78. The provenance of *1 Enoch* 69:14, however, may be questioned.

[28] G. G. Scholem, *Major Trends in Jewish Mysticism* (New York: Schocken, 1941), 212-17; cf. H. Odeberg, *3 Enoch or the Hebrew Book of Enoch* (New York: KTAV, 1928), 144.

presence of God.²⁹ In the alteration of the first person suffix to that of the third person masculine in *1QIs^a* 51.5, there is the strong hint that the Dead Sea sectarians understood God's ethical qualities and attributes in the eschatological portions of Isaiah as descriptive names for the Messiah.³⁰ Thus the cry "O Lord, we await your Name" of *1QIs^a* 26.8 is probably to be read with messianic import. It is possible that we should understand the profaning of "the Name" and references to God's "Great Name" in the other Scrolls as having messianic significance as well.³¹ Evidencing his Jewish background, though blending into it extraneous elements, Philo employs τὸ ὄνομα as one of the names of the Logos.³²

Extrapolating into the New Testament, instances of the use of "the Name" take on greater significance. And significantly, as I believe, it is the Jewish-Christian writings of the New Testament that evidence both a greater interest in the name of Jesus generally and an almost exclusive use of "the Name" as a christological designation.

In the Gospel of Matthew there is an emphasis on the name of Jesus such as is not found in the other Synoptic Gospels. While both Matthew and Luke tell of the circumstances in the naming of Jesus, only Matthew speaks of the significance of the name.³³ Also, only Matthew records Jesus' promise of his presence in any gathering, however small, that meets "in my name" (εἰς τὸ ἐμὸν ὄνομα).³⁴ All three Synoptic Gospels recount Jesus' words regarding leaving everything, house, family, and relatives for his sake and the purposes of the Gospel. But whereas Mark's account reads "for my sake and for the

---

²⁹ E.g., Deut 12:11, 21; 14:23-24; 16:2, 6, 11; 26:2; Neh 1:9; Ps 74:7; Isa 18:7; Jer 3:17; 7:10-14, 30.

³⁰ Cf. D. Barthélemy, "Le grand rouleau d'Isaïe trouvé près de la Mer Morte," *RB* 57 (1950) 530-49 (548, n. 2); J. V. Chamberlain, "The Functions of God as Messianic Titles in the Complete Qumran Isaiah Scroll," *VT* 5 (1955) 369-70.

³¹ *CDC* 15.3 (19:4). T. H. Gaster fills in the lacuna of line 2 to read: "for the name of God is spelled out in that law" (*The Dead Sea Scriptures in English Translation* [Garden City: Doubleday, 1964], 95). See also *1QM* 11.2-3; 18.6, 8; *1QH* 11.6; 12.3.

³² Of the Logos, Philo says: "And many names are his, for he is called "the Beginning" (ἀρχή), and the Name of God (ὄνομα θεοῦ), and His Word (λόγος), and the Man after His image (ὁ κατ' εἰκόνα ἄνθρωπος), and "he that sees" (ὁ ὁρῶν), that is Israel" (*De confusione linguarum* 146).

³³ Matt 1:21-25; cf. Luke 1:31; 2:21.

³⁴ Matt 18:20.

Gospel,"[35] and Luke's "for the sake of the kingdom of God,"[36] Matthew's wording is "for my name's sake" (ἕνεκεν τοῦ ὀνόματός μου).[37] In the sending out of the twelve to evangelize the countryside, only Matthew records the apocalyptic portion that includes the warning: "And you will be hated by all people because of my name" (διὰ τὸ ὄνομά μου).[38] Matthew alone describes pseudo-Christians rejected by Jesus as those preaching and working wonders "in your [Jesus'] name" (thrice: τῷ σῷ ὀνόματι).[39] And in the last three verses of the First Gospel, it is the name of the triune God, together with the authority of Jesus, that is central.[40]

John's Gospel stresses believing "in his name" (εἰς τὸ ὄνομα αὐτοῦ),[41] life "in his name" (ἐν τῷ ὀνόματι αὐτοῦ),[42] and Jesus' invitation to ask "in my name" (ἐν τῷ ὀνόματί μου).[43] Acts tells of Jewish exorcists at Ephesus who wanted to profit by the power of the name of Jesus,[44] and of "the name of the Lord Jesus" being held "in high honor" among both Jews and Gentiles of that city when dire consequences came on those exorcists because of their misuse of Jesus' name.[45] It also reports Paul's account of the Jewish-Christian Ananias telling him to call "on his name"—which, in context, may also be a christological ascription.[46] And the Johannine Apocalypse evidences an interest in "a new name" and "the name of my God" given to Christians.[47]

---

[35] Mark 10:29.
[36] Luke 18:29.
[37] Matt 19:29.
[38] Matt 10:22; though in a later apocalyptic section the warning is repeated, and all three Synoptic Gospels include the phrase διὰ τὸ ὄνομά μου (Matt 24:9, Mark 13:13, and Luke 21:17; cf. also Luke 21:12).
[39] Matt 7:21-23; cf. Luke 6:46.
[40] Matt 28:18-20. Cf. H. Kosmala, "The Conclusion of Matthew," *ASTI* 4 (1965) 140-41, with whom I agree with respect to centrality, though without accepting his exclusively christological treatment of the passage.
[41] John 1:12; 2:23; 3:18.
[42] John 20:31.
[43] John 14:13-14; 15:16; 16:23-26.
[44] Acts 19:13-16.
[45] Acts 19:17.
[46] Acts 22:16.
[47] Rev 2:17; 3:12.

Paul, of course, refers to the name of Jesus as well: in appeal to the Corinthians "by (διά) the name of our Lord Jesus Christ,"[48] in alluding to his converts' baptism in Jesus' name,[49] in speaking of their gathering together "in the name of our Lord Jesus,"[50] in exorcising an evil spirit,[51] and in teaching on prayer and diligence.[52] But his use of the expression seems to be largely traditional and is relatively infrequent.

As a christological designation, "the Name" appears almost exclusively in materials that reflect the Jewish-Christian mission and Jewish-Christian interests. The three uses of Joel 3:5 (MT; 2:32 in LXX) in Acts 2:21, 4:12, and Rom 10:13, where the calling on the "name of the Lord" refers to God in the Old Testament and the exalted Jesus in the New Testament, are all within a Jewish-Christian context—even the latter, set as it is in Paul's discussion of the "Jewish Question" in Romans 9–11. The strange wording of Acts 3:16 ("His name, through faith in his name, has made this man strong"), which has often been declared to be a mistranslation on the part of the author of Acts,[53] is rather to be explained as an archaic remnant of an early Jewish-Christian Christology. Likewise James's reference to the rich who blaspheme "the good name (τὸ καλὸν ὄνομα) by which you are called," which plainly has reference to blaspheming the name of Jesus.[54] And the opening lines of the second part of the christological hymn reproduced by Paul in his Philippian letter carry a similar significance: "Therefore God has highly exalted him and given him the name that is above every name, that at the name of Jesus every knew should bow."[55]

In John's Gospel, Jesus' prayers regarding declaring, manifesting, and glorifying God's name have christological import as well, for the

---

[48] 1 Cor 1:10.

[49] 1 Cor 1:13.

[50] 1 Cor 5:3-5, though with which clause "in the name of our Lord Jesus" is to be associated is somewhat problematic.

[51] Acts 16:18.

[52] Col 3:17; Eph 5:20.

[53] Cf., e.g., C. C. Torrey, *The Composition and Date of Acts* (HTS 1; Cambridge, MA: Harvard University Press, 1916), 14-16; F. J. Foakes Jackson and K. Lake, *The Beginnings of Christianity*, 5 vols. (London: Macmillan, 1920–1933), 2.142.

[54] Jas 2:7.

[55] Phil 2:9-10a.

evangelist's intent is clearly to demonstrate that in the person and redemptive ministry of Jesus exactly this was accomplished.[56] And this archaic understanding of the significance of "the Name" is probably the basis for Jesus' statement in John 8:58 that "before Abraham was, I am"—as well as for the "I am" analogies of the Fourth Gospel—whether we take these as dominical or later expressions of an earlier consciousness.[57]

Just as "the Name" was a pious Jewish surrogate for God, so for early Jewish Christians it became a designation for Jesus, the Lord's Christ. And as in its Jewish usage, so for Christians it connoted the divine presence and power.[58] It had a definite history. And while used more widely and combined with other emphases as the Christian message spread, it seems to have been originally employed meaningfully in a Jewish-Christian context.[59] When divorced from its Jewish associations, however, it appears to have suffered subordinationistic interpretations.

4. Expressions of Primacy and Priority

The Christian conviction regarding the primacy and priority of Jesus in the redemptive activity of God comes to expression in the Jewish-Christian materials of the New Testament in various ways and forms. At times, the language of Old Testament devotion is employed; at times, motifs drawn from Israel's wisdom literature are invoked; and at times, terms in common coin from the Hellenistic world are used. While lines are not clearly drawn, there are features that should be noted as being fairly distinctive.

In the first place, there is the imagery of "the stone"—especially the "rejected stone–copestone" motif. All three of the Synoptic Gospels

---

[56] John 12:28; 17:6, 26.

[57] John 6:35; 8:12; 10:7, 9, 11, 14; 11:25; 14:6; 15:1; cf. also 8:23-24, 28; 13:19. For a denial of dominical status set in the context of a high view of Johannine historicity generally, see A. J. B. Higgins, *Historicity of the Fourth Gospel* (London: Lutterworth, 1960), 73-74. In defense of the absolute "I am" on the lips of Jesus and its correlation with the divine Name, see H. Zimmermann, "Das absolute 'Ich bin' in der Redeweise Jesu," *TTZ* 69 (1960) 1-20; *idem*, "Das absolute ἐγώ εἰμι als die neutestamentliche Offenbarungsformel," *BZ* 4 (1960) 54-69 and 266-76.

[58] Cf., e.g., Acts 3:16; 4:7, 10; 16:18; 19:13-17.

[59] *Contra* R. Bultmann, *Theology of the New Testament*, 2 vols., trans. K. Grobel (London: SCM, 1952), 1.40.

record that Jesus applied Ps 118:22 to himself: "The stone that the builders rejected has become the 'head of the corner'."⁶⁰ And the New Testament evidences three christological variations on the stone theme, with three different Old Testament texts used in support: (1) the "rejected stone that has become the head of the corner" (ὁ λίθος ὁ ἐξουθενηθείς ... ὁ γενόμενος εἰς κεφαλὴν γωνίας) based on Ps 118:22; (2) the "cornerstone" (λίθος ἀκρογωνιαῖος) based on Isa 28:16; and, (3) the "stone of stumbling and rock of offense" (λίθος προσκόμματος καὶ πέτρα σκανδάλου) based on Isa 8:14. The first is confined to materials having a Jewish-Christian base—that is, Acts 4:11 and 1 Pet 2:4, 7, with both instances credited to Peter. The second is implicit in 1 Cor 3:11, and comes to expression in Eph 2:20 and 1 Pet 2:5-6. The third is found in Rom 9:33, Luke 20:18, and 1 Pet 2:8.

Joachim Jeremias has argued that both "cornerstone" (λίθος ἀκρογωνιαῖος) and "stone at the head of the corner" (λίθος ... κεφαλὴ γωνίας) should be understood as a "copestone" or "topstone" (*Abschlussstein*), and not as a "foundation stone" (*Grundstein*).⁶¹ And he has marshaled a number of texts in support—the most significant of these being the Jewish *Testament of Solomon* 22:7–23:4, which can be dated to the first century CE, where both λίθος ἀκρογωνιαῖος and λίθος ... κεφαλὴ γωνίας are unambiguously used with reference to the final copestone at the summit of the Jerusalem temple and where Ps 118:22 is applied to it.⁶² New Testament scholarship has largely followed Jeremias here, with many interpreters even going beyond him to understand the reference to be to a keystone of an archway that serves as a locking-stone for the whole structure.⁶³

Nonetheless, it should be noted, as well, that "cornerstone" and Isa 28:16 are also used in Jewish literature with reference to a founda-

---

⁶⁰ Matt 21:42; Mark 12:10-11; Luke 20:17-18.

⁶¹ J. Jeremias, "κεφαλὴ γωνίας—ἀκρογωνιαῖος," *ZNW* 29 (1930) 264-80; idem, "Eckstein—Schlussstein," *ZNW* 36 (1937) 154-57; idem, "γωνία, ἀκρογωνιαῖος, κεφαλὴ γωνίας," *TWNT* 1.792-93; idem, "λίθος," *TWNT* 4.275-83.

⁶² Cf. Symmachus's translation of 2 Kgs 25:17, which reads ἀκρογωνιαῖος; also note the Peshitta rendering of Isa 28:16 as "head of the wall."

⁶³ See the bibliography in R. J. McKelvey, "Christ the Cornerstone," *NTS* 8 (1962) 352-59 (352-53). Note the translation "keystone" in the Jerusalem Bible at Acts 4:11 and 1 Pet 2:7, as well as in the text of the New English Bible at Acts 4:11 and footnote to Eph 2:20.

tional stone on which a building is erected, as is clear in *1QS* 8.4 and *b. Yoma* 54ᵃ.[64] It seems therefore that while Jeremias has demonstrated a very important point, particularly with regard to a first-century Jewish understanding of the figure in Ps 118:22, his conclusion cannot be applied rigidly in every instance where λίθος appears as a christological ascription. Variations existed within contemporary Judaism on the stone theme, and an understanding of its use in the New Testament must depend on the individual contexts.

In Jesus' use of Ps 118:22, as well as its employment in Acts 4:11 and 1 Pet 2:4, 7, it is probable that the idea of the rejected stone that has become the copestone or topstone of the building, thereby consummating all previous building activity and standing supreme over the whole structure, is in mind. And very likely this "rejected stone–copestone" motif, finding its basis in the teaching of Jesus and having pertinence to the fulfillment message of the earliest Christians, was the original theme in the Jerusalem Church, to which were added the "foundational" and "stumbling" motifs. The inclusion of all three in 1 Pet 2:4-8 probably indicates a later development—possibly under Pauline influence, which may be partially explained by the acknowledgment in 1 Pet 5:12 of Silas's hand in the composition, though just as possibly due to variations on the theme current in Jewish circles. But even here it should be noted that the "rejected stone–capstone (head of the corner)" motif is dominant in the passage, as witness both the order of listing and the relative frequency of occurrence.

Paul's development in 1 Cor 10:4 of the rabbinical legend of the accompanying rock in the wilderness,[65] which he calls a "spiritual rock" and identifies with Christ, may have been inspired to some extent by an early Christian "stone" theme, though it evidences no necessary connection. But whatever the history of the rabbinic legend and however Paul was inspired to use it, his allusion points to a contemporary Jewish tendency to conceptualize the divine presence in terms of a rock or stone.

---

[64] Cf. also *1QS* 5.6; 9.5-6; *j. Sanh.* 29ᵃ; *Exodus Rabbah* 15.7. See McKelvey, "Christ the Cornerstone," as a corrective to Jeremias. In fairness, however, Jeremias's one-paragraph qualification on Isa 28:16 should be noted (*TWNT* 4.279), though, admittedly, it is far too reserved.

[65] On the rabbinic legend, see E. E. Ellis, *Paul's Use of the Old Testament* (Edinburgh: Oliver & Boyd; Grand Rapids: Eerdmans, 1957), 66-70.

In the second century Christ is spoken of as a "stone," "rock," and "corner-stone" by Justin, the author of the *Shepherd of Hermas*, and the author of the *Epistle of Barnabas*.⁶⁶ Here are witnesses to "stone" as an early christological ascription, though it is also evident that by the time of these "apostolic fathers" the earlier variations in that designation had either vanished or become amalgamated. Logion 66 of the *Gospel of Thomas* reads: "Jesus said: 'Show me the stone that the builders have rejected; it is the cornerstone.'" Though set in a gnostic framework, and perhaps not meant to be a christological affirmation in that context, this saying seems to have carried into the second century elements of the original Jewish-Christian identification of Jesus as the "rejected stone who has become the copestone"—thereby preserving to some extent the dual emphasis found in the earliest christological stone ascription of rejection and of primacy.

In writings of the patristic period, Christ is also often designated by such terms as ἀρχή and πρωτότοκος, and their cognates. For example, to cite some significant second-century instances, Theophilus of Antioch appealed to the LXX of Gen 1:1 (ἐν ἀρχῇ ἐποίησεν ὁ θεός; "in the beginning God created") in support of ἀρχή ("beginning") as being a christological ascription.⁶⁷ And Gen 1:1 was the usual proof-text for such an assertion—though Justin had earlier used also Prov 8:22, "the Lord created me in the beginning (ἀρχή) of his way."⁶⁸

Clement of Alexandria calls Christ the ἀρχή and πρωτότοκος, crediting the early second-century *Preaching of Peter* as his source and attributing to Peter's "accurate understanding" of Gen 1:1 the origin of these ascriptions.⁶⁹ Similarly, Jerome speaks of "the Gospel written in the Hebrew speech that the Nazarenes read" as calling Christ the Spirit's "firstborn Son that reignest forever."⁷⁰ Not only Theophilus of Antioch's geographical proximity to Jewish-Christian centers and Justin's evident acquaintance with Jewish motifs, but also the direct assertions of Clement of Alexandria and Jerome as to their

---

⁶⁶ Justin, *Dialogue* 126:1-2; *Shepherd of Hermas*, *Similitudes* 9.12.1ff.; *Epistle of Barnabas* 6:2ff.
⁶⁷ *Ad Autolycum* 2.10.
⁶⁸ *Dialogue* 61:1; 62:4.
⁶⁹ *Stromata* 6.7.58.
⁷⁰ *Commentary on Isaiah* 4, on Isa 11:2; cf. E. Hennecke, *New Testament Apocrypha* 1.163-64.

source lend credence to the idea that the connection of ἀρχή and πρωτότοκος, and their cognates, with Christ took place first in Jewish-Christian circles, and then spread more widely.

There are a number of expressions denoting primacy and priority in the New Testament that are applied to Jesus. I refer especially to ἀρχή ("beginning"), ἀρχηγός ("chief one," "leader," "prince," "founder," "originator," "pioneer"), πρωτότοκος ("firstborn"), μονογενής ("unique," "one and only"), κεφαλή ("head"), μορφή ("express form"), and εἰκών ("image," "likeness," "form"). And, interestingly, the majority occur in material that is either Jewish-Christian in nature or polemical against certain Jewish-Christian errors—the only exceptions being the use of πρωτότοκος in Rom 8:29, εἰκών in 2 Cor 4:4, and κεφαλή in Ephesians. Omitting consideration of the much discussed Col 1:15-20 for the moment, Peter is recorded as speaking of the exalted Jesus as "the ἀρχηγός of life" in Acts 3:15, "ἀρχηγός and savior" at God's right hand in Acts 5:31, and "κεφαλή of the corner" in Acts 4:11 and 1 Pet 2:7. In the hymn of Phil 2:6-11, Jesus is spoken of as being "in the μορφή of God" (v 6) and exalted (vv 9-11). He is the πρωτότοκος who is worthy of angelic worship in Heb 1:6, the ἀρχηγός of the believer's salvation in Heb 2:10, and the ἀρχηγός of faith in Heb 12:2. He is the μονογενής Son of God the Father in John 1:14, 3:16, 18, and 1 John 4:9—perhaps even the μονογενής θεός in John 1:18. He is ἀρχὴ καὶ τὸ τέλος ("the beginning and the end") in Rev 21:6 and 22:13 (also 1:8 in Codex Sinaiticus) and "the ἀρχή of the creation of God" in Rev 3:14. Perhaps also "the Alpha and the Omega" of Rev 1:8, 21:6, and 22:13 should be joined to these expressions.[71] And the description in Heb 1:3 of the Son as "the effulgence (ἀπαύγασμα) of the glory [of God] and the very stamp of his nature" is only a paraphrase of the concept of "image" (εἰκών).

---

[71] W. H. Brownlee has suggested that the Hebrew letter *aleph* of *1QS* 10.1 should be understood as an abbreviation for Elohim, forming an acrostic with the letters *men* and *num* of the following lines (*The Dead Sea Manual of Discipline*, BASOR Suppl.Studies 10–12 [1951] 50-51; idem, "Messianic Motifs of Qumran and the New Testament," NTS 3 (1956) 12-30; 3 (1957) 195-210 [201-203]). Cf. also Gaster's translation (*Dead Sea Scriptures*, 126). If so, the use of the Greek letter *alpha* for Christ in the Johannine apocalypse would have a Palestinian foundation as well as hellenistic parallels. The problem here in reading *1QS* 10.1 is that the Hebrew letter *aleph*, with no space before it, may simply be understood as connected to the preceding word as a third person singular suffix.

It has been commonly asserted that since these terms originated in a hellenistic milieu, their presence in the New Testament indicates the hellenistic Christian character of those portions in which they are found.[72] But to this it must be said: (1) that these are terms which, though first coined in the cosmological speculations of Greek philosophy, were in common circulation among Jews during the period of Second Temple Judaism, both in the homeland and the Diaspora;[73] (2) that the presence of these terms in the LXX and the popular literature of pre-Christian Judaism would have guaranteed their wide disemination in Palestine, should they have needed any such aid in propagation;[74] and (3) that their transference to the status of christological ascriptions in the early church was motivated chiefly by religious rather than cosmological interests.

Where these terms of primacy and priority do seem to evidence gnostic or proto-gnostic influence, however, is in Col. 1:15-20—though that influence should probably be described differently than is usually the case. Assuming (1) a Jewish sectarian basis for the heresy at Colosse, as comparison with the Qumran material reveals, (2) incipient gnostic elements to have been incorporated into the heresy during its syncretistic development, and (3) Paul's use of some of the heretics' own terminology in dealing with their thought, perhaps even to the recasting of a hymnodic portion employed by them, it is plausible to view the basic problem in the Colossian church as that of the harmonization of a primarily religious conviction with an interest that is dominantly cosmological. It was the problem of reconciling the Christian conviction of the primacy and priority of Jesus—which hitherto had been considered mainly in religious and historical terms, but without any real thought given to questions of cosmology—with a Grecian understanding of gradations and relative

---

[72] E.g., Bultmann, *Theology of the New Testament*, 1.132-33 and 177-78.

[73] They were, of course, common to Philo in his descriptions of the Word (cf. esp. *De confusione linguarum* 146). Similarly, however, *1 Enoch* 15:9 speaks of evil spirits born of men and the Holy Watchers as "the beginning of creation and primal origin" (ἡ ἀρχὴ τῆς κτίσεως [cf. Rev 3:3, 14] καὶ ἀρχὴ θεμελίου)—which is a tautology, employing ἀρχή twice. *Wisdom of Solomon* 7:22-26 attributes to wisdom the terms μονογενής ("unique"), ἀπαύγασμα ("effulgence"), and εἰκών ("image"). Cf. also *1 Enoch* 106:10 on the use of εἰκών in connection with an awesome apocalyptic figure.

[74] Note, e.g., Exod 4:22; Jer 38:9 (MT 31:9); *1 Enoch* 15:9; 106:10; *Wisdom of Solomon* 7:22-26.

orders of primacy in the universe. Inherent in the problem was the conflict of differing *Weltanschauungen*: the one religious and historical, the other philosophic and cosmological. And it was a conflict that probably became exceedingly confused, for undoubtedly many of the same terms were used in the expression of these differing orientations. It was this commonness of terminology, in fact, that probably facilitated the submerging of the religiously based conviction of the primacy of Jesus into the maze of cosmological stratification in hellenistic thought, and made the heresy so difficult to treat at Colosse.

Paul's response to this challenge was the insistence that if one is to think philosophically as well as religiously, then indeed the primacy and priority of Jesus must be asserted in the cosmological sphere as well. No speculation, whatever its merits (and Paul seems to have had little inclination to enter into a discussion of relative merits on a philosophic basis), must be allowed to detract from the absolute supremacy of Jesus Christ. While the primacy of Jesus had hitherto been asserted in contexts that were primarily religious and historical, it had legitimate import for cosmology as well. Thus, in this context of thought, Paul insisted that Jesus is "the εἰκών of the invisible God," "the πρωτότοκος of all creation" and "from the dead," "the κεφαλή of the body," and "the ἀρχή." Further, in him "are hid all the treasures of wisdom (σοφία) and knowledge (γνῶσις)," in him "dwells the whole fullness (πᾶν τὸ πλήρωμα) of deity bodily," and he is "the head (κεφαλή) of all rule and authority (πάσης ἀρχῆς καὶ ἐξουσίας)," as the apostle goes on to say in Col 2:1-10 in answer to the specifically gnostic features of the heresy.[75]

In the Letter to the Colossians, Paul is not originating new christological designations. These, in the main, had been used of Jesus by Jewish Christians before him. What he is doing is extending their reference to the field of cosmological consideration. In response to

---

[75] C. F. Burney has argued that in Col 1:16-18 Paul is giving an elaborate midrashic exposition of the first word of Genesis, *bereshith*, and interpreting the *reshith* of Gen 1:1 and Prov 8:22 as referring to Christ ("Christ as the ΑΡΧΗ of Creation," *JTS* 27 (1926) 160-77; cf. also W. D. Davies, *Paul and Rabbinic Judaism: Some Rabbinic Elements in Pauline Theology* [London: SPCK, 1948[1], 1955[2], 1970[3]; Philadelphia: Fortress, 1980[4]], 150-52). What is said above is not meant to oppose Burney's highly significant thesis, but only to point out in addition that Paul's argument, while possibly following a rabbinic pattern exegetically, was circumstantially determined.

tendencies that would qualify the supremacy of Jesus by the imposition of a system of emanated and gradated primacies, Paul asserts the absolute primacy and priority of his Lord over all that may be envisaged. That his argument is circumstantially conditioned is evidenced by the letter to the Ephesians, where, assuming Pauline authorship, the apostle continues to use κεφαλή of Jesus but has turned from cosmology to ecclesiology.

And that this extension from categories of religious and historical primacy to one of cosmic supremacy was considered legitimate within the cycle of Jewish Christianity is seen in the somewhat similar treatment of the opening sentences of Hebrews and the Prologue to the Fourth Gospel. In Heb 1:2-3, the fact that the Son is "heir of all things" gives rise to the accompanying claim that he was *also* (note the extension of thought implied in the Greek connective καί) involved in the creation of all that exists (τοὺς αἰῶνας), and since he is "the effulgence of the glory [of God] and the very stamp of his nature" it follows that he is involved in the sustaining of the universe "by the word of his power." The Prologue of John's Gospel, which is conceptually subsequent to the body of the Gospel and may very well have been added later, speaks of Jesus as a pre-existent cosmic figure and connects him with the wisdom motif of the Logos.[76] It is significant that in both these cases the addressees have a similar background and seem to be influenced by similar ideas as expressed in the heresy at Colosse; and in both there is a similar extension of the ascriptions of primacy and priority as in Paul's Colossian response. But it should also be noted that all of these extensions into the cosmological sphere presuppose earlier christological attributions of religious primacy and historical priority. And while they were originally coined in the context of hellenistic philosophy, there is good reason to believe that such terms as ἀρχή, ἀρχηγός, πρωτότοκος,

---

[76] As has often been pointed out, the ascription λόγος in the Prologue differs from the rest of the Gospel. Probably, as V. Taylor has suggested, "if we infer that the Prologue was written last, as a summary of St. John's apprehension of the significance of the incarnation of the Son of God, we account better for the traditional element combined with interpretation present in the Gospel. The same inference is warranted if, as some have thought, he took over and adapted in i.1-18 a pre-Johannine hymn" (*The Person of Christ in New Testament Teaching* [London: Macmillan, 1958], 21). This connection of ἀρχή and its cognates with λόγος and its cognates is continued in such passages as Justin, *Dialogue* 61:1, and Clement of Alexandria, *Stromata* 4.7.58.

μονογενής, κεφαλή, μορφή, and εἰκών were early used of Jesus by Jewish Christians as well.

5. The "Katabasis–Anabasis" Theme

A further feature of early Jewish Christianity appears to have been the description of Jesus and the redemption accomplished by him in terms of the *"katabasis* (κατάβασις, 'descent')*–anabasis* (ἀνάβασις, 'ascent')" theme.

The hymn of Phil 2:6-11 begins in its first half (vv 6-8) with Christ as being "in the form of God," and then goes on to develop details of his humiliation: "form of a servant," "likeness of human beings," "obedient unto death," "even death on a cross." In its second half (vv 9-11), however, it concludes with an acclamation of his exaltation. In John's Gospel, this theme of *katabasis–anabasis* Christology comes to definite expression in two "Son of Man" sayings of Jesus: (1) "No one has ascended (οὐδεὶς ἀναβέβηκεν) into heaven except he who descended (ὁ καταβάς) from heaven, the Son of Man," of John 3:13; and (2) "What if you were to see the Son of Man ascending (ἀναβαίνοντα) where he was before?" of John 6:62. The first half of the motif underlies the Prologue of the Fourth Gospel, speaking as it does of pre-existence, divinity, and incarnation, while the second half is basic to the portrayal of the exalted Jesus throughout the Johannine Apocalypse.

The Epistle to the Hebrews indicates familiarity with this conceptual pattern in its presentation of the lowering, obedience, and temptations of Jesus in chapters 2 and 5, and in its doctrine of the heavenly high priesthood of Jesus in 4:14–10:18. Likewise, Eph 4:8-10—which is a midrashic explication of the statement "he ascended on high" of Ps 68:18, with applications to both Christ's "descent" and his "ascent"—probably incorporates a traditional understanding among early believers in Jesus, for both the citation of Ps 68:18 and the midrash that follows are given in such a manner as though commonly assumed.[77] Evidently, to judge by the manner of citation in these verses and their broader context, a statement of the obvious is made in order to bridge the gap in the argument from the "gift of Christ" in verse 7 to a discussion of the "gifts of Christ" in verses 11-

---

[77] Possibly the text form of Ps 68:18 as it appears in Eph 4:8 was traditional within pre-Pauline Christian circles as well.

13. And so, probably, the references to Christ's descent (κατέβη, ὁ καταβάς) and ascent (ἀνέβη, ὁ ἀναβάς) reflect something of an early Christian tradition.

In Rom 10:5-6 Paul evidences acquaintance with a *katabasis–anabasis* christological ascription in his quotation, with comments, of Deut 30:12-13: "Do not say in your heart, 'Who will ascend (τίς ἀναβήσεται) into heaven?'—that is, to bring Christ down—or, 'Who will descend (τίς καταβήσεται) into the abyss?'—that is, to bring Christ up from the dead." It is a use of Scripture that evidences almost as many textual and interpretive difficulties as found in Eph 4:8-10 (cited above), as well as reflecting an earlier *katabasis– anabasis* Christology. But what also needs to be noted is that in this passage Paul directly leaves such a *katabasis–anabasis* understanding—even disparages it—in favor of an emphasis on the presence of the word of faith," as based on the following verse in Deut 30:14. Evidently what Paul feared was that a *katabasis–anabasis* understanding of Christ, even though traditional among certain Christians of the day, could lead in this particular circumstance to a concept of remoteness, and he wanted to forestall any such false inference. Nonetheless, in so doing he provides some evidence for the pre-Pauline nature of the theme in question.

The traditional nature of a *katabasis–anabasis* Christology is also suggested in the early Christian confessional material incorporated into the affirmation of 1 Tim 3:16:

> Beyond all question, the mystery of godliness is great:
> "He appeared in a body,
> > was vindicated by the Spirit,
> was seen by angels,
> > was preached among the nations,
> was believed on in the world,
> > was taken up in glory."[78]

---

[78] Other passages in the Pauline corpus where this theme is sometimes found cannot with sufficient certainty be so credited. 1 Cor 15:3-5 may fit in and reflect an earlier consciousness, but its correspondence is rather meager. 1 Cor 2:8 and Col 2:15 can be credited along these lines only by first classing the *katabasis–anabasis* motif as a distinctly gnostic theme, and then identifying any terminology that remotely savors of gnosticism as based on a *katabasis–anabasis* concept. I have already indicated a circumstantial rationale for the gnostic features of Colossians, and would deny that "ignorance" (as in 1 Cor 2:8) is an exclusively gnostic note. The polarity of "riches" and "poverty" in 2 Cor 8:9 may reflect an earlier

7. Distinctive Early Christological Motifs 169

And it may underlie the argument of 1 Pet 3:18-22 regarding Christ's proclamation "to the spirits in prison," though the difficulties involved in interpreting 3:19-20 and 4:6 defy delineation here as to how the aspect of descent may have been conceptualized.[79]

It has been commonly asserted that *katabasis–anabasis* Christology arose under the influence of gnostic mythology in a hellenistic ideological milieu and was "completely foreign" to early Palestinian Christianity.[80] But while a case can be made for such a view, it should also be noted:

1. That chapters 12–16 of *1 Enoch* offer a plausible prototype for certain elements of this biblical motif. And this is true whether the descent in particular New Testament passages is understood as a *descensus ad inferos*, a penetration into the transcendental sphere of spirits, the incarnation, or Pentecost—though, admittedly, easier for the former two options than the latter two. In *1 Enoch* 12–16, Enoch is sent to "the Watchers," who are the fallen angels of Genesis 6, to proclaim to them their judgment. Terror-stricken, they implore him to draw up a petition on their behalf asking for forgiveness. Enoch is then lifted up to heaven and appears in the fiery courts of God, where he is given the terrible words to convey to his petitioners: "You will have no peace." The theology varies considerably, but the apocalyptic imagery—at least in the local aspect—bears a resemblance to features in certain passages where this theme appears in the New Testament. And at least this portion of 1 Enoch was sufficiently well known in

---

"descent—ascent" conceptualization. But, if so, it also indicates a re-working of the theme in the Pauline message.

[79] On Patristic, Augustinian, Catholic, Reformation, and modern Protestant interpretations, with a detailed treatment of considerable merit in advocacy of the view that 1 Pet 3:18-20 teaches Christ's proclamation of triumph to spirits in the transcendental sphere, see B. Reicke, *The Disobedient Spirits and Christian Baptism: A Study of 1 Pet. III. 19 and its Context* (Copenhagen: Munckgaard, 1945). For similar treatments, see E. G. Selwyn, *The First Epistle of St Peter* (London: Macmillan, 1946), 314-62; J. Jeremias, "Zwischen Karfreitag und Ostern," *ZNW* 42 (1949) 194-201; Daniélou, *Theology of Jewish Christianity*, 233-35; A. M. Stibbs, *The First Epistle General of Peter* (London: Tyndale, 1959), 138-52.

[80] Cf., e.g., Bultmann, *Theology of the New Testament*, 1.175-77; F. Hahn, *Christologische Hoheitstitel: Ihre Geschichte im frühen Christentum* (Göttingen: Vandenhoeck & Ruprecht, 1964), 126-32; R. H. Fuller, *The Foundations of New Testament Christology* (London: Lutterworth Press, 1965), 234, 257.

Palestine to warrant our keeping chapters 12–16 in mind when dealing with the motif in the New Testament.

2. That the *katabasis–anabasis* theme—both in its earlier form of the descent of Christ from heaven to earth and in its developed form of a descent from earth to hades—was prominent in Jewish Christianity of the second and third centuries. Jean Daniélou has collected the passages of pertinence here and adequately demonstrated this point.[81] Representative is the *Gospel of Peter* 10:41-42, where, after a description of two heavenly creatures coming out of the tomb sustaining a third whose head reached to heaven (the resurrected Jesus), "a cross following them," it is said: "And they heard a voice out of heaven saying, 'Hast thou preached to them that sleep?' And from the cross there was heard the answer, 'Yes'."[82]

3. That *katabasis–anabasis* Christology appears prominently in Jewish-Christian canonical materials, and that where it appears in Paul it is with the suggestion of its pre-Pauline character—which is what I have attempted to demonstrate above.[83]

In the canonical *katabasis–anabasis* passages there is, on the one hand, an ambivalence that defies precise designation of the nature of the descent involved, and, on the other, a comprehensiveness that allows for the amalgamation of the two aspects of a "descent from heaven to earth" and a "descent from earth to hades"—and for the development of the latter.[84] Probably the original motif had to do only with the humiliation of incarnation, servitude, temptation, and death, as seen in Phil 2:6-11, John 1:1-18, 3:13, 6:62, Hebrews 2 and 5, and probably Eph 4:8-10. Very soon, however, it appears to have been extended to include a *descensus ad inferos* understanding, as seen at

---

[81] Daniélou, *Theology of Jewish Christianity*, 205-63.

[82] Note, as well, Irenaeus's citation of traditional material from the teaching of "the Elder" in *Adversus haereses* 4.27.2; likewise the passage from the *Apocryphon of Jeremiah* quoted by Justin, *Dialogue* 72:4, and by Irenaeus, *Adversus haereses* 3.20.4; 4.22.1; 4.33.1; 5.31.1. Also *Similitudes* 9.16.5-7 of the *Shepherd of Hermas* and *Testament of Levi* 4:1.

[83] Mention could also be made of the "humiliation—exaltation" theme in Jewish thought with regard to the pious man (cf. E. Schweizer, *Lordship and Discipleship* [London: SCM, 1960], 23-28, and *passim*)—though, while evidencing a similar pattern, the "humiliation–exaltation" of the pious is not as far-reaching as *katabasis–anabasis* Christology.

[84] Cf. esp. Phil 2:10: "that at the name of Jesus every knee should bow, in heaven and on earth and under the earth."

7. Distinctive Early Christological Motifs

least in second-century materials if not already in 1 Pet 3:19 and 4:6.[85] But however these two elements are to be related, there is good reason for believing that *katabasis–anabasis* Christology was a distinctive feature of early Palestinian Jewish Christianity.

6. Conclusion

Other themes, further data, and additional observations should undoubtedly be presented before any claim for adequacy of treatment in regard to our topic could be made. Certainly such motifs as the following lend themselves to a similar approach: (1) "The Eschatological Mosaic Prophet," (2) "The New Exodus," (3) "The New Law," (4) "The Righteous One," and (5) "Shepherd." It is in the Jewish-Christian materials of the New Testament, as I have defined them, that these particular themes and titles come to expression. Each has its own history in Jewish thought, and each is continued to some extent in the Jewish-Christian materials of the second and third centuries. Further, each has received extensive scholarly treatment, and there is fairly widespread agreement on the primitive nature of many of these christological expressions.[86] What I have attempted to do in this article is to deal with motifs that are not commonly treated in this manner, but which I believe ought to be.

If, then, the evidence presented above is anywhere close to the mark, it must be concluded that there are distinctive christological motifs in the New Testament that are peculiar to early Jewish Christianity, as I am using that term. This is not to deny that there are

---

[85] As Vincent Taylor observed: "There is no need to assign this teaching to a late date. It is the kind of reflection that could have arisen at any time in the first generation of Christianity when questions connected with Christ's resurrection and ascension were considered and when baptism, which is expressly mentioned in [1 Peter] iii.21 in connexion with the deluge and the story of Noah, was in mind" (*Person of Christ in New Testament Teaching*, 87-88). In response to the problem of the fate of pre-Christian worthies, which undoubtedly concerned the earlier generations of believers in Jesus, it may be postulated that some Jewish Christians developed a doctrine of a pre-incarnational proclamation or a post-resurrection proclamation in Hades. Gentile Christians, on the other hand, seem to have used the Johannine Prologue to develop a pre-Christian "Logos enlightenment" explanation.

[86] I have treated many of these latter themes and titles, along with a number of others, in my *The Christology of Early Jewish Christianity* (SBT, 17; London: SCM, 1970).

images and expressions common to both the Jewish and the Gentile Christian missions, or to minimize the fact that some differences are merely verbal. Nor is it necessarily to pit the Jewish mission against the Gentile mission, or *vice versa*.

And if the features noted above be accepted as elements in that distinctive body of early Jewish-Christian christological imagery and expression, this must affect procedures in our reconstruction of christological affirmation in the New Testament. Therefore, before subtracting hellenistic elements from the whole in order to arrive at the earliest stratum of conviction—or allowing our presuppositions to dominate in the determination of what we think was possible in a Palestinian milieu—we ought to approach the subject from the perspective of these distinctive features in the Jewish cycle of conceptualization and expression. Otherwise, in our deletion of the supposedly extraneous and in our quest for what we believe ought to be there, we may be found to be removing the very evidence of pertinence for a proper reconstruction.

SELECT BIBLIOGRAPHY

This bibliography contains materials published through 1970. A more extensive listing can be found in my *The Christology of Early Jewish Christianity* (London: SCM, 1970; repr. Grand Rapids: Baker, 1981; repr. Vancouver: Regent College Publishing, 2001).

Black, Matthew. *The Scrolls and Christian Origins: Studies in the Jewish Background of the New Testament*. London: Nelson, 1961.
Brownlee, William H. "Messianic Motifs of Qumran and the New Testament," *NTS* 3 (1956) 12-30; 3 (1957) 195-210.
Bultmann, Rudolf. *Primitive Christianity in its Contemporary Setting*, trans. R. H. Fuller. London: Thames & Hudson, 1956.
_____. *Theology of the New Testament*, 2 vols., trans. K. Grobel. London: SCM, 1952.
Burney, Charles F. "Christ as the APXH of Creation," *JTS* 27 (1926) 160-77.
Chadwick, Henry. *The Circle and the Ellipse*. Oxford: Clarendon, 1959.
Cullmann, Oscar. *The Earliest Christian Confessions*, trans. J. K. S. Reid. London: Lutterworth, 1949.
_____. *The Christology of the New Testament*, trans. S. C. Guthrie and C. A. M. Hall. London: SCM; Philadelphia: Westminster, 1959, 1963^2.
Daniélou, Jean. *The Theology of Jewish Christianity*, trans. J. A. Baker. Chicago: Regnery, 1964.

_____. *The Dead Sea Scrolls and Primitive Christianity*, trans. S. Attanasio. Baltimore: Helicon, 1958.
Fitzmyer, Joseph A. "Jewish Christianity in Acts in Light of the Qumran Scrolls," in *Studies in Luke–Acts*, ed. L. E. Keck and J. L. Martyn. Nashville: Abingdon, 1966, 233-57.
Flusser, David. "The Dead Sea Sect and Pre-Pauline Christianity," in *Aspects of the Dead Sea Scrolls*, ed. C. Rabin and Y. Yadin. SH, 4. Jerusalem: Hebrew University, 1958, 215-66; repr. in his *Judaism and the Origins of Christianity*. Jerusalem: Magnes Press, Hebrew University, 1988, 23-74.
_____. "Two Notes on the Midrash on 2 Sam. vii," *IEJ* 9 (1959) 99-109; repr. in his *Judaism and the Origins of Christianity*. Jerusalem: Magnes Press, Hebrew University, 1988, 88-98.
Hort, Fenton J. A. *Judaistic Christianity*. London: Macmillan, 1894.
Jeremias, Joachim. "κεφαλὴ γωνίας—ἀκρογωνιαῖος," *ZNW* 29 (1930) 264-80.
_____. "Eckstein—Schlussstein," *ZNW* 36 (1937) 154-57.
_____. "γωνία, ἀκρογωνιαῖος, κεφαλὴ γωνίας," *TWNT*, 1.792-93 (ET: *TDNT*, 1.791-93).
_____. "λίθος," *TWNT*, 4.272-83 (ET: *TDNT*, 4.268-80).
Longenecker, Richard N. "Christianity in Jerusalem," Appendix in *Paul, Apostle of Liberty*. New York: Harper & Row, 1964; repr. Grand Rapids: Baker, 1976; Vancouver: Regent College Publishing, 2003, 103-16.
_____. *The Christology of Early Jewish Christianity*. SBT, 17. London: SCM, 1970; repr. Grand Rapids: Baker, 1981; repr. Vancouver: Regent College Publishing, 2001.
McKelvey, Richard J. "Christ the Cornerstone," *NTS* 8 (1962) 352-59.
Moule, Charles F. D. "The Influence of Circumstances on the Use of Christological Terms," *JTS* 10 (1959) 247-63; repr. in his *Essays in New Testament Interpretation*. Cambridge: Cambridge University Press, 1982, 165-83.
_____. *The Phenomenon of the New Testament*. London: SCM, 1967.
Quispel, Gilles C. "The Jung Codex and Its Significance," in *The Jung Codex. A Newly Recovered Gnostic Papyrus* ["Three Studies by H. C. Puech, G. Guispel, and W. C. van Unnik"], trans. F. L. Cross. London: Mowbray, 1955, 37-78.
Schweizer, Eduard. *Lordship and Discipleship*. London: SCM, 1960.
Strugnell, John. "The Angelic Liturgy at Qumran—4Q Serek Sirot 'Olat Hassabbat'," *Congress Volume: Oxford, 1959* (VTSup 7; Ledien: Brill, 1960, 318-45.
Taylor, Vincent. *The Person of Christ in New Testament Teaching*. London: Macmillan, 1958.
Teeple, Howard M. *The Mosaic Eschatological Prophet*. Philadelphia: Society of Biblical Literature, 1957.
Vermes, Geza. *Scripture and Tradition in Judaism*. Leiden: Brill, 1961.

_____. "The Use of בר נש / בר נשא in Jewish Aramaic," Appendix E in M. Black, *An Aramaic Approach to the Gospels and Acts*, 3rd ed. Oxford: Clarendon, 1967, 310-28.

8

WHOSE CHILD IS THIS?

Christians at Christmas focus on the Infancy Narratives of Matt 1:18–2:23 and Luke 1:5–2:52. The two narratives are quite different. Neither evangelist seems to have known the other's account. Yet one major point they agree on is that Jesus was born of a virgin through the power of the Holy Spirit. And this agreement, amidst otherwise diverse and independent presentations, suggests that a common tradition regarding the virgin birth antedates the writing of both narratives.

To speak of the virgin birth, however, immediately raises a definitional ambiguity. Roman Catholics have traditionally taken the term to have reference to "the threefold virginity of Mary"—that is, (1) the virginal conception of Jesus without a human father (*virginitas ante partum*); (2) the virginal birth of Jesus without the rupture of Mary's hymen (*virginitas in partu*); and (3) Mary's perpetual virginity, with neither marital relations nor further children after the birth of Jesus (*virginitas post partum*). Protestants, however, use "virgin birth" to refer only to what Romans Catholics speak of as "the virginal conception of Jesus," since only a virginal conception has any basis in Scripture—speculations regarding Jesus' "virginal birth" (*in partu*) or Mary's "perpetual virginity" (*post partum*) being not only *extra*-biblical but also *contra*-biblical (cf. Matt 1:25; Mark 3:31-32, par.; Mark 6:3 // Matt 13:55-56; John 7:3-5; Acts 1:14; 1 Cor 9:5; Gal 1:19). And it is in the Protestant sense that the virgin birth will be discussed in what follows.

1. *Contemporary Debate*

From at least Ignatius of Antioch (writing about 110 CE) to the nineteenth century, the virgin birth was accepted by almost all Christians as both a fact of history and a datum of theology. It was expected that the marvelous would accompany God's actions among people, and so the miraculous served to support faith. In addition, the virgin birth of Jesus fit nicely with doctrines regarding Jesus' divine sonship and sinless nature.

After the Enlightenment, however, the miraculous created suspicion rather than faith among many Christians. This stemmed from more than mere rationalism or the association of miracles with credulity. It also arose from the dual convictions that (1) God is the God of history who works in and through a history like our own, and (2) a history studded with miracles is not the kind of history we know. So in the nineteenth and twentieth centuries many Christians refused to believe that Jesus was conceived any differently than any one else. Further, it seemed to many that a doctrine of the virgin birth was unable to be reconciled with the true humanity of Jesus.

Today there exists a rather sharp division among Christians regarding the virgin birth. Should it be viewed as a fact of history—that is, that Jesus was conceived in the womb of a virgin without the intervention of a human father? Or should it be considered a *theologoumenon*—that is, a theological statement of the early church that was meant to translate the mystery of the incarnation into terms intelligible to unsophisticated people, and so to be taken as a symbol of the truth that Jesus' birth was God's gift to humanity given entirely by grace, without any necessary reference to the mechanics of procreation? This difference of opinion has been clearly drawn among Protestants for over a century and a half. It has also, of late, been rising to prominence among Roman Catholics, first in the Netherlands in the mid-60s and widespread elsewhere since Vatican II.

2. Lack of Reference in Early Christian Preaching and Confessions

The preaching of the earliest Christians, to judge by the sermons recorded in Acts, did not include a reference to Jesus' virgin birth, but began with Jesus' adult ministry and focused on his death, resurrection and ascension (cf., e.g., Peter's Pentecost sermon of Acts 2:14-36). In fact, in choosing a replacement for Judas, the qualification stated was that he must be one who had "been with us the whole time the Lord Jesus went in and out among us, beginning from John's baptism to the time when Jesus was taken up from us" (1:21-22). And it is the redemptive events that transpired during this period that the early Christian preachers proclaimed—not, evidently, dealing with matters in the life of Jesus before his baptism by John.

8. Whose Child Is This?

Likewise, there can be found no reference to the virgin birth in the early Christian confessional portions that have been incorporated by the authors of the New Testament into their writings. Two expressions in these confessional materials have sometimes been claimed to allude to Jesus' virgin birth. The first is "born of a woman" with reference to Jesus that appears in Gal 4:4, which has been taken by some to imply a virgin birth since reference is made only to "a woman" without also her husband. But "born of a woman" is simply a Jewish locution for being human—as, for example, Job 14:1, "Man born of woman is of few days and full of trouble"; Matt 11:11 // Luke 7:28, "Among those born of women there has not arisen anyone greater than John the Baptist" (see also Josephus, *Antiq.* 7.21 and 16.382). The phrase itself provides no information, either explicit or implied, regarding the biological factors having to do with Jesus' birth. Rather, in context, "born of a woman" speaks of Jesus' true humanity and representative quality—that is, that he was truly one with us, who came as "the Man" to stand in our place.

A second expression sometimes taken as alluding to Jesus' virgin birth is found in the confession of Rom 1:3-4, which, in speaking of our Lord's human credentials, says that he was "the seed [or, descendant] of David according to the flesh" (v 3). Since the word "seed" (*sperma*) is used, some have claimed that here Davidic male seed or sperm is what is in mind, and that royal *sperma*, according to Luke's genealogy (as it is argued), came only through Mary's line and not Joseph's. But "seed" here means no more than it does elsewhere in Scripture—that is, simply a descendant, as in 2 Sam 7:12; Ps 89:3-4; John 7:42; Gal 3:16, 29; and 2 Tim 2:8. What Rom 1:3-4 sets out is a two-stage Christology: (1) humanly, Jesus was a descendant of David; (2) because of the resurrection, he is legitimately declared to be God's Son and humanity's Lord. There is nothing said here, either directly or allusively, about Jesus' virginal conception.

A particularly significant case in point is Phil 2:6-11, for here is a passage that almost everyone takes to be an early Christian confession, hymn, or liturgical portion, which was used by Paul to assert Christ's pre-existence, abasement, obedience, and post-resurrection exaltation. Here, in fact, is a christological portion that runs the gamut from pre-existence to exaltation and that seems to come from the very heart of early Christian conviction. Yet no reference is made in this "Christ-hymn" to Jesus' virgin birth. Though fully human ("born of a woman") and with Davidic blood in his veins ("seed of David"), Jesus the Christ was also pre-existent and divine ("the divine nature was his from the first," NEB; "being in very nature God," NIV) and has become the Lord over all ("every knee should bow ... and every tongue confess that Jesus Christ is Lord, to the glory of God the Father"). No reference is made in this early confessional portion, however, to the virginal conception of Jesus. The virgin birth, evidently, was not understood by early Christians as a necessary topic for treatment when speaking about our Lord's becoming "the very nature of a servant, being made in human likeness" (v 7). Certainly it functions in no way in this early Christ hymn as either the basis for or evidence of the incarnation.

3. Lack of Reference in the Rest of the New Testament—Apart from the Infancy Narratives

Apart from the Infancy Narratives of Matthew and Luke (which we will treat later), the whole of the New Testament has, in fact, no direct statement regarding the virgin birth. Paul's letters, which were probably the first materials of the New Testament that were written, incorporate various confessional portions from the early church. But those portions, while not opposed to such an understanding, do not either explicitly or implicitly speak about Jesus' virgin birth. And it is significant, I believe, that Paul makes no attempt to correct or improve on those early Christian confessions in terms of a virginal conception. Nor does he come anywhere close to speaking about the virgin birth elsewhere in his letters.

Mark's Gospel, which was probably the first written of our canonical Gospels, likewise is silent about Jesus' virgin birth. For Mark "the beginning of the gospel about Jesus Christ, the Son of God" (1:1) has to do with (1) Jesus' ministry as the fulfillment of prophecy (1:2-3), (2) John the Baptist's testimony (1:4-8), (3) the baptism of Jesus (1:9-11), and (4) the temptation of Jesus (1:12-13)—perhaps also (5) Jesus' announcement of the kingdom (1:14-15) and (6) Jesus' call to four fishermen to follow him (1:16-20). In agreement with what was identified as the essential scope of the apostolic witness in Acts 1:21-22 ("beginning from John's baptism to the time when Jesus was taken up from us"), Mark's Gospel begins with the baptism of John and concludes with the resurrection of Jesus.

8. Whose Child Is This?

The only possible hint of a virgin birth in the Gospel of Mark may be found in 6:3, where it is reported that the people of Nazareth, which was Jesus' hometown, called him "the carpenter, Mary's son"—for, as has often been argued, it would have been unusual in a patriarchal society to identify someone by reference only to his mother, and so to speak of Jesus as "Mary's son" should be seen as a veiled allusion to his virgin birth. But the statement is somewhat cryptic. It may have been something of a taunt on the lips of the local townsfolk, suggesting that Jesus' birth was in some way improper or illegitimate—and so may witness indirectly to rumors that were then current. If that was the case, then Mark's inclusion of their taunt may be taken to signal something of his own consciousness of some sort of unusual circumstances associated with Jesus' birth. On the other hand, it may be that the people's statement and Mark's inclusion of it are to be seen in a more innocuous light. At any rate, both Matthew and Luke, who seem to be dependent here on Mark's Gospel, rephrase the people's question to read either: "Isn't this the carpenter's son? Isn't his mother's name Mary?" (so Matt 13:55) *or* "Isn't this Joseph's son?" (so Luke 4:22)—which seems to suggest that neither of these evangelists understood the designation "Mary's son" of Mark 6:3 as carrying any necessary connotation regarding impropriety or illegitimacy.

Apart from their infancy narratives, the virgin birth of Jesus receives no attention at all in either Matthew or Luke, the two Synoptic Gospels that appear to be built on the narrative of Mark. In fact, as we have just noted, even though Matt 1:18-25 and Luke 1:26-38 depict the birth of Jesus as coming about without the aid of a human father, the evangelists elsewhere in their Gospels recast Mark 6:3 in a manner that has the townsfolk of Nazareth speak of Jesus as "the carpenter's son" (Matt 13:55) or "Joseph's son" (Luke 4:22). And nowhere else in their Gospels, apart from their respective infancy narratives, is the topic of the virgin birth raised, either directly or allusively.

Likewise, there is no teaching about Jesus' virgin birth in John's Gospel, which seems to have been the last of our canonical Gospels written but probably preserves material about Jesus that circulated among the earliest believers in Jesus. For John the evangelist, Jesus is "the Word" who was pre-existent ("with God in the beginning"), divine ("was God"), creator ("through him all things were made"), and the source of life ("in him was life"), but the One who "became flesh and made his dwelling among us" (1:1-14). For others, as portrayed by the fourth evangelist, Jesus was "the son of Joseph" (1:45; 6:42). But neither from the author of the Fourth Gospel nor from those he presents is there any direct statement regarding the virgin birth. The only possible allusion to some such occurrence is the response of the people to Jesus recorded in John 8:41, "We are not illegitimate children." It is more likely, however, that that statement, rather than being an allusion to Jesus' virgin birth, reflects a degree of suspicion on the part of the Jewish leaders regarding some type of irregularity in connection with Jesus' birth, and so should be understood as a veiled insinuation regarding illegitimacy.

One minor variant of the text of John 1:13 is sometimes introduced into the discussion here. All our Greek manuscripts, virtually all the early versions, and most of the Church Fathers read this verse as "*those* who were born not (οἳ οὐκ ... ἐγεννήθησαν) of natural descent, nor of human decision or a husband's will, but born of God" (NIV), with the antecedent of "those" being understood as "those who believe" to whom God has given the right to become "children of God" (cf. v 12). One Old Latin manuscript of the third century, however, reads *qui natus est*, which reflects the Greek phrase ὃς οὐκ ... ἐγεννήθη or "*he* who was not born"—with the implied antecedent being Jesus. This reading was accepted by Tertullian and some of the Latin Fathers, who charged the Valentinians with changing the singular to the plural in order to deny the virgin birth. But although a few modern textual critics and exegetes have argued for the originality of the singular (without, however, always seeing it as support for a virgin birth), such a reading has little textual warrant and so has been rejected by almost all New Testament scholars.

4. *The References in the Infancy Narratives of Matthew and Luke*

Yet despite the lack of any explicit reference to his virgin birth elsewhere in the New Testament, the infancy narratives of Matthew and Luke proclaim quite clearly Jesus' virginal conception in the womb of Mary without the involvement of Joseph in the procreation process. In Matt 1:18-25 Mary is discovered to be already pregnant before having sexual relations with her betrothed husband Joseph; Joseph contemplates divorcing her so as not to put her to "public disgrace"; but "an angel of the Lord" assures Joseph that Mary's pregnancy is the result of God's design through the action of the Holy

Spirit, and so Joseph "took Mary home as his wife, but had no union with her until she gave birth to a son," whom he named Jesus. In Luke 1:26-38 the angel, who is here identified as Gabriel, announces to Mary the conception of a son in her womb through the intervention of God's Holy Spirit; calms her fears regarding the unnaturalness of such a conception by assuring her of divine providence; and points to her relative Elizabeth's pregnancy in old age as a sign that "nothing is impossible with God."

The infancy narratives of Matthew and Luke have, of course, a number of fairly obvious common features in their respective accounts: (1) the principal characters are Jesus, Mary and Joseph; (2) Jesus' birth occurred during the reign of Herod the Great; (3) Mary was betrothed to Joseph; (4) Joseph was of Davidic descent; (5) Jesus was born in Bethlehem; (6) Jesus was given his name by heavenly direction; (7) Jesus as (reputedly) Joseph's son was also of Davidic descent; and (8) the family finally settled in Nazareth. In many other respects, however, principally with regard to perspective and organization, the two accounts are decidedly different. Neither evangelist, it seems, was dependent on the other's account—nor, in all probability, did either evangelist even know of the other's account.

Yet the one major item that both Matthew and Luke, despite their diversities of presentation, include in their respective infancy narratives—which item goes far beyond such expected matters in the story line as characters, date, lineage, circumstances and final residence—is that concerning Jesus' virginal conception by the action of the Holy Spirit. Despite the lack of reference to the virgin birth elsewhere in the New Testament, the fact of its appearance in these two so otherwise different and independent accounts, as well as the place of prominence it holds in both, suggest that a common tradition regarding the virginal conception of Jesus circulated within the early church prior to the writing of both Matthew's Gospel and Luke's Gospel.

A number of questions, of course, immediately arise when talking about an early Christian tradition that appears only in the two infancy narratives of the New Testament. Historically, it must be asked: From whence this tradition of Jesus' virgin birth? Why does it not appear in the confessional materials and preaching of the early church, or in the earliest letters we have from the early church (i.e., Paul's letters), or in our earliest canonical Gospel (i.e., Mark's Gospel)? And why does it appear only in the infancy narratives of the evangelists Matthew and

8. *Whose Child Is This?*

Luke, with attention being focused on it in both? Likewise, doctrinally it must be asked: Of what significance was the virgin birth for first-century believers in Jesus, and of what significance should it be for Christians today?

Often the accounts of a virgin birth in Matthew and Luke are seen as having been motivated by the evangelists' desire to counter a rising docetism within the early church, much as later Christians used the creedal statements "Born of the Virgin Mary" and "Suffered under Pontius Pilate" to refute the docetic claim that Jesus was not really human but only appeared to be human. Such a view would explain, to some extent, why there is no reference to Jesus' virgin birth in the earlier materials of the New Testament and why it appears only later when the docetic heresy arose (cf. 1 John 4:2-3). Yet that explanation, while a possible rationale for the inclusion of infancy accounts by both Matthew and Luke, does not adequately treat the question as to why there is an emphasis on Jesus' virgin birth in these two narratives—for a virgin birth would seem, *prima facie*, to separate Jesus from the rest of humanity rather than identify him as being truly human.

A more likely explanation for the stress on the virgin birth of Jesus in the infancy narratives of Matthew and Luke, as well as in the traditions that presumably underlie these two accounts, has to do with the need of first-century believers in Jesus to counter certain suggestions of irregularity and certain rumors of illegitimacy that were probably then circulating regarding his birth—hints of which may appear in the Gospels themselves (cf. Mark 6:3, the seeming taunt of the people of Jesus' own hometown that he was "Mary's son"; also, perhaps, John 8:41, the response of the Jewish leaders to Jesus, "We are not illegitimate children"). Rumors about Jesus' birth as being illegitimate were widespread among both pagans and Jews in the second and third centuries (cf. Origen, *Contra Celsum* 1.28, 32, 69; Tertullian, *De spectaculis* XXX. 3; *m. Yebamoth* 4:13; *t. Hullin* 2:22-23; *j. Abodah Zarah* 40d; *j. Sabbath* 14d; *b. Sabbath* 104b; *b. Sanhedrin* 67a), and it is highly probable that such rumors had their origins in Jesus' own day.

The early Christians, it seems, had only two choices when faced with such rumors: either (1) to accede to them, which they could not; or (2) to affirm the supernatural character of Jesus' birth in a manner that accepted the fact of unusual circumstances associated with his birth but explained those circumstances in terms of divine intervention. And Christians today, when they stop to really think about it, are faced with the same alternative choices, unpleasant as the options may seem to many.

Yet while apologetic interests may have motivated Matthew and Luke to lay stress on the virgin birth in their infancy narratives, equally important is the need to recognize distinctions between early Christian proclamation (*kerygma*) and early Christian teaching (*Didache*) that was given in support of that proclamation. As far as we know from the New Testament itself, the early Christian confessional materials and the early Christian preaching did not include the virgin birth as a feature of importance. Nor did Mark's Gospel, which is kerygmatic in nature; nor John's Gospel, which is evangelistic; nor Paul's letters, which deal with specific pastoral problems. The evangelists Matthew and Luke, however, seem to have more distinctly teaching interests, which would have necessitated fuller portrayals of Jesus. So they included in their narratives not only material drawn from Mark's Gospel, but also a great many of the teachings of Jesus, which seem to have been drawn from a "Sayings" source, and other details about Jesus' person and ministry, which would have been incorporated from other traditions that had been kept and cherished among the early Christians. And it may be reasonably postulated that among these other traditions were some infancy materials that Matthew and Luke used in the composition of their respective infancy narratives.

In support of the Christian kerygma, Matthew and Luke suited their portrayals of the life, ministry and teaching of Jesus to the particular mindsets of their respective audiences. So each in his own way has reorganized Mark's kerygmatic presentation in line with his own instructional purposes, has augmented Mark's Gospel with additional narrative material, and has inserted many more sayings of Jesus (about one-sixth of the material in each of these two Gospels) than Mark has given. And so both Matthew and Luke have not only set out the basic Christian proclamation about Jesus ("beginning from John's baptism to the time when Jesus was taken up from us," cf. Acts 1:22), but also provided an introductory infancy narrative that focuses on Jesus as having been born of a virgin—which is a feature, we suggest, understandable when seen as part of their teaching purpose, but also able to be appreciated in light of probable rumors of illegitimacy that were then current.

5. *The Virgin Birth in Christian Thought Today*

Martin Luther once, somewhat lightly, observed (citing Benedict and Bernhard) that the incarnation consists of three miracles: "the first, that God became man; the second, that a virgin was a mother; and the third, that the heart of man should believe this" (cf. *Luther's Meditations on the Gospels*, trans. R. H. Bainton [London: Lutterworth, 1963], 26, on Luke 1:26-38). Thinking about miracles, however, has always been plagued by predispositions, presuppositions and personal prejudices. And thinking about the virgin birth has suffered the same fate—though there are indications of a changing attitude toward the miraculous, and even toward Jesus' virgin birth, among many New Testament scholars and theologians today.

Indeed, Christians must always affirm that "born of the virgin Mary" is a theological statement (a *theologoumenon*) that signals the fact that Jesus of Nazareth was (and is) God's Son in a unique sense. We may also, however, affirm that the God of the miraculous has accomplished his purpose in the incarnation in the manner portrayed by Matthew and Luke in their nativity accounts. It is the incarnation itself, of course, that is the far greater miracle and must always be the primary focus of Christian proclamation. The virgin birth, while a facet of Christian teaching, has to do only with the means that God used to bring about the incarnation. No doubt God could have brought about a true union of divinity with humanity in a number of ways, some quite natural and others quite extraordinary. In a Christian theology that is biblically based, the virgin birth is neither the basis for nor the evidence of the incarnation. Nonetheless, the fact of Jesus' virginal conception may be understood as a further sign in the whole story of Christmas about God's great gift to humanity given entirely by grace—a sign that seems to have been brought to the fore in the Christian message only when that proclamation was under specific attack and to counter that attack, but which continues today even apart from that apologetic interest as a sign of divine grace.

At Christmas it is the incarnation of our Lord that we celebrate. And in Christian proclamation and pastoral care it is that incarnation, together with work and person of Christ, that we proclaim and contextualize. But the virgin birth may also be understood as having a

8. Whose Child Is This?

place in our understanding of how God brought about the "good news" of the Christian message. It may, of course, be an offense to those who consider themselves "too modern to believe such nonsense." It is, however, hardly as inherently offensive to the modern world as are such features of the gospel as (1) the incarnation itself, (2) "the preaching of the cross," (3) belief in the resurrection of Jesus, or (4) trust in Christ's promised return, which are matters that form the basis of Christian belief as presented in the New Testament. So at Christmas we celebrate what God has done in bringing about the incarnation of his Son—understanding something of how the proclamation of the incarnation was clarified by the early Christians and accepting the virgin birth as one facet of that marvelous story.

SELECT BIBLIOGRAPHY

Boslooper, Thomas D. *The Virgin Birth*. Philadelphia: Westminster, 1962.
Brown, Raymond E. *The Virginal Conception and Bodily Resurrection of Jesus*. New York: Paulist, 1973.
_____. "Luke's Description of the Virginal Conception," *TS* 35 (1974) 360-62.
_____. *The Birth of the Messiah: A Comentary on the Infancy Narratives in Matthew and Luke*. Garden City: Doubleday, 1977.
Campenhausen, Hans. *The Virgin Birth in the Theology of the Ancient Church*, trans. F. Clarke. London: SCM, 1964.
Daniélou, Jean. *The Infancy Narratives*. New York: Herder & Herder, 1968.
Derrett, J. Duncan M. "Further Light on the Narratives of the Nativity," *NovT* 17 (1975) 81-108.
Fitzmyer, Joseph A. "The Virginal Conception of Jesus in the New Testament," *TS* 34 (1973) 541-75; repr. with "Postscript" in his *To Advance the Gospel: New Testament Studies*. New York: Crossroad, 1981, 41-78..
Fuller, Reginald H. "The Virgin Birth: Historical Fact or Kerygmatic Truth?" *Biblical Research* 1 (1956) 1-8.
Machen, J. Gresham. *The Virgin Birth of Christ*. New York: Harper, 1930.
Mann, Christopher S. "The Historicity of the Birth Narratives," in *Historicity and Chronology in the New Testament*. Theological Collection, 6. London: SPCK, 1965, 46-58.
Michel, Otto, and Otto Betz, "Von Gott gezeugt," in *Judentum, Urchristentum, Kirche. Festschrift J. Jeremias*. BZNW, 26. Berlin: Töplemann, 1960, 3-23.
Miguens, Manuel. *The Virgin Birth: An Evaluation of Scriptural Evidence*. Westminster, MD: Christian Classics, 1975.
Minear, Paul S. "The Interpreter and the Birth Narratives," *SBU* 13 (1950) 1-22.

Nolan, Brian M. *The Royal Son of God: The Christology of Matthew 1–2 in the Setting of the Gospel.* Göttingen: Vandenhoeck & Ruprecht, 1979, 63-71, 121-22, 232-33.

Orr, James. *The Virgin Birth of Christ.* New York: Scribner's; London: Hodder & Stoughton, 1907.

Piper, Otto A. "The Virgin Birth: The Meaning of the Gospel Accounts," *Int* 18 (1964) 131-48.

Stauffer, Ethelbert. *Jesus and his Story.* London: SCM, 1960, 22-43.

Taylor, Vincent. *The Historical Evidence for the Virgin Birth.* Oxford: Clarendon, 1920.

Walker, Thomas. *Is Not This the Son of Joseph? An Exposition of the Relevant Chapters of the Gospels in the Light of Jewish Culture.* London: James Clarke, 1937.

9

THE MELCHIZEDEK ARGUMENT OF HEBREWS
A Unique Christological Presentation for a Particular Situation

There is probably no more enigmatic a figure in all of Scripture than Melchizedek, and no more difficult task in biblical studies than tracing the Melchizedek tradition through its various developments in Jewish and Christian writings. He appears in the Old Testament only in Gen 14:18-20 and Ps 110:4; in the New Testament only in Heb 5:6, 10 and 6:20–7:28 (principally, of course, in chapter 7, where the writer's argument is developed). He also appears in a number of writings that can be assigned to the period of Second Temple Judaism—with *Jubilees*, *Assumption of Moses*, Philo, Josephus, and various Aramaic Targumim suggesting, either explicitly or by inference, that he was the subject of rather fervent debate in various Jewish quarters just prior to and during the first Christian century. The Talmud and its cognate writings also lend support to the existence of such a discussion and add their evidence as to an earlier Pharisaic attitude toward his person and significance.

But references and allusions to Melchizedek in the materials of Second Temple Judaism and later rabbinic Judaism are, at best, somewhat indeterminate, allowing for a wide range of opinion among scholars as to the nature of pre-Christian Jewish views on the subject. With the discovery and publication of the Melchizedek text from Qumran, however, interest in the subject has been renewed and a measure of clarification has come about—both as to the various attitudes toward Melchizedek within Second Temple Judaism and as to the use of Melchizedek by the writer of the Epistle to the Hebrews.

It is not my purpose here to take up the thorny questions regarding (1) the identification of Melchizedek in the narrative of Genesis 14 or (2) his significance in Psalm 110. Nor is it my purpose to set out a history of the use of the Melchizedek figure in later Christian theology, whether "orthodox" or "heretical."[1] I will assume, with most commentators, that Melchizedek was originally an early Canaanite king-priest who ruled over the Palestinian city-state of Salem and was used by God for his own purposes in dealing with Abram.[2] And I accept that Psalm 110 was composed as something of a "royal" psalm during the time of the United Monarchy, probably during the early reign of David.[3] Beyond that, I am willing to leave the further Old Testament issues and the additional Christian materials from the patristic period to others more qualified.

What I am interested in here, however, and what I want to explicate in what follows, are three matters: (1) the various attitudes that were taken toward Melchizedek during the period of Second Temple

---

[1] For informed treatments of Melchizedek in the Old Testament, the patristic materials, and later Christian writings, see G. Bardy, "Melchisédech dans la tradition patristique," *RB* 35 (1926) 496-509; 36 (1927) 25-45; G. Wuttke, *Melchisedech der Priesterkönig van Salem: Eine Studie zur Geschichte der Exegese* (Giessen: Topelmann, 1927); M. Delcor, "Melchizedek from Genesis to the Qumran Texts and the Epistle to the Hebrews," *JSJ* 2 (1971) 115-35; F. L. Horton, Jr, *The Melchizedek Tradition: A Critical Examination of the Sources to the Fifth Century A.D. and in the Epistle to the Hebrews* (Cambridge: Cambridge University Press, 1976); and B. Demarest, *A History of the Interpretation of Hebrews 7,1-10 from the Reformation to the Present*. Tübingen: Mohr, 1976.

[2] Melchizedek's title "Priest of 'El 'Elyon" (translated τοῦ θεοῦ τοῦ ὑψίστου, "of God Most High") suggests first of all the Phoenician deity 'El 'Elyon, with the title being later used by the Hebrews in attribution of Yahweh (Ps 78:35; Dan 3:26; 4:32; 5:18, 21) and by the Greeks of Zeus (cf. C. Roberts, T. C. Skeat, and A. D. Nock, "The Guild of Zeus Hypsistos," *HTR* 29 [1936] 39-88). While often debated, recent evidence tends to increase the probability that as "King of Salem" Melchizedek ruled over the Canaanite city-state that the Hebrews later called Jerusalem. This equation of Salem with Jerusalem is not only made in Ps 76:2 and by Josephus in *Antiq.* 1.10.2, but has been attested by the *Genesis Apocryphon* from Qumran (*1QApoc* 22.18) and the Targums *Onkelos* and *Neofiti* on Gen 14:18. Further, the Ebla texts speak of a Palestinian "Salem" as being in existence in the third millennium BCE (see G. Pettinato, "The Royal Archives of Tell Mardikh–Ebla," *BA* 39 [1976] 44-52 [46]).

[3] Recent scholarship has tended to push the date of Psalm 110 back to the time of the United Monarchy, favoring a provenance in the early days of David's reign (cf. H. H. Rowley, "Melchizedek and Zadok (Gen. 14 and Ps. 110)," in *Festschrift für Alfred Bertholet zum 80. Geburtstag*, ed. O. Eissfeldt, K. Elliger, W. Baumgartner, L. Rost [Tübingen: Mohr, 1950], 461-72; A. Weiser, *The Psalms: A Commentary* [Philadelphia: Westminster, 1962], 693; and Horton, *Melchizedek Tradition*, 29-34).

9. The Melchizedek Argument of Hebrews

Judaism; (2) the argument of the author of Hebrews vis-à-vis the varied strands of thought about Melchizedek that were then current; and (3) the unique christological presentation that is made in Hebrews by way of both comparing and contrasting the priesthood of Jesus to that of Melchizedek, and so arguing in the particular situation addressed that Jesus "has become a high priest forever according to the order of Melchizedek" (Heb 6:20b: κατὰ τὴν τάξιν Μελχιζέδεκ ἀρχιερεὺς γενόμενος εἰς τὸν αἰῶνα). In the process I would also like to highlight certain features of christological development and circumstantial expression that appear in the sermonic material that is commonly called "The Epistle to the Hebrews."

1. Melchizedek in Second Temple Judaism

The expression "Second Temple Judaism" is roughly synonymous with the Christian designation "Intertestamental," which has been widely used to identify the period from about 200 BCE to approximately 120 CE—though, of course, with reference to events and developments within Judaism itself, apart from Christianity, that occurred from the Maccabean rebellion through to the second destruction of Jerusalem by the Romans. It coincides with the period of Jewish national independence (such as it was) under the Hasmoneans and the Herodians, and it bridges the span religiously between "the Religion of Israel" (as represented in the Old Testament) and "Rabbinic Judaism" (as represented in the Talmud and cognate materials). It is probably best known to Christians as the period that saw the rise of such groups as the Sadducees, the Pharisees, and the Essenes. And it is within such groups that various attitudes toward the person and significance of Melchizedek can be discerned.

Hasmonean–Sadducean Views

There are a number of indications in various Jewish writings that the Hasmoneans began to think of their reign in messianic terms and that they justified their priestly-royal prerogatives by reference to Melchizedek. And from suggestions in cognate materials, it appears that their successors, the Sadducees, continued to view matters in the same light.

The writer of *Jubilees*, who wrote sometime during the reigns of Jonathan, Simeon, and John Hyrcanus (i.e., 152–104 BCE), appears to have viewed the messianic kingdom as already inaugurated with the

Hasmonean supremacy. This is suggested by his portrayal of the Messianic Age as a process that will come to final realization only gradually in history (23:23-30), by his depiction of the ascendancy of Levi over Judah in the messianic blessings of the patriarch Isaac (31:9-20), and by his use of the Melchizedekian title for Jacob and his two sons, Levi and Judah: "they ordained and made him the priest of the Most High God, him and his sons for ever" (32:1)—with particular emphasis in the context on Levi. If we only knew what had been originally written in what is now the lacuna of 13:25a (of which lacuna we must speak later), our understanding of the attitude of the author of *Jubilees* toward the Hasmonean claim would undoubtedly be clarified. Suffice it here to say, *Jubilees* suggests that sometime during the reign of Jonathan (152–142 BCE), Simeon (142–134 BCE), or John Hyrcanus (134–104 BCE), an identification of the Messianic Age with the Hasmonean dynasty began to be made.

Such a consciousness seems to come to the fore in the hymn of praise to Simeon in *1 Macc* 14:4-15—particularly in the attribution to his reign of the prophetic words about "the last days" in verse 12, which are taken from Mic 4:4 and Zech 8:4 ("each sat under his own vine and his own fig tree, and there was none to make them afraid"). It may also be involved in the designation of Simeon in *1 Macc* 14:41 as "ethnarch and high priest for ever" (εἰς τὸν αἰῶνα), which carries nuances of the Melchizedekian title.[4]

That the Hasmoneans claimed Melchizedekian support for their prerogatives is indicated rather directly in materials that have no Sadducean connections. *Assumption of Moses* 6:1, for example, after detailing the sacrilege of the Seleucids and before describing Herod the Great, summarizes the Hasmonean period in the following terse words: "Then there shall be raised up unto them kings bearing rule, and they shall call themselves 'Priests of the Most High God' (ἱερεὺς τοῦ θεοῦ ὑψίστου)"—which is the title of Melchizedek in Gen 14:18. Josephus in *Antiq.* 16.163, speaking of Caesar Augustus, writes that Augustus decreed that "the Jews may follow their own customs in accordance with the law of their fathers, just as they followed them in the time of Hyrcanus, high priest of the Most High God (ἀρχιερέως θεοῦ ὑψίστου)"; and *b. Rosh Hashanah* 18b relates: "The Grecian

---

[4] Though, admittedly, the qualification of 14:41b, "until a faithful prophet should arise" (ἕως τοῦ ἀναστῆναι προφήτην πιστόν), seems somewhat out of harmony with the apparent "realized" messianology of the rest of the chapter.

[Seleucid] government had forbidden the mention of God's name by the Israelites, but when the government of the Hasmoneans became strong and defeated them, they ordained that they should mention the name of God even on bonds; and they used to write thus: 'In the year so-and-so of Johanan, High Priest of the Most High God'." Likewise, there are suggestions of this joining of the Melchizedekian appellative and the Hasmonean dynasty in *t. Sotah* 13:5, *b. Sotah 33a*, and *Testament of Levi* 18:14 (if, indeed, the Greek *Testament of Levi* reflects a pre-Christian stance at this point).

Psalm 110, of course, has been commonly associated with the Hasmonean rise to supremacy, usually on the basis of its perceived acrosticon "Simeon" that is formed by the first letters of each of the four verses in the oracle (i.e., the Hebrew letters ש, מ, ע, נ), and therefore understood as a piece of Maccabean propaganda written in support of Simeon's claim to priestly and kingly powers in 141–140 BCE.[5] The acrostic argument for Maccabean provenance, however, has been widely judged as being weak. Further, the psalm in its ascription of priesthood to a royal figure does not quite fit the Hasmoneans, who were priests by birth and required legitimacy for their royal assertions.[6] Nevertheless, as David M. Hay has pointed out, "while the Hasmoneans probably did not compose the psalm, they probably did use it to defend their claims to priestly and royal prerogatives."[7]

Mattathias's initial rebellion against the Seleucids is supported in *1 Macc* 2:26 and 54 by appeal to the action of the righteous and zealous priest Phinehas, who received for himself and his posterity the promise of a perpetual priesthood because of his valiant activity in rooting out apostasy and protecting his people (cf. Num 25:12-13). But Phinehas was not a king! Thus when Jonathan, Simeon, John Hyrcanus, and their successors assumed kingly powers, it became necessary to find a more substantial biblical prototype. And it was just such a prototype that the Hasmoneans and their Saducean descendants seem to have found in the Canaanite king-priest of Gen 14:18-20.

---

[5] Cf., e.g., B. Duhm, *Die Psalmen* (Tübingen: Mohr, 2nd ed., 1922), 398-399; R. H. Pfeiffer, *Introduction to the Old Testament* (New York: Harper, 1948), 161; idem, *History of New Testament Times, with an Introduction to the Apocrypha* (New York: Harper, 1949), 19n.

[6] Cf. D. M. Hay, *Glory at the Right Hand: Psalm 110 in Early Christianity* (Nashville, New York: Abingdon, 1973), 19, 24.

[7] *Ibid.*, 24.

Melchizedek in Psalm 110 had already been disinfected from his earlier Canaanite associations and rebaptized into the religion of Israel. The Hasmoneans and their descendants, therefore, could re-employ him in support of their priestly-kingly position. So it seems that we should understand both Psalm 110 and its Melchizedekian ascription as having "entered the NT age trailing associations of the dusty glory of the Hasmoneans."[8]

Quietistic Reactions
Not every Jew living in the time of Second Temple Judaism, however, seems to have been prepared to concede the legitimacy of the Hasmonean–Sadducean claim or to accept their appeal to Melchizedek in support of that claim. The copyist of the *Book of Jubilees* evidently could not, as is indicated by the absence of an entire line at what should be Jub 13:25a—a line that, in context, would have undoubtedly said something about the meeting of Abraham with Melchizedek. Just when this lacuna first appeared in the text of *Jubilees* is difficult to determine. The Latin version of *Jubilees* offers no help here, for only about one fourth of the text of *Jubilees* is extant in that version and chapter 13 is not one of those portions preserved. Nor does the existing Greek fragment of *Jubilees* (i.e., 2:2-21), or the Greek quotations of the book in the patristic writings, or the recently discovered Aramaic portions, since none of these materials contains either this verse or its context. Nonetheless, the fact that in all four extant Ethiopic manuscripts of *Jubilees* there is a whole line omitted at what should be 13:25a—with no such lacuna appearing anywhere else in the entire text—suggests that (1) the lacuna was present in the Greek manuscript of the book from which the Ethiopic version was translated, and (2) it probably appeared as well in an Aramaic transcription.

The question, of course, is: How are we to understand this omission of an entire line of text at *Jub* 13:25a? Certainly the author of *Jubilees*, as R. H. Charles appropriately theorized, "would naturally be interested in the first man who bore the title assumed by his heroes, the Maccabees."[9] But what about the copyist? Why did he omit the line at 13:25? It seems too much to believe that it occurred only through "technical inadvertence," as some have rather lightly

---

[8] *Ibid.*, 25.
[9] R. H. Charles, *APOT*, 2.33 n.

proposed. Rather, probably the copyist was so opposed to something in the original text itself or some contemporary usage of the text that he could not bring himself even to copy out the line that spoke of Abraham's meeting with Melchizedek. And in view of the Hasmonean–Sadducean use of the Melchizedekian figure in support of their combining cultic and royal prerogatives, it does not seem too much to postulate that at least one quietistic Jew with a priestly background (perhaps an Essene and/or a member of the Qumran community), while generally applauding the message of *Jubilees*, found the explicit reference to Melchizedek in *Jub* 13:25*a* just too much to take—either because of what it said directly or of how it was then being used.

The *Assumption of Moses*, which was written sometime between 6–30 CE, probably characterizes such a quietistic attitude as well, though in this case from a more Pharisaic perspective than the priestly stance of either the author or the copyist of *Jubilees*. The *Assumption of Moses* expresses its attitude toward the Hasmonean claims not only in its very brief reference to Hasmonean supremacy, saying only in 6:1*a* (as noted above), "Then there shall be raised up unto them kings bearing rule, and they shall call themselves 'Priests of the Most High God'," but more directly in its rather caustic comment by way of evaluation in 6:1*b*: "And they shall assuredly work iniquity in the holy of holies."

Pharisaic Stances

The Talmud and its cognate writings, which are codifications of earlier Pharisaic teachings, treat Melchizedek in three ways. First, in *b. Nedarim* 32*b* he is identified by Rabbi Zechariah, in the name of the early second-century teacher Rabbi Ishmael, as Shem, the son of Noah. And this is supported by *Targum Neofiti* on Gen 14:18, which reads: "And Melchizedek, king of Jerusalem—that is the great Shem—brought bread and wine, for he was a priest and exercised the sovereign priesthood before the Most High God";[10] also by *Targum*

---

[10] Cf. A. Díez Macho, *Neophyti 1: Targum palestinense, Ms de la Biblioteca Vaticana*. I: *Genesis*, trans. R. Le Déaut, M. McNamara, and M. Maher (Madrid: Consejo superior de investigaciones científicas, 1968).

Pseudo-Jonathan on the same passage: "And Melchizedek, who is Shem, the son of Noah, went out to meet Abraham."[11]

A second way in which Melchizedek is treated is found in *Song of Songs Rabbah* 2.13.4 and *b. Sukkah* 52*b*, where he is included among the four "eschatological craftsmen" by whom the Age to Come is to be built:

> It is written in Zechariah [2:3]: "The Eternal showed me four workmen." R. Hanna ben Gizna says in the name of R. Simeon the Hasid: "these four workmen are the Messiah the son of David, the Messiah the son of Joseph, Elijah and Melchizedek."

Later in *b. Sukkah* 52*b*, however, Rabbi Shesheth is recorded as strenuously objecting to the inclusion of Melchizedek.

The third way that the rabbis, and presumably their predecessors the Pharisees, dealt with Melchizedek can be found in *Leviticus Rabbah* 25.6 and *b. Nedarim* 32*b*, where he is portrayed as an irreverent priest who relinquished the rights of his office to Abraham because of his inappropriate action of first blessing Abraham and then blessing God:

> Rabbi Zechariah said in the name of Rabbi Ishmael: God wanted to derive the priestly line from Shem, as it is said, "He was priest of God Most High" [Gen 14:18]. But God derived (the priestly line) from Abraham, when Shem placed the blessing of Abraham before the praise of God, as it is said, "Blessed be Abram by God Most High, maker of heaven and earth; and blessed be God Most High" [Gen 14:19].
>
> Said Abraham to him: "Does one place the blessing of a servant before that of his master?"
>
> Immediately (the priesthood) was given to Abraham, as it is said, "The Lord says to my lord: 'Sit at my right hand, until I make your enemies your footstool'" [Ps 110:1]. And after this it is written, "The Lord has sworn and will not change his mind, 'Thou art a priest forever after the order of Melchizedek'" [Ps 110:4].
>
> This means, on account of what Melchizedek had said. And that is why it is written, "He was a priest of God Most High" [Gen 14:18]. He was a priest, but his descendants were not priests.

While there may be "nothing more than innocent midrashic play in the identification of Melchizedek with Shem,"[12] the polemical tone is

---

[11] Cf. J. Bowker, *The Targums and Rabbinic Literature* (Cambridge: Cambridge University Press, 1969), 193-99.

[12] As J. J. Petuchowski insists ("The Controversial Figure of Melchizedek," *HUCA* 28 (1957) 127-36 [129]).

strong in (1) the disparagement of Melchizedek's eschatological status and (2) the renunciation of his continuing priesthood. Perhaps, on reevaluation, it should also be seen in the Melchizedek–Shem equation.

But against whom was this polemic against Melchizedek and the Melchizedekian priesthood directed? Louis Ginzberg, R. Travers Herford, Marcel Simon, and many others have understood it as directed against the Christian use of Melchizedek in the Epistle to the Hebrews and as continued in Justin Martyr's *Dialogue with Trypho* 19 and 33.[13] On such a view, it is argued (1) that Melchizedek, priest of the Most High God, who was a foreigner by birth, sees humbled before him one whom the chosen people claimed as their father and whom the Christians now recognized as such; (2) that Melchizedek is the true father of the Gentiles, of whom the titles are in consequence older than those of Israel; and (3) that in his person, the Gentiles are mingled with the church, which triumphs over the Jews.[14] Kaufmann Kohler, on the other hand, viewed the polemic as directed against "Jewish propagandists of Alexandria, who were eager to win proselytes for Judaism without submitting them to the rite of circumcisions," and who therefore appealed to Melchizedek in support of their "cosmopolitan monotheism."[15]

The problem with viewing the polemic of *b. Nedarim* 32*b* and its parallels as being directed against Christians, whether Gentile or Jewish believers in Jesus, is that, as Victor Aptowitzer and Hans Windisch long ago noted, there is nothing in the statement of Rabbi Zechariah given in the name of Rabbi Ishmael that specifically interacts with the depiction of Melchizedek in the Epistle to the Hebrews.[16] And to speak of a "cosmopolitan monotheism" among the Jews of Alexandria that was prepared to omit the practice of circumcision by an appeal to a universal Melchizedekian figure is to deduce from later

---

[13] L. Ginzberg, *The Legends of the Jews*, 7 vols. (Philadelphia: Jewish Publication Society of America, 1909–1938), 5.226, n. 104; R. T. Herford, *Christianity in the Talmud and Midrash* (London: Williams & Norgate, 1903), 265, 338-40; M. Simon, "Melchizedek dans la polémique entre Juifs et Chrétiens et dans la légende," *RHPR* (1937) 58-93; idem, *Verus Israel* (Paris: de Boccard, 1948), 110-11. See also Delcor, "Melchizedek from Genesis to the Qumran Texts and the Epistle to the Hebrews," 132.

[14] To paraphrase Marcel Simon, *ibid*.

[15] K. Kohler, "Melchizedek," *JE*, 8.450.

[16] V. Aptowitzer, "Malkizedek," *MGWJ* 70 (1926) 93-113; H. Windisch, *Der Hebräerbrief* [HNT; Tübingen: Siebeck-Mohr, 1931], 61.

Christian sources what the Jewish propagandists of Alexandria must have been arguing—which is a supposition totally without warrant. Certainly Philo, the most prominent allegorist among the Jews of Egypt, never thought of an allegorical understanding of the Mosaic law as setting aside its literal practice—as seen, for example, in *De migratione Abrahami* 92, where he specifically insists that though circumcision should be understood allegorically, it must always be practiced literally.

It therefore seems that we must interpret Pharisaic stances with regard to Melchizedek, as they have been incorporated into the later rabbinic materials, as arising initially in opposition to the Hasmonean–Sadducean preemption of this Old Testament king-priest in support of their own priestly-kingly prerogatives—though, of course, such stances may also have been expressive of the attitude of later rabbis toward the Christians. Jakob Petuchowski has cogently represented what was probably the true situation:

> If, then, we find Rabbi Ishmael, in the second century C.E., making a statement the import of which is to make impossible the claim that the established levitical line can be superseded by another "after the order of Melchizedek," the Rabbi may well have given expression to the opposition voiced against the Hasmonean use of Psalm 110 by the early Hasidim, and transmitted by the Pharisees. ... The Pharisaic-rabbinic attempts to put the old priest-king of Salem in his place considerably ante-date the second century polemics against Christianity.[17]

Evidence from Qumran
Melchizedek is mentioned in two of the scrolls that represent the distinctive views of the Qumran covenanters: the *Genesis Apocryphon* from Cave 1 (*1QApoc*) and the *Melchizedek Scroll* from Cave 11 (*11QMelch*). *1QApoc* 22.14-17 retells the biblical story of Abraham's encounter with Melchizedek, without embellishment and with the inclusion of the title "Priest of God Most High." Beyond that, however, it adds nothing to our understanding of the person or significance of Melchizedek in Jewish sectarian circles. But the situation with *1QMelch* is quite different, and for our purposes needs to be highlighted

---

[17] Petuchowski, "Controversial Figure of Melchizedek," 136; see also 130-32.

9. The Melchizedek Argument of Hebrews

In 1956 Bedouin shepherds found thirteen fragments of a single scroll in what is now known as Cave 11 at Qumran. When pieced together, the fragments comprise the better part of one column of text made up of twenty-six lines, with extensive lacunae both within and between the lines. One third of the material in the reconstructed text consists of Old Testament quotations—that is, Lev 25:9-10, 13; Deut 15:2; Pss 7:8-9; 82:1-2; and Isa 52:7; 61:1—with the remainder being an exposition on these *testimonia* passages that deals with the final salvation of the elect and the retribution that will be meted out on the wicked. The text was first published by A. S. van der Woude in 1965, together with a German translation and explanatory annotations.[18] Since then it has become the subject of extensive investigation and discussion.

Melchizedek (מלכי צדק) first emerges in the scroll's portrayal of the final eschatological drama at line 5, and thereafter he appears repeatedly as the one who brings back the elect, who proclaims liberty, who makes atonement for those bound by the powers of wickedness, and who executes judgment on Belial and his band of perverse spirits. Lines 10 and 11*a*, however, constitute the most significant section of the scroll for our purposes and have become the focus of scholarly debate. Quoting Ps 82:1-2, the lines read (*à la* van der Woude's translation):

> ... as it is written [line 10] concerning him in the hymns of David, who says: "The heavenly one (אלוהים) standeth in the congregation of God; among the heavenly ones (אלוהים) he judgeth" and concerning him he says: "Above them [line 11] return thou on high; God shall judge the nations."

Van der Woude argues that here the writer of the scroll applies Ps 82:1-2 to Melchizedek, with the first אלוהים referring to Melchizedek himself and the second אלוהים referring to angels of lower rank than Melchizedek.

Van der Woude's reasons for so understanding the passage are basically four: (1) that the expression "concerning him" (לו) has as its logical antecedent the Melchizedek of lines 5 through 9, which immediately precede; (2) that God is consistently designated elsewhere in the column not by אלוהים but by אל; (3) that line 13 expressly

---

[18] A. S. van der Woude, "Melchisedek als himmlische Erlösergestalt in den neugefundenen eschatologischen Midraschim aus Qumran Höhle XI," *OTS* 14 (1965) 354-73.

differentiates Melchizedek from God in the activity of judging ("Melchizedek will avenge with the vengeance of the judgments of God"), which distinction allows for understanding a similar distinction in lines 10-11a; and (4) that the motif of the return to heaven by the אלוהים would have been understood by Jews of the day most readily in terms of a return of angels.

As A. S. van der Woude, therefore, understands the text of this one column scroll, Melchizedek is depicted as a Heavenly Redeemer Figure ("ein himmlische Erlösergestalt") who functions as an Archangel Warrior with certain priestly characteristics. And in this judgment van der Woude has been substantially joined by such scholars as Marinus de Jonge,[19] Yigael Yadin,[20] Joseph Fitzmyer,[21] and F. du Toit Laubscher[22]—though without always continuing the identification of Melchizedek with the archangel Michael, as van der Woude originally proposed.

Jean Carmignac's understanding of *1QMelchizedek*, however, is quite different from that proposed by van der Woude.[23] According to Carmignac, the principal theme of the so-called Melchizedek Scroll is not Melchizedek but rather the execution of judgment by God himself on the powers of Belial and the consequent liberation of the righteous. Carmignac insists that the lacuna of line 9 allows for another subject other than Melchizedek as the antecedent for the expression "concerning him" of line 10, and argues that that antecedent must be God himself. And by the double use of אלוהים in line 10 the writer is not referring first to Melchizedek and then to the angelic hosts, but first to God and then to the saints of the congregation, who will be assumed into the Messianic Age when God executes judgment on the nations. The distinction made by many scholars between אלוהים and אל Carmignac believes to be both inexact and inappropriate, since the writer of the scroll is utilizing אלוהים where the tetragrammaton יהוה appears in the biblical text but simply prefers to use אל where he

---

[19] M. de Jonge and A. S. van der Woude, "11Q Melchizedek and the New Testament," *NTS* 12 (1966) 301-26.

[20] Y. Yadin, "A Note on Melchizedek and Qumran," *IEJ* 15 (1965) 152-54.

[21] J. A. Fitzmyer, "Further Light on Melchizedek from Qumran Cave 11," *JBL* 86 (1967) 25-41.

[22] F. du Toit Laubscher, "God's Angel of Truth and Melchizedek: A Note on 11Q Melch 13b," *JSJ* 3 (1972) 46-51.

[23] J. Carmignac, "Le document de Qumran sur Melkisedeq," *RQ* 7 (1970) 343-78.

comments himself—without any difference of meaning or designation being intended in the two forms for "God."

Further, Carmignac argues that Melchizedek is not being presented in this text as the king-priest of Abraham's day; rather, he is portrayed as someone who was at that time present within the Qumran community itself—that is, not some sort of celestial being comparable to an angel who would come to judge in the future, but a historical person who was recognized by the sect as reproducing the character of the biblical Melchizedek. He was thought of by the covenanters at Qumran as "King of Justice" (מלכי meaning "my king"; צדק meaning "justice"). So he was probably the community's "king" or "military leader," who may well be identical with the "Messiah" or "Anointed One of the Spirit" (משיח הרו[ח]) of line 18—even, perhaps, considered one of the Messiahs who were expected at Qumran.

Indeed, Carmignac may be right. There are just too many lacunae within and between the lines of the text to be dogmatic. Yet the bulk of scholarship, to date, has judged his case to be weak and concluded that the more natural reading of the text in its present form supports the interpretation of A. S. van der Woude, *et al.*

It appears, then, that what we have in *11QMelchizedek* is a partial portrayal of the messianology of the Qumran sectarians. It may be postulated that this particular feature of Jewish messianism came about at some time later in the history of the community, when such an intensive antagonism to the Melchizedekian figure as caused the scribe who copied the *Book of Jubilees* to omit 13:25a became somewhat abated—and therefore at a time roughly contemporaneous with the rise of Christianity. At such a time, understanding the text of *11QMelchizedek* as A. S. van der Woude and others have, Melchizedek seems to have been brought back into the messianic expectations of the covenanters at Qumran and thought of in terms of an Archangel Warrior-Redeemer from Heaven, who in making atonement for sins was to exhibit certain priestly characteristics.

Philo of Alexandria
Philo (c. 20 BCE–50 CE) refers to Melchizedek in three of his extant writings: *Legum allegoriae* 3.79-82, *De congressu eruditionis gratia* 99, and *De Abrahamo* 235, though without naming him in the latter. In *De congressu* 99 and *De Abrahamo* 235, Melchizedek is presented as a historical personage. In *Legum allegoriae* 3.79-82, however, all of

the details of his appearance in Genesis 14 are used to portray him as a representation of the eternal Logos.

Three matters in Philo's treatment deserve comment here. First, the name "Melchizedek" is treated etymologically in *Legum allegoriae* 3.79-82 to mean "Righteous King" (βασιλεὺς δίκαιος) and the title "King of Salem" to mean "King of Peace" (βασιλεὺς τῆς εἰρήνης). Second, evidently building on the fact that Melchizedek is the first priest mentioned in Holy Writ, all three of Philo's references highlight the uniqueness of Melchizedek's priesthood. In *De congressu* 99 and *De Abrahamo* 235, his historical priesthood is described as being a "self-taught" (αὐτομαθῆ) and "instinctive" (αὐτοδίδακτον) priesthood; in *Legum allegoriae* 3.79-82 the fact that he was the first priest in Scripture, and therefore without antecedents, leads to the conclusion that he was the Logos. And so, third, Melchizedek became for Philo the manifestation of the high-priestly Logos who intoxicates the soul with esoteric virtues.

Many commentators have focused on Philo's treatment of Melchizedek as a representation of the eternal Logos. Hans Windisch in 1913, for example, correlated the use of Melchizedek in *Legum allegoriae* 3.79-82 with the priestly Logos speculation of *De vita Mosis* 2.2-7 and argued that such a view (1) must have been fairly widespread among Jews generally, and (2) should be seen as the primary basis for the Melchizedekian Christology of the Epistle to the Hebrews.[24] In 1970, however, Ronald Williamson demonstrated that though Logos speculations played a part in both Philo and Hebrews—more prominently in Philo, where the word λόγος appears some 1,300 times, than in Hebrews—"Philo and the Writer of Hebrews represent quite different (perhaps even entirely unconnected) strands in the intricate pattern of Jewish-Christian Logos speculation."[25]

In fact, as Williamson went on to show, Hebrews seems to owe little to Philonic thought beyond the rather common etymological treatment of the names "Melchizedek" and "Salem" and a general appreciation for the uniqueness of the person and priesthood of Melchizedek. In his use of etymology and his appreciation of Melchizedek's uniqueness, therefore, Philo seems to be reflecting attitudes that were fairly widespread among Jews of his day (as will be noted

---

[24] Windisch, *Hebräerbrief*.
[25] Williamson, *Philo and the Epistle to the Hebrews*, 430.

again in the discussion of Josephus below). It may be questioned, however, as to just how much he represented or influenced other Jews of his day, whether Hebraic or hellenistic, with respect to his distinctive Logos speculations and his particular treatment of Melchizedek.

Flavius Josephus

Josephus (c. 37–100 CE) speaks of Melchizedek in two passages of his four writings: *Jewish War* 6.10.1 and *Antiquities of the Jews* 1.10.2. In relating the history of Jerusalem, Josephus says:

> Its original founder was a Canaanite chieftain (Χαναναίων δυνάστης, "a potent man among the Canaanites"), who was called in the native tongue "Righteous King" (βασιλεὺς δίκαιος), for such indeed he was. In virtue thereof he was the first to officiate as priest of God and, being the first to build the temple, gave the city, previously called Solyma [i.e., the biblical "Salem"], the name "Jerusalem."[26]

And in recounting the story of Abraham's encounter with Melchizedek in Genesis 14, he writes:

> He was received by the king of Solyma [Salem], Melchizedek. This name means "Righteous King" (βασιλεὺς δίκαιος), and such he was by common consent, insomuch that for this reason he was moreover made priest of God. Solyma was, in fact, the place afterwards called Hierosolyma [the hellenized form of "Jerusalem"]. Now this Melchizedek hospitably entertained Abraham's army, providing abundantly for all their needs, and in the course of the feast he began to extol Abraham and to bless God for having delivered his enemies into his hand. Abraham then offered him the tithe of the spoil, and he accepted the gift.[27]

For Josephus, then, Melchizedek was a Canaanite chieftain who became a priest of Israel's God because of the uprightness of his character. He was the first to officiate as a priest of God at Jerusalem, actually building there the first temple to God, and his name means etymologically "Righteous King." In addition, Josephus refers to Melchizedek blessing first Abraham and then God, but he does not elaborate any Pharisaic polemic against Melchizedek on this basis.

A number of questions, of course, immediately arise about these portrayals of Melchizedek by Josephus, the renegade Jewish historian.

---

[26] *War* 6.10.1.
[27] *Antiq.* 1.10.2.

For example, it must be asked: To what extent was Josephus adjusting first-century Jewish views for the ears and sensibilities of his Roman audience?, and, How many Jews of that day (or any day) would have spoken of a Canaanite chieftain as having been the first to build a temple at Jerusalem? Further: Should not Josephus's portrayal of Melchizedek as extolling Abraham, for which reason Abraham reciprocates by offering him a tithe of the spoil, be considered more propaganda than conviction? Nonetheless, that Josephus (1) speaks of Melchizedek as a Canaanite chieftain, (2) highlights the priority and uniqueness of his priesthood, and (3) takes pains to emphasize the etymological significance of his name indicates that at least one first-century Jew thought of Melchizedek along these lines, and there may have been others who did so as well.

Summation

What, then, can be said regarding attitudes toward Melchizedek among the Jews during the period of Second Temple Judaism? No longer can it be assumed that "the normal idea" was that Ps 110:1 describes a heavenly monarch, as has been commonly proposed,[28] or that Melchizedek was a very insignificant figure during the first century, as has been sometimes stated.[29] Rather, Psalm 110 seems to have "entered the NT age trailing associations of the dusty glory of the Hasmoneans."[30] Further, the person and significance of Melchizedek seem to have been hotly disputed in various quarters.

From the evidence now available, it can be argued that (1) for the Hasmoneans and their Saddurean successors, Melchizedek was seen as the prototype for their priestly-kingly prerogatives; (2) for certain quietists drawn from both Saddurean and Pharisaic backgrounds, such Hasmonean associations were personally revolting; (3) for the Pharisees, he was to be identified with Shem and demoted from any continuing priestly succession because of his irreverence; (4) for

---

[28] As, e.g., S. A. Cook, *The Old Testament: A Reinterpretation* (London: SPCK, 1936) 205-206; C. H. Dodd, *According to the Scriptures* (London: Nisbet, 1952), 120; B. Lindars, *New Testament Apologetic* (London: SCM, 1961), 45-46.

[29] As was affirmed just before the publication of *11QMelchizedek* in 1965 by H. Braun, "Qumran und das Neue Testament: Ein Bericht über 10 Jahre Forschung (1950–1959)—Hebräer," *TRu* 30 (1964) 1-38, 89-127 (20), and by H. Montefiore, *A Commentary on the Epistle to the Hebrews* (BNTC / HNTC; London: Black; New York: Harper, 1964), 117-18.

[30] To quote again Hay, *Glory at the Right Hand*, 25.

Philo, he was a manifestation of the eternal Logos; (5) for Josephus, he was an early Canaanite chieftain who became God's priest at Jerusalem because of his piety; and (6) for the covenanters at Qumran, he was reinstated as an important eschatological personage—probably a heavenly, eschatological Archangel Warrior-Redeemer messianic figure, who exercised certain priestly characteristics in atoning for sin. The list could probably be extended if only more of the writings of Second Temple Judaism were extant.[31] Nonetheless, though the evidence is scanty and we know only in part, it is against such a background that we must consider the treatment of Melchizedek in the Epistle to the Hebrews.

2. Melchizedek in the Epistle to the Hebrews

A rather radical reevaluation of the Epistle to the Hebrews has taken place during the past few decades, principally due to discoveries at Qumran. But reevaluations of the epistle have also come about because of renewed studies of relationships between Hebrews and Philonic thought.

Based on the striking parallels that exist between the distinctive tenets of the Qumran community and the argument of Hebrews, Yigael Yadin insisted in 1958 that "the addressees of the Epistle must have been a group of Jews originally belonging to the Dead Sea Sect who were converted to Christianity carrying with them some of their previous beliefs."[32] Shortly thereafter, Ceslas Spicq, impressed by

---

[31] Mythical material preserved in the third (and last) part of Slavonic Enoch (i.e., 2 Enoch 21–23), which concerns "The Priesthood of Methuselah, Noah and Melchizedek," depicts the miraculous conception of Melchizedek (i.e., his mother conceived "without having slept with her husband") and his birth from the corpse of his mother, Sophonim, the wife of Nir and sister of Noah, and goes on to predict that this Melchizedek will reign as a priest and a king in the middle of the earth as the prototype of the Messiah. But this is a Christian midrash on the statements "without father, without mother, without beginning of days or end of life" of Heb 7:3, and need not detain us here. For a treatment of 2 Enoch that argues for its Christian authorship in the ninth or tenth centuries CE, see J. T. Milik, *The Books of Enoch: Aramaic Fragments of Qumran Cave 4* (Oxford: Clarendon, 1976), 110, 114-16.

[32] Y. Yadin, "The Dead Sea Scrolls and the Epistle to the Hebrews," in *Aspects of the Dead Sea Scrolls*, ed. C. Rabin and Y. Yadin (SH 4; Jerusalem: Hebrew University, 1958), 36-55 (38); see also idem, "Note on Melchizedek and Qumran," 152-54.

Yadin's evidence, retracted in 1959 his earlier Philonic approach in favor of a position that lays emphasis on such parallels, while still holding to a degree of Alexandrian influence on the epistle through Apollos its author.[33] And John Wick Bowman sought to popularize what he called an "Essene Thesis" in his 1962 "Layman's Bible Commentary" on Hebrews.[34]

Running concurrent to such studies based on the Dead Sea materials, though working independently, C. K. Barrett argued in 1954 that with regard to eschatology "certain features of Hebrews which have often been held to have been derived from Alexandrian Platonism were in fact derived from apocalyptic symbolism,"[35] and George Caird asserted in 1959 that the scriptural exegesis of Hebrews, rather than being "Alexandrian and fantastic," was, in reality, "one of the earliest and most successful attempts to define the relation between the Old and New Testaments, and that a large part of the value of the book is to be found in the method of exegesis which was formerly dismissed with contempt."[36] In fact, in what is probably the most extensive and penetrating analysis to date of the linguistic, conceptual, and hermeneutical affinities between Philo and Hebrews, Ronald Williamson has argued in a work published in 1970 that Hebrews "differs radically from the outlook and attitude of Philo. Neither in his basic judgment about the essential character of the O.T. nor in his chief method of scriptural exegesis does the Writer of Hebrews appear to owe anything to Philo."[37]

Not everyone, of course, agrees with what has been called "the Qumran hypothesis" for the Epistle to the Hebrews. Some have over-

---

[33] C. Spicq, "L'Epître aux Hébreux, Apollos, Jean-Baptiste, les Hellénistes et Qumran," *RQ* 1 (1959) 365-90; cf. his earlier views in his *L'Epître aux Hébreux*, 2 vols. (Paris: Gabalda, 1952, 1953).

[34] J. W. Bowman, *Hebrews, James, I & II Peter* (Richmond: John Knox, 1962), esp. 9-10 on "A New Solution."

[35] C. K. Barrett, "The Eschatology of the Epistle to the Hebrews," in *The Background of the New Testament and its Eschatology*, ed. W. D. Davies and D. Daube (Cambridge: Cambridge University Press, 1954), 363-93 (393).

[36] G. B. Caird, "The Exegetical Method of the Epistle to the Hebrews," *CJT* 5 (1959) 44-51 (45).

[37] R. Williamson, *Philo and the Epistle to the Hebrews*, 538. See also idem, "Hebrews and Doctrine," *ExpT* 81 (1970) 371-76; idem, "The Background of the Epistle to the Hebrews," *ExpT* 87 (1976) 232-37.

played it;[38] others have denied it.[39] Nonetheless, I believe that Yigael Yadin's form of that thesis provides a better basis for the interpretation of Hebrews than any other proposed. Therefore I suggest that in *11QMelchizedek* we have an important key for understanding the treatment of Melchizedek in Hebrews. Particularly is this so, I propose, in the following four areas.

1. *The Place of Melchizedek in the Structure and Thought of Hebrews.* The Epistle to the Hebrews is unique in both the emphasis it gives to the priesthood of the Son and its explication of this priesthood as being "after the order of (κατὰ τὴν τάξιν) Melchizedek." The focal point of and the watershed for the exposition of Hebrews 1–10, in fact, is the Melchizedek argument of chapter 7, culminating, as it does, the discussion of the superior priesthood of Jesus that was mentioned in 2:17–3:1 and then developed in 4:14– 5:10, and preparing the way for the detailing of Christ's high-priestly ministration in 8:1–10:39.

Questions, however, have always been raised regarding: (1) What gave rise to such a high-priestly Christology? and (2) Why did the writer climax his exposition with the Melchizedek argument? Some have viewed these questions as only two parts of the same basic issue—thereby connecting the high-priestly motif and the Melchizedek argument in such a fashion that what is said about the one applies also to the other. Others, rightly I believe, consider two issues to be involved here.

As for the high-priestly motif of 3:1b and 4:14–5:10, it may well be that Hebrews is unique only in the emphasis that is given. Olaf Moe has demonstrated that the idea of the priesthood of Jesus lies implicit

---

[38] E.g., H. Kosmala, *Hebräer–Essener–Christen* (Leiden: Brill, 1959); cf. also J. Daniélou, *The Dead Sea Scrolls and Primitive Christianity* (Baltimore: Helicon, 1958).

[39] E.g., J. Coppens, "Les affinités qumraniennes de l'Epître aux Hebreux," *NRT* 84 (1962) 128-41, 257-82; F. F. Bruce, "'To the Hebrews' or 'To the Essenes'?," *NTS* 9 (1963) 217-32—though, unfortunately, usually on the basis of lumping together Yigael Yadin's thesis with that of Hans Kosmala, and then demolishing the former by association with the latter. F. F. Bruce's later review of the question is much more nuanced than his earlier article and contains a good summation of the current state of scholarly opinion: "Recent Contributions to the Understanding of Hebrews," *ExpT* 80 (1969) 260-64.

elsewhere in the New Testament;[40] Hugh Montefiore has related the priestly ascription of Jesus in Hebrews to the consciousness of Jesus as portrayed in the canonical Gospels;[41] and George Buchanan, following E. Brandenburger, has built a case for the confessional nature of Heb 5:7 ("Who during the days of his flesh offered up prayers and petitions ...") and Heb 5:8-9 ("Although he was a son, he learned obedience through what he suffered ..."), thereby rooting in the early church some consciousness of a high-priestly activity for the Christ.[42] Indeed, therefore, there are reasons to believe that the high-priestly motif of Hebrews is unique in the New Testament not in the fact of its appearance but in the emphasis it receives. Nonetheless, with regard to the Melchizedek argument of Hebrews, its uniqueness resides not just in the emphasis it receives in the epistle but in the fact of its employment, for nowhere else does it appear in the writings of the New Testament.

With *11QMelchizedek*, however, we now have a plausible explanation as to why the writer to the Hebrews built his argument in such a manner—if, that is, "the Qumran hypothesis" be anywhere close to the mark. As M. Delcor has argued:

> Indeed, since Melchizedek played an eschatological and celestial role in the speculations of the members of the Qumran community, it was quite normal for the author of an epistle addressed to priests of an Essene origin to use this *theologoumenon* as a pivot for his argument. It was a proof of apologetic skill to take his starting-point for an exposition of Christ's priesthood in the very beliefs shared by those with whom he was discussing the question of Melchizedek who was to play a role at the time of the judgment in the eschatological age.[43]

What the writer to the Hebrews seems to be doing is not only climaxing his presentation of Jesus as high priest in 3:1*b* and 4:14–5:10 with the Melchizedek argument, but also culminating his portrayal of the superiority of the Son to angels in chapters 1 and 2—all

---

[40] O. Moe, "Das Priesterthum Christi im NT ausserhalb des Hebräerbriefes," *TLZ* 72 (1947) 335-37; see also O. Cullmann, *The Christology of the New Testament*, trans. S. C. Guthrie and C. A. M. Hall (London: SCM; Philadelphia: Westminster, 1959, 1963²), 104-107.

[41] Montefiore, *Epistle to the Hebrews*, 95-96.

[42] G. W. Buchanan, *To the Hebrews: Translation, Comment and Conclusions* [AB; Garden City: Doubleday, 1972], 98-100.

[43] Delcor, "Melchizedek from Genesis to the Qumran Texts and the Epistle to the Hebrews," 126-27.

with an eye to what his addressees may have held in great esteem prior to their conversion to Christianity, and now were being tempted to return to. In so doing, of course, he was speaking situationally and circumstantially. But also, in so doing, he was attempting to direct his addressees' attention back to what he believed to be the true significance of the Melchizedekian figure of Gen 14:18-20 and Ps 110:4—though of this we must speak more extensively in what follows.

2. *The Initial Hesitancy of the Writer in Presenting his Melchizedek Argument.* The first reference to Melchizedek in Hebrews is the quotation of Ps 110:4 in Heb 5:6. Then, after two short confessional portions in 5:7 and 5:8-9 (*à la* Brandenburger and Buchanan), the writer comes to the apex of his presentation in 5:10: "And he was designated by God to be high priest, after the order of (κατὰ τὴν τάξιν, perhaps best rendered 'in line with' or 'just like') Melchizedek." Yet though he has come to the climax of his argument, the writer immediately backs off from the discussion, saying "concerning whom (περὶ οὗ) we have much to say, but it is hard to explain because you are slow to learn" (v 11). There then follows a rebuke of the addressees' inability to understand and an extended warning regarding apostasy in 5:12–6:20, after which the writer takes up the Melchizedek argument with great relish in chapter 7.

The question, of course, is: Why this initial hesitancy to enter directly into the full-blown portrayal of Melchizedek as given eventually in chapter 7? If the relative pronoun in the expression περὶ οὗ of 5:11 is understood as a neuter pronoun, then the reference would be back to the antecedent discussion of high priesthood, and the writer would be saying, in effect, that the topic of the priestly nature of Jesus is a difficult one. But the use of a neuter relative pronoun to capture the entirety of a previous discussion is not really in the style of Hebrews elsewhere. On the other hand, if the pronoun οὗ is understood as a masculine relative pronoun, then Christ as typified by Melchizedek may be what the writer is characterizing as being difficult to present to his addressees—and many commentators would readily agree. Yet the masculine relative pronoun could just as readily refer to its immediate masculine antecedent "Melchizedek." Linguistically, this is preferable. And in light of the various and sometimes competing attitudes toward Melchizedek in Second Temple Judaism—and particularly in view of a possible early ambivalence toward him at Qumran, but then a later near-veneration—such a reading has much to commend it.

The writer is both (1) dealing with a topic about which there seems to have been a great many conflicting opinions in his day, and (2) writing to a particular group of people who, prior to their allegiance to Jesus as Israel's Messiah, seem to have held Melchizedek in very high esteem. He is at the heart of his argument. More importantly, however, he is at a crucial point of difference between commitment to Jesus, which he is calling his addressees to reaffirm, and old allegiances, to which they were being enticed again. In such a situation, the writer's initial hesitancy to elaborate a Melchizedekian argument is somewhat understandable.

3. *The Biblical Argument of the Writer with Respect to Melchizedek.* The Epistle to the Hebrews is structured along the lines of an "anticipation–consummation" theme. From the perspective of the Messiah's presence among his people in "these last days," Israel's life and worship are viewed as preparatory for the coming of the Lord's Christ. A more profound significance is seen in the prophetic words and the redemptive experiences recorded in Scripture, and these words and events are understood to be looking forward to the consummation of God's salvific program in the work and person of Jesus. For the author of Hebrews, as B. F. Westcott has pointed out,

> the O.T. does not simply contain prophecies, but ... it is one vast prophecy, in the record of national fortunes, in the ordinances of a national Law, in the expression of a national hope. Israel in its history, in its ritual, in its ideal, is a unique enigma among the peoples of the world, of which the Christ is the complete solution.[44]

In spelling out this theme, the argument of the letter is built around five biblical portions: (1) a catena of verses drawn from the Psalms, 2 Samuel 7, and Deuteronomy 32 (LXX and *4QDeut*), on which Heb 1:3–2:4 is based; (2) Ps 8:4-6, on which Heb 2:5-18 is based; (3) Ps 95:7-11, on which Heb 3:1–4:13 is based; (4) Ps 110:4, on which Heb 4:14–7:28 is based; and (5) Jer 31:31-34, on which Heb 8:1–10:39 is based.[45] All the exhortations of Hebrews 11–13 depend on the

---

[44] B. F. Westcott, *The Epistle to the Hebrews* (London: Macmillan, 1889), 493.

[45] Cf. Caird, "Exegetical Method of the Epistle to the Hebrews," 47-51; see also my *Biblical Exegesis in the Apostolic Period* (1975), 174-85; (1999), 155-65.

exposition of these five biblical portions, and all the other verses quoted in the letter are ancillary to these.

In approaching each of these biblical portions, the writer to the Hebrews asks basically the same question, and always from a christocentric perspective: What do these enigmatic passages really mean when viewed from a Christian perspective? That is, What do the Scriptures mean when they speak of God's Son (Ps 2:7; 2 Sam 7:14), of One whom all the angels of God are to worship (Deut 32:43 LXX and *4QDeut*), and of One who is addressed as God by God, yet is distinguished from God (Ps 45:6-7; 102:25-27; 110:1)? What does the psalmist mean when he talks about humanity's creatureliness and subordination, yet also of humanity's destined glory, honor, and universal authority (Ps 8:4-6)? What does the psalmist mean when he speaks about entering God's rest (Ps 95:7-11)? What did Jeremiah mean by a New Covenant (Jer 31:31-34)? And in Hebrews 7, which is the direct concern of this article, he does the same with respect to Melchizedek.

George Caird has somewhat overstated the case in arguing that "it is important to recognize that throughout his treatment of Melchizedek our author is concerned *solely* with the exegesis of Ps. 110,"[46] for the narrative of Gen 14:18-20—both with regard to what is said about Melchizedek and what is not said—plays a significant role in the author's argument as well. But Caird is certainly right to insist that "he carries us back to the story of Genesis 14 not to compose a fanciful and allegorical midrash on that chapter after the manner of Philo, but rather because he wishes to answer the very modern question: 'What did the words "priest for ever after the order of Melchizedek" mean to the psalmist who wrote them?'"[47]

The writer to the Hebrews is working with two traditions. In the first place, he accepts Psalm 110 as being messianic, as had become traditional within the church (e.g., Acts 2:34-35) and as credited to the impetus of Jesus himself (cf. Mark 12:36, par.), and he seeks to explicate verse 4 of that psalm along these lines. But he also, secondly, has an eye toward the figure of Melchizedek as revered at Qumran. Thus on the basis of his Christian perspectives, in line with

---

[46] G. B. Caird, "Exegetical Method," 48 (italics his).
[47] Ibid.

certain current and widespread Jewish exegetical procedures,[48] and with a view to his addressees' understanding of the enigmatic personage of Gen 14:18-20, he asks: Who is this Melchizedek and what was the nature of his priesthood—particularly in view of the fact that the psalmist speaks of him in a messianic psalm? And, further: How does he serve as a prototype of the Christ? And how may Jesus, the Messiah and Son of God, be appropriately compared to him?

We need not here become diverted into a psychoanalysis of the psalmist's intention at this point, as though millennia later we could assemble the exact details of his consciousness when writing. Nor need we become carried away with the writer's allegorical-etymological treatment of the name "Melchizedek" and the title "King of Salem." As we have seen above, Josephus as well as Philo can treat Melchizedek's title in much the same fashion, which indicates something of the widespread nature of this type of exposition. And as Richard P. C. Hanson has observed, our author's treatment of these names is "so simple and obvious" that their use in his epistle hardly signals anything specifically Alexandrian or Philonic.[49]

For the writer to the Hebrews, the Melchizedek of Genesis 14 is an enigma that finds its solution in Psalm 110:4—but only when Psalm 110 is recognized as having messianic relevance. From this Christian understanding of the psalm, the typological correspondences that lie inherent in the redemptive history of Genesis 14 can be drawn out and a "fuller sense" in the narrative explicated by means of commonly accepted exegetical procedures.

The writer to the Hebrews, it seems, did not consider himself to be inventing any new interpretation or using any deviant exegetical procedures. He was simply extending the application of a psalm that had already been identified within the church as having messianic relevance, and was doing so with an eye to the interests and appreciation of his addressees. In the process, of course, he used a mild allegorical-etymological treatment of the name "Melchizedek" and the title "King of Salem" (7:2). But that kind of exposition seems to have been somewhat common in his day. Likewise, he argued for the eternality of Melchizedek on the basis of the silence of Scripture regarding his ancestors and his descendants (7:3). But the principle

---

[48] Cf. my *Biblical Exegesis in the Apostolic Period* (1975), 28-50; (1999), 14-35.

[49] R. P. C. Hanson, *Allegory and Event* (London: SCM, 1959), 86.

quod non in thora non in mundo ("what is not in the Torah is not in the world") was also quite widespread in the Jewish hermeneutics of the day.⁵⁰ Given his presuppositions, his precedents, and his audience, in fact, our author's exposition of the Melchizedekian priesthood of Jesus may be judged to be quite straightforward and telling.

4. *The Theological Significance of the Melchizedek–Christ Comparison in Hebrews.* The writer to the Hebrews seems to have found himself confronted by two basic necessities: (1) the need to support a high-priestly acclamation of Jesus the Messiah on some explicit biblical basis, for being from the tribe of Judah Jesus had no inherited priestly rights; and (2) the need to set out the superiority of Jesus, the high-priestly Messiah, over the Arch-angel, Warrior-Redeemer figure of Qumran messianology, who was evidently being turned to again by his addressees in their desperation to find something or someone on whom to build their hopes. What priestly claims were made for Jesus prior to our writer's time were evidently made principally on a functional rather than a speculative basis (e.g., Gal 3:10-14; Rom 3:21-26; 2 Cor 5:18-21; Eph 5:2). But our writer was not willing to leave it at that. Having accepted Psalm 110 as possessing messianic relevance, he found in verse 4 the explicit biblical support he needed for a high-priestly Christology.

---

⁵⁰ The triad ἀπάτωρ, ἀμήτωρ, ἀγενεαλόγητος ("without father, without mother, without genealogy") of 7:3 has often been viewed as a strictly Philonic argument from silence (cf., e.g., J. Moffatt, *A Critical and Exegetical Commentary on the Epistle to the Hebrews* [MNTC; New York: Scribner's, 1924], 92). Paul Billerbeck, however, has demonstrated that for the rabbis—and, presumably, also for the earlier Pharisees—what is not said in the Torah was just as significant as what is said, and that therefore rabbinic hermeneutics also argued from silences in the biblical accounts (H. L. Strack and P. Billerbeck, *Str-Bil* 3.694-95). An example that is somewhat comparable to the treatment of Melchizedek in Hebrews can be found in the treatment of the parentage of Cain in *Targum Pseudo-Jonathan*, where on Gen 4:1 the targumic exposition speaks of Eve having "conceived from Sammael the angel, and she became pregnant and bare Cain" and on Gen 5:3 says that Eve bore Cain "who was not like Adam." The biblical rationale that is invoked for Cain being a child of Sammael, from whom he inherited his evil character, and not Adam's own son, is the statement in Gen 5:3: Adam "begat a son in his own likeness, after his image; and called his name Seth." Such a direct statement of lineage, however, is not given earlier with respect to the birth of Cain, and therefore the targumist drew from that silence the conclusion that Cain was not Adam's true son (cf. Bowker, *Targums and Rabbinic Literature*, 132, 136).

This acclamation of Jesus as "high priest forever according to the order of Melchizedek" seems to have been the writer's own contribution to the ongoing development of early Christian apologetic and the church's Christology. Methodologically, it involved only a broadening of focus from a messianic interpretation of Ps 110:1, as had been given by Jesus himself (cf. Mark 12:35-37, par.) and was accepted within the early church (cf. Acts 2:34-35), to include the explicit reference in that same messianically relevant passage only three verses later in Ps 110:4. In so doing, Melchizedek seems to have become important to the writer as a prototype of messianic redemption.

In agreement with his addressees, he acknowledges the legitimacy of considering Melchizedek as a heavenly figure of continuing priestly significance.[51] This is suggested by the characterization of 7:3: "Without father, without mother, without genealogy, without beginning of days or end of life, like the son of God he remains a priest forever." The verse may very well be poetic in structure, originally appearing in some such form as the following:

ἀπάτωρ, ἀμήτωρ, ἀγενεαλόγητος,
μήτε ἀρχὴν ἡμερῶν μήτε ζωῆς τέλος ἔχων,
ἀφωμοιωμένος δὲ τῷ υἱῷ τοῦ θεοῦ,
μένει ἱερεὺς εἰς τὸ διηνεκές. [52]

Such a structure suggests that these words were drawn, either wholly or in part, from some previous oral or written midrashic treatment of Gen 14:18-20—perhaps even from a catechetical or hymnodic portion used previously by his addressees. But whether our author used an earlier formulation that was known to his addressees or composed the wording himself, there can be no doubt from his manner of usage that he had at least some commitment to what is said. And though some have argued that the statements have reference only to Melchizedek's

---

[51]. Agreeing with de Jonge and van der Woude, "11QMelchizedek," 321; though Horton has argued that "the Epistle to the Hebrews should not be reckoned with the literature in which Melchizedek is considered a divine or heavenly figure" (*Melchizedek Tradition*, 164).

[52] Cf. de Jonge and van der Woude, "11QMelchizedek," 319. Michel also considered Heb 7:3 to be poetic (*Brief an die Hebräer*, 164). Also to be noted is the fact that in verse 3 Melchizedek is compared to "the Son of God," whereas elsewhere in the chapter the reverse is true.

priestly qualifications and not at all to his person,[53] it is by far more natural to read them as referring to his person.

The whole discussion of 7:1-10 is, in fact, encapsulated in the exclamation of 7:4a: "Just think how great he was!" And thus the writer speaks of Melchizedek in 7:2 as the "King of Righteousness" (βασιλεὺς δικαιοσύνης) and the "King of Peace" (βασιλεὺς εἰρήνης), and in 7:4-10 as one who is greater than Abraham and the Levitical cultus in that both Abraham and Levi ("one might even say") paid tithes to him.

More than that, however, the writer takes pains to point out in 7:11-22 that Melchizedek was the priest of "God Most High" *prior to* and *apart from* the Aaronic priesthood, being appointed by God on the basis of his character, and that it is of such a priesthood as based on character rather than on lineage that Psalm 110 speaks of in connection with the Messiah. And it is at this point in his argument that the comparisons between Christ and Melchizedek are drawn, for Jesus' priesthood, too, is (1) based on "the power of an indestructible life" apart from any Aaronic lineage, and (2) given by divine oath apart from any Mosaic legislation.

It is worth noting, as well, that while our author agreed with his addressees in 7:1-10 as to the nature of Melchizedek's person, he did not attempt to correlate the person of Christ with the person of Melchizedek—rather, in fact, with respect to their persons, he did just the opposite in relating Melchizedek to "the Son of God." But now in 7:11-22 he presents Melchizedek as the precedent for and prototype of an eternal priesthood based on character apart from lineage and ordained by God apart from law. And having thus established the precedent and prototype, he goes on to elucidate Jesus' high priesthood in these terms.

Yet while agreeing with his addressees as to the nature of Melchizedek's person, the writer to the Hebrews profoundly disagrees with them as to the place of Melchizedek in redemptive history and as to the significance of his ministry. For his addressees, it seems, at least to judge by *11QMelchizedek*, Melchizedek would be an Archangel, Warrior-Redeemer figure of some importance in the Messianic Age, who would in his priestly activities atone for sin and for whom the epithets אלוהים (*11QMelch*, line 10) and perhaps משיח הרוח (*ibid.*, line

---

[53] As does Michel, *Brief an die Hebräer*, 162-63; also Horton, *Melchizedek Tradition*, 162-63.

18) apply. For the writer to the Hebrews, however, Melchizedek serves only as the precedent for and prototype of a greater high priesthood that is also based on character apart from lineage and ordained by God apart from law. In addition, in the warfare of the Son with the devil in 2:14-18, it is a fully human and suffering Messiah who became "a merciful and faithful high priest" in order to be able "to help those who are being tempted"—which is in sharp contrast to the military figure of *11QMelchizedek* who bests Belial in the final cosmic battle.

The addressees of the Epistle to the Hebrews were, it seems, beginning to think more of Melchizedek than of Christ in connection with redemption and the fulfillment of God's promises. The writer, however, convinced regarding the messianic relevance of Psalm 110 and agreeing with his addressees as to the nature of their hero's person, finds in Ps 110:4 the key to understanding relationships between Melchizedek and Jesus the Christ. For the one, Melchizedek, is the precedent for and prototype of the much greater One, Jesus the Messiah, who having been made "perfect through suffering" is the far superior and only "Pioneer (ἀρχηγός) of their salvation" (2:10; cf. 12:2). In so arguing, of course, the writer speaks in ways that are circumstantially conditioned to meet his addressees' interests and appreciation. But he also, both through providential insight and challenge, develops the motif of the priestly nature and ministry of Jesus in ways beyond what was heretofore expressly stated in the New Testament and presumably explicitly taught by other Christian teachers of his day.

3. *Christological Development and Circumstantial Expression in Hebrews*

Our interest in this article has been principally in the christological comparisons and contrasts made between Jesus and Melchizedek in Hebrews. In the process we have attempted, as well, to highlight certain features of christological development and circumstantial expression that appear in this New Testament epistle. Such primary and secondary purposes have required (1) that we first sketch out the various attitudes toward Melchizedek that are able to be discerned in the extant materials representative of Second Temple Judaism, and (2) that we then attempt to understand our author's use of the Melchizedek figure both in the light of his Christian commitments and vis-à-vis the situation he was addressing. The detailing of the particular situation addressed and of the argument presented has, of course, value of itself for exegesis and for biblical theology. We have, however, been primarily interested in these matters in order to gain from them some appreciation of the christological development and circumstantial expression that appear in this particular New Testament writing.

The New Testament does not come to us as a treatise on theology or compendium of ethics. It presents itself as the record of God's redemptive activity in first-century Palestine through the ministry, death, and resurrection of Jesus of Nazareth (i.e., in its four Gospels) and as the apostolic interpretation of that activity to various people in their somewhat diverse cultural situations and ideological environments (i.e., in its Acts, Pauline letters, sermonic epistles, and Apocalypse). As such it speaks in the language of the day to the issues and interests of the day, using such exegetical methods and arguments in support as were then current, in order to win the allegiance of those it addresses to Jesus, who is Israel's Messiah and humanity's Lord. The message it proclaims appears in the record in various stages of development and in various cultural forms, dependent not only on the perceptions of the particular writers involved but also on the interests, appreciation, and understanding of the particular addressees.

Students of the New Testament, therefore, find themselves confronted by a multifaceted flow of thought and a variety of presentations in the primary materials that often seem to yield no clearly definable system of doctrine but from which they seek to extract something approaching a coherent understanding. In addition, they are faced with the issue of how the normative principles of the gospel relate to the specific situations to which they were originally directed and to the particular forms into which they were first cast, asking always how to distill those principles from the situations and cultural forms of that day—and then, by God's grace, how to recast them into forms that will speak meaningfully to the interests, appreciations, and understandings of people today in their varying cultural situations and ideological environments, so that the same gospel might confront the thought and lives of people today with something of the same force as it did in apostolic times.

It is no mean task that students of the New Testament take on themselves. It requires all the scientific, artistic, and theological acumen that can be marshaled, together with a constant dependence on God's Spirit for illumination and discernment. It necessitates, as well, interaction with the many and various attempts to understand the New Testament that have been advanced, both in the past and today. And as one current proposal, I would like to offer the following by way of understanding the flow of New Testament thought generally and the Melchizedek argument of Hebrews in particular.

It is possible to understand the multifaceted flow of New Testament thought and the variety of presentations within the New Testament canon along the lines of the following four captions: (1) revelational immediacy; (2) historical continuity; (3) theological development; and (4) circumstantial expression. Foundational to all New Testament proclamation, and the ultimate rationale for the writing of the New Testament itself, is the fact that God has acted redemptively and revealed himself uniquely in the person and work of Jesus of Nazareth. Everything in the New Testament stems from this initial note of revelational immediacy: that in Jesus men and women have experienced the presence of God in their midst; that to know him is to know the One who sent him; that God was in Christ effecting humanity's redemption; and that by the Spirit relationship with the risen Christ is established and maintained. The proclamation of the earliest apostles was based on and validated by their having been commissioned directly by Jesus—whether during his earthly ministry (Mark 3:13-19, par.; John 15:27), immediately after his ascension (Acts 1:21-26), or later on the road to Damascus (Gal 1:12, 15-16; 1 Cor 9:1)—and their business was to bear witness to the revelation they had received.

But while that apostolic message was rooted in the revelation of God in Jesus Christ, it was filled out providentially through the continued ministry of the Spirit, just as the Lord had promised (cf. John 16:12-15). Thus the earliest believers in Jesus sought for continuity with the past redemptive activity of God by means of a reevaluation of the Old Testament Scriptures, taking Jesus' own exegetical practice as the paradigm for their hermeneutical procedures. Thus they were led to explicate their convictions in ways that developed from a more functional manner of speaking to include more speculative and ontological affirmations, finding that the issues they faced in making their gospel message intelligible often forced them to think in such ways. And thus they expressed their convictions in terminology suited to the interest, appreciation, and understanding of

9. The Melchizedek Argument of Hebrews

their audiences, discovering that the various cultural situations and ideological environments they confronted often caused them to refine the terms of that message so as better to convey its truth—and sometimes supplied them with certain vehicles of expression that could be appropriately employed in their proclamation.

In particular, as we have argued before and now formally propose, the argument of Hebrews regarding the relationship of Jesus the Messiah to the legendary king-priest Melchizedek is, to an extent, a good example of the general approach outlined above as to the flow of New Testament thought. It may fail to do full justice to the theory in that, though he assumes a decidedly christocentric perspective in treating the Old Testament, the writer does not root his presentation in any revelation that he himself received personally. Rather, in 2:3-4 he explicitly speaks of having received the basic gospel traditions from the apostles, and he seems to reserve such revelational immediacy for the apostles alone. But in matters having to do with historical continuity, theological development, and circumstantial expression, our author reveals quite clearly how one early Christian leader—perhaps Apollos, who was associated with the apostolic ministry (cf. 1 Cor 1–4)—understood and explicated such features.

Throughout his sermonic epistle the writer demonstrates his interest in historic continuity, particularly in highlighting the five biblical portions around which he builds his argument. Theological development, however, reaches its zenith in the Melchizedek argument itself, where our author expands on the theme of the high priesthood of Christ—first by bringing Ps 110:4 explicitly into the orbit of messianically relevant passages; then by explicating our Lord's priestly ministry in ways that go beyond the dominantly functional statements of the earliest Christians and begin to move into more distinctly ontological and metaphysical realms; and finally by treating Melchizedek as the precedent for and prototype of Jesus' high priesthood. And it is in the Melchizedek argument that his circumstantial expression comes most to the fore in agreeing with his addressees as to the nature of Melchizedek in order that he might then go on to draw such comparisons and contrasts between Melchizedek and Christ as to enhance the superiority and supremacy of our Lord's high priesthood and priestly ministry.

We may not today feel entirely comfortable with the writer's views regarding the nature of Melchizedek. Nor may we feel the same necessity to root the high priesthood and priestly ministry of Christ in some such explicit precedent and prototype. In accepting such a view regarding the enigmatic king-priest of Genesis 14 and in searching for such an explicit precedent, our author, it seems, was trying to relate to his addressees' particular understanding and to speak along the lines of their interests. In so arguing, we propose, he committed himself as well (at least to some extent) to the correctness of his addressees' opinions—much as he does elsewhere in speaking of the Mosaic law as having been mediated by angels (2:2), or in acknowledging the tabernacle as Israel's ideal place of worship (8:5; 9:2-5, 21), or in referring to the post-biblical martyrs (11:35-37) (or, for that matter, as Paul does with reference to the rock that followed the Israelites in the wilderness in 1 Cor 10:1-4). But these are matters having to do with the circumstances of his argument, which he uses to explicate within a specific ideological environment the priestly nature and ministry of Jesus the Messiah in a more developed manner. We may appreciate the writer's circumstantial expression, but we must not become so weighted down by it as to lose the significance and impact of the theological and christological development represented.

SELECT BIBLIOGRAPHY

Bardy, Gustave. "Melchisédech dans la tradition patristique," *RB* 35 (1926) 496-509; 36 (1927) 25-45.
Barrett, C. Kingsley. "The Eschatology of the Epistle to the Hebrews," in *The Background of the New Testament and its Eschatology*, ed. W. D. Davies and D. Daube. Cambridge: Cambridge University Press, 1954, 363-93.
Bowman, John Wick. *Hebrews, James, I & II Peter*. Richmond: John Knox, 1962.
Bruce, Frederick F. "'To the Hebrews' or 'To the Essenes'?," *NTS* 9 (1963) 217-32.
_____. "Recent Contributions to the Understanding of Hebrews," *ExpT* 80 (1969) 260-64.
Buchanan, George W. *To the Hebrews. Translation, Comment and Conclusions*. AB. Garden City: Doubleday, 1972, 96-100.
Caird, George B. "The Exegetical Method of the Epistle to the Hebrews," *CJT* 5 (1959) 44-51.
Carmignac, Jean. "Le document de Qumran sur Melkisedeq," *RQ* 7 (1970) 343-78.
Delcor, Mathias. "Melchizedek from Genesis to the Qumran Texts and the Epistle to the Hebrews," *JSJ* 2 (1971) 115-35.

Demarest, Bruce. *A History of the Interpretation of Hebrews 7,1-10 from the Reformation to the Present*. Tübingen: Mohr, 1976.

Fitzmyer, Joseph A. "Now this Melchizedek (Hebr 7:1)," *CBQ* 25 (1963) 305-21.

_____. "Further Light on Melchizedek from Qumran Cave 11," *JBL* 86 (1967) 25-41.

Hanson, Richard P. C. *Allegory and Event*. London: SCM, 1959.

Hay, David M. *Glory at the Right Hand: Psalm 110 in Early Christianity*. Nashville, New York: Abingdon, 1973.

Horton, Fred L., Jr, *The Melchizedek Tradition: A Critical Examination of the Sources to the Fifth Century A.D. and in the Epistle to the Hebrews*. Cambridge: Cambridge University Press, 1976.

Jonge, Marinus de, and Adam S. van der Woude, "11Q Melchizedek and the New Testament," *NTS* 12 (1966) 301-26.

Koester, Craig R. *Hebrews: A New Translation and Commentary*. AB. New York: Doubleday, 2001, 338-74.

Laubscher, F. du Toit. "God's Angel of Truth and Melchizedek: A Note on 11Q Melch 13b," *JSJ* 3 (1972) 46-51.

Longenecker, Richard N. *Biblical Exegesis in the Apostolic Period*. Grand Rapids: Eerdmans, 1975, 158-85; 2nd ed., 1999, 140-65.

Michel, Otto. *Der Brief an die Hebraer*. Gottingen: Vandenhoeck & Ruprecht, 1957; rev ed., 1960.

Petuchowski, Jakob J., "The Controversial Figure of Melchizedek," *HUCA* 28 (1957) 127-36.

Simon, Marcel. "Melchizedek dans la polémique entre Juifs et Chrétiens et dans la légende," *RHPR* (1937) 58-93.

Spicq, Ceslas. "L'Epître aux Hebreux, Apollos, Jean-Baptiste, les Hellénistes et Qumran," *RQ* 1 (1959) 365-90.

Westcott, Brooke F. *The Epistle to the Hebrews*. London: Macmillan, 1889.

Williamson, Ronald. *Philo and the Epistle to the Hebrews*. Leiden: Brill, 1970.

_____. "Hebrews and Doctrine," *ExpT* 81 (1970) 371-76.

_____. "The Background of the Epistle to the Hebrews," *ExpT* 87 (1976) 232-37.

Woude, Adam S. van der. "Melchisedek als himmlische Erlösergestalt in den neugefundenen eschatologischen Midraschim aus Qumran Höhle XI," *OTS* 14 (1965) 354-73.

Wuttke, G. *Melchisedech der Priesterkönig van Salem: Eine Studie zur Geschichte der Exegese*. Giessen: Topelmann, 1927.

Yadin, Yigael. "The Dead Sea Scrolls and the Epistle to the Hebrews," in *Aspects of the Dead Sea Scrolls*, ed. C. Rabin and Y. Yadin. SH, 4. Jerusalem: Hebrew University, 1958, 36-55.

_____. "A Note on Melchizedek and Qumran," *IEJ* 15 (1965) 152-54.

Part III

DISCIPLESHIP

10

"Son Of Man" Imagery
Some Implications for Theology and Discipleship

In her little book of poems translated *Prayers from the Ark*,[1] Carmen Bernos de Gasztold expresses, as she imagines, the prayers and observations of Noah and twenty-six of his animal companions on that fateful diluvian voyage. Noah's prayer begins:

> Lord,
> What a menagerie!
> Between Your downpour and these animal cries
> one cannot hear oneself think!

And it concludes with the dual requests:

> Guide Your Ark to safety;
> Lead me until I reach the shore of Your covenant.

The cock's prayer, however, begins and ends on a somewhat different note:

> Do not forget, Lord,
> it is I who make the sun rise ...
> I am Your servant,
> only do not forget, Lord,
> I make the sun rise.

The giraffe cannot deign to bow his neck, and rather loftily lectures the Lord—and any who might overhear—on his superior qualities:

> Lord,
> I who see the world from above
> find it hard to get used to its pettiness.
> I have heard it said
> You love humble creatures.
> Chatter of apes!

---

[1] New York: Viking Press, 1962.

10. "Son of Man" Imagery

> It is easier for me
> to believe in Your greatness.
> I feed on exalted things
> and I rather like
> to see myself so close to Your heaven.
> Humility?
> Chatter of apes!

The cat, without seeking to be presumptuous, asks only:

> If You have by some chance, in some celestial barn,
> a little white mouse,
> or a saucer of milk,
> I know someone who would relish them.

And then she offers but one small suggestion:

> Wouldn't You like someday
> to put a curse on the whole race of dogs?
> If so, I should say,
>   Amen.

And so it goes throughout each of the twenty-seven prayers: each viewing life from its own perspective; each voicing its own prejudices; and each circumscribed by its own interests. After vicariously entering into the individual situations represented by the prayers, one can't help agreeing with Noah in the opening lines of his petition to God: "Lord, what a menagerie!"

The analogy is obvious. How like the Noah's ark is the church, and Christians like its inhabitants—all too provincial, all too limited by our own interests, and viewing everything from our own perspectives. This is particularly true, I suggest, in our work as Christian theologians and in our lives as Christian disciples. What we need, of course, is some objective standard by which we can check our all-too-human notions and our all-too-worldly lifestyles. And this is exactly what we have been given, we believe, in the Word made flesh (Jesus Christ) and in "the word" inscripturated (Scripture). Yet given these revelational standards, the hermeneutical question as to what is central in them for Christian thought and life still remains.

In what follows, I would like to focus on one dominant feature in the Gospels' portrayal of Jesus—that of Jesus as "the Son of Man"—and to suggest that a proper understanding of this image has important implications for the construction of our theologies and the expression of our convictions in life as Christians. My justification for raising this issue in this form is twofold: (1) while much has been written on the Son of Man by a vast number of New Testament specialists, there seems to be emerging a new thrust in the discussion that I believe to be highly commendable; and (2) while the importance of this motif for the shaping of early Christian theology is widely recognized by New Testament scholars (whatever their views as to how exactly it occurred), little of this seems to have spilled over into the theological and devotional literature of our day.

I would, therefore, first of all like to report on the state of Son of Man studies today, spelling out in the process what I believe to be a growing and laudatory new thrust in the discussion.[2] In particular, I want to focus on three areas of concern: (1) the appearance of Son of Man imagery in the writings of Second Temple Judaism; (2) the dominical status of Son of Man imagery in the New Testament; and (3) Jesus' understanding and use of Son of Man imagery (if, indeed, we can believe it to have had dominical status). These three areas, of course, overlap considerably, yet may be treated somewhat separately for purposes of analysis. Then I want to indicate what I believe to be some rather important implications of all of this for the construction of our Christian theologies and for the living of our lives as followers of Christ. I cannot hope to set out anything like a programmatic proposal in these latter regards, for that goes far beyond the measure of my poor abilities. But I do hope to be suggestive in these matters, pointing the way toward a type of theological construction that I believe would be more biblically based and a lifestyle that would be more like that of Christ's.

1. *Son of Man Imagery in Second Temple Judaism*

Many modern treatments of "Son of Man" have begun on the premise that there existed in Second Temple Judaism a generally well-defined concept of a transcendent, eschatological Redeemer figure and Judge, who was spoken of as the Son of Man and whose coming to earth would be a feature of the drama of the End Time, and that evidence for such a conception can be found in Daniel 7, 1 Enoch 37–71 and 4

---

[2] Admittedly, I am here covering some of the same ground I covered earlier in my article "'Son of Man' as a Self-Designation of Jesus," *JETS* 12 (1969) 151-58, and my monograph *The Christology of Early Jewish Christianity* (SBT, 17; London: SCM, 1970), though, hopefully, with a bit more perception and as a necessary prolegomenon to highlighting certain implications.

Ezra 13.[3] To begin with such an understanding is to control all further considerations in terms of these categories—which, of course, is true of any premise, and so requires that every premise be carefully scrutinized before proceeding. However there is much, I believe, that can be said against this particular premise.

The major difficulty with beginning any christological discussion with the Enochian Son of Man is that, to date, there is no evidence of a pre-Christian Jewish provenance for chapters 37–71 of *1 Enoch* (i.e., Book 2 of *Ethiopic Enoch*, the "Parables" or "Similitudes of Enoch," where this expression occurs repeatedly, but does not appear elsewhere in the other four sections of the work), and it is precarious to deduce the existence of a firm Son of Man concept in pre-Christian Judaism on the basis of Daniel 7 and 4 Ezra 13 alone. Of the twenty-nine or so extant manuscripts of *Ethiopic Enoch*, which consists of five sections with a total of 108 chapters, most belong to the eighteenth century CE and none can be confidently dated earlier than the fifteenth or sixteenth centuries. Even if R. H. Charles's guess be accepted that the Ethiopic version was translated in the sixth or seventh centuries, or F. C. Burkitt's speculation that this may have occurred as early as the fourth century, we are still centuries removed from pre-Christian times. And none of the few Greek portions of the work discovered in 1886–1887 contains material from Book 2 of so-called 1 Enoch. It is for this reason that C. H. Dodd and a few British scholars influenced by him at this point have refused to erect any

---

[3] Cf., e.g., O. Cullmann, *The Christology of the New Testament*, trans. S. C. Guthrie and C. A. M. Hall (London: SCM, 1959, 1963), 139-44; A. J. B. Higgins, *Jesus and the Son of Man* (London: Lutterworth, 1964), 15; idem, *The Son of Man in the Teaching of Jesus* [SNTSMS, 39; Cambridge: Cambridge University Press, 1980), 12-28; F. H. Borsch, *The Son of Man in Myth and History* (NTL; London: SCM, 1967), 145-56; idem, *The Christian and Gnostic Son of Man* (SBT, 2/14; London: SCM, 1970), 116-18, *passim*. See also F. Hahn, *Christologische Hoheitstitel* (Göttingen: Vandenhoeck & Ruprecht, 1963), 13-53; R. H. Fuller, *The Foundations of New Testament Christology* (New York: Scribner's, 1965), 34-43; P. Vielhauer, "Gottesreich und Menschensohn," in *Festschrift für Günther Dehn*, ed. W. Schneemelcher (Neukirchen: Moers, 1957), 51-79; idem, "Jesus und der Menschensohn," *ZTK* 60 (1963) 133-77; idem, "Ein Weg der neutestamentlichen Theologie: Prüfung der Thesen Ferdinand Hahns," *EvT* 25 (1965) 24-72.

arguments on evidence drawn from the Similitudes[4]—though there has often been little reticence in accepting a pre-Christian provenance for these chapters 37–71 of 1 Enoch on the continent and in North America.

In addition, while the caves of Qumran have produced portions of ten or so manuscripts whose content corresponds to every other chapter in *Ethiopic Enoch* (with the possible exception of chapters 105 and 108), they have yielded no fragments from the Similitudes themselves (i.e., chapters 37–71).[5] This fact has compelled such scholars as J. T. Milik, Frank M. Cross, Jr, Jean Daniélou, Joseph A. Fitzmyer, C. F. D. Moule, Ragnar Leivestad, J. C. Hindley and Lloyd Gaston to suggest a late first-century or early second-century CE date for the composition of the Enochian Similitudes and to view them as possibly representative of some type of early Jewish Christianity.[6] And I argued this position in 1970 myself.[7]

Since the meetings of the "Pseudepigrapha Seminar" of the *Studiorum Novi Testamenti Societas* at Tübingen in 1977 and Paris in 1978,

---

[4] Cf. C. H. Dodd, *According to the Scriptures* (London: Nisbet, 1952), 116-17; idem, *The Interpretation of the Fourth Gospel* (Cambridge: Cambridge University Press, 1954), 242-43. See particularly T. F. Glasson, *The Second Advent: The Origin of the New Testament Doctrine* (London: Epworth, 1945), 25-62.

[5] Cf. M. Black, "The Fragments of the Aramaic Enoch from Qumran," in *La littérature juive entre Tenach et Mischna*, ed. W. C. van Unnik (Leiden: Brill, 1974), 15-28.

[6] J. T. Milik, *Ten Years of Discovery in the Wilderness of Judaea*, trans. J. Strugnell (London: SCM, 1959), 33-34; F. M. Cross, Jr, *The Ancient Library of Qumran* (London: Duckworth, 202-203; J. Daniélou, *The Dead Sea Scrolls and Primitive Christianity*, trans. S. Attanasio (New York: New American Library, 1958), see esp. appendices; J. A. Fitzmyer, *Essays on the Semitic Background of the New Testament* (London: Chapman, 1971), 136-37 and 152-53; C.F.D. Moule, in review of H. E. Todt's *The Son of Man in the Synoptic Tradition*, *Theol* 69 (1966) 173-75; idem, "Neglected Features in the Problem of the Son of Man," in *Neues Testament und Kirche*, ed. J. Gnilka (Freiburg: Herder, 1974), 413-28; R. Leivestad, "Der apokalyptische Menschensohn ein theologisches Phantom," *ASTI* 6 (1968) 49-105 (English summary: "Exit the Apocalyptic Son of Man," *NTS* 18 [1972] 243-67); J. C. Hindley, "Towards a Date for the Similitudes of Enoch," *NTS* 14 (1968) 551-65; L. Gaston, *No Stone on Another: Studies in the Significance of the Fall of Jerusalem in the Synoptic Gospels* (NovTSup, 23; Leiden: Brill, 1970), 370ff.

[7] See my *Christology of Early Jewish Christianity*, 82-88.

however, which sessions focused attention on the provenance and date of the Enochian Similitudes, a consensus has grown among scholars that these "parables" or "similitudes" should not be viewed as having a Jewish-Christian provenance but are to be credited to a Jewish writer or writers who composed them some time in the middle or latter part of the first Christian century—and that probably they were included within the composite work known as *1 Enoch* (i.e., as later represented by *Ethiopic Enoch*) by the end of that century.[8] But however matters of provenance and date may be finally settled (if ever)—whether a late first century or early second century Jewish-Christian provenance or a middle to late first century strictly Jewish provenance—it needs to be recognized that, in all probability, the treatment of "Son of Man" in *1 Enoch* 37-71 had little, if any, impact on the portrayals of Jesus as the "Son of Man" in the Gospels of the New Testament. It may have been something of a parallel phenomenon in certain Jewish apocalyptic circles of the day. But its omission in the Greek fragments of the *Book of Enoch* and its absence in the Dead Sea texts published to date strongly suggests that its Enochian usage should not be employed in any discussions regarding Son of Man imagery in the New Testament—except, perhaps, as a parallel phenomenon in certain Jewish circles.

Admittedly, to argue from omissions in the extant Greek fragments and the absence of these chapters in the evidence to date from the Dead Sea texts is to argue only negatively. Such an argument, of course, always suffers from the inability of conclusive demonstration. Who, for instance, can argue from the lack of evidence that something could not have existed? It is also a tenuous argument in the sense that a great deal of material from Qumran has yet to be identified and published, and more texts may even yet be found, with some of these materials possibly giving evidence to the contrary. What would happen if, say, material from chapter 46 of *Ethiopic Enoch* were to be identified in the Aramaic portions from Qumran? Well, undoubtedly, we would have to revise considerably our thesis as here stated—perhaps even renounce it altogether. But as matters stand today, such an argument based on the absence of evidence is of sufficient import as to be highly significant. And it should give pause and cause for concern to those who erect on the basis of the Enochian Similitudes

---

[8] See, e.g., E. Isaac, "1 (Ethiopic Apocalypse of) Enoch," in *OTP* 1.6-7.

such imposing christologies as have been rather fashionable in some quarters in the recent past and continue so even today.

In actual fact, the only instances of the expression in Jewish writings that can be demonstrated to be certainly pre-Christian are to be found in the canonical Old Testament and once in the Qumran texts: (1) Ps 8:4 where it appears as a locution for humanity generically ("What is man that you are mindful of him, or the son of man that you should visit him?"); (2) Ps 80:17 where in context and in association with "the vine" imagery it is to be understood as a locution for the nation Israel; (3) the prophecy of Ezekiel as a vocative addressed by God to the prophet; (4) Dan 7:13-14 as a symbolic representation of the One who comes before the Ancient of Days and is given dominion, glory and a kingdom; and (5) *1QGen Apoc* 21.13 as a semitism for humanity generically ("I will make your descendants as the dust of the earth which no man [literally, 'son of man'] can number, so your descendants will be without number"). Probably also Geza Vermes' demonstration that the Aramaic expression בר נש ("son of man"), in both its indefinite and its definite forms, was used by the rabbis not only in the sense of humanity generally but also as a deferential locution for the first person pronoun "I" should be viewed as having been true as well for the earlier Pharisees—and, presumably, for other Jews during the time of Jesus.[9]

We must return in the discussions below to questions regarding the meaning of the expression in the Old Testament, the Qumran texts, and the Talmud. Suffice it here to say that no longer should scholars be dominated in their understanding by the categories of the Enochian eschatological Redeemer and Judge, for there is no evidence to date that the "Parables" or "Similitudes" of *1 Enoch* are pre-Christian in either their date of composition or their characterization of theological conviction. And *4 Ezra* 13, which bears some resemblance to *1 Enoch* 37–71 in its Son of Man portrayals (though is more directly dependent on Daniel 7), cannot be dated before the end of the first century CE.

---

[9] G. Vermes, "The Use of בר נש / בר נשא in Jewish Aramaic," Appendix E in M. Black, *An Aramaic Approach to the Gospels and Acts* (Oxford: Clarendon, 3rd ed., 1967), 310-28.

2. The Dominical Status of Son of Man Imagery in the New Testament

It has been commonly asserted, particularly since Rudolf Bultmann's *Theology of the New Testament*, that (1) Jesus never used the expression "Son of Man" of himself, (2) Jesus only used the title with regard to a coming Enochian apocalyptic Redeemer figure who would vindicate his own earthly ministry at some time in the future and with whom he would be associated in some manner (the so-called Son of Man "A" sayings), (3) it was the early church, via a series of misconceptions, that applied the title directly to Jesus, first identifying him as the coming Son of Man (the so-called Son of Man "B" sayings) and then identifying him as the Son of Man in his earthly ministry and sufferings (the so-called Son of Man "C" sayings), and (4) all evidence to the contrary must be discounted as having been fabricated by the church in order to justify its own later ascriptions of Jesus as the Son of Man.[10] But though this line of argument is reasonably convincing on its own presuppositions, it runs roughshod over more *prima facie* interpretations of the evidence and bases itself on hypothetical reconstructions in favor of a more normal reading of the data.

We must not deny that there were theological motives and tendencies at work in the composition of the canonical Gospels, so that the reporting of the words of Jesus was conditioned in each case by the evangelists' own backgrounds, interests, purposes and audiences. But we handle the evidence much too loosely in our redaction criticism if we interpret the records as indicating the exact reverse of what they purport. "The Gospels," as Frederick Borsch has rightly insisted, "do not offer it [i.e. the Son of Man title] to us as one title among many; they clearly state that this is the designation of which Jesus spoke, and spoke consistently, as most revelatory of his work."[11]

The expression itself occurs eighty-one times in the Gospels, sixty-nine times in the Synoptic Gospels (i.e., thirty-seven instances with their parallels) and twelve times in John. And with just two excep-

---

[10] Cf. R. Bultmann, *Theology of the New Testament*, trans. K. Grobel (London: SCM, 1952), 1.29-31, 49. For detailed expositions of this position, see the works by Todt, Higgins, Hahn and Fuller cited above. For an extension of the position beyond the guidelines set out by Bultmann, see Vielhauer (cited above) and H. M. Teeple, "The Origin of the Son of Man Christology," *JBL* 84 (1965) 213-50.

[11] Borsch, *Son of Man in Myth and History*, 16.

tions—Luke 24:7 (where an angel at the empty tomb quotes Jesus' words) and John 12:34 (where people ask Jesus regarding what he meant by his use of the expression), neither of which are true exceptions since they both reflect Jesus' own usage—all of the occurrences are attributed to Jesus himself. In no instance in the four Gospels is the title recorded as having been given to Jesus by others; nor is it used in any explanatory manner by the evangelists.[12] Apart from the Gospels, it appears only in the quotation of Ps 8:4-6 in Heb 2:6-8, on the lips of the dying Stephen in Acts 7:56, and in the description of the exalted Jesus in Rev 1:13 and 14:14. It is only in the latter three cases (Acts 7:56, Rev 1:13 and 14:14), however, that it is used outside of the Gospels as a christological title.[13] On the face of it, therefore, it would seem that there is in the New Testament a widely based tradition that Jesus used the expression of himself and very little evidence to suggest any use of it on the part of Christians during the first century.

Further, when the currently proposed literary criteria in Life-of-Jesus research are applied to the Son of Man sayings in the Gospels,[14] the case for the authenticity of the expression on the lips of Jesus

---

[12] Cf. W. L. Lane's argument to the contrary regarding the use of the expression in Mark 2:10, which, by extension, also applies to its appearance in Mark 2:28 (*The Gospel according to Mark* [Grand Rapids: Eerdmans, 1974], 26, 96-98). On the basis of the verse's awkward syntactical structure and the patterning of the Son of Man expression in Mark's Gospel, Lane proposes that Mark 2:10 should not be seen as dominical, but rather as "a parenthetical statement addressed by the evangelist to the *Christian* readers of the Gospel to explain the significance of the closing phase of the healing *for them* (ibid., 98, italics his). It needs to be noted, however, that both the evangelists Matthew and Luke, who are our earliest "commentators" on Mark, treat these words as being dominical, not only taking over the expression Son of Man as a self-designation of Jesus but also reproducing the very awkward syntax as something they seem to have felt best to be left as it is, and not a Markan editorial comment, which they would probably (to judge by their usual practice) have felt no hesitancy about either altering or dropping altogether.

[13] The context of Hebrews 2 makes it evident that Son of Man is used in Heb 2:6-8 in exactly the same way as it is in Ps 8:4-6—that is, as a locution for humanity, to whom many promises were made but not all have as yet been fulfilled.

[14] Cf. my article "Literary Criteria in Life-of-Jesus Research: An Evaluation and Proposal," in *Current Issues in Biblical and Patristic Interpretation: In Honor of Merrill C. Tenney*, ed. G. F. Hawthorne (Grand Rapids: Eerdmans, 1975), 217-29.

comes off rather well—unless, of course, one is disposed to deny such authenticity whatever the evidence. The criterion of multiple attestation (or, "the cross-section method"), which arose in conjunction with the discipline of source criticism, argues that our assessment of the authenticity of any particular saying of Jesus can be heightened when that saying appears in more than one tradition (i.e., Q and Mark), in all or most of the Gospels in the same manner, or within one tradition or Gospel in more than one form (e.g., a parable and an aphorism). Son of Man sayings appear in all the strata of the Gospel tradition: in Mark, in the non-Marcan material common to Matthew and Luke ("Q"), in the material distinctive to Matthew ("M"), and in the material distinctive to Luke ("L"). In addition, they appear in all of the Synoptic Gospels in the same manner, with the same blend of suffering and future elements present (the blend of elements in John's Gospel being somewhat different, but not contradictory).

A second criterion of contemporary literary criticism focuses on the Semitic features in the teaching of Jesus, and argues that the retention of such features in Gospels written in Greek is, to quote J. Jeremias, "of great significance for the question of the reliability of the gospel tradition."[15] And in this regard, the authenticity of the expression Son of Man on the lips of an Aramaic-speaking Jesus comes off again quite well, for the cumbersome and rather inelegant ὁ υἱὸς τοῦ ἀνθρώπου was hardly coined in a Greek milieu and seems rather to be solidly based on the Aramaic בר נש.

A third criterion, and with the rise of form criticism probably the most extensively used criterion in Gospel criticism today, is that of dissimilarity (or, "distinctiveness"), which asserts that "material may be ascribed to Jesus only if it can be shown to be distinctive to him, which usually will mean dissimilar to known tendencies in Judaism before him or the church after him."[16] The criterion has been often grossly misused. And when applied in a ham-fisted manner, it tends to give us only a caricature of Jesus rather than a characterization of him. But if there is any feature in the Gospels' portrayal of Jesus that can be legitimately validated by the criterion, I suggest that the dominical status of the term Son of Man ought to be it—for, as we have pointed out, there is no evidence that it had currency in pre-Christian Judaism

---

[15] J. Jeremias, *New Testament Theology*, 2 vols., trans. J. Bowden (London: SCM, 1971), 1.8.

[16] N. Perrin, *What is Redaction Criticism?* (Philadelphia: Fortress, 1970), 71.

as a title and little evidence that it was carried on as a christological ascription among first-century Christians. And the other various literary criteria in vogue today in the analysis of the New Testament Gospels (e.g., "eschatological context" and "coherence") are similarly able to be employed in defense of the dominical status of the expression as well.

The Bultmannian position that asserts that Jesus only spoke of a future Son of Man who was distinct from himself—and that the identification of this Son of Man with Jesus and all references to a suffering Son of Man must be credited to the early church as it placed later christological titles of its own manufacture back on the lips of Jesus—is unconvincing. Why, if this be true, should the evangelists of the New Testament have been so careful in the composition of their Gospels to have the expression only on the lips of Jesus, and not also on the lips of others in the accounts or in the editorial comments of the evangelists, when (as the Bultmannians believe) it really represented the church's own Christology and not his? And why were the early Christians so circumspect as to preserve such a saying as that of Luke 12:8 ("Everyone who acknowledges me before men, the Son of Man also will acknowledge before the angels of God"), which Bultmannians point to as a definite instance of Jesus' distinction between himself and the coming Son of Man, when for them (as Bultmannians insist) there existed no such distinction between Jesus and the Son of Man?[17]

The expression, as Ernest Best has observed, "is varied very little by Matthew and Luke in their adoption of the passages in which it occurs in Mark," which suggests "a particular reverence for it" and supports the conclusion that "it was continued because it lay deep in the tradition."[18] We cannot, therefore, speak of the Gospels' use of Son of Man as being simply editorial or the product of community theology. It may have had meaning for the evangelists, or it may have been almost as ambiguous to them as when Jesus first used it. But though it was not a current designation for Jesus in their circles at the time of writing, the evangelists received it and preserved it—probably

---

[17] Rephrasing slightly the question put by E. Schweizer, "Son of Man Again," *NTS* 9 (1963), 256-61 (257n.).

[18] E. Best, *The Temptation and the Passion: The Markan Soteriology* (SNTSMS, 2; Cambridge: Cambridge University Press, 1965), 162.

3. Jesus' Understanding and Use of Son of Man Imagery

No christological ascription has been more variously understood by Christians than that of Son of Man. Since Ignatius, Justin Martyr, and the Gentile Fathers who followed them, it has been commonly viewed as simply a locution for the humanity of Jesus. And that is how it often appears in our systematic theologies, devotional literature, and hymns today. On the other hand, many biblical theologians of the past decades have taken it as signaling to some extent the eschatological Redeemer figure and Judge of the Enochian Similitudes. Such confusion has not been, however, reserved for the church. Only in the generic usage of *1QGen Apoc* 21.13 does the expression demonstrably appear in the pre-Christian writings of Second Temple Judaism (assuming Daniel 7 to be earlier). And the question of the people in John 12:34, "Who is this Son of Man?," indicates further something of the ambiguity of the term. Nonetheless, the Gospels report that Son of Man was the favorite self-designation of Jesus.

Perhaps, as Eduard Schweizer and I. H. Marshall have suggested, Jesus "adopted the term Son of Man just because it was an ambiguous term, revealing as well as hiding."[20] Though in view of his explicit reference to Daniel's "abomination of desolation" in the Olivet Discourse (Mark 13:14; Matt 24:15)—as well as his allusions to the imagery of Dan 7:13 in that same discourse (Mark 13:26, par.) and in his reply before the Sanhedrin later (Mark 14:62, par.), both with explicit reference to the Son of Man—it can hardly be doubted that Daniel 7 was the primary biblical source on which Jesus based his own understanding of the expression and to which he pointed in his use of the term. It seems, in fact, as Gustaf Dalman long ago insisted, that what Jesus meant to say in using this expression of himself was

---

[19] *Ibid.*, 163.
[20] E. Schweizer, "Son of Man," *JBL* 79 (1960) 119-29 (128); *idem*, "Son of Man Again," 359. Also I. H. Marshall, "Divine Sonship of Jesus," *Int* 21 (1967) 87-103 (93); *idem*, "The Synoptic Son of Man Sayings in Recent Discussion," *NTS* 12 (1966) 327-51.

"that He was that one in whom this vision of Daniel was to proceed to its realisation."[21]

But the question yet remains: How did Jesus understand the Son of Man imagery of Daniel 7? Various answers, of course, have been and can be given. C. F. D. Moule has argued, cogently I believe, that the Son of Man in Daniel 7 is not only a figure who is vindicated and glorified, as in 7:13-14, but that suffering is also involved, for "in Dan. 7:21, 25, the specially aggressive 'horn' on the beast's head 'made war with the saints and prevailed over them' and was destined to 'wear out the saints of the Most High'; and it is precisely with these saints of the Most High that the Son of Man is identified."[22] Further, in his article for the Rudolf Schnackenburg *Festschrift*, Moule reminds us that "it is important to recollect a broad background of thought about man's function and destiny in general and Israel's function and destiny in particular, and to see both Daniel and his successors in the light of this background."[23]

It may legitimately be argued, I suggest, that Jesus saw in the Danielic Son of Man imagery an ascription (1) that highlighted the situation of humanity, both generically and corporately, as men and women exist in lowliness and under the ordination of God, and (2) that combined features of both suffering and glory that he could use to signal a number of aspects concerning his redemptive ministry. And by reaching back to the enigmatic figure of Daniel 7 (a figure so enigmatic that neither pre-Christian Judaism nor the early church knew exactly what to make of it), he sought to explicate his person and ministry in terms of vindication and glory through suffering, in fulfillment of the prophet's vision. In so doing, it may be theorized, he provided for his followers and for all who have succeeded them an interpretive key into the nature of his person and ministry. Or, as Dalman has more aptly expressed it: "In using the title He purposely furnished them with a problem which stimulated reflection about His

---

[21] G. H. Dalman, *Words of Jesus*, trans. D. M. Kay (Edinburgh: T. & T. Clark, 1902), 258.

[22] Moule, review of H. E. Todt, *Theol* 69 (1966) 174. On a suffering motif in Daniel 7 and Psalm 80, see also W. D. Davies, *Paul and Rabbinic Judaism* (London: SPCK, 1955), 280; Dodd, *According to the Scriptures*, 117; Best, *Temptation and Passion*, 163-64.

[23] C. F. D. Moule, "Neglected Features in the Problem of 'The Son of Man'," in *Neues Testament und Kirche*, ed. J. Gnilka (Freiburg: Herder, 1974), 413-28 (415).

person, and gave such a tendency to this reflection that the solution of the problem fully revealed the mystery of the personality of Jesus."[24]

This is not to say that Jesus only used Son of Man as a title (in line with Daniel's prophecy), for certainly there are places in the portrayals of the Gospels where a case can be made that he used it, as well, as a locution for the personal pronoun "I" (in line with contemporary Aramaic usage, as Geza Vermes has demonstrated). Nor is it to assert that when Jesus used Son of Man of himself as a title he was thereby setting aside an understanding of his person and ministry in terms of Messiah or the Servant of Yahweh—though until his resurrection there was a decided reticence on his part to allow himself to be acclaimed in messianic terms, and the laying out of a servant motif in Jesus' self-consciousness depends more on inference and allusion than direct statement. Indeed, even granting these concessions, I personally believe that an excellent case can be made for all three of these motives—that is, "Son of Man," "Messiah," and "Servant of Yahweh"—as having been intertwined in Jesus' self-consciousness and underlying his ministry.[25]

What I am attempting to point out here, however, is that when Jesus wanted to set before his disciples the nature of his person and ministry he did so repeatedly in terms of his being the Son of Man. Probably nowhere is this seen more clearly than in Mark's portrayal. Mark's Gospel begins, of course, with the affirmation: "The beginning of the gospel about Jesus Christ, the Son of God"; and the first half of the evangelist's presentation is given over to a gradual unfolding of the "messianic secret" that reaches a climax in Peter's Caesarean confession: "You are the Christ (i.e., the Messiah)." But according to Mark's Gospel, Jesus was not content with such an affirmation regarding his person and status. For immediately after this most significant of confessions (Mark 8:29), and after Jesus' injunction to silence (Mark 8:30), the evangelist portrays in three parallel cycles of material our Lord as reinterpreting what Messiahship means for himself and for his disciples[26]—and this he did in terms of referring to himself as the Son of Man:

---

[24] Dalman, *Words of Jesus*, 259.

[25] Cf. my *Christology of Early Jewish Christianity*, 63-82 and 104-109.

[26] Cf. Lane's observation that "Son of Man" in its twelve occurrences in Mark after Peter's confession "provides the key to Jesus' self-disclosure *to his disciples*" (*Gospel according to Mark*, 96, italics his).

Mark 8:31: He then began to teach them that the Son of Man must suffer many things and be rejected by the elders, chief priests and teachers of the law, and that he must be killed and after three days rise again.

Mark 9:31: He said to them: "The Son of Man is going to be betrayed into the hands of men. They will kill him, and after three days he will rise."

Mark 10:32-34: Again he took the Twelve aside and told them what was going to happen to him. "We are going up to Jerusalem," he said, "and the Son of Man will be betrayed to the chief priests and teachers of the law. They will condemn him to death and will hand him over to the Gentiles, who will mock him and spit on him, flog him and kill him. Three days later he will rise."

In each case the evangelist makes it a point to note that the disciples failed to grasp the significance of Jesus' words, both as to the nature of his Messiahship and as to the nature of their discipleship (Mark 8:32b-33; 9:32-34; 10:35-39). And, sadly, we are all too often their successors in this blindness as well.

What Jesus was evidently telling his disciples—and through them and the evangelists' narratives, the church—was that his person and ministry are not to be defined according to popular Jewish expectations of Messiahship (whether political, nationalistic, or even militaristic) and not first of all in terms of glory or ontology, but rather that he should be understood first of all in terms of his redemptive identification with humanity and his sufferings for people. Such a "functional theology" (as it is often called) is inevitably based on ontology and carries with it overtones that are metaphysical in nature. One cannot speak religiously of function without also saying something about person and metaphysics. But Jesus' starting point and emphasis in defining his person and ministry to his disciples had to do with the functional nature of his redemptive activity for people in his suffering, and that only through such suffering was he to enter into his glory. And he signaled this by his repeated use of the Danielic imagery of the Son of Man.

4. Some Implications of Son of Man Imagery for Theology and Discipleship

As followers of Christ, we are, of course, quite prepared to acknowledge that Jesus' declaration of himself as "the Son of Man" has implications of some type for Christian thought and life today. Theoretically, we can hardly say less—though historically and at present, both collectively and as individuals, we habitually seem at a loss to say exactly what and how. As a faltering attempt, allow me here to propose that Jesus' favorite self-designation of himself as the Son of Man serves as something of a paradigm for both our theological formulations and our discipleship, and to make some suggestions along these lines.

For Theology
Dogmatic theology has classically organized its material according to some logical principle: usually beginning with a discussion of epistemology; then moving on to a treatment of theism; then turning to questions of revelation and authority; then to the nature, purposes and activity of God, etc.—and somewhere about halfway along dealing with the person and work of Jesus Christ. We are inheritors of Greek rationality, and so seem to demand some such sort of logical formulation. There is, therefore, abundant reason for continuing the classical order of investigation, arrangement and presentation, rearranging the topics only slightly when confronted by some particular issue of the day.

But Jesus presented himself first of all in terms of the Danielic Son of Man who becomes vindicated and glorified only through suffering. And the early church proclaimed him in terms that were first of all functional in nature—though, of course, within that functional proclamation were ontological overtones, which became more fully expressed in the ongoing of revelation and the continuing work of illumination by God's Spirit.

Witness, for example, the preaching of Peter at Pentecost in Acts 2. It begins with a declaration of fulfillment (vv 16-21); it speaks of Jesus as "a man accredited by God," crucified according to God's purpose by the hands of wicked men, and raised from the dead by God himself (vv 22-24); it relates what happened in the resurrection experience of Jesus to the prophetic message of the Old Testament (vv 25-35); and it calls for a response (vv 36, 38-40). Its thrust is dominantly functional, and its message is set out within the context of its audience's background and appreciation. The only ontological hint it seems to contain is found in the explanation of verse 24b, "because it was impossible for death to keep its hold on him." But the rationale as to why it was impossible is not spelled out, though we might guess from the rest of the New Testament's proclamation that it has something to do with Jesus' own person and his relationship to God the Father.

A similar emphasis can be found in the hymnodic portion of Phil 2:6-11, which may be the earliest piece of Christian composition now extant. That Christ hymn begins with an ontological affirmation, "Who, being in very nature God" (or, as NEB has it, "the divine nature was his from the first"). But it goes on to speak almost entirely in functional terms of Christ's obedience and humiliation—such an obedience as to extend to "even death on a cross!"—and of God's exaltation of him because of his obedience and of God's giving him "the name that is above every name," with the result "that at the name of Jesus every knee should bow, in heaven and on earth and under the earth, and every tongue confess that Jesus Christ is Lord, to the glory of God the Father." When viewed only from an ontological perspective, the hymn has appeared to many to incorporate "kenosis" and "adoptionistic" themes. But the hymn of Phil 2:6-11 is not primarily dealing with ontology but with function, and so it is neither a kenosis nor an adoptionistic view that is being expressed but a functional Christology. And a number of other examples of this same type of functional understanding could be cited from the early Christians' proclamation and writing as well.[27]

In suggesting that as Christian theologians we begin our treatments of theology on the basis of a functional Christology, I am not arguing that we should commence every theological discourse with a formal treatment of the Son of Man motif. After all, the earliest Christians didn't. And judging by the facts that (1) outside of the Gospels the expression appears only three times as a christological title in the entire rest of the New Testament (i.e., Acts 7:56, Rev 1:13 and 14:14; denying, as we have, that its appearance in Heb 2:6-8 is of the same order) and (2) Son of Man imagery is never included in any of the evangelists' own editorial comments within the Gospels, it seems that the earliest Christians were somewhat at a loss to know what to do with the term themselves.[28]

---

[27] See my *New Wine into Fresh Wineskins: Contextualizing the Early Christian Confessions* (Peabody: Hendrickson, 1999), Parts 1 and 2, pp. 5-131.

[28] Noting that for the early Christians Jesus in his earthly ministry *was the suffering Son of Man* and when he returns to complete the prophetic picture *would*

10. *"Son of Man" Imagery*

But though they might not have understood exactly what their Lord meant by his repeated use of Son of Man, they captured the essence of the matter in their emphases on (1) his identification with humanity, (2) his obedience and faithfulness to God the Father, (3) his redemptive sufferings on behalf of all people, (4) his subsequent vindication and glory, and (5) people being reconciled to God and ultimately glorified with Christ through what he accomplished. And this is, I propose, where our formal theologies might profitably start—or, at least, where some of our writing of Christian theology could start: beginning with the functional themes of Christ's identification with humanity, his obedience and faithfulness to God, his sufferings on our behalf, his vindication and glorification through suffering, and our being reconciled to the Father and ultimately glorified with Christ by being "in Christ."

All of this, of course, is basic Christian proclamation. But it needs to be set forth clearly at the beginning of our formal theologies, and not just shuffled somewhere into the midst of our logical development only to be leveled out as to its importance in the process. From this, then, we can go on to develop the ontological ramifications of Christology, and then move on from that to the other areas of a full blown theology. For, after all, it is only from a knowledge of what Christ has accomplished redemptively that we come to understand who he is; and it is only from a christocentric perspective that we truly know regarding revelation, theism, the nature of God, the purposes of God, the nature of man, the nature and purpose of the church, hope for the future, and most other matters—if not, indeed, all other matters—of importance that go to make up a complete Christian theology.

This is where, as a matter of fact, most of us began our thinking psychologically regarding the Christian faith, and it may be of great value to bring our formal logic into line with our psychological

---

be the glorified Son of Man, C. F. D. Moule has observed: "Half its content was already a thing of the past, and half was—at any rate in the eyes of the early Church—yet in the future ... And wherever this view prevailed, there it was naturally assumed that the Church was in a *Zwischenzeit*, between the going and the return; and what relevance has the term Son of Man to that?" ("The Influence of Circumstances on the Use of Christological Terms," *JTS* 10 [1959] 247-63 [257]; repr. in his *Essays in New Testament Interpretation* [Cambridge: Cambridge University Press, 1982], 165-83 [176]).

experience. In so doing we could well be allowing others to retrace our steps theologically, and not force them to take a possibly "alien path" to arrive at the same conclusions. And in so doing, I believe, we would be closer to the mind of Jesus and to the proclamation of the early church.

To some, I suppose, such a proposal sounds like a "unitarianism of the Second Person." That is not my intention. All I am suggesting is that just as some systems of Christian theology begin on the basis of a trinitarian theism, others commence with a specific concept of revelation, others with a particular view of humanity, others with a distinctive understanding of the church, and still others with a doctrine regarding the future—and all of those who propose such systems believe themselves able to find biblical support for their positions, for the Scriptures speak to each of these topics—so we ought to give consideration to the formulation of a Christian system of theology that starts with the functional emphases of the early apostolic proclamation. Such a conclusion, I believe, lies implicit in what we have proposed to be a proper understanding of Jesus' favorite self-designation: Son of Man.

For Discipleship
To understand the pattern of Jesus' ministry according to the Danielic Son of Man imagery, however, is not only significant for the pattern of our theological formulations, it is also significant for the pattern of our Christian discipleship. For in naming him Lord, we also take on as our own the pattern of his life.

The Gospel of Mark, again, is quite explicit in this regard. In the three cycles of material in chapters 8, 9 and 10 (to which we referred above), Mark not only presents Jesus as three times defining the nature of his ministry in terms of the suffering Son of Man and three times depicting the disciples as unable to apprehend Jesus at this point, but also three times portrays Jesus as setting forth the nature of true discipleship:

> Mark 8:34-35: Then he called the crowd to him along with his disciples and said: "If anyone would come after me, he must deny himself and take up his cross and follow me. For whoever wants to save his life will lose it, but whoever loses his life for me and for the gospel will save it."

> Mark 9:35: Sitting down, Jesus called the Twelve and said, "If anyone wants to be first, he must be the very last, and the servant of all."
>
> Mark 10:42-45: Jesus called them together and said, "You know that those who are regarded as rulers of the Gentiles lord it over them, and their high officials exercise authority over them. Not so with you. Instead, whoever wants to become great among you must be your servant, and whoever wants to be first must be slave of all. For even the Son of Man did not come to be served, but to serve, and to give his life a ransom for many."

Jesus' pattern of ministry as the Son of Man is to be our pattern of life as his disciples. And while it seems that the early church, for one reason or another, did not latch on to the title Son of Man as one of its christological ascriptions, nonetheless there certainly was in the early church a lively consciousness that to be one of Christ's people—that is, a Christian or "Christ Follower"—was to accept for one's life this pattern of discipleship. It is the consciousness that lies behind the words of Paul in Rom 8:17, where, when speaking of Christian believers as being both "children of God" and "heirs with Christ," the apostle cannot help but also exclaim: "if indeed we share in his sufferings in order that we may also share in his glory." It is the pattern of life that underlies Paul's desire for himself as expressed in Phil 3:10-11: "I want to know Christ and the power of his resurrection and the fellowship of sharing in his sufferings, becoming like him in his death, and so, somehow, to attain to the resurrection of the dead." It is the pattern that is expressed in such a sermonic epistle as that of 1 Peter, which sets forth the life of a true follower of Jesus as modeled according to the life of suffering of his or her Lord. And it is the pattern of life that is to be ours as we are committed to and reflect the concerns of Jesus, the Son of Man.

Postscript
The history of Christendom has witnessed a readiness on the part of all-too-many believers in Jesus to think in all-too-human terms and live in all-too-worldly a fashion—not just in our techniques and methods, nor just in our lifestyles and fashions, but more importantly in our basic orientations and attitudes. We have tried to get Jesus to think our thoughts rather than we his, and so to mold him into our image and to have him respond to us. We have often failed to realize that our ministry, like his, is to be one of complete identification with people, one of strenuous exertion on behalf of the kingdom of God,

and one of suffering in the extension of the "Good News" that he brought into existence. We all too often appear to think and act like those deluded Christians at Laodicea who boasted: "I am rich; I have acquired wealth and do not need a thing" (Rev 3:17).

Now, however, as we confront the fact that Jesus defined himself and his ministry in terms of the Danielic Son of Man, we come face to face with the realization that he desires to fit us into his mold, to conform us to his image—both in our theological formulations and in our lives of discipleship. It is a humbling and a challenging demand. But so it has always been where the claims of Christ are properly understood.

SELECTED BIBLIOGRAPHY

Black, Matthew. "The 'Son of Man' in the Teaching of Jesus," *ExpT* 60 (1948) 32-36.

_____. "Servant of the Lord and Son of Man," *SJT* 6 (1953) 1-11.

_____. "The Son of Man Problem in Recent Research and Debate," *BJRL* 45 (1963) 305-18.

_____. "The 'Son of Man' Passion Sayings in the Gospel Tradition," *ZNW* 60 (1969) 1-8.

_____. "The Theological Implications of Dr. Vermes' Observations" [a postscript to Geza Vermes's article in Appendix E of M. Black, *An Aramaic Approach to the Gospels and Acts*, 3rd. ed. Oxford: Clarendon, 1967, 328-30].

Borsch, Frederick H. *The Son of Man in Myth and History*. NTL. London: SCM, 1967.

_____. *The Christian and Gnostic Son of Man*. SBT, 2/14. London: SCM, 1970.

Bowman, John Wick. "The Background of the Term 'Son of Man'," *ExpT* 59 (1948) 283-88.

Cullmann, Oscar. *The Christology of the New Testament*, trans. S. C. Guthrie and C. A. M. Hall. London: SCM, 1959, 1963.

Dalman, Gustaf H. *The Words of Jesus*, trans. D. M. Kay. Edinburgh: T. & T. Clark, 1902.

Fitzmyer, Joseph A. "The New Testament Title 'Son of Man' Philologically Considered," in his *A Wandering Aramean: Collected Aramaic Essays*. Chico: Scholars, 1979, 143-60.

Higgins, Angus J. B. *Jesus and the Son of Man*. London: Lutterworth, 1964.

_____. "Is the Son of Man Problem Insoluble?," in *Neotestamentica et Semitica*, ed. E. E. Ellis and M. Wilcox. Edinburgh: T. & T. Clark, 1969, 70-87.

_____. *The Son of Man in the Teaching of Jesus*. SNTSMS, 39. Cambridge: Cambridge University Press, 1980.

Hooker, Morna D. *The Son of Man in Mark*. London: SPCK, 1967.
Lane, William L. *The Gospel according to Mark.* Grand Rapids: Eerdmans, 1974.
Leivestad, Ragnar. "Der apokalyptische Menschensohn ein theologisches Phantom," *ASTI* 6 (1968) 49-105; an English summary by the same author appears under the title "Exit the Apocalyptic Son of Man," *NTS* 18 (1972) 243-67.
Longenecker, Richard N. "'Son of Man' as a Self-Designation of Jesus," *JETS* 12 (1969) 151-58.
_____. *The Christology of Early Jewish Christianity.* SBT, 17. London: SCM, 1970; repr. Grand Rapids: Baker, 1981; repr. Vancouver: Regent College Publishing, 2001.
Marshall, I. Howard. "The Synoptic Son of Man Sayings in Recent Discussion," *NTS* 12 (1966) 327-51.
_____. "The Divine Sonship of Jesus," *Int* 21 (1967) 87-103.
Moule, Charles F. D. "The Influence of Circumstances on the Use of Christological Terms," *JTS* 10 (1959) 247-63; repr. in his *Essays in New Testament Interpretation.* Cambridge: Cambridge University Press, 1982, 165-83.
_____. *The Phenomenon of the New Testament*. London: SCM, 1967.
_____. "Neglected Features in the Problem of 'the Son of Man'," in *Neues Testament und Kirche*, ed. J. Gnilka; Freiburg: Herder, 1974, 413-28; repr. in his *Essays in New Testament Interpretation.* Cambridge: Cambridge University Press, 1982, 75-90.
Schweizer, Eduard. "Der Menschensohn," *ZNW* 50 (1959) 185-210.
_____. "Son of Man," *JBL* 79 (1960) 119-29.
_____. "Son of Man Again," *NTS* 9 (1963) 256-61.
Teeple, Howard M. "The Origin of the Son of Man Christology," *JBL* 84 (1965) 213-50.
Tödt, Heinz E. *The Son of Man in the Synoptic Tradition*, trans. D. M. Barton. London: SCM, 1965.
Vermes, Geza. "The Use of בר נש / בר נשא in Jewish Aramaic," Appendix E in M. Black, *An Aramaic Approach to the Gospels and Acts*, 3rd ed., Oxford: Clarendon, 1967, 310-28.

11

TAKING UP THE CROSS DAILY
Discipleship in Luke–Acts

Luke's use of the term "disciple" (μαθητής) is less frequent and less nuanced than that of the other canonical evangelists. But his treatment of the theme of discipleship is more extensively developed, more radically expressed, and more consistently sustained. As one of the so-called Synoptic Gospels, Luke's Gospel may be presumed to have many points in common with Mark's Gospel and Matthew's Gospel. It also has features in common with some of the material of John's Gospel, particularly the Johannine passion narrative. Yet Luke's treatment of discipleship is unique, with a number of distinctive features—not only in his Gospel but also in his Acts, which together comprise about thirty percent of the New Testament.

We are, of course, quickly alerted to the distinctiveness of Luke's treatment by the fact that he alone among the New Testament writers has given his readers not only an account of Jesus' ministry but also a narrative sequel to that account, which sets out the ministries of Peter and Paul in roughly comparable fashion. More important, however, is the redactional "spin" that Luke gives to the materials he has derived from his sources. For in analyzing how he treats his sources, we are often confronted with data that indicate quite clearly not only how Luke wanted his readers to respond to the question "Who is Jesus?" but also how he wanted them to answer the question "What does it mean to be a follower of Jesus?"

In what follows, therefore, we will first set out the basic lines of the structure of Luke's two volumes, suggesting what such a structure signals for the topic of discipleship (Section 1). Second, we will survey how the disciples of Jesus are portrayed in Luke's Gospel, comparing the Lukan portrait with that of the other Synoptic Gospels and giving attention to the disciples' didactic function as models of Christian discipleship (Section 2). Following that, we will highlight a number of distinctive features in Luke's use of his sources in the writing of his Gospel, with those features selected because of what they tell us about the evangelist's understanding of discipleship (Sections 3–6). Then we will do likewise for certain distinctive features in Luke's Acts (Section 7). And finally, we will identify some ten lessons that Luke seems to have wanted to teach his readers regarding the nature of Christian discipleship today, whether that "today" be taken as only Luke's day or also ours (Section 8).

Throughout our depiction of discipleship in Luke–Acts, it needs also to be noted, there will appear something of a crescendo in the explicitness, development and intensity of the data dealt with. That is not a pedagogical ploy on our part. Rather, that is how, it seems, Luke himself treated the subject, being more restrained—though frequently quite suggestive—when controlled more by his sources, but more expansive when feeling free to go beyond them.

Our method will be largely redaction-critical in nature, assuming, in the process, that Luke used a number of literary sources in his writing. In the preface to his two volumes he says that he knew of such sources (Luke 1:1-4), implying, as well, that he had studied them and used them in his own account—at least for the writing of his Gospel, but probably also in Acts. Presumably, as seems most critically supportable, the major literary sources for the writing of his Gospel were Mark's Gospel and a Sayings collection, which has commonly been designated "Q" (from the German word *Quelle*, or "source"). From Mark, evidently, he derived the account of Jesus' ministry in Galilee and the basic narrative for Jesus' final week and passion in Jerusalem; from Q, he received sayings of Jesus that were not included in Mark but are shared by Matthew—with those sayings constituting about one sixth of both Matthew's Gospel and Luke's Gospel. Possibly Luke also used a "parable-travel" source for the writing of his travel narrative (9:51–19:27), or perhaps materials drawn from such a source or sources. It appears that he used other source materials, as well, in addition to Mark's Gospel in his passion narrative (22:1–24:53), which materials seem also to have been used in the composition of the Fourth Gospel.

As for his writing of Acts, we will proceed on the assumption that source materials from the early Jewish-Christian mission were at his disposal for Acts 1–12, however he may have come to have them. Also, reminiscences from various participants in the Pauline mission and his own travel notes may have served as the bases for Acts 13–28 (cf. the "we" sections of 16:10-17, 20:5-15, 21:1-18 and 27:1– 28:16).

1. *The Structure of Luke–Acts vis-à-vis Discipleship*

What immediately strikes the reader of Luke–Acts is the basic architectural structure of the work. For not only are the two volumes almost equal in size (the Gospel being the longest of our New Testament writings, with Acts about one-tenth shorter) and almost identical in chronological coverage (about thirty-three years for both), they also, more importantly, exhibit, as Charles Talbert has stated matters, "a remarkable series of correspondences between what Jesus does and says in Luke's Gospel and what the disciples [mainly Peter and Paul] do and say in the Acts" ("Discipleship in Luke–Acts," 63). Talbert has set out in quite detailed fashion a large number of parallels of event and expression—even of sequence—that can be found in Luke's two volumes: (1) parallels in his first volume between Jesus' Galilean ministry (Luke 4:14–9:50) and Jesus' Perean–Judean ministry in the travel narrative (Luke 9:51–19:10); (2) parallels in his second volume between the church's mission to the Jewish world (Acts 2:42–12:24) and the church's mission to the Gentile world (Acts 12:25–28:31); and (3) parallels between the two volumes themselves (cf. *Literary Patterns*, 1-65). Talbert has also argued that the literary genre of Luke–Acts "is similar to the biographies of certain founders of philosophical schools, that contained within themselves not only the life of the founder but also a list or brief narrative of his successors and selected other disciples" ("Discipleship in Luke–Acts," 63; cf. *idem*, *Literary Patterns*, 125-40; *idem*, *What Is a Gospel? The Genre of the Canonical Gospels* [Philadelphia: Fortress, 1977]; *idem*, "The Gospel and the Gospels," in *Interpreting the Gospels*, ed. J. L. Mays [Philadelphia: Fortress, 1981], 14-26; building on a suggestion of H. von Soden, *Geschichte der christlichen Kirche*, vol. 1: *Die Entstehung der christlichen Kirche* [Leipzig: Teubner, 1919], 73).

Talbert has been criticized for overdrawing the redactional parallels that can be found both within and between Luke's Gospel and his Acts. Likewise, for identifying too precisely the literary genre of Luke's two-volume work. But his main points have certainly been established: (1) that the architectural structure of Luke–Acts requires the two volumes be read together, the first interpreted by the second and the second by the first; and (2) that the ministry of the early church, as depicted in Luke's second volume, be seen as having been shaped by the Jesus tradition, as portrayed in his first. Indeed, in setting out numerous parallels between Jesus' mission and the church's mission, Luke must be seen to be actually proposing the thesis that Jesus' ministry and the church's mission *together* constitute the fullness of God's redemptive activity on behalf of humanity. For though Jesus' mission and the church's mission are not to be taken as identical, they are, nonetheless, comparable and inseparable—that of Jesus being the announcement and effecting of redemption; that of the church being the proclamation, extension and application of what Jesus effected.

Just how Luke first came to think of relating the mission of the church to the ministry of Jesus, juxtaposing the two as comparable and inseparable entities, will always remain a mystery. Perhaps it was by association with the apostle Paul, from whom he would have heard such things as: "We are children and heirs—heirs of God and co-heirs with Christ, if indeed we share in his sufferings, in order that we may also share in his glory" (as in Rom 8:17), or "I want to know Christ and the power of his resurrection and the fellowship of sharing in his sufferings, becoming like him in his death, and so, somehow, to attain to the resurrection of the dead" (as in Phil 3:10-11), or "I rejoice in what was suffered for you [understanding the Greek phrase ἐν τοῖς παθήμασιν ὑπὲρ ὑμῶν as referring to Christ's sufferings, which were highlighted earlier in vv 20b and 22a], and I fill up in my flesh what is still lacking in regard to Christ's afflictions, for the sake of his body, which is the church" (Col 1:24). But however it came about in Luke's mind, once formed, such a conception would have had explosive consequences for an understanding of Christian discipleship. For now the thesis could be made that what was foundational in Jesus' ministry—being often, it appears, only rather embryonically present there—was (and is) to be explicated and more fully expressed in the church's mission.

It is, in fact, just such an idea that Luke expresses over and over again, both explicitly and implicitly, throughout the length and breadth of his two volumes, showing that what was basic in Jesus' ministry has been and should continue to be the pattern for all of the church's life and ministry. The major topics that Luke treats in this fashion are: (1) the Spirit's presence and power, (2) the inauguration of a prophetic ministry, (3) the universality of the gospel, (4) the importance of the apostles and their witness, (5) the necessity of dependence on God, and therefore of prayer, and (6) concern for the poor, the imprisoned, the blind, and the oppressed, whom sociologically we would call "the disenfranchised"—all of which needs to be explicated more fully in what follows.

2. The Twelve in Luke–Acts vis-à-vis Discipleship

Our canonical Gospels were written to tell the story of Jesus. Yet that story also includes the story of Jesus' disciples, who are repeatedly designated "the Twelve" by Mark and Luke (e.g., Mark 4:10; 6:7; 9:35; 10:32; 11:11; 14:10, 17, 20; Luke 8:1; 9:12; 18:31; 22:3, 47; cf. Acts 6:2; 1 Cor 15:5)—though less frequently by Matthew and John (Matt 26:14, 20, 47; John 6:67, 70, 71; 20:24). There is no doubt that all four evangelists meant their readers to identify, in one way or another, with the disciples, and so learn from them what it means to follow Jesus.

Each of the evangelists, however, portrays the disciples somewhat differently. In Mark's Gospel, after being initially called (cf. 1:16-20; 2:14) and appointed to be with Jesus (3:13-19), the Twelve are presented, for the most part, quite negatively. Indeed, after those first positive portrayals having to do with their call and appointment, the picture of the disciples in Mark becomes rather dark—culminating, as it does, with accounts of Judas' betrayal (14:43-45), the disciples' desertion (14:50-52), and Peter's threefold denial (14:66-72).

In Matthew's Gospel the portrait is not quite as bleak. For while Matthew takes over from Mark many of the passages that depict Jesus' disciples rather negatively (e.g., 8:23-27; 14:15; 15:16-17; 16:5-12; 17:16, 19; 19:13; 20:20-24; 26:36-46, 56), he also portrays them elsewhere in his Gospel in a somewhat more favorable light—both by deleting some of Mark's negative comments and by saying things about them of a more positive nature. So, for example, Matthew omits Mark's reference to the disciples being unable to understand (13:18; cf. Mark 4:13). Likewise, he omits Mark's derogatory statements about their hearts being "hardened" (14:32; 16:9; cf. Mark 6:52; 8:17). And while he continues to speak in some places of the disciples being slow to understand (e.g., 15:16-17; 16:8-9), he also reports that, at times, they did indeed understand what Jesus was teaching them (e.g., 13:51; 16:12; 17:13). Moreover, more clearly than in Mark's Gospel, Matthew points to the significant role that the disciples will play in the post-resurrection era (cf. 17:9; 18:18-20; 19:28; 24:14; 27:64; 28:16-20). The portrait of the disciples presented by Matthew, therefore, is somewhat brighter than that given by Mark—though, admittedly, not much brighter.

In Luke's Gospel, however, the Twelve are portrayed much more positively. True, Luke retains some of Mark's negativism. For example, Luke also reports that the disciples were unable to cast out an evil spirit (Luke 9:40; cf. Mark 9:18)—though Luke omits Mark's later reference to the disciples asking Jesus why they could not cast it out (cf. Mark 14:28). Further, following Jesus' second passion prediction, Luke says of the disciples: "They did not understand what this meant. It was hidden from them, so that they did not grasp it, and they were afraid to ask him about it" (9:45; cf. Mark 9:32). Similarly, Luke reproduces Mark's story about the disciples rebuking those who brought children to Jesus for his blessing (18:15-17; cf. Mark 10:13-16). And he retains Mark's account of their dispute about who would be the greatest (22:24-27; cf. Mark 10:35-45), though he abbreviates it and relocates it.

On the other hand, Luke omits much of Mark's harsh treatment of the disciples. For example, he omits (1) Mark's statement about them being unable to understand Jesus' parables (8:11; cf. Mark 4:13), (2) Mark's references to their "hardened hearts" (cf. Mark 6:52; 8:17), and (3) Mark's account of Peter's rebuke of Jesus (cf. Mark 8:32-33). He also tones down the failure of three of their number to stay awake and pray with Jesus in Gethsemane, reporting only once that they fell asleep—and then somewhat excusing them with the comment that they slept because they were "exhausted from sorrow" (22:45-46).

More significant, however, are (1) Luke's omission of Jesus' prediction: "You will all fall away; for it is written, 'I will strike the shepherd, and the sheep will be scattered'" (cf. Mark 14:27, quoting Zech 13:7), and (2) Luke's depiction of the Twelve (minus, of course, Judas) as actually remaining faithful to Jesus in his hour of trial (*contra* Mark 14:50). In fact, Jesus in Luke's Gospel actually declares to the Eleven at the Last Supper: "You are those who have stood by me in my trials" (22:28). And the disciples are probably to be seen in Luke's account as being present at Jesus' crucifixion, for the evangelist states: "All those who knew him [Jesus], ... stood at a distance, watching these things" (23:49).

The portrayal of Jesus' disciples in John's Gospel is rather unique. Never does the author of the Fourth Gospel give a list of the disciples, as can be found in all three of the Synoptic Gospels. Only six of the disciples, in fact, are referred to by John (in various settings) by name: Andrew, Peter, Philip, Nathanael, Judas, and Thomas. And only in four verses does John speak of them as "the Twelve" (6:67, 70, 71; 20:24). Rather, in John's Gospel (as also in Matthew's Gospel) the disciples are, for the most part, referred to as a unified group, who are distinguished from the followers of John the Baptist, from "the Jews," from "the world," and from some "secret believers" such as Nicodemus (3:1-15; 7:50-51; 19:39), Joseph of Arimathea (19:38-40) and "others" (12:42-43).

Further, the term "disciples" is also used in John's Gospel to designate a larger group than "the Twelve" (as also in Matthew's Gospel). This is evident, for example, in the following comment on the part of the evangelist: "From this time on, many of his disciples turned back and no longer followed him" (6:66). Such an ambiguity seems to suit the fourth evangelist's purpose, for the term can thus, as well, have a more direct application to members of the Johannine community. One disciple in particular, the "Beloved Disciple," is depicted in John's Gospel as the ideal or model disciple, for he followed Jesus in a close, believing relationship (cf. 13:23; 19:26-27; 21:7, 20).

In Luke's depiction of the disciples, however, the Twelve are several times also referred to as "apostles" (cf. Luke 6:13; 9:10; 17:5; 22:14; 24:10; see also 11:49). This feature, together with his more positive treatment of Jesus' disciples in both his Gospel and his Acts (cf. Acts 6:2), is probably to be explained by the fact that Luke sees the Twelve—minus Judas, but later augmented by Matthias—as being prepared (in his Gospel) for their roles as leaders of the church (in Acts). It is also important to note that Luke, like Matthew and John, does not limit the term "disciple" to the Twelve (cf. 6:17; 19:37; see also 24:9, 33), as is more or less true of Mark. For Luke, evidently, viewed discipleship in somewhat broader categories—such as would include Matthias later as the replacement for Judas (Acts 1:26), but also believers in Jesus generally (cf. his twenty-eight masculine uses and one feminine use of the term in Acts).

Despite, however, the somewhat differing portrayals of Jesus' disciples in our four canonical Gospels, each evangelist, it seems, meant for his readers to identify with the disciples and to learn from them—both in their failures and in their successes—what it means to be a follower of Jesus. Admittedly, Luke's portrait of the Twelve is less detailed and less developed than those of Mark or Matthew; likewise, less than John's treatment of the "Beloved Disciple," whoever he was. But it is certainly far more positive than the portrait given by Mark, who seems to have been Luke's main narrative source—even than that of Matthew, who follows in the same narrative tradition. For Luke views the disciples as modeling the essential characteristics of Christian discipleship. It is not their failures that he highlights. Rather, what he emphasizes are the new commitments, orientation and lifestyle that the disciples reflected in their lives by association with Jesus their Master. And so, as Luke reports it, Jesus' statement about discipleship applies not only to his immediate disciples but also to all succeeding believers who will identify with them: "Disciples are not above their teachers, but all those who are fully trained will be like their teachers" (6:40; cf. Matt 10:24-25).

3. *Luke's Use of Mark vis-à-vis Discipleship*

Luke's use of Mark vis-à-vis the theme of discipleship can be seen at the very beginning of the Synoptic Gospels' common narrative, that is, in his portrayal of the ministry of John the Baptist in 3:1-6 (cf. Mark 1:2-6). For while Luke knows that believers in Jesus originally called themselves "Those of the Way" (cf. Acts 9:2; 19:9, 23; 22:4; 24:14, 22), he seems not to put any emphasis on the word "way" (ὁδός) here in this context—even though it appears twice in Mark's quotations of Mal 3:1 and Isa 40:3, being what linguistically ties those two *testimonia* passages together. Rather, Luke's stress in 3:1-6 is on (1) the proclamation of "the word of God," and (2) the universality of the gospel. The first, that of the proclamation of "the word of God," is depicted as meaning for John the Baptist the preaching of "a baptism of repentance for the forgiveness of sins" (vv 2-3). Elsewhere in Luke's volumes, however, it has to do with proclaiming "the kingdom of God" as focused in Jesus (as is prominent in the Gospel, but also in Acts) and/or the proclamation of "God's salvation" as focused in Jesus (as is prominent in Acts, but also in the Gospel). The second, that of the universality of the gospel, is seen in Luke's extension of Mark's quotation of Isa 40:3 to include verses 4 and 5 of Isaiah's prophecy, which speak of "every valley," "every mountain," and "all humanity" being involved in God's redemptive activity. Also to be noted in Luke's quotation of Isaiah's prophecy is the fact that the evangelist transposes "the glory of the Lord" motif of the prophecy (Isa 40:5a) to the theme of "God's salvation" (Luke 3:6), thereby highlighting further the universality of the gospel at the conclusion of the prophetic portion with the ringing affirmation: "And all flesh shall see the salvation of God."

These two themes, of course, are only somewhat embryonically set out in Luke 3:1-6, for the evangelist's purpose, it seems, was only to lay the basis for them at this point in his presentation and then to develop them more fully later. Nonetheless, they serve here to inaugurate two very important features in Luke's overall profile of Christian discipleship: (1) that of being involved in the proclamation of "the word of God," which focuses preeminently on the work and person of Jesus; and (2) that of having a universal view, not a parochial perspective, regarding the outreach and application of the Christian message.

After going on to present the ministry of John the Baptist in further detail (3:7-20), the baptism of Jesus by John the Baptist (3:21-22), the genealogy of Jesus (3:23-28), and the temptation of Jesus by the devil in the wilderness (4:1-13)—with each of these four presentations evidencing a number of redactional features of importance for all sorts of other issues—Luke then focuses on the Nazareth pericope of 4:14-30. It is important to note here not only that Luke has moved this passage up from where he found it in Mark's narrative (cf. Mark 6:1-6a), but also that he has (1) set it in a distinctive context, (2) expanded it to include the central features of Jesus' preaching, and (3) used it as the introductory episode or frontispiece for all that he wants to portray throughout his two volumes concerning the ministries of both Jesus and the church.

The Lukan context for the Nazareth pericope focuses on the presence and power of the Spirit: "Jesus returned in the power of the Spirit into Galilee" (v 14a). This context is unique, since Mark (also Matthew) has only "Jesus came [or, 'withdrew'] into Galilee." The important features highlighted in Luke's account of Jesus' reading of Isa 61:1-2a in the Nazareth synagogue, which only Luke presents, are (1) that "the Spirit of the Lord" is present on God's servants (v 18a), and (2) that the good news of redemption is to be proclaimed to the poor, the captives, the blind and the oppressed, with release and blessing for them (vv 18b-19). Also highlighted in Luke's portrayal of Jesus' preaching at Nazareth—which is considerably expanded in Luke's account—are the themes of (1) the universality of God's grace, particularly by references to God's acceptance of a Gentile widow and a Syrian general (vv 25-27), and (2) the rejection of Jesus by his own people, mainly because they saw that a universality of divine grace included an acceptance of Gentiles (vv 23-24, 28-30).

It is the Nazareth pericope of 4:14-30, with its distinctive context and themes, that Luke uses as the introduction to all that he desires to present regarding the ministry of Jesus (in his Gospel) and the ministry of the church (in his Acts). Moreover, it is these themes that he highlights throughout his two volumes as being vitally important for Christian discipleship: (1) the presence and power of the Spirit; (2) release and blessing for the poor, the captives, the blind, and the oppressed; (3) the universality of God's grace (with that universality, of course, expressed preeminently in the Christian gospel); and (4) rejection experienced by Jesus (with that rejection extended also to followers of Jesus).

It also needs to be noted that there is a greater emphasis in Luke's Gospel on Jesus' disciples as "apostles" (ἀπόστολοι) than can be found in Mark (or Matthew or John)—with, then, that emphasis being unfolded in Luke's Acts in terms of apostolic teaching and authority, and so the apostolic tradition. In Luke 6:13 the statement is made that the twelve disciples were designated "apostles" by Jesus himself. Probably, however, the appearance of the term "apostle" here in Luke 6:13, as well as the reference to Jesus as having originated the term for his disciples, is Luke's addition to his Markan narrative source. For though the external textual tradition (esp. the major fourth century codices Sinaiticus and Vaticanus) largely supports the reading "whom he also named apostles" in Mark 3:14, which is the passage that Luke evidently had before him when he wrote, the wording of that Markan passage is less cumbersome without the seemingly intrusive "whom he also named apostles" between "he appointed twelve" and "in order that they might be with him." So most scholars, for internal reasons, have viewed the reference to "apostles" in Mark 3:14 as a scribal harmonization under the influence of Luke 6:13 (as well, perhaps, an attempt to parallel the verb "sent out," ἀποστέλλω, in v 14b), with the result that most have taken "whom he also named apostles" in

Luke 6:13 to be Luke's own addition to the Markan narrative he worked from.

The term "apostle" appears six times in Luke's Gospel (here at 6:13; also 9:10; 11:49; 17:5; 22:14; and 24:10) and twenty-nine or thirty times in Acts. It is, however, used only once by each of the other evangelists (assuming its absence at Mark 3:14): in Mark 6:30, Matt 10:2, and John 13:16. We may take it, therefore, that apostleship was a major theme in Luke's mind. It is signaled here in 6:13 only by Luke's comment "whom he also named apostles." But it becomes developed, principally in Acts, with a stress on the apostles' teaching and authority, and thus on the apostolic tradition. For Luke, the church is only faithful to its calling as it perseveres in the teaching and tradition of the apostles, who constitute the human link with Jesus. And Christian discipleship is only authentic as it does likewise.

Much more could be derived from a study of how Luke redacted Mark for an understanding of his treatment of discipleship. We have only highlighted some of the differences—whether of arrangement, addition, emphasis, or omission. But before leaving this section, two observations need be made. The first is that, while we have highlighted differences, the agreements between Luke and Mark are also significant. For by including Markan narrative materials into his account, Luke makes many of Mark's points on discipleship his own as well. The second is that where Luke effects changes of Mark, often those changes are more subtle than overt, often more suggestive than definitive, with adroit hints given of what might be expected in the narration in Acts of developments later. But this phenomenon is in line with what seems to be Luke's general policy and approach: that in his Gospel—particularly where he is using Mark as his narrative source—the foundations of the gospel proclamation are set out, with the inclusion of various suggestive hints and embryonic statements that will lay the basis for further developments; whereas in Acts are portrayed the explications, applications and extensions of what was effected by Jesus in his teaching, death, resurrection and ascension.

4. *Luke's Use of Q vis-à-vis Discipleship*

Luke's other main source for the writing of his Gospel, it seems, was a collection of the sayings of Jesus that was either written or retained in the church's collective memory and that has been dubbed "Q." Matthew seems to have used this source as well. So by comparing the non-Markan sayings in Luke's Gospel with the non-Markan sayings in Matthew's Gospel—which make up about one sixth of what each of the evangelists Matthew and Luke present—we are able to arrive at some approximation of what was contained in the original, postulated Q used by both Matthew and Luke (whether they worked from closely similar copies of Q or from somewhat different recensions).

The Q sayings evidently included teachings of Jesus regarding discipleship. In a study of Luke's treatment of the theme of discipleship, therefore, it is necessary to note how he used Q (his major "sayings" literary source), just as it was necessary to observe how he used Mark (his major "narrative" literary source). For by comparing Luke and Matthew in their respective uses of Q, it is possible to identify certain of Luke's emphases in the editing of this material. Three Q passages in Luke's Gospel are particularly significant for such a study: (1) "the beatitudes" in 6:20b-26 (cf. Matt 5:3-12); (2) the "conditions for following Jesus" in 9:57-62 (cf. Matt 8:18-22); and (3) "the cost of discipleship" in 14:25-33 (cf. Matt 10:37-38).

The differences between Matt 5:3-12 and Luke 6:20b-26 are well known. The most important are (1) that Matthew speaks of those who are blessed by God as being "the poor in spirit," "those who hunger and thirst for righteousness," and "the pure in heart," thereby stressing more spiritual qualities, whereas Luke has "the poor" and "the hungry" as blessed by God and "the rich" and "the full" as under God's curse, thereby emphasizing economic and social conditions; and (2) Matthew has a list of nine situations that deserve the appellative "blessed" (μακάριοι), whereas Luke sets out four conditions that are designated "blessed" (μακάριοι) and four that call for the prophetic denunciation "woe" (οὐαί).

It may be debated as to which evangelist has most closely reproduced the actual words found in Q—whether Matthew with his emphasis on spiritual qualities or Luke with his focus on economic and social conditions. Most have concluded that Luke is closest, since here Jesus' words, both in form and in content, closely parallel Jewish ethical teaching as found in Jer 22:13-17, *Sirach* 11:18-19, and *1 Enoch* 94:8-10, 96:4-8 and 97:8-10. And with that opinion I agree, and so view Matthew's portrayal as having been reworked by him for his own purposes. But even when we judge Luke's Beatitudes to be closest to the actual words recorded in Q, it is important to remember that all of what Luke has taken over from his source or sources was incorporated by him into his Gospel because it fit his own interests and his own purposes.

Luke has a definite interest in the poor, in captives, in those who are afflicted and oppressed, and in the disenfranchised, as witness his inclusion of the words of Isa 61:1-2a in the Nazareth pericope of 4:14-30 and his emphases at many places throughout his two volumes (which we will refer to later). And Luke also has a number of things to say about the rich, those of the establishment, and the well-off, constantly setting them in a bad light and calling on them to repent. The infancy narrative of 1:5–2:52 provides us with quite a few illustrations of his attitude with regard to these matters. For there, in material that is certainly Luke's own, (1) women—even a widow—have a significant part in God's redemptive program, (2) the pious poor are lauded, and (3) the rich are condemned. The Magnificat of 1:46-55 epitomizes such attitudes, particularly in Mary's statements: "he ['God my Savior'] has been mindful of the humble state of his servant"; "he has brought down rulers from their thrones, but lifted up the humble"; and "he has filled the hungry with good things, but sent the rich away empty" (1:48a, 52-53). Likewise, John the Baptist's responses to questions asked him by "the crowds," the "tax collectors," and "some soldiers" in 3:10-14—a passage that is found only in Luke's Gospel—are all framed in terms of one's attitude toward money and material goods. And elsewhere throughout Luke's two volumes (as we will see later), such attitudes come repeatedly to the fore.

While the Lukan Beatitudes can be paralleled in both form and content with some of the material found in *1 Enoch* 94–104/105 (the so-called "Epistle of Enoch," which is very old Jewish material), Jesus' teachings on poverty and riches in Luke's Gospel and those of the church in Luke's Acts differ in a number of respects. Most prominently, while the sage of *1 Enoch* 94–104/105 only condemns the rich and their riches, Jesus and the church call on believers to have a new attitude toward possessions and their use—that is, not just to dispense with possessions, but to repent of selfishness and to use their riches for the benefit of others (cf., e.g., Acts 2:45; 4:32-37; 5:1-11). Or as Joseph Fitzmyer has said with regard to Jesus' warning about riches in Luke 18:24-25, which uses the metaphor of a camel going through the eye of a needle: "The reason why it is hard for the rich to get through the eye of the needle (18:25) is not because of amassing in itself, but because of the iniquitous seduction that invariably comes with it, distracting that person from the consideration of what life is all about"—which Fitzmyer admits "may sound like bourgeois piety," but which he insists "is part of the message of the Lucan Jesus" (*Gospel according to Luke* 2.972).

In Luke's version of the Beatitudes, therefore, concerns for the poor and the hungry are highlighted, with corresponding denunciations of the rich and the well-off. Luke shares with Matthew interests in the spiritual disposition and religious persecution of believers (so the third and fourth sets of his "blessings" and "woes"). But he differs from Matthew in that he expressly presents Jesus as being vitally concerned about the economic and social conditions of people—in fact, he brings these concerns directly to the fore in Jesus' teaching (so the first and second sets of his "blessings" and "woes"). In so doing, of course, he carries on themes previously emphasized in the Nazareth pericope of Luke 4:14-30, particularly those set out in Jesus' quotation of Isa 61:1-2a. And in so doing, he points up issues regarding poverty and riches that he sees to be important for any who would be a follower of Jesus.

There are, however, two other major Q passages in Luke's Gospel where Jesus speaks directly regarding Christian discipleship. The first is 9:57-62 (cf. Matt 8:18-22), where "conditions for following Jesus" are enumerated; the second, 14:25-33 (cf. Matt 10:37-38), where "the cost of discipleship" is detailed. Both of these passages are in Luke's travel narrative, and so could be reserved for a later discussion. But both are from Q, and so can rightfully be treated here. More importantly, both evidence distinctive Lukan redactional interests.

In the pericope on "conditions for following Jesus" (Matt 8:18-22; Luke 9:57-62), Matthew and Luke set out in fairly comparable fashion two sayings of Jesus. The contexts for the sayings, of course, differ, with each evangelist introducing what was said in terms of the narrative development of his own Gospel—that is, Matthew speaks of "great crowds," of going over to the other side of the Sea of Galilee, of a "scribe," of another "disciple," and of Jesus being addressed as "teacher"; whereas Luke speaks of "a certain person" (τις) and "another" (ἕτερον) who spoke to Jesus as he and his disciples were "going along the road" (or "on the way"). But the words addressed to Jesus in the two Gospels are identical: "I will follow you wherever you go" and "Lord, let me first go and bury my father." More significantly, the two sayings of Jesus in response are also identical: "Foxes have holes, and birds of the air have nests; but the Son of man has nowhere to lay his head!" and "Follow me! Leave the dead to bury their own dead." So in portraying what Jesus said in these two responses, Matthew and Luke agree: Christian discipleship has as its conditions (1) the willingness to live an unsettled and insecure lifestyle for Jesus' sake, and (2) being unencumbered by other allegiances.

But Luke adds more to his portrayal of Jesus' words on discipleship, attaching an addendum to the second saying and going on to present a third saying. The addendum gives a positive spin to the subject of discipleship, for not only are Jesus' followers not to be encumbered by other allegiances but they are also to "go and proclaim the kingdom of God" (9:60b). The third saying, however, which is not included in Matthew's account, heightens the radicalism of what it means to be unencumbered by other allegiances in following Jesus. For it speaks not just of letting others bury a deceased father but also of not being detained by farewells to one's own family at home—using the aphorism "No one who takes hold of the plow and looks back is fit for the kingdom of God" (9:61-62).

And as though this were not enough, Luke intensifies this note of radicalism in his treatment of "the cost of discipleship" (Matt 10:37-38; Luke 14:25-33). For whereas Matthew presents Jesus as speaking of loving Jesus more than one loves one's own father and mother and of taking up one's cross and following Jesus, Luke has it: "If anyone comes to me and does not hate father and mother, wife and children, brothers and sisters—yes, even life itself—such a person cannot be my disciple! Those who do not carry their cross and follow me cannot be my disciples!" (14:26-27). And then, as though to reinforce that radicalism, Luke adds a further saying of Jesus about builders needing to consider carefully the cost of building before beginning construction and kings needing to consider carefully the cost of warfare before going to war, with the application for discipleship being: "So, therefore, those of you who do not give up everything you have cannot be my disciples" (14:28-33).

It may never be conclusively determined whether, when Matthew and Luke differ in their selection of Q materials, the one added or the other deleted certain sayings—or, when they differ in wording or emphasis, which is closest to Q. Nonetheless, analyzing Luke's use of

11. *Taking up the Cross Daily*

Q vis-à-vis the theme of discipleship, it is clear that Luke wants his readers to know that being a follower of Jesus requires (1) new attitudes toward wealth, poverty and the use of riches for the benefit of others, and (2) a radical new type of lifestyle that puts following Jesus before every other allegiance—so radical, in fact, that every other allegiance, of whatever nature, can be characterized by comparison as "hate."

5. *Luke's Travel Narrative vis-à-vis Discipleship*

The so-called travel narrative of Luke's Gospel, that is, 9:51–19:27, is a lengthy section that has numerous references to Jesus and his disciples traveling from Galilee to Jerusalem (cf. 9:51, 52-56, 57; 10:1, 38; 11:53; 13:22, 33; 17:11; 18:31, 35; 19:1, 11). Some have seen it as ending earlier at 18:30 or 19:10; others, at 19:44. But the wording of 19:28—"After Jesus had said these things [understanding the Greek demonstrative pronoun ταῦτα, 'these things', as referring to all of the parabolic teachings of the travel narrative], he went on ahead, going up to Jerusalem"—seems to function as a hinge between "travel to Jerusalem" and "ministry in Jerusalem," with the travel narrative, therefore, ending just before this statement, that is, at 19:27. Luke had earlier portrayed Jesus as traveling about in Judea (e.g., 4:42; 8:1). Now, however, Jerusalem comes into view as the goal of his travels.

Up through 9:50 (minus the infancy narrative and genealogy), Luke's Gospel has been largely dependent on Mark for its narrative and on Q for its (non-Markan) sayings. From 9:51 through 19:27, however, most of the evangelist's material appears to have been drawn from other sources, with only a limited use of Mark (i.e., some use of Mark 10:1-52) and Q (i.e., Luke 9:57-62 // Matt 8:18-22 and Luke 14:25-33 // Matt 10:37-38, as treated above). Debate has been extensive as to whether Luke's source material for the travel narrative was one connected "parable" or "travel" source, either written or oral, or various sources that contained both parables of Jesus and further information about his ministry in Transjordan. Yet whatever the source or sources of this section, most of what Luke presents here must be considered as being unique to the evangelist, for it appears neither in any of the other Gospels nor in what can be postulated about Q. And as distinctive to Luke, it must be seen as incorporating the evangelist's own understanding of how Jesus' ministry progressed and his own emphases on how Jesus' teaching should be understood—particularly, for our purposes, of what Jesus taught about discipleship.

The narrative of 9:51–19:27 is fragmentary and only loosely joined together. It seems to skip about somewhat, in almost a haphazard manner (e.g., first in Samaria, 9:52-56; then at Bethany, outside of Jerusalem, 10:38-42; then "passing along between Samaria and Galilee," 17:11; and finally at Jericho before entering Jerusalem, 18:35, 19:1). Numerous parallels are set up between Jesus' ministry in Galilee and his ministry in Perea and Judah—for example, a leper is healed in 5:12-16 and ten lepers are healed in 17:11-19; controversies with the Pharisees in 5:17–6:11 and further controversies with the Pharisees in 11:14-54; the "Sermon on the Plain" in 6:17-49 and other sermonic materials in 17:1-10 (and *passim*); the sending out of the Twelve in 9:1-11 and the sending out of the Seventy in 10:1-24; and two passion predictions in 9:22-27, 43-45 and a third passion prediction in 18:35-43. But the main content of the travel narrative is made up of fifteen or sixteen parables—sometimes two or three just strung together, though usually the parables are framed by the rather loose travel narrative.

Some of the parables in the travel narrative are addressed to the crowd and some to opponents, but most are told by Jesus to his disciples. Mark, of course, after recounting Jesus' seed parables (i.e., "the sower and the seed," "the growing seed," and "the mustard seed" of 4:1-32), concluded by saying: "With many such parables Jesus spoke the word to them, as much as they could understand. He did not say anything to them without using a parable. But when he was alone with his own disciples, he explained everything" (4:33-34). So having Mark's Gospel before him, Luke well knew—if not, of course, also from Christian tradition generally—that Jesus often used parables in his teaching, even though Mark himself records only the three seed parables (4:1-32) and the parable of the wicked tenants (12:1-12). Luke, in fact, uses three of the Markan parables, distributing them throughout his Gospel: "the sower and the seed" in his section on Jesus' Galilean ministry (8:4-15; cf. Mark 4:1-20), "the mustard seed' in his travel narrative (13:18-19; cf. Mark 4:30-32); and "the wicked tenants" in his section on the ministry of Jesus in Jerusalem (20:9-19; cf. Mark 12:1-12). But Luke obviously knew of a number of other parables of Jesus—as did also Matthew, though Matthew included fewer additional parables in his Gospel than did Luke.

11. *Taking up the Cross Daily*

What Luke seems to have intended in setting out the parables of his travel narrative was to give his readers something of a column-lage—or, a number of multi-faceted pictorial representations—of what Jesus taught his disciples about following him, with not too veiled applications about how the readers, as well, should conduct their lives as Christians. Matthew's Gospel presents Jesus as telling parables mostly about (1) the nature of the kingdom ("the sower," "the mustard seed," "the weeds and the grain," "the yeast/leaven," "the hidden treasure," and "the net" in 13:1-50; also, perhaps, "the unmerciful servant" in 18:21-35), (2) Israel's rejection ("the wedding banquet" in 22:1-14 and "the two sons" in 21:28-32; and, of course, "the wicked tenants" in 21:33-46), and (3) future eschatological judgment ("the ten virgins," "the talents," and "the sheep and goats" in 25:1-46). But Luke's parables in his travel narrative are instructional for how believers should live their lives here and now—and so function as themselves parables of the Christian life.

The parables of Luke's travel narrative have often been used for devotional and homiletical purposes. That is not only because of their multivalent imagery, but also because they have been tailored by Luke—as well as, it may be presumed, by Jesus—for easy application to living as a follower of Jesus. It is impossible in short compass to deal with all that is taught in these parables (for a full coverage by thirteen authors, see now *The Challenge of Jesus' Parables* [MNTS 4], ed. R. N. Longenecker [Grand Rapids: Eerdmans, 2000]). Suffice it here merely to set out their major topics:

1. loving and helping others ("the good Samaritan," 10:25-37),

2. prayer ("the persistent friend," 11:5-13; "the persistent widow," 18:1-8),

3. possessions and true riches ("the rich fool," 12:13-34; "the rich man and Lazarus," 16:19-31),

4. service to God ("the unproductive fig tree," 13:1-9; "the proper attitude in serving God," 17:7-10; "the ten minas/pounds," 19:11-27 [cf. Matt 25:14-30]),

5. the importance of response to God ("the great supper," 14:15-24 [cf. Matt 22:1-14]; "the rich man and Lazarus," 16:19-31 [see also 3 above]),

6. God's love for the lost ("the lost sheep," 15:1-7 [cf. Matt 18:12-14]; "the lost coin," 15:8-10; "the prodigal son," 15:11-32),

7. humility ("The Pharisee and the tax collector," 18:9-14; also the "parable" in 14:7-14, which is without imagery), and

8. shrewdness in one's affairs ("the shrewd manager," 16:1-12).

Almost all of these parables are multivalent in their imagery and application. But their main point or points are usually readily understandable—though, admittedly, the parable of the shrewd manager is somewhat perplexing. All of them, however, were evidently intended by Luke to teach regarding what it means to follow Jesus, and so to provide pictorial patterns for Christian discipleship.

6. *Luke's Passion Narrative vis-à-vis Discipleship*

The greatest degree of agreement between the four Gospels is to be found in their respective passion narratives (Mark 14:1–15:47; Matt 26:1–27:66; Luke 22:1–23:56; John 18:1–19:42). This might not be too surprising for the Synoptic Gospels. For they seem to represent, in the main, a single tradition regarding the events of Jesus' passion—one that, evidently, Mark used as the basis for his Gospel, which then both Matthew and Luke essentially followed. It is, however, somewhat surprising for John's Gospel. For while the Fourth Gospel is quite different from the Synoptic Gospels in its portrayal of the ministry of Jesus, its account of Jesus' passion is remarkably similar—in fact, of the six percent of material in John's Gospel that may be said to be comparable to that of the Synoptics, almost all of it is to be found in John's passion narrative.

Such a commonality suggests that the events of Jesus' passion, more than any other events of the Jesus story, were relatively fixed in the proclamation and traditions of the early church. That does not mean, however, that the passion narratives of the four Gospels should be assumed to be identical. Certainly the Fourth Gospel, while comparable in its overall presentation, is different from the others in its selection, arrangement and wording of material; and the Synoptic Gospels differ among themselves, to some extent, on such matters as well. Nor should it be assumed that the four evangelists interpreted the events of Jesus' passion in exactly the same way.

At least two major traditions regarding the telling of the passion story seem evident in our Gospels: (1) that incorporated by Mark, which was basically followed by Matthew and Luke, and (2) that incorporated by John, with some features of this tradition appearing also in Luke. Moreover, each evangelist appears to have included some data that only he, for one reason or another, seems to have been interested in—for example, Mark's telling of the flight of the naked young man at Jesus' arrest (14:51-52) and Luke's report of Jesus being sent to Herod by Pilate (mark 23:6-12). Of even more importance in reading the passion narratives of the four Gospels, however, is the recognition that each evangelist has given his own redactional "spin" to the data presented, following out his own interests and speaking to the concerns of his addressees. So it is necessary when studying any particular passion narrative to ask: (1) What tradition seems to be represented? (2) What additional data is presented? and (3) How has the evangelist portrayed the data he incorporates?

Luke's passion narrative has much in common with Mark's, as well as that of Matthew. Its narrative follows, in the main, the order and structure of Mark's narrative, omitting only four episodes recorded by Mark: the anointing of Jesus at Bethany (Mark 14:3-9); Jesus' prediction of the desertion of his disciples (Mark 14:27-28); the flight of the naked young man (Mark 14:51-52); and the mocking of the soldiers (Mark 15:16-20)—with each omission probably explainable in terms of Luke's own interest (or lack of interest), as can be seen elsewhere in his two volumes. Luke adds only the four sets of statements at the end of the Last Supper (22:21-23, 24-30, 31-34, 35-38) and the two reports of Jesus being sent to Herod (23:6-12) and then again to Pilate (23:13-16). Yet at some places in their respective narratives, Luke and John share details not found in Mark (or in Matthew). Further, the percentage of Markan words in Luke's passion narrative is far less (about twenty-seven percent) than in Luke's portrayal of Jesus' Galilean ministry (about fifty percent).

Some have surmised from the above data that Luke knew and used John's Gospel in the writing his passion narrative. Others have concluded that he used, in addition to Mark's account, another connected account of Jesus' passion—one used by John as well. And still others, that he knew and used "an early form" or "earlier forms" of material about Jesus' passion that had not as yet been organized into a connected account—though later it might have been, and so used in the composition of the Fourth Gospel. That Luke's narrative depends on John seems highly debatable; that it is based on Mark and another account also used by John is possible. More likely, however, is the hypothesis that Luke's passion narrative is based mainly on

Mark, with supplementary data added from other developing traditions within the church and one Q saying (i.e., 22:28-30).

More significant for our purposes, however, is to note how Luke portrays Jesus in his passion narrative. For in Luke's Gospel, Jesus' passion and the cross are not depicted so much in terms of vicarious suffering, human redemption, or the expiation of sins, as they are in Mark's account (also Matthew's). Rather, they are presented primarily in exemplary fashion as the culmination of Jesus' unconditional obedience to God, and so as a pattern for the lives of Jesus' followers.

Luke has already hinted at such an understanding in 9:23 by the addition of the adverbial expression "daily" (καθ' ἡμέραν) to Jesus' words of Mark 8:34: "Those who would come after me must deny themselves and take up their cross *daily* and follow me." And he has also suggested such an understanding by his inclusion of Q material in 14:27: "Those who do not carry their cross and follow me cannot be my disciples." It may be thought, of course, that the addition of only one small expression to a saying found in Mark is a very minor matter and that the repetition of a saying reported also by Matthew is of little consequence. In reality, however, 9:23 and 14:27—which, it may be observed, are nicely balanced in the two parts of Luke's Gospel—provide the reader with two rather deft touches in Luke's use of his sources that serve to signal what the evangelist wanted to emphasize later in his writings, especially here in his passion narrative (and also, as we will note, throughout his Acts).

This is not to say that suffering, sacrifice, or soteriology are absent in Luke's portrayal of Jesus' passion. The evangelist has earlier spoken in 9:31 about Jesus going to Jerusalem in order to fulfill his "departure"—or, more literally, his "exodus" (ἔξοδος), which is a term that would certainly have evoked ideas about the redemptive significance of Jesus' passion to anyone knowing the Old Testament. And here in his passion narrative he explicitly refers to the Last Supper as a Passover meal (22:7, 8, 11, 13, 15) and repeats Jesus' words of institution at that meal: "This is my body given for you … This cup is the new covenant in my blood, which is poured out for you" (22:19-20). But in his omission in 22:24-30 of the Markan ransom saying "to give his life a ransom for many" (Mark 10:45b; cf. also Matt 20:28b), Luke indicates that what he wanted his readers to think about when they thought of Jesus' passion, of his service for others, and of their service for God was not just a soteriological theory. And throughout Luke's passion narrative the theme of Jesus' passion and cross as being exemplary for Christian living and service is to the fore.

The theme of exemplary service is highlighted in the distinctly Lukan portrayal in 22:27, where, at the Last Supper, Jesus resolves a conflict among his disciples by saying: "Who is greater, the one who is at the table or the one who serves? But I am among you as one who serves." Admittedly, Jesus does not here explicitly refer to his suffering on the cross as being exemplary for discipleship. But his approaching passion provides the setting for what is said. Likewise, Luke's depiction of Jesus praying on the Mount of Olives in 22:39-46 (cf. Mark 14:32-42; Matt 26:36-46) is set out in distinctly exemplary fashion. For though verses 43 and 44 ("an angel from heaven appeared to him and strengthened him"; "his sweat was like drops of blood falling to the ground") may be textually in doubt (being omitted by the early third-century Chester Beatty papyrus P^{75}, the fourth-century codex Vaticanus, and the fifth-century codex Alexandrinus), the twice-repeated exhortation to his disciples to "pray so that you will not fall into temptation" is certainly authentic. Here, in fact, is a clear echo of the Lord's Prayer in its request "Lead us not into temptation" (Luke 11:4; Matt 6:13). And here Jesus exhorts his disciples to take on in their lives an important feature of his ministry: that of prayer, particularly at the crisis points of life.

More directly associated with the cross, however, is Luke's rather cryptic reference to Simon of Cyrene (23:26), who was made to bear the cross of Jesus (cf. Mark 15:21; Matt 27:32). For Luke adds to the Markan reference the observation that Simon carried the cross "behind" (ὄπισθεν) Jesus. It seems, therefore, that what the evangelist saw in Simon's carrying of Jesus' cross and following after him was a concrete example of Jesus' teaching that Luke incorporated earlier in 9:23: "Those who would come after (ὀπίσω) me must deny themselves and take up their cross daily and follow me." For Luke, Simon of Cyrene, it appears, symbolized the attitude of the Christian disciple, carrying the symbol of Jesus' suffering—which, as Luke's addition to Jesus' instruction in 9:23 highlights, must be an attitude and action that takes place "daily."

7. Luke's Acts vis-à-vis Discipleship

At the end of Luke's Gospel, Jesus tells "the Eleven and those with them" (24:33): "You are witnesses of these things. I am going to send you 'the promise of my Father' (τὴν ἐπαγγελίαν τοῦ πατρός μου); but stay in the city until you have been clothed with power from on high" (24:48-49). At the beginning of Luke's Acts, "the promise of the Father, which you heard me speak about" is first explained as being "baptized with the Holy Spirit" (1:4-5) and then spoken of as being "filled with the Holy Spirit" (2:4). And with the coming of God's Spirit to believers on the Day of Pentecost, the gift of prophecy is given and believers in Jesus begin to proclaim "the word of God" about Jesus of Nazareth—who was accredited by God throughout his ministry, who was crucified, but whom God raised from the dead—as being both Lord and Christ (cf. Peter's sermon in 2:14-40).

So as Acts begins, the two basic themes of Luke's Nazareth pericope (Luke 4:14-30), which are themes that he carried on throughout his Gospel, are again highlighted: (1) the presence of God's Spirit on his servants and (2) the proclamation of the good news of God's redemptive activity. The joining of these two themes is, in fact, claimed to be rooted in Old Testament prophecy. For Peter is presented in Acts 2 as quoting Joel 2:28-32 (MT = 3:1-5) to the effect that it is precisely these two features, which were prophesied to characterize "the last days" of eschatological fulfillment, that can now be seen to be actually occurring: "'In the last days' [MT: 'afterward'], God says, 'I will pour out my Spirit on all people. Your sons and your daughters will prophesy, your young men will see visions, and your old men will dream dreams. Even on my servants, both men and women, I will pour out my Spirit in those days'" (vv 17-18a).

In quoting Joel, Peter breaks into the quotation, evidently for the sake of emphasis and to highlight what was at that time taking place in his preaching, with the added words: "and they will prophesy" (v 18b). In addition, it needs to be noted that the quotation from Joel ends with a statement regarding the universality of God's grace as expressed in the gospel: "And everyone who calls on the name of the Lord will be saved" (v 18b)—which is, of course, a further important theme of the Nazareth pericope (cf. Luke 4:25-27).

Each of these themes—the Spirit's presence, the proclamation of God's redemptive activity, and the universality of God's grace—is not only an important feature of Luke's writing, but also is presented in both his Gospel and his Acts as factors that are to characterize the self-consciousness of a follower of Jesus, and so to be accepted and worked out in Christian discipleship. Further, it needs also to be observed that all of the other major themes of discipleship that appear in Luke's Gospel recur, with greater explication, in his Acts. This is true, in particular, for such themes as: being rooted in and shaped by the apostolic tradition (cf. 2:42, *passim*); being dependent on God in prayer (cf. 1:14, 24-25; 2:42; 6:4; 12:5); being committed to a lifestyle that allows no allegiance to take the place of allegiance to Jesus (*passim*); and being concerned for the poor, the imprisoned, the blind, and the oppressed (cf. 2:44-46; 4:32–5:11).

In Acts, however, Luke never calls the twelve disciples (Judas having been replaced by Matthias) by the term "disciple" (μαθητής). He calls them that less frequently than the other evangelists in his Gospel, and he never does so in Acts. Nor in the early part of Acts does he call believers "disciples" (μαθηταί). Rather, in 1:16 he refers to believers as "brothers" (ἀδελφοί, or "brothers and sisters" inclusively understood). It is only in Acts 6:1-7, when dealing with the problems that arose with the influx of hellenistic Jewish believers, that Luke first uses "disciples" of believers in Jesus. Further, it is in that passage that he first brings all of these designations together in describing the constituency of the early church: "In those days when the number of *the disciples* was increasing, ... *the Twelve* gathered all *the disciples* together and said ... *Brothers and sisters* ... So the word of God spread, and the number of *the disciples* in Jerusalem increased rapidly." After that passage, Luke then uses "disciple/disciples" and "brothers and sisters" interchangeably for believers in Jesus ("disciple/disciples" some twenty-nine times; "brothers and sisters" thirty-two times). He also reports that the apostles addressed Jewish audiences as "men and brothers," "men, brothers, and fathers," or simply "brothers" (e.g., 2:29; 3:17; 7:2; 13:26, 38; 22:1; 23:1, 6; 28:17) and that Jews referred to one another as "brothers" (e.g., 2:37; 13:15; 28:21; cf. Luke 6:41-42).

Just what to make of (1) Luke's non-use of "disciple/ disciples" for the Twelve in Acts, whereas they were so designated in his Gospel, and (2) his interchangeable use of "disciples" (μαθηταί) and "brothers and sisters" (ἀδελφοί) for believers in Jesus, with the latter seeming to be his preference, may be debated. Perhaps it was because "disciple," though common among the various philosophical schools

11. *Taking up the Cross Daily* 268

of the day, had only recently become acceptable in religious associations. On such an understanding, one could argue that being more controlled in the writing of his Gospel by his sources, which reflected a rising use of "disciple" in the religious parlance of Palestine, Luke used that language in his Gospel; but being freer in the writing of Acts, and knowing that "disciple" was not a common designation for a follower of a religious figure in the hellenistic world, he may have wanted to tone down that term somewhat in favor of the expression "brother." And that is certainly a possible and plausible explanation.

Just as likely, however, is the explanation that Luke, for both theological and egalitarian reasons, felt some reticence in the post-resurrection period about using "disciple/disciples" for the Twelve and for believers in Jesus. For the term "disciple," while carrying many important nuances, also suggests ideas about subordination and inequality, whereas "brother" carries more of the nuances of familial oneness and equality. On such a rationale, it could be argued that Luke saw no problem in describing relations between Jesus and his followers during his earthly ministry in "master–disciple" or "teacher–pupil" language, but that in describing relations within the church he preferred to speak of believers as "brothers and sisters"—while continuing, as well, to refer to them as "disciples," evidently trusting that his interchangeable use of the terms would be self-defining and so aid his readers' understanding. In all likelihood, it may be further proposed that both explanations should be seen as being, at least in some manner, complimentary rather than mutually exclusive.

Of more importance for our consideration here, however, is that with Luke's preference for designating believers in Jesus as "brothers and sisters"—though, again, without refusing to call them "disciples"—two somewhat inchoate features of discipleship in Luke's Gospel take on greater significance in his Acts. The first is that of Luke's exemplary emphasis, which is worked out in his Gospel in terms of following Jesus and in Acts in terms of patterning one's life by the example of the apostles, particularly Paul. In his Gospel Luke has highlighted Jesus' exemplary life of service (cf. 22:27; also 6:40), his exemplary praying (cf. 22:39-46), and his exemplary cross-bearing (cf. 23:26; also 9:23). But without denying the importance of Jesus in the evangelist's thought, Paul was, in reality, Luke's great hero. And so in the portrayals of Paul's strenuous exertions in carrying out his missions, his magnanimous attitudes toward his colleagues, his staunch defenses against opposition, and his magnificent missionary sermons (cf. esp. Acts 13–14) and trial speeches (cf. Acts 22–26)—all of which are lauded by Luke, though probably more than they were by Paul himself and certainly more than they were by some of his converts (esp. at Corinth)—the example is set before believers of the one who "turned the world upside down" (cf. 17:6, as freely translated).

A second feature of discipleship that Luke expresses more fully in his Acts is that of a developing life of relationship with Christ and of service to others. Development is a theme that Luke hinted at in his Gospel, particularly in closing off his infancy narrative with the words: "The child grew and became strong; he was filled with wisdom, and the grace of God was upon him" (2:20) and "Jesus grew in wisdom and stature, and in favor with God and people" (2:52). But it underlies all of Acts as Luke seeks to show how "the word of God" progressed from its earliest Jewish-Christian roots to its full expression in Paul's ministry to Gentiles, with finally "the kingdom of God" being preached in the capital city of the Roman empire, even Rome itself, "boldly and without hindrance" (Acts 28:31). And implicit in all of these depictions of progress and development is the exemplary exhortation for believers also to progress and develop in their lives of faith and service.

8. *Patterns of Discipleship for Today*

Luke has frequently been accused of shifting the focus of early Christian thought from the eschatological future (ἡ ἔσχατος) to the present "today" (ἡ σήμερον ἡμέρα). Many, in fact, have seen him perverting the original gospel by a shift from an imminent coming of Christ to the everyday life of Christian living, from the charismatic to the ecclesiastical, from following Jesus (i.e., orthopraxis) to preaching about and believing in Jesus (i.e., orthodoxy), and from worship to mission. To some extent, of course, much of this is true. We may acknowledge the truthfulness of many of these observations without also acceding to the accusations that they imply. For Luke has not set aside eschatological expectations (cf. Luke 17:22-37; 21:5-36; Acts 11), nor has he minimized in any way the work of the Spirit, following Jesus, or the worship of God by his people. Nonetheless, it is quite true that Luke's major interest in the writing of his two volumes seems to have been the everyday matter of Christian discipleship—that is, of setting out for his readers the self-consciousness that one should have and the manner in which one should live as a follower of Christ.

Luke makes no catalogue of the qualities, characteristics, attitudes, or actions involved in Christian discipleship. What he presents are portrayals of the ministry of Jesus and the missions of the early church—particularly, the missions of his hero Paul. But those portrayals evidence throughout their author's distinctive redactional "spin" in their telling. And from those redacted portrayals one can infer that Luke meant to teach his readers, whether of his day or ours, at least the following things about Christian discipleship:

1. Discipleship is based on what Christ has effected for the redemption of humanity.
2. Discipleship must always be rooted in and shaped by the apostolic tradition.
3. Discipleship needs always to be dependent on God and submissive to his will, and so the importance of prayer.
4. Discipleship must always recognize the presence and power of the Holy Spirit.
5. Discipleship is to be involved in prophetic proclamation, with that proclamation focused on the work and person of Jesus.
6. Discipleship is to cherish, both in thought and in action, the understanding of God's grace and the gospel as being universal.
7. Discipleship is to be committed to a lifestyle that allows no allegiance to take the place of allegiance to Jesus.
8. Discipleship is to be concerned for the poor, the imprisoned, the blind, and the oppressed.
9. Discipleship is to follow the examples of Jesus and the apostles, particularly Paul, in matters of service, prayer, and cross-bearing.
10. Discipleship is to be a life of development in both one's faith and one's practice.

11. *Taking up the Cross Daily*

SELECT BIBLIOGRAPHY

Beck, Brian E. "*Imitatio Christi* and the Lucan Passion Narrative," in *Suffering and Martyrdom in the New Testament. Studies Presented to G. M. Styler*, ed. W. Horbury and B. McNeil. Cambridge: Cambridge University Press, 1981, 28-47.

Blomberg, Craig L. *Neither Poverty Nor Riches: A Biblical Theology of Material Possessions*. London: Apollos; Grand Rapids: Eerdmans, 1999.

Cassiday, Richard J. *Jesus, Politics, and Society: A Study of Luke's Gospel*. Maryknoll: Orbis, 1978.

_____ and P. J. Scharper, eds. *Political Issues in Luke–Acts*. Maryknoll: Orbis, 1983.

Fleddermann, Harry T. "The Demands of Discipleship: Matt 8,19-22, par. Luke 9,57-62," in *The Four Gospels 1992. Festschrift Frans Neirynck*, 3 vols., ed. F. van Segbroeck, C. M. Tuckett, G. van Belle, J. Verheyden. Leuven: University Press, 1992, 1.541-61.

Fitzmyer, Joseph A. *The Gospel according to Luke: Introduction, Translation, and Notes*. 2 vols. AB. New York: Doubleday, 1981, 1985.

_____. "Discipleship in the Lucan Writings," in *Luke the Theologian: Aspects of his Teaching*. New York, Toronto: Paulist, 1989, 117-45.

_____. *The Acts of the Apostles. A New Translation with Introduction and Commentary*. AB. New York: Doubleday, 1998.

Hengel, Martin. *The Charismatic Leader and his Followers*, trans. J. Greig. Edinburgh: T. & T. Clark; New York: Crossroad, 1981.

Johnson, Luke Timothy. *The Literary Function of Possessions in Luke–Acts*. Missoula: Scholars, 1977.

Karris, Robert J. "Women and Discipleship in Luke," *CBQ* 56 (1994) 1-20.

Longenecker, Richard N. "Acts," in *The Expositor's Bible Commentary*, 12 vols., ed. F. E. Gaebelein. Grand Rapids: Zondervan, 1981, 9.205-573 (one volume paperback edition, 1995); 2nd ed., 2005.

_____, ed. *Patterns of Discipleship in the New Testament*. MNTS. Grand Rapids: Eerdmans, 1996.

Marshall, I. Howard. *The Gospel of Luke: A Commentary on the Greek Text*. NIGTC. Grand Rapids: Eerdmans, 1978.

_____. *The Acts of the Apostles*. Grand Rapids: Eerdmans, 1980.

Martin, Ralph P. "Salvation and Discipleship in Luke's Gospel," *Int* 30 (1976) 366-80.

Nickelsburg, George W. E., "Riches, the Rich and God's Judgment in 1 Enoch 92–105 and the Gospel according to Luke," *NTS* 25 (1979) 324-44.

Rengstorf, Karl H. "μαθητής," *TDNT*, 4.415-61 (ET from *TWNT*, 4.417-65).

Schweizer, Eduard. *Lordship and Discipleship*. SBT, 28. London: SCM, 1960.

_____. *Luke: A Challenge to Present Theology*. Atlanta: John Knox, 1982.

Segovia, Fernando F., ed. *Discipleship in the New Testament*. Philadelphia: Fortress, 1985.

Talbert, Charles H. *Literary Patterns, Theological Themes, and the Genre of Luke–Acts*. Missoula: Scholars, 1974.

———. "Discipleship in Luke–Acts," in *Discipleship in the New Testament*, ed. F. F. Segovia. Philadelphia: Fortress, 1985, 62-75.

Wilkins, Michael J. "Disciples" and "Discipleship," in *Dictionary of Jesus and the Gospels*, ed. J. B. Green, S. McKnight, and I. H. Marshall. Downers Grove: InterVarsity, 1992, 176-89.

———. *Following the Master: A Biblical Theology of Discipleship*. Grand Rapids: Zondervan, 1992.

INDEX OF AUTHORS

Albright, W. F., 20, 58
Aleith, E. H., 17
Allison, D. C., 86, 119, 144
Aptowitzer, V., 196, 197
Argyle, A. W., 20
Aristobulus, 7, 45
Attwater, D., 17
Aulén, G., 122, 144
Bandstra, A. J., 86
Bardy, G., 189, 219
Barr, J., 54
Barrett, C. K., 86, 205, 219
Barth, K., 126, 144
Barthélemy, D., 157
Bateman, H. W., 86
Baumgärtel, F., 64
Beare, F. W., 21
Beasley-Murray, G. R., 101, 102, 120, 144
Beck, B. E., 273
Berger, K., 93
Berkhof, L., 65
Bernos de Gasztold, C., 224
Best, E., 234, 236
Bierberg, R., 66
Bigg, C., 17
Billerbeck, P., 212
Black, M., 2, 6, 56, 71, 86, 134, 173, 175, 203, 228, 230, 244
Blackman, E., 17
Bloch, R., 37
Blomberg, C. L., 273
Bock, D. L., 87
Bonsirven, J., 46, 70
Borsch, F., 227, 231, 244
Boslooper, T. D., 186
Bowker, J., 196, 212
Bowman, J. W., 205, 219, 244

Brandenburger, E., 207, 208
Brandon, S. G. F., 154
Braun, H., 203
Brown, R. E., 43, 66, 70, 87, 96, 108, 111, 186
Brownlee, W. H., 39, 40, 44, 70, 164, 173
Bruce, F. F., 32, 38, 42, 43, 49, 61, 70, 87, 104, 206, 219
Buchanan, G. W., 207, 208, 219
Bultmann, R., 14, 30, 64, 96, 131, 160, 165, 170, 173, 230, 231
Buri, F., 17
Burkill, T.A., 32
Burkitt, F. C., 227
Burney, C. F., 166, 173
Burrows, M., 40
Butterworth, G. W., 17
Caird, G. B., 59, 87, 205, 210, 220
Calvin, J., 26, 77
Campenhausen, H., 186
Carmignac, J., 199, 200, 220
Cassiday, R. J., 273
Chadwick, H., 173
Chadwick, O., 32
Chamberlain, J. V., 157
Charles, R. H., 28, 147, 193, 194, 227
Chase, F. H., 17
Chrysostom, 11, 12, 13, 29
Clarke, W. K. L., 51, 186
Clement of Alexandria, 7, 8, 29, 45, 154, 163, 167
Coccejus, J., 65
Cook, S. A., 203

Coppens, J., 206
Cross, F. M., 50, 59, 70, 92, 148, 156, 174, 228
Cullmann, O., 144, 173, 207, 227, 244
Cyril of Jerusalem, 3
Dalman, G., 235, 236, 244
Daniélou, J., 17, 32, 149, 156, 170, 171, 174, 186, 206, 228
Daube, D., 46, 59, 68, 70, 205
Davies, W. D., 38, 57, 70, 166, 205, 236
Deichgräber, R., 87, 120, 144
Deissmann, A., 125, 144
Delcor, M., 189, 196, 207, 208, 220
Demarest, B., 189, 220
Derrett, J. D., 186
Díez Macho, A., 195
Dodd, C. H., 54, 57, 70, 87, 93, 100, 104, 120, 203, 227, 236
Donahue, J. R., 120
Dormeyer, D., 97
Duhm, B., 192
Dupont, J., 101, 102, 120
Eichrodt, W., 65
Elliger, K., 43, 189
Ellis, E. E., 57, 59, 60, 67, 68, 87, 162
Eusebius, 107, 110
Farrar, F. W., 65
Filson, F. V., 20
Fitzmyer, J. A., 43, 53, 56, 70, 174, 186, 199, 220, 228, 244, 258, 273
Fleddermann, H. T., 273

Index of Authors

Flusser, D., 174
Ford, D., 101, 102, 120
France, R. T., 87
Fuller, R. H., 170, 186, 227, 231
Gaster, T. H., 38, 41, 157, 164
Gaston, L., 228
Gerhardsson, B., 37, 38, 56
Ginzberg, L., 196
Glasson, T. F., 228
Goltz, E. von der, 113
Goppelt, L., 87
Gordan, P., 17
Grant, F. C., 17, 21
Gundry, R. H., 49
Hahn, T., 170, 227, 231
Hanson, R. P. C., 17, 32, 211, 220
Harnack, A., 18, 27, 32, 87
Hartman, L., 101, 102, 120
Hay, D. M., 192, 203, 220
Hays, R. B., 87, 144
Hengel, M., 144, 273
Herford, R. T., 196
Higgins, A. J. B., 145, 160, 227, 231, 244
Hill, D., 20
Hindley, J. C., 228
Holtzmann, H. J., 28, 108
Hooker, M. D., 93, 94, 98, 100, 120, 244
Horovitz, S., 35
Hort, F. J. A., 67, 174
Horton, F. L., 189, 213, 214, 220
Ignatius, 176, 235
Irenaeus, 3, 4, 7, 10, 11, 12, 171
Isaac, E., 229
Jackson, F. J. F., 51, 159
Jeremias, J., 59, 70, 93, 95, 96, 120, 161, 162, 170, 174, 233
Jerome, 4, 9, 16, 26, 163
Johnson, L. T., 273

Jonge, M. de, 155, 199, 213, 220
Josephus, 45, 153, 178, 188, 189, 191, 202, 203, 204, 211
Juel, D., 87
Justin, 151, 163, 164, 167, 171, 196, 235
Kähler, M., 91
Karris, R., 87, 121, 144, 273
Käsemann, E., 131
Kelly, J. N. D., 32
Kennedy, H. A. A., 7, 45, 153
Kingsbury, J. D., 19
Kloppenborg, J. S., 121
Koester, C. R., 220
Kosmala, H., 158, 206
Kuhlmann, G., 44
Kuhn, K. G., 53, 54
Lachmann, K., 108
Ladd, G. E., 100
Lake, K., 51, 159
Lane, W. L., 232, 237, 244
Laubscher, F. du T., 199, 220
Lauterbach, J. Z., 36, 45, 46, 70
Lawson, J., 18
Le Déaut, R., 70, 195
Leenhardt, F., 134
Leivestad, R., 122, 144, 228, 245
Lightfoot, J. B., 18, 28
Lindars, B., 59, 70, 71, 93, 98, 121, 203
Linnemann, E., 96
Lohse, E., 131
Longenecker, B. W., 144
Longenecker, R. N., 13, 24, 57, 68, 72, 80, 85, 87, 113, 118, 121, 131, 144, 149, 172, 174, 210, 220, 226, 228, 232, 237, 240, 245, 263, 273
Lüdemann, H. K., 27
Luther, M., 15, 16, 26, 123, 133, 185
Machen, H. G., 186

Maher, M., 195
Maimonides, 26
Mann, C. S., 186
Manson, T. W., 60, 145
Marcion, 2, 3, 4, 5, 6, 8, 13, 14
Marshall, I. H., 20, 235, 245, 273
Martin, R. P., 155, 273
Matheson, G., 28
Maurer, C., 93, 121
McCasland, S. V., 64
McGrath, A. E., 32
McKelvey, R. J., 161, 162, 174
McNamara, M., 195
Melanchthon, P., 16, 134
Michaelis, W., 155
Michel, O., 45, 57, 70, 88, 187, 213, 214, 220
Miguens, M., 187
Milik, J. T., 41, 204, 228
Minear, P. S., 187
Moe, O., 207
Moffatt, J., 124, 212
Montefiore, C. G., 152, 203, 207
Moo, D., 94, 121
Moore, G. F., 36, 37, 152
Moule, C. F. D., 56, 69, 71, 88, 145, 174, 228, 236, 240, 245
Munck, J., 154
Newman, J. H., 27, 29, 32
Nickelsburg, G. W. E., 273
Nock, A. D., 189
Nolan, B. M., 187
Norden, E., 112, 127, 145
Odeberg, H., 156
Origen, 3, 4, 7, 8, 9, 10, 11, 12, 16, 29, 150, 154, 183
Orr, J., 27, 29, 32, 187
Papias, 97, 107, 110, 111, 112
Pelagius, 3

Pelikan, J., 16, 33
Pettinato, G., 189
Petuchowski, J. J., 196, 197, 220
Pfeiffer, R. H., 192
Pfleiderer, O., 27
Philo, 7, 44, 45, 152, 153, 157, 165, 188, 197, 201, 202, 204, 205, 206, 210, 211
Piper, O. A., 187
Przybylski, B., 19
Quispel, G. C., 147, 148, 156, 174
Rainy, R., 27, 29, 33
Rashi, 26
Reicke, B., 170
Rengstorf, K. H., 273
Roberts, B. J., 71
Roberts, C., 189
Robinson, T. H., 20
Roth, C., 39, 42, 43
Rowley, H. H., 189
Sabatier, A., 27, 33
Sandmel, S., 44
Sauer, A. von R., 56
Schelkle, K. H., 18
Schenke, L., 96
Schneemelcher, W., 18, 154, 227
Schoeps, H. J., 154
Scholem, G., 156
Schweizer, E., 18, 21, 130, 171, 174, 234, 235, 245, 274
Seeberg, A., 113
Seeseman, H., 18
Segovia, F. F., 274
Selwyn, E. G., 109, 170

Siegfried, C., 7, 45
Simon, M., 196, 220
Skeat, T. C., 189
Smith, B. T. D., 21
Soden, H. von, 248
Souter, A., 18
Sowers, S., 44
Spicq, C., 205, 220
Stauffer, E., 113, 187
Stendahl, K., 39, 40, 48, 49, 54, 60, 71
Strugnell, J., 41, 153, 174, 228
Sutcliffe, E. F., 66
Talbert, C. H., 248, 274
Tasker, R. V. G., 20
Taylor, V., 96, 167, 172, 174, 187
Teeple, H. M., 174, 231, 245
Teichmann, E. G. G., 27
Tertullian, 3, 4, 5, 6, 7, 10, 11, 12, 149, 181, 183
Thackeray, H. StJ., 28, 57, 59, 71
Theodore of Mopsuestia, 11, 29
Theodoret, 11
Theophilus of Antioch, 163
Thiselton, A. T., 33
Tödt, H. E., 245
Toon, P., 33
Torrey, C. C., 159
Turner, C. H., 18

Vermes, G., 37, 71, 74, 88, 174, 230, 237, 245
Vielhauer, P., 227, 231
Volf, M., 76
Waard, J. de, 51, 52, 53, 71
Walgrave, J. H., 33
Walker, T., 187
Weiser, A., 189
Weiss, B., 27, 108, 112
Weisse, C. H., 108
Wenham, D., 102, 121
Werner, M., 18, 155
Westcott, B. F., 209, 220
Wickert, U., 18
Wilcox, M., 51, 59
Wiles, M. F., 3, 11, 18, 28, 29, 30, 33
Wilkins, M. J., 274
Williamson, R., 201, 205, 206, 220
Windisch, H., 196, 197, 201
Wolff, H. W., 65
Wolfson, H. A., 71
Woude, A. van der, 155, 198, 199, 200, 213, 220
Wright, A. G., 38, 71
Wuttke, G., 189, 220
Yadin, Y., 199, 204, 205, 206, 221
Zahn, T., 134
Zimmerli, W., 120
Zimmermann, H., 160

BIBLICAL REFERENCES
(INCLUDES APOCRYPHAL AND PSEUDEPIGRAPHICAL WORKS)

Genesis
1:1, 163, 166
3:15, 22
4:1, 212
5:3, 212
6, 170
13:15, 59
14, 188
14:18-20, 188, 193,
    208, 210, 211, 213
14:18, 1 91, 194, 195
14:19, 195
16:7-11, 152
17:7, 59
21:17, 152
22:11, 152
22:15, 152
24:7, 59
31:11, 152
48:16, 152

Exodus
3:2, 152
4:22, 165
14:19, 152
15:1-18, 118
18:21, 118
23:20-21, 156
34:33-35, 59

Leviticus
11:44, 52
19:2, 52
20:7, 52
23:29, 53
25:9-10, 198
25:13, 198

Numbers
21:17, 59
22:22-35, 152
24:24, 42
25:12-13, 192

Deuteronomy
12:11, 157
12:21, 157
14:23-24, 157
15:2, 198
16:2, 157
16:6, 157
16:11, 157
18:15, 22, 53
18:18, 22, 53
21:22-23, 128
21:23, 92
26:2, 157
30:11-14, 59
30:12-13, 169
30:14, 169
32, 209
32:8, 152
32:43, 141, 210
33:2, 152, 154

Judges
2:1, 152
2:4, 152
5:1-31, 118
5:23, 152
6:11-22, 152
6:20, 152
13:3-21, 152
13:6, 152
13:9, 152

2 Samuel
7, 209
7:12, 178
7:14, 141, 210

2 Kings
25:17, 161

Nehemiah
1:9, 157

Job
14:1, 178

Psalms
1:1, 38
2:1-2, 38, 53
2:7, 141, 210
7:8-9, 198
8–9, 118
8:4-6, 141, 210, 232
8:4, 230
8:5, 152
16:8-11, 53
22, 93, 94
29, 118
31, 94
33, 118
34, 94
34:12-16, 52
35:19, 56
40:6-8, 142
41, 94
41:9, 56
45:6-7, 141, 210
65, 118
67–68, 118
68:18, 59, 168
69, 94
69:4, 56
69:9, 23
69:25, 53
74:7, 157
76:2, 189
78:35, 189
78:36-37, 55
80:17, 230
82:1-2, 198
89:3-4, 178
95:7-11, 141, 210
96, 118
97:7, 141
98, 118
100, 118
102:25-27, 141, 210
103–105, 118
109, 94
109:8, 53
110, 188, 192, 193, 210

Index of Biblical References

110:1, 53, 56, 195, 203, 210, 213
110:4, 22, 141, 188, 195, 208, 210, 213, 215, 218
111, 118
113–14, 118
117, 118
118:22-23, 55
118:22, 53, 161, 162
118:25-26, 23
118:25, 50
135–36, 118
145–50, 118

Proverbs
3:34, 52
8:22, 163, 166

Isaiah
6:3, 150
6:9-10, 55
7:10-12, 77
8:14, 53, 161
11:2, 163
18:7, 157
28:16, 53, 161, 162
29:13, 55
40:3-5, 254
40:3, 50, 55, 253
40:6, 52
40:8, 52
49:8, 61
52:7, 198
52:13–53:12, 93
53, 94, 98
53:7-8, 53, 56
53:12, 55, 56
54:13, 55
61:1-2, 54, 254, 258, 259
61:1, 198

Jeremiah
3:17, 157
7:1-15, 104
7:10-14, 157
7:30, 157
22:13-17, 257
25:1-3, 22
25:11-12, 42
25:12-14, 22
25:20-27, 22

29:10, 42
31:9, 165
31:31-34, 22, 141, 210
31:33, 55

Ezekiel
24:15-23, 104

Daniel
2, 42
2:4–7:28, 42
3:26, 189
4, 42
4:32, 189
5, 42, 44
5:18, 189
5:21, 189
7, 42, 226, 227, 235, 236
7:13-14, 230, 236
7:13, 155, 235
7:21, 236
7:25, 236
9:24-27, 41
11:30, 42

Joel
3:1-5, 53, 268
3:5, 159

Micah
4:4, 191

Habakkuk
1:8, 39
1:11, 39
1:15-16, 39
2:1-2, 41
2:3, 41
2:16, 39
2:17, 46

Zechariah
1:12, 153
2:3, 195
8:4, 191
9–14, 93, 94
9:9, 23
13:7, 55, 251

Malachi
3:1, 22, 55, 253

Matthew
1:18–2:23, 176
1:18-25, 180, 181
1:18-23, 140
1:21-25, 157
1:25, 176
2:1-18, 140
2:15, 140
2:19-21, 140
3:13-17, 140
3:17, 138
4:1-17, 140
4:1-11, 137
4:18-22, 140
5:1–7:28, 140
5:3-12, 257
6:13, 267
7:21-23, 158
7:22-24, 100
8:1–9:38, 140
8:18-22, 257, 259, 261
8:23-27, 250
9:17, 83
10:1-42, 140
10:2, 256
10:22, 158
10:24-25, 253
10:25, 20
10:37-38, 257, 259, 260, 261
11:10, 55
11:11, 178
13:1-50, 263
13:14-15, 55
13:18, 250
13:51, 32, 251
13:52, 19, 21
13:55-56, 176
13:55, 180
14:15-21, 140
14:15, 250
14:32, 250
15:16-17, 250
15:32-39, 140
16:5-12, 250
16:8-9, 251
16:9, 250
16:12, 251
16:19, 21
17:1-8, 140
17:5, 139
17:9, 251
17:13, 251

Index of Biblical References 278

17:16, 250
17:19, 250
18:12-14, 264
18:18-20, 251
18:18, 21
18:20, 157
18:21-35, 263
19:13, 250
19:28, 251
19:29, 158
20:20-24, 250
21:28-32, 263
20:28, 267
21:33-46, 263
21:42, 161
22:1-14, 263, 264
22:41-46, 56
23:34-36, 100
24–25, 99
24, 102
24:6, 102
24:9, 158
24:14, 251
24:15, 101, 103, 235
24:24, 102
25:1-46, 263
25:14-30, 263
26:1–27:66, 264
26:14, 250
26:20, 250
26:31, 55
26:36-46, 250, 267
26:39, 140
26:43, 267
26:44, 267
26:47, 250
26:56, 250
27:32, 267
27:57, 19
27:64, 251
28:16-20, 251
28:18-20, 79, 158
28:19, 19

Mark
1:1, 138, 143, 179
1:2-6, 253
1:2-3, 55, 179
1:4-8, 179
1:9-11, 179
1:11, 138
1:12-13, 179
1:14-15, 179

1:16-20, 179, 250
2:10, 232
2:14, 250
2:28, 232
3:13-19, 217, 250
3:14, 255, 256
3:31-32, 176
4:1-20, 262
4:10, 250
4:13, 250, 251
4:30-32, 262
6:1-6, 254
6:3, 176, 180, 183
6:7, 250
6:30, 256
6:52, 250, 251
8:17, 250, 251
8:29, 138, 237
8:30, 237
8:31–10:52, 138
8:31, 237
8:32-33, 238, 251
8:34-35, 242
8:34, 266
9:7, 138
9:18, 251
9:31, 238
9:32-34, 238
9:32, 251
9:35, 242, 250
10:1-52, 261
10:13-16, 251
10:29, 158
10:32-34, 238
10:32, 250
10:35-45, 251
10:35-39, 238
10:42-45, 243
10:45, 267
11:1–13:37, 138
11:11, 250
12:1-12, 263
12:10-11, 55, 161
12:35-37, 56, 213
12:36, 211
13, 99, 100, 102, 103
13:5-22, 103, 106
13:7, 102
13:9-11, 101
13:13, 158
13:14, 101, 103, 235
13:22, 102
13:26, 235

13:28-29, 101
13:34-36, 101
14:1–15:47, 264
14:1–15:39, 138
14:3-9, 265
14:3, 95
14:5, 95
14:10, 250
14:17, 250
14:20, 250
14:27-28, 265
14:27, 55, 251
14:28, 251
14:32-42, 267
14:36, 140
14:43-45, 250
14:50-52, 250
14:50, 251
14:51-52, 265
14:54, 95
14:62, 235
14:66-72, 250
14:67, 95
15:14, 95
15:16-20, 265
15:21, 267
15:28, 56
15:39, 138, 143
15:42, 95

Luke
1–2, 118, 119
1:1-4, 118, 247
1:4-5, 268
1:5–2:52, 176, 258
1:26-38, 180, 182, 185
1:31, 157
1:46-55, 258
1:48, 258
1:52-53, 258
2:4, 268
2:14-40, 268
2:20, 271
2:21, 157
2:49, 137
2:52, 271
3:1-6, 253, 254
3:2-3, 253
3:6, 254
3:7-20, 254
3:10-14, 258
3:16-17, 111
3:21-22, 254

3:22, 138
3:23-28, 254
4:1-32, 262
4:1-13, 137, 254
4:14–9:50, 248
4:14-30, 254, 255, 258, 259, 268
4:14, 254
4:16-21, 54
4:18-19, 255
4:18, 254
4:22, 180
4:23-24, 255
4:25-27, 255, 269
4:28-30, 255
4:33-34, 262
4:42, 261
5:12-16, 262
5:17–6:11, 262
6:13, 252, 255, 256
6:17-49, 262
6:17, 252
6:20-26, 257
6:40, 253
6:41-42, 269
6:46-49, 111
6:46, 158
7:18-23, 111
7:28, 178
7:31-35, 111
8:1, 250, 261
8:4-15, 262
8:11, 251
9:1-11, 262
9:10, 252, 256
9:12, 250
9:22-27, 262
9:23, 266, 267
9:31, 266
9:35, 139
9:40, 251
9:43-45, 262
9:45, 251
9:50, 261
9:51–19:27, 247, 261, 262
9:51–19:10, 248
9:51, 261
9:52-56, 261, 262
9:57, 261
9:57-62, 257, 259, 261
9:57-60, 111
9:60, 260

9:61-62, 260
10:1-24, 262
10:1, 261
10:22, 111
10:25-37, 263
10:38-42, 262
10:38, 261
11:4, 267
11:5-13, 263
11:14-54, 262
11:31-32, 111
11:49, 252, 256
11:49-51, 100
11:53, 261
12:1-12, 262
12:8, 234
12:13-34, 263
13:1-9, 263
13:1-5, 100
13:18-19, 262
13:22, 261
13:33, 261
13:34-35, 111
14:7-14, 264
14:15-24, 264
14:25-33, 257, 259, 260, 261
14:26-27, 111, 260
14:27, 266
14:28-33, 260
15:1-7, 264
15:8-10, 264
15:11-32, 264
16:1-12, 264
16:19-31, 263, 264
17:1-10, 262
17:5, 252, 256
17:7-10, 263
17:11-19, 262
17:11, 261, 262
17:22-37, 272
17:23-27, 111
17:30, 111
17:37, 111
18:1-8, 263
18:9-14, 264
18:15-17, 251
18:24-25, 258
18:29, 158
18:30, 261
18:31, 250, 261
18:35-43, 262
18:35, 261, 262

19:1, 261, 262
19:10, 261
19:11-27, 263
19:11, 261
19:27, 261
19:28, 261
19:37, 252
19:41-44, 100
19:44, 261
20:9-19, 263
20:17-18, 161
20:18, 161
20:41-44, 56
21, 99, 102
21:5-36, 272
21:12, 158
21:17, 158
22:1–24:53, 247
22:1–23:56, 264
22:3, 250
22:7, 266
22:8, 266
22:11, 266
22:13, 266
22:14, 252, 256
22:15, 266
22:19-20, 267
22:21-23, 265
22:24-30, 265, 267
22:24-27, 251
22:27, 267
22:28-30, 266
22:28, 251
22:29-30, 111
22:31-34, 265
22:35-38, 265
22:37, 55
22:39-46, 267
22:42, 140
22:45-46, 251
22:47, 250
23:6-12, 265
23:13-16, 265
23:26, 267
23:27-31, 100
23:49, 252
23:53, 95
24:7, 231
24:9, 252
24:10, 252, 256
24:33, 252, 268
24:36-49, 95
24:48-49, 268

Index of Biblical References

John
1:1-18, 167, 171
1:1-14, 117, 181
1:12, 158, 181
1:13, 181
1:14, 139, 164
1:18, 139, 164
1:23, 50
1:45, 181
2–12, 24
2:1-3, 50
2:13, 50
2:17, 23, 50
2:22, 23
2:23, 158
3:1-15, 252
3:13, 168, 171
3:16, 139, 164
3:18, 158, 164
5:1, 50
5:39-47, 50, 55
6:4, 50
6:35, 160
6:42, 181
6:45, 50, 55
6:62, 168, 171
6:66, 252
6:67, 250, 252
6:70, 250, 252
6:71, 250, 252
7:2, 50
7:3-5, 176
7:37-39, 50
7:42, 178
7:50-51, 252
8:12-14, 50
8:12, 160
8:23-24, 160
8:28, 160
8:41, 181, 183
8:58, 160
10:7, 160
10:9, 160
10:11, 160
10:14, 160
10:22, 50
11:25, 160
11:55, 50
12:1, 50
12:2-4, 50
12:3, 95
12:5, 95
12:13, 50
12:15, 50
12:27-28, 140
12:28, 160
12:34, 231, 235
12:36, 50
12:37, 50
12:38, 50
12:40, 50
12:42-43, 252
13:1–18:1, 50
13:1, 50
13:16, 256
13:18, 50, 56
13:19, 160
13:23, 252
14–16, 23
14:6, 160
14:13-14, 158
14:26, 78
15:1, 160
15:16, 158
15:25, 50
15:27, 62, 67, 217
16:12-15, 217
16:12-13, 23
16:23-26, 158
17:6, 160
17:26, 160
18:1–19:42, 264
18:15, 95
18:18, 95
18:25, 95
19:14, 50
19:15, 95
19:26-27, 252
19:31, 95
19:38-40, 252
19:39, 252
19:41, 95
20:19-29, 95
20:24, 250, 252
20:30, 118
20:31, 158
21:7, 252
21:20, 252

Acts
1–12, 247
1:14, 176, 269
1:15-26, 85
1:16, 269
1:20, 53
1:21-26, 217
1:21-22, 62, 177, 179
1:22, 98, 184
1:24-25, 269
1:26, 252
2:14-36, 177
2:16-21, 239
2:17-21, 53
2:17-18, 268
2:18, 268
2:21, 159
2:22-24, 22, 239
2:24-36, 98
2:24, 239
2:25-35, 239
2:25-28, 53
2:29, 269
2:34-36, 56
2:34-35, 53, 210, 213
2:36, 239
2:37, 269
2:38-40, 239
2:42–12:24, 248
2:42, 269
2:44-46, 269
2:45, 258
3:13-15, 98
3:15, 164
3:16, 159, 160
3:17, 269
3:22-23, 51, 53
3:23, 53
4:2, 98
4:7, 160
4:10-11, 98
4:10, 160
4:11, 53, 56, 161, 162, 164
4:12, 159
4:25-26, 53
4:32–5:11, 269
4:32-37, 258
4:33, 98
5:1-11, 258
5:30-32, 98
5:31, 164
5:40-41, 98
6:1-7, 269
6:2, 250, 252
6:4, 269
6:40, 271
7, 53
7:2, 269
7:43, 51

www.ingramcontent.com/pod-product-compliance
Lightning Source LLC
Chambersburg PA
CBHW071658160426
43195CB00012B/1505